HOUGHTON MIFFLIN

English

HOUGHTON MIFFLIN

English

Authors
Robert Rueda
Tina Saldivar
Lynne Shapiro
Shane Templeton
C. Ann Terry
Catherine Valentino
Shelby A. Wolf

Consultants
Jeanneine P. Jones
Monette Coleman McIver
Rojulene Norris

 HOUGHTON MIFFLIN

BOSTON

Acknowledgments

For each of the selections listed below, grateful acknowledgment is made for permission to excerpt and/or reprint original or copyrighted material as follows:

Published Models

From *Bats: Night Fliers* by Betsy Maestro, illustrated by Giulio Maestro. Text copyright ©1994 by Betsy Maestro. Illustrations copyright ©1994 by Giulio Maestro. Reprinted by permission of Scholastic Inc.

From *The Changing World: Jungles & Rainforests* by John A. Burton. Copyright ©1996 by Dragon's World Ltd. Reprinted by permission of Belitha Press Ltd.

From *Charlotte's Web* by E.B. White, illustrated by Garth Williams. Text copyright 1952 and renewed ©1980 by E.B. White. Illustrations copyright 1952 and renewed ©1980 by Garth Williams. Used by permission of HarperCollins Publishers.

"Crows" from *Legends of the Seminoles* as told by Betty Mae Jumper, illustrated by Guy LaBree. Text copyright ©1994 by Betty Mae Jumper and Peter B. Gallagher. Illustrations copyright © by Guy LaBree. Used by permission of Pineapple Press, Inc.

Acknowledgments are continued at the back of the book following the last page of the Index.

ISBN-13: 978-0-618-61120-1
ISBN-10: 0-618-61120-7

20 0868 18
4500742556

HOUGHTON MIFFLIN
English

Just follow the colors . . .

Part 1

Grammar, Usage, and Mechanics

Part 2

Writing, Listening, Speaking, and Viewing

Part 3

Tools and Tips

Part 1
Grammar, Usage, and Mechanics

In the blue grammar units, look for these ways to make your writing stronger.

Revising Strategies

Writing Wrap-Up

Part 2

Writing, Listening, Speaking, and Viewing

In the green writing units, look for these grammar links for help as you write.

GRAMMAR CHECK

GRAMMAR TIP

GRAMMAR LINK

Revising Strategies

Proofreading Checklist

Grammar and Spelling Connections

Look for these parts, too!

Special Focus

COMMUNICATION LINK

Part 3

Tools and Tips

Use these Tools and Tips whenever you need them.

- Listening and Speaking Strategies
- Building Vocabulary
- Research and Study Strategies
- Test-Taking Strategies
- Using Technology
- Writer's Tools

- Guide to Capitalization, Punctuation, and Usage
- Spelling Guide
- Diagramming Guide
- Thesaurus Plus
- Glossary of Language Arts Terms
- Index

Visit Kids' Place for Houghton Mifflin English at www.eduplace.com/kids/hme for activities like these.

- Bright Ideas for Writing
- Grammar Blast
- Evaluation Station
- Net's Best for Research
- Authors and Illustrators
- Graphic Organizers
- Writers' Showcase

TABLE OF CONTENTS

Unit 2 Nouns 63

Part 1

WRITING TRAITS

Unit 5 Capitalization and Punctuation 165

WRITING TRAITS

Unit 6 Pronouns 203

Unit 7 — Adverbs and Prepositions 233

Part 2
Writing, Listening, Speaking, and Viewing

Unit 9 · Writing a Story 297

Part 2

SECTION 2 Explaining and Informing

Getting Started

WRITING TRAITS

Unit 10 | Writing Instructions 338

WRITING TRAITS

Unit 11 Writing a Research Report 368

SECTION 3 Expressing and Influencing

WRITING TRAITS

Unit 12 · Writing to Express an Opinion 412

Part 3 — Tools and Tips

Listening, Speaking, and Viewing

Learning from Each Other

Each one of you has your own skills, experiences, interests, and opinions. As a boy or a girl, you're like a book full of great information and ideas to share. Together as a class, you're a whole encyclopedia!

Together, we can find the Big Dipper, tell a stegosaurus from a pterodactyl, juggle oranges, and cook tamales!

By learning from each other, you can make school—and life—easier and much more fun. You will be able to rely on one another to solve problems, to think of new ideas, and to offer encouragement. How can you best learn from each other? SPEAK, LISTEN, and VIEW! Speaking lets you share what you know. Listening and looking, or viewing, help you learn from others. Here are some of the most common reasons for speaking, listening, and viewing.

Speaking	Listening and Viewing	Examples
to entertain	for enjoyment	telling a joke or a story, attending an art exhibit, a movie, or the circus
to inform	to get information	listening to a weather report, explaining a math problem to a friend, reading someone's body language
to persuade	to form an opinion	asking parents for permission to stay up late, selecting a movie at the video store

Think and Discuss

- Look back at the pictures on page 1. What reason does each person have for listening? for speaking? for viewing?
- At what other times do you listen, speak, and view during the day?

Discussion Breakdown

These students are trying to choose a class pet, but they are not using good listening and speaking skills. What's wrong?

Think and Discuss

- What is each student doing wrong in this discussion?
- What could the students do to improve their discussion?

Breakthrough Discussion

The students are still trying to choose a class pet. How have they improved their listening and speaking skills?

Think and Discuss

● What has each student done to improve his or her listening or speaking skills?

Being a Good Listener and Speaker

Here are some basic guidelines for listening and speaking with others. They will help you communicate at school, on the soccer field, in the mall, or around the dinner table!

When You Listen

▶ Face the speaker. Look him or her in the eye.
▶ Listen carefully. Don't daydream.
▶ Don't create distractions—no foot-tapping, whistling, or waving!
▶ If you get confused, repeat in your own words what was said. Ask if you've understood.

When You Speak

▶ Share your ideas with the group, not just your neighbor.
▶ Look at your listeners.
▶ Ask others what they think of your ideas. Say what you think about theirs.
▶ If you disagree, politely explain why.
▶ Stick to the subject being discussed.
▶ Don't interrupt or try to take over the conversation.
▶ Speak loudly and clearly enough for your listeners to hear and understand your words.

Try It Out Read the statements below. Choose one that interests you. Decide whether or not you agree with the statement. Discuss your opinions in small groups.

- Kids today watch too much TV.
- Summer is the best season.
- Animals are happy living in zoos.

Being a Good Viewer

When you view, you look carefully and learn from what you see. What are these students learning by viewing?

When You View

Viewing the World Around You
► First, open your eyes wide! Notice all that you can.
► Then focus. What is the most important part of what you see?
► Then refocus. What interesting or important details do you see?

Viewing Others
► Watch for hand gestures that help explain what someone is saying.
► Watch people's faces for clues to how they feel.
► When you speak, watch your listeners' body language to see how they are reacting.

Viewing Still or Moving Images
► Notice the main focus of the image. What catches your eye?
► Look more closely. What details are important? Why?
► Look for the purpose of the image. Is it to entertain? inform? persuade?
► Who is the audience? How do you know?
► Does the image send the audience a message? What message?

Try It Out Using books and other materials in your classroom, look for images whose purpose is to entertain, inform, and persuade. Try to find one of each. Discuss your images with a small group. How can you tell the purpose? What is the main focus? What details are important?

The Writing Process

A Day in the Life of a Student

What Is the Writing Process?

The writing process takes you step by step from a blank sheet of paper to an interesting piece of writing. The writing process gives you many chances to make your writing better.

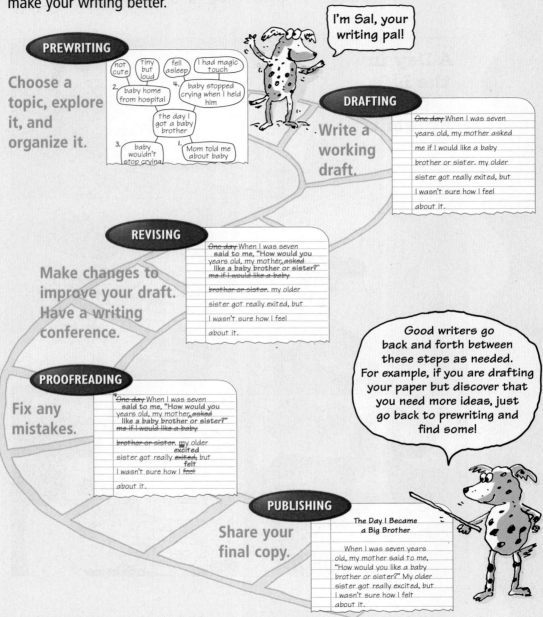

PREWRITING

Choose a topic, explore it, and organize it.

I'm Sal, your writing pal!

DRAFTING

Write a working draft.

REVISING

Make changes to improve your draft. Have a writing conference.

Good writers go back and forth between these steps as needed. For example, if you are drafting your paper but discover that you need more ideas, just go back to prewriting and find some!

PROOFREADING

Fix any mistakes.

PUBLISHING

Share your final copy.

Looking Ahead In this section, you will learn about the writing process as you write a description. To get ready, you will first read a description that was published in a book.

Read the following description of a barn from *Charlotte's Web.* As you read, try to imagine yourself standing inside this barn. What would you see, smell, and feel?

The Barn

from *Charlotte's Web*, by E. B. White

The barn was very large. It was very old. It smelled of hay and it smelled of manure. It smelled of the perspiration of tired horses and the wonderful sweet breath of patient cows. It often had a sort of peaceful smell—as though nothing bad could happen ever again in the world. It smelled of grain and of harness dressing and of axle grease and of rubber boots and of new rope. And whenever the cat was given a fish-head to eat, the barn would smell of fish. But mostly it smelled of hay, for there was always hay in the great loft up overhead. And there was always hay being pitched down to the cows and the horses and the sheep.

more ▶

Go to www.eduplace.com/kids/ for information about E. B. White.   A Published Model   **9**

The barn was pleasantly warm in winter when the animals spent most of their time indoors, and it was pleasantly cool in summer when the big doors stood wide open to the breeze. The barn had stalls on the main floor for the work horses, tie-ups on the main floor for the cows, a sheepfold down below for the sheep, a pigpen down below for Wilbur, and it was full of all sorts of things that you find in barns: ladders, grindstones, pitch forks, monkey wrenches, scythes, lawn mowers, snow shovels, ax handles, milk pails, water buckets, empty grain sacks, and rusty rat traps. It was the kind of barn that swallows like to build their nests in. It was the kind of barn that children like to play in. And the whole thing was owned by Fern's uncle, Mr. Homer L. Zuckerman.

Reading As a Writer

Think About the Description

- What sense—sight, sound, or smell—does E. B. White use to describe the barn in the paragraph on page 9?
- What are four smells that the writer describes?
- What does the barn feel like during the winter? during the summer?
- Where are the stalls, the sheepfold, and the pigpen found in the barn?

Think About Writer's Craft

- In the paragraph on page 10, which sentence names the most things found in the barn? What mark separates each thing listed in this sentence?

Think About the Picture

- Look at the picture on page 10. What shows you that the girl and the animals are friends?

Looking Ahead

Now you are ready to write your own description. Starting on the next page, you will find many ideas to help you. You will see how one student, Jack Welch, used the writing process to write a description of his oboe.

Using the Writing Process

What Is Prewriting?

Prewriting has three parts. First, you choose your topic. Next, you explore your topic. Then you organize, or plan, your writing.

Start thinking about **audience** and **purpose**. Who will read or listen to your writing? What kind of paper will you write?

Think about how you are going to **publish** or **share** your paper. This may make a difference in how you write your paper.

How Do I Choose a Topic?

Here are a few ways to find an idea to write about.

Ways to Think of Topics		
Try this!	**Here's how.**	
Remember your experiences or those of others.	You fell off your bike into a huge, deep puddle of mud.	• Write a **personal narrative** about what happened. • Add this event to a **story**. • **Describe** how you looked when you stood up out of the puddle.
Read a book.	You enjoyed reading about the life of a baseball player.	• Write a **research report** about an athlete you like. • **Persuade** your classmates to play baseball.
Reread your journal.	You wrote a journal entry about your summer vacation.	• Write an **opinion essay** about why summer is the best season. • **Compare and contrast** summer and winter.
Use your imagination.	What would it be like to be a pioneer?	• Write a **story** about a pioneer family. • Write a **research report** about pioneer life.

Write a Description

Choosing a Description Topic

Learning from a Model Jack's school newspaper has a section called "My Favorite Things." Jack wanted to write a description for this section of the paper. First, he made a list of ideas and thought about each idea.

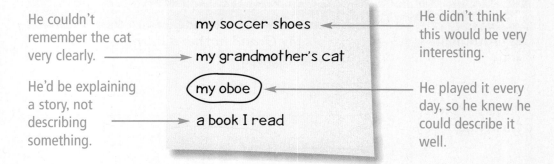

He couldn't remember the cat very clearly. ——————→ my soccer shoes ←————————— He didn't think this would be very interesting.

→ my grandmother's cat

He'd be explaining a story, not describing something. ——————→ my oboe ←————————— He played it every day, so he knew he could describe it well.

→ a book I read

► Choose Your Topic

As you choose your topic, think about your **purpose**, your **audience**, and how you will **publish** or **share** your description.

❶ List five topics that you would like to describe, such as a special person, a pet, or a place you love. Use the chart on page 12 to think of ideas.

❷ Discuss your topics with a partner. Which ideas does your partner like? Why?

❸ Ask yourself these questions about each topic.

- Can I observe it before I write about it?
- Can I use at least three senses to describe it?
- Which topic would I most like to write about?

❹ Circle the topic you will write about.

 Keep all your work for your description in one place, such as a writing folder.

Tech Tip
See page H39 for ideas for using a computer at each stage of the writing process.

What Is Exploring?

The second part of prewriting is exploring. You remember events, collect facts, and think of details to elaborate, or tell more, about your topic.

How Do I Explore My Topic?

This chart shows different strategies you can use to explore a topic.

Exploring Strategies	
Try this!	**Here's how.**
Brainstorming a list	My Grandmother's Farm barn goat cows mosquitoes stream tractor hay barbecues
Clustering	what they eat where they live what they look like GRIZZLY BEARS
Making a chart	Snowstorm Touch — cold snow on my face Sound — whistling wind
Drawing and labeling	We spent all day paddling around!
Interviewing with a partner	How long was your dog lost?
Asking *Who? What? When? Where? Why? How?*	Hitting the Winning Run What? last baseball game of the season When? the bottom of the last inning

📖 See page H50 for more graphic organizers.

Exploring a Description Topic

Learning from a Model Jack drew a picture of his oboe. Then he wrote words to describe how it looked, felt, and sounded.

looks like a bell at the bottom

pipes connect keys   The sound scared our cat once.

hard keys   squishy pad

black tube   shrieking noise

▲ Jack's picture and list

▶ Explore Your Topic

❶ **Think** about what you are describing.

❷ **Draw** a picture of your topic.

❸ **Use your five senses** to brainstorm sense words and details to write beneath your picture. Use words from the chart below, or think of your own.

Sight	Sound	Smell	Touch	Taste
fluffy	buzz	fruity	squishy	oily
teal	chirp	fishy	slimy	sweet
oval	grunt	nutty	damp	tart
dull	bellow	rotten	lumpy	tangy
enormous	thump	musty	prickly	bitter
glossy	rattle	fresh	scalding	spicy
pointed	crash	burnt	silky	buttery
muddy	honk	moldy	fuzzy	sour
dusty	whimper	flowery	sticky	peppery
foamy	croak	vinegary	crisp	sugary

If you can't think of details for three senses, try describing something else.

What Is Organizing?

The third part of prewriting is organizing, or planning. You choose what ideas and details to include. Then you group them and put the groups in order.

How Do I Organize My Writing?

Group facts, events, or ideas. Put related details into separate groups, such as how two things are alike and how they are different.

Choose an organization. Put the groups of details in an order that fits your purpose. It often helps to chart, diagram, or outline your plan.

Ways to Organize	
Try this!	**Here's how.**
Time order First Next Last	Tell events in the order they happen.
Place order	Describe things from top to bottom, bottom to top, right to left, left to right, near to far, or far to near.
Comparison and contrast	Describe how two subjects are alike. Then describe how they are different. You can also tell the differences first and the likenesses next.
Order of importance LEAST → MOST MOST → LEAST	Tell the least important reason first, or tell the most important reason first.
Question and answer Q? A . . . Q? A . . .	Ask a question and tell the answer. Then ask another question and answer that.
Logical order	Group details that belong together. Present the groups in an order that makes sense.

Organizing a Description

Learning from a Model Jack needed to group the details he had listed. He decided to group them by sense.

- First, he circled details about each sense with a different colored pen.
- Next, he made an Observation Chart showing each group of details.
- Then he numbered the groups in a logical order.
- Finally, he added more details.

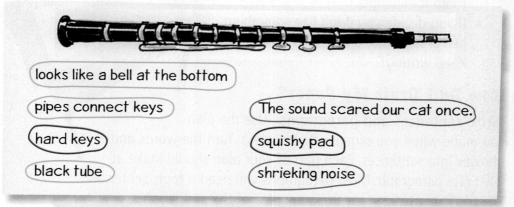

looks like a bell at the bottom

pipes connect keys

The sound scared our cat once.

hard keys

squishy pad

black tube

shrieking noise

① How It Looks	③ How It Sounds	② How It Feels
looks like a bell at the bottom	The sound scared our cat once.	squishy pad
pipes connect keys	like an elephant's cry shrieking noise ∧	cold, hard keys ∧
about two feet long black tube ∧		

▲ Jack's Observation Chart

Organize Your Description

❶ **Group** the details about your topic that belong together.

❷ **Organize** your details. Make an Observation Chart.

❸ **Number** your details in the order you will write about them.

❹ **Add** any more details you think of. Use exact words.

Go to www.eduplace.com/kids/hme/ for graphic organizers.

What Is Drafting?

When you draft, you just write. Don't worry about mistakes. You can fix them later because this is a **working draft**.

- Keep your audience and purpose in mind.
- Keep adding details. A new idea can come at any time.
- Write on every other line to leave room for changes.
- If you decide you don't like something, just cross it out. Don't start over. Keep writing!

How Do I Draft My Paper?

Write sentences and paragraphs. Use the plan you made when you organized your ideas. Turn the words and phrases into sentences. Each part of your plan should make at least one paragraph. Most paragraphs will need a topic sentence. The **topic sentence** tells the main idea of the paragraph.

Write a beginning and an ending. Write an interesting beginning that introduces your topic. Write an ending that finishes your paper by making a final comment about your topic.

Make connections. Use connecting words to tie your sentences and paragraphs together.

Ways to Make Connections	
Try this!	**Look at these examples.**
Use time clues.	finally, until, often, first, tomorrow, Friday, during the day, before, then, after, next, when
Link causes and effects.	because, as a result, so that, therefore, if … then
Use place clues.	above, around, down, here, there, beside, inside, outside, over, under
Signal likenesses and differences.	however, although, in contrast, similarly
Signal another idea.	also, too, another, in addition

Drafting a Description

Learning from a Model Jack wrote his working draft. He introduced his topic in an interesting way. Then he started with the part he had numbered *1* on his Observation Chart: *How It Looks.* He wrote a topic sentence and used details from his chart to write his other sentences.

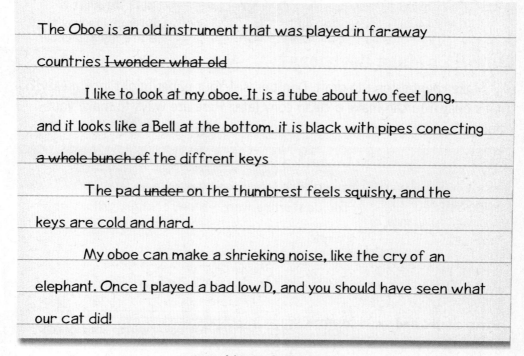

The Oboe is an old instrument that was played in faraway

countries ~~I wonder what old~~

　　　I like to look at my oboe. It is a tube about two feet long,

and it looks like a Bell at the bottom. it is black with pipes conecting

~~a whole bunch of~~ the diffrent keys

　　　The pad ~~under~~ on the thumbrest feels squishy, and the

keys are cold and hard.

　　　My oboe can make a shrieking noise, like the cry of an

elephant. Once I played a bad low D, and you should have seen what

our cat did!

▲ **Jack's working draft**

▶ Draft Your Description

❶ **Write** an interesting beginning.

❷ **Use** your Observation Chart to help you write the main part of your paper. Skip every other line. Don't worry about mistakes yet.

❸ **Think** about the main idea of each paragraph, and write a topic sentence. Write other sentences that fill in the details about the main idea.

❹ **Write** an ending that makes a final comment about your topic.

What Is Revising?

When you revise, you change your writing to make it clearer or more interesting. Ask yourself the Big Questions. Don't worry about fixing mistakes yet.

How Do I Make Revisions?

Make changes on the draft. Don't erase! Your paper might look messy, but that's okay. You can make a clean copy later. Here are ways to make your changes.

Ways to Mark Your Revisions	
Try this!	**Look at these examples.**
Cross out parts that you want to change or take out.	The costumes were ~~yellow~~ red, orange, yellow, and purple.
Use carets to add new words or sentences.	The clown had on baggy yellow pants and a flowered hat.
Draw circles and arrows to move words, sentences, or paragraphs.	Don't forget clothes for both warm and cold weather. Be sure to pack carefully for the trip.
Use numbers to show how sentences should be ordered.	②Draw a picture on heavy paper. ③Then cut it into puzzle pieces. ①This is how you make a puzzle.
Add wings to add sentences that won't fit on your paper.	Last night I couldn't sleep. Could a tiny animal be scampering between the walls? I kept hearing a scratching sound behind my bed.

Revising a Description

Learning from a Model Jack reread his working draft. To help his readers picture his oboe, he added details and more exact words. He added a topic sentence. He also added a comparison to make his description more vivid.

> musical
> The Oboe is an old instrument that was played in faraway
>
> countries ~~I wonder what old~~
>   slender
>   I like to look at my oboe. It is a tube about two feet long,
>
> and it looks like a Bell at the bottom. it is black with pipes conecting
>
> ~~a whole bunch of~~ the diffrent keys The keys look like little manhole
>   covers.
> When I pick it up, my oboe feels both soft and hard.
>   The pad ~~under~~ on the thumbrest feels squishy, and the
>   as   as marbles
> keys are cold and hard.

▲ **Part of Jack's revised draft**

▶ Revise Your Description

Reread your description. Use the Revising Checklist to help you make changes. Think about what you meant to say. Use a thesaurus to find exact, descriptive words. Don't worry about fixing any mistakes yet!

Revising Checklist

✔ Did I write clear topic sentences?
✔ Did I use details that support the topic sentences in each paragraph?
✔ Did I order the details so my readers can follow them easily?
✔ Where do I need to add sense words or details?
✔ Did I make a final comment about my topic in my ending?

📖 See the Thesaurus Plus on page H79.

Don't be afraid to mark up your paper!

What Is a Writing Conference?

In a writing conference, a writer reads his or her paper to a partner or a group. The listeners tell what they like, ask questions, and make suggestions. Your conference partners might be a classmate, a small group, your teacher, or someone who knows about your topic.

How Do I Have a Writing Conference?

In a writing conference, you will be either the writer or the listener. The following guides can help you.

Guides for a Writing Conference	
When You're the Writer . . .	**When You're the Listener . . .**
• Read your paper aloud. • Pay attention to your listeners' comments and suggestions. Keep an open mind. • Take notes to remember any compliments, questions, or suggestions. • Reread your paper after the conference. • Use your notes. Make any other changes you want.	• Look at the writer. • Listen carefully. Don't let your thoughts wander. • Retell what you have heard. • Then tell two things that you like about the paper. • Next, ask questions about things you don't understand. • Finally, give one or two suggestions to help the writer. • Always be positive and polite.

Could you tell me more about that detail?

Why do you think that? Could you explain?

How else could you say that?

Try to understand what the writer meant to say.

Having a Writing Conference

Learning from a Model Jack had a conference with a partner, Jorge.

▶ Have Your Writing Conference

❶ **Find** a partner or a small group, and have a writing conference. Use the guides on page 22.

❷ **Use** your conference notes to make any other changes you want.

What Is Proofreading?

When you proofread, you correct any mistakes. You check spelling, capitalization, and punctuation. You also check that you have used words correctly, written complete sentences, and indented paragraphs.

How Do I Proofread?

Choose from these ideas to help you.

- Use proofreading marks.
- Proofread for one skill at a time.
- Read one line at a time. Hold a ruler or a strip of cardboard under the line to help you focus on the spelling of each word.
- Say each word aloud to yourself.
- Read your paper aloud. You may notice mistakes when you hear them.
- Circle any word that might be misspelled. Check spellings in a dictionary.

HELP ?

Proofreading Tip

Remember **CUPS** when proofreading.
Capitalization
Usage
Punctuation
Spelling

Proofreading Marks		
Try this!	**Here's when.**	**Look at these examples.**
¶	to begin a new paragraph; to indent the paragraph	¶ All eyes were looking up. Everyone was begging the kitten to come down. The frightened animal wouldn't budge.
∧	to add letters, words, or sentences	Bring your scissors ∧*and* glue to class.
ᵔ	to take out words, sentences, and punctuation marks; to correct spelling	Mrs. Jones asked, me to work at the book sail. *sale* ∧
/	to change a capital letter to a small letter	We pitched our tent near a small /Stream.
≡	to change a small letter to a capital letter	Last summer we went to Yellowstone ≡national Park.

Proofreading a Description

Learning from a Model Jack made more changes to his description after talking to Jorge. Then he proofread it.

¶ The Øboe is an old *musical* instrument that was played in faraway

countries. ~~I wonder what old~~

I like to look at my oboe. It is a *slender* tube about two feet long,

and it looks like a ~~B~~bell at the bottom. ~~i~~it is black with *a dull, sooty / shiny silver* pipes ~~conecting~~ *connecting*

~~a whole bunch of~~ the ~~diffrent~~ *different* keys. The keys look like little manhole *covers.*

When I pick it up, my oboe feels both soft and hard. The pad ~~under~~ on the thumbrest feels squishy, and the

keys are cold *as* and hard. *as marbles*

▲ **Part of Jack's proofread draft**

▶ Proofread Your Description

Proofread your description, using the Proofreading Checklist. Use the proofreading marks shown on page 24.

Proofreading Checklist

Did I
✔ indent all paragraphs?
✔ use complete sentences?
✔ use capital letters and punctuation correctly?
✔ use the correct form of adjectives when comparing?
✔ use nouns and verbs correctly?
✔ correct any spelling errors?

📖 Use the Guide to Capitalization, Punctuation, and Usage on page H55 and the Spelling Guide on page H65 for help.

What Is Publishing?

When you publish your writing, you prepare to share it with your audience.

How Do I Publish My Writing?

Here are some ideas for sharing your writing.

Write It

- Turn your paper into a book. Add pictures and a cover.
- Send your paper as a letter or an e-mail.
- Create a class book of writing with your classmates.
- Post your paper on the Internet.
- Send your paper to a magazine or a newspaper that publishes student writing.

Say It

- Record your paper on tape. Add sound effects.
- Read your paper aloud from the Author's Chair.
- Read your paper as a speech.

Show It

- Add photographs or drawings to your paper.
- Make a diorama and attach your paper to it.
- Act out your writing with a small group. Have a teacher or other adult videotape your performance.
- Show slides about your topic to the class while reading your paper aloud.

Tech Tip
Make a multimedia presentation. See page H45 for ideas.

How Do I Reflect on My Writing?

When you reflect, you think about what you have written. You can think about what you did well, what you could do better next time, and what your goals are for your next writing assignment.

 You might want to keep a collection of some of your writing, such as favorite or unusual pieces.

Publishing a Description

Learning from a Model Jack made a neat, correct final copy of his description. He sent it to the editor of his school newspaper.

Jack Welch

My Oboe
by Jack Welch

The oboe is an old musical instrument that was played in faraway countries.

I like to look at my oboe. It is a slender tube about two feet long, and it looks like a bell at the bottom. It is a dull, sooty black with shiny silver pipes connecting the different keys. The keys look like little manhole covers.

When I pick it up, my oboe feels both soft and hard. The pad on the thumbrest feels squishy, and the keys are as cold and hard as marbles.

My oboe makes a smooth, clear sound, like someone singing. It also can make a shrieking noise, like the cry of an elephant. Once I played a bad low D, and you should have seen what our cat did! Even when I play badly, I like to play my oboe.

I love all your comparisons!

I can almost hear it!

Great! You end by making a final comment about your oboe.

▶ Publish Your Description

❶ **Check** that you fixed all mistakes. Make a neat final copy of your description. Give your description a title.

❷ **Publish or share** your description. Look at page 26 for ideas.

Will you keep this description? Use the paragraph on page 26 to help you reflect on your writing experience.

Part

1

Grammar, Usage, and Mechanics

What You Will Find in This Part:

Informal Language

When you're with your friends or in other informal situations, you may not worry about using every word correctly. That's fine.

When you write in your diary or do other personal writing, it doesn't matter if every word or punctuation mark is correct. YOU know what you mean.

To Do

✓ permission slip signed

☆ lab report – due Thurs.

? call Coach Sever

A Turtle Makes Its Mark

...y favorite pastimes in Oklahoma was
...least until one crazy day last
...e with my brother, Andy, and my
...snapping turtle. Andy and my
...re messing around in the book yard
lunch, but I stayed behind.
I was petting the turtle. I put my left index
finger in front of him and said, "Here, turtle, turtle!
Come and get my finger!" He did, and it really hurt! The
turtle wouldn't let go. I yelled as loud as I could—no
words, just a long, drawn-out wail.
When they heard me screaming, Andy and Sara
came running. "What's wrong?" they shouted. I held
up my finger with the turtle stuck to it. My hand was
shaking, but the turtle seemed calm.

Formal Language

In school and in many situations outside of school, though, you need to use more formal language, for both speaking and writing. This section of the book will help you develop your ability to use formal language when you need it.

Where else can a kid have this much fun going this fast? What a blast you can have on a corkscrew coaster! The first ride is always the best. Promise that you'll come with me.

The Sentence

1 What Is a Sentence?

One-Minute Warm-Up

Read the sentence below. Whom or what is the sentence about? What happened?

The hottest flames clawed up the trunks of large trees.

—from *The Great Yellowstone Fire,*
by Carole G. Vogel and Kathryn A. Goldner

A **sentence** is a group of words that tells a complete thought. In order to tell a complete thought, a sentence must tell *who* or *what.* It must also tell *what is* or *what happens.*

Who or What	What Is or What Happens
Mr. Nolan	rolled up the sleeping bags.
Your backpack	is too heavy!

Sentences	Not Sentences
Jason likes camping.	Likes camping by the lake.
Our new tent leaks.	Our new green tent.

Try It Out

Speak Up Which groups of words are sentences? Which are not sentences?

1. At Yellowstone National Park.
2. The park has famous hot springs.
3. The first national park in the world.
4. Flows through the park into the canyon.
5. Many different kinds of wildlife.
6. Jason's family camped at Yellowstone.
7. They saw a fossil forest.
8. Hot springs, waterfalls, and canyons.

Old Faithful erupts.

For each pair, write the group of words that is a sentence.

Example: Lisa visited a national park. Camping in a park last summer.
Lisa visited a national park.

9. Planned the trip ahead of time.
Lisa's family planned the trip.

10. Her parents sent for information.
Maps about the park.

11. The family camped in a meadow.
Enjoyed the mountain view.

12. Hiked together along the trail.
They admired the rocks.

13. Over sixty kinds of animals.
The hikers saw deer and bears.

14. Skiing in winter.
The park is open all year.

15–20. Read these notes from a science journal. Write each group of words that is a sentence.

Example: March 1 Snow flurries this morning. I saw many deer tracks.
I saw many deer tracks.

March 31
The last snow finally melted.
Saw a rabbit under a bush.

April 15
More buds on the trees.
Heavy rain fell all day.

May 6
Picked violets and dandelions.
Two robins built a nest.

May 29
Tulips are in bloom everywhere.
Five baby birds in the nest.

June 18
Swam in the lake with my brother.
We nearly froze in the cold water!

July 9
Hot, sticky weather the whole month.
Blueberries are almost ready to pick.

Writing Wrap-Up WRITING • THINKING • LISTENING • SPEAKING

DESCRIBING

Write a Journal Entry

Write an entry describing today's weather for a science journal.
Write complete sentences. Find a partner and read your descriptions
to each other. Listen for any sentences that are not complete.

Writing Good Sentences

Writing Complete Sentences You have learned that a group of words is not a sentence unless it tells a complete thought. Sometimes you can fix an incomplete sentence by adding it to a complete sentence.

Many clues to American history
lie buried underwater.
In old shipwrecks.

Many clues to American history lie buried underwater in old shipwrecks.

Sometimes you can fix two incomplete sentences by combining them.

Many amazing sights.
Are found in national parks.

Many amazing sights are found in national parks.

Apply It

1–4. Rewrite the picture captions below to make complete sentences.

Revising

National Park Highlights

The saguaro cactus can survive in the Arizona desert. Because it can hold two tons of water.

Have you ever seen caribou grazing? Near Alaska's tallest mountain?

A national park ranger. Explores a historical underwater site.

A river inside Mammoth Cave. Flows 360 feet underground.

When you write, make sure your sentences state a complete thought. Incomplete sentences can confuse your reader.

The saguaro produces white flowers. In May and June. Its juicy red fruits are good to eat.

The incomplete sentence above makes the meaning unclear. Does the saguaro produce white flowers or good fruit in May and June? The writer can revise by adding the incomplete sentence to the first sentence.

The saguaro produces white flowers in May and June.

Be sure your new sentences make sense.

Apply It

5–10. Rewrite this part of a report. Fix each incomplete sentence by adding it to a complete sentence or to another incomplete sentence.

Revising | Cactus

Desert Survival

How does a cactus survive in the desert? With so little water? It can usually find enough water because its roots are very long. Cactus stems are hollow or spongy inside. For storing the water. A waxy coating. Makes them waterproof. The stems may also have sharp thorns that keep thirsty animals away.

One fascinating kind of cactus. Is the giant saguaro. Don't expect to see the saguaro's lovely blossoms. Until it is at least fifty years old! The saguaro may still be less than an inch tall. When it is ten years old. However, it reaches a height of at least thirty feet when it is about one hundred years old! The largest saguaros live to be 200 years old. They can reach fifty feet in height. This is as tall as a five-story building!

2 Statements and Questions

Riddle: Why was the plane so tired in the morning?

Answer: It stayed up all night.

Think of a riddle to try out on your classmates. Use a question to ask and a statement to answer the riddle.

- Different kinds of sentences have different jobs. **A sentence that tells something is a statement**. A statement ends with a period (.).

- **A sentence that asks something is a question.** A question ends with a question mark (?).

- A sentence always begins with a capital letter.

Statements	Questions
The airport was crowded.	Was the airport crowded?
Her plane landed on time.	When did her plane land?
Carlos bought a ticket.	Did Carlos buy a ticket?

Try It Out

Speak Up Is each sentence a statement or a question? What end mark should follow each sentence?

1. The flight attendant welcomed the passengers
2. I pushed my small brown bag under the seat
3. Have you fastened your seat belts
4. Can you see out the window
5. What city is below
6. The cars look like ants
7. Now everything looks foggy
8. Are we flying through a cloud
9. How high will the plane climb
10. We will land in about an hour
11. Is this your first flight

Write *statement* if the sentence is a statement. Write *question* if it is a question.

Example: Who made the first flight alone across the Atlantic? *question*

12. Charles Lindbergh was the pilot's name.
13. A prize of $25,000 was offered.
14. What kind of plane did he fly?
15. His plane was called the *Spirit of St. Louis*.
16. Lindbergh flew from New York to Paris.
17. How long did the flight take?
18. The flight took thirty-three and one-half hours.
19. Have you ever seen Lindbergh's plane?
20. His plane is in the Smithsonian Institution.

21–28. This ad has three missing capital letters and five missing or incorrect end marks. Write the ad correctly.

Example: can anyone learn to fly   *Can anyone learn to fly?*

LEARN TO FLY!

Did you ever dream of flying like a bird. Would you like to see the world? the Ace Pilot School is the answer to your dreams Our teachers are experts You will learn the skills of safe flying. lessons are half-price in January. you cannot afford to wait? Isn't it time to make your dream come true

Writing Wrap-Up   WRITING • THINKING • LISTENING • SPEAKING

PERSUADING

Write an Ad

Write an ad that would convince people to learn to juggle, use a yo-yo, or learn some other fun or unusual skill. Include questions and statements in your ad. Then read it to a partner. Is your ad convincing? Work together to check for capital letters and end marks.

3 Commands and Exclamations

Read these sentences about the picture aloud. Use your voice to express the meaning of each sentence.

The bus is going to leave!
Get on now.

You have learned about two kinds of sentences called statements and questions. Now you will learn about two other kinds of sentences.

- **A sentence that tells someone to do something is a command.** A command ends with a period.

- **A sentence that shows strong feeling such as surprise, excitement, or fear is an exclamation.** It ends with an exclamation point (!).

- Remember to begin every sentence with a capital letter.

Commands	Exclamations
Please wait at the bus stop.	The bus finally arrived!
Meet me at Paige's Bookstore.	What a huge store it is!
Take the subway home.	How fast the train travels!

Try It Out

Speak Up Is each sentence a command or an exclamation? What end mark should be put at the end of each sentence?

1. Plan your trip carefully
2. Apply for your passport
3. Please bring a photo of yourself
4. How excited I am
5. My dream is coming true
6. We're leaving at last
7. Lock the door

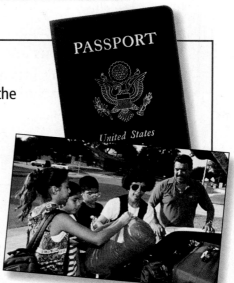

Write *command* if the sentence tells someone to do something. Write *exclamation* if it shows strong feeling.

Example: What a perfect day it is to fly to England!   *exclamation*

8. Be at the airport early.
9. Show your ticket at the gate.
10. How hard it is to stay calm!
11. I can't wait to fly!
12. Find your seat quickly.
13. Let me fasten your seat belt.
14. What a smooth takeoff that was!
15. How tiny everything looks!
16. Please stay in your seat.
17. We have arrived at last!

18–24. This page from a travel brochure has two missing capital letters and five missing end marks. Each sentence is a command or an exclamation. Write the page correctly.

Example: what delicious food Mexico has   *What delicious food Mexico has!*

Proofreading

Unforgettable Mexico

How exciting it is to visit Mexico

◆ Explore Aztec temples
◆ swim in the warm Pacific Ocean.
◆ Shop for handmade jewelry
◆ Enjoy lively festivals.

what a land of surprises Mexico is   It is a place you will never forget

Writing Wrap-Up   WRITING • THINKING • LISTENING • SPEAKING

DESCRIBING

Write a Travel Brochure

Write a paragraph about your city or town for a travel brochure. What will you say to make people want to visit? Include commands and exclamations. Add pictures. Read your paragraph to a partner. Make your voice show the types of sentences you used. Ask your partner to supply the end marks.

4 Subjects and Predicates

Read the sentence below. Whom or what is the sentence about? What happened?

A large trout leapt in the air.

—from *A River Dream*, by Allen Say

- **The subject tells whom or what the sentence is about. The predicate tells what the subject does or is.**

- All the words in the subject make up the **complete subject**. All the words in the predicate make up the **complete predicate**. A complete subject or a complete predicate may be one word.

Complete Subjects	Complete Predicates
Angela Kelly	is the captain of the boat.
We	waited at the dock.
The red ferryboat	stops.
Passengers	get off the boat.

- Ask whom or what the sentence is about to find the subject. Ask what the subject does or is to find the predicate.

Try It Out

Speak Up What are the complete subject and the complete predicate of each sentence?

1. Henry Delgado fished from the wharf.
2. The ocean was calm.
3. Several gulls flew overhead.
4. The gulls squawked noisily.
5. Henry cast his line into the sea.
6. He waited.
7. A large fish tugged on his line.

Write each sentence. Draw a line between the complete subject and the complete predicate.

Example: Many people enjoy the ocean. *Many people | enjoy the ocean.*

8. Children splash in the waves.
9. Two older children swim to the raft.
10. Geneva Simpson works at the beach.
11. She is a lifeguard.
12. Lifeguards watch the swimmers carefully.
13. Mr. Mota runs the snack bar.
14. His children help.

15–22. Write this poem. Draw a line between the complete subject and the complete predicate in each sentence.

Example: Bright pebbles tumble on the shore.
Bright pebbles | tumble on the shore.

The Beach

Green waves toss their foamy heads.
Clams sleep in their sandy beds.
A lonely man wades. A girl skips by.
They look at clouds up in the sky.
The wind is cool. Big white birds glide.
Footprints wash away in the tide.

Writing Wrap-Up
WRITING • THINKING • LISTENING • SPEAKING

CREATING

Write a Poem

Write a poem made up of sentences. The poem does not have to rhyme, but each sentence should have a complete subject and a complete predicate. With a small group, take turns reading your poems aloud. Which poems did you like the best? Why?

5 Simple Subjects

Three _____ broke the record!

How many different ways can you complete this headline?

- You have learned that the complete subject includes all the words that tell whom or what the sentence is about. In every complete subject, there is one main word that is the simple subject. **The simple subject tells exactly whom or what the sentence is about.**

- Sometimes the complete subject and the simple subject are the same. The simple subjects below are shown in yellow.

Complete Subjects	Complete Predicates
Many people	watch ball games at the park.
Marcus Johnson	slides into third base.
He	pitched five innings.
The palm of his glove	is torn.

Try It Out

Speak Up The complete subject of each sentence is underlined. What is the simple subject?

1. <u>James Naismith</u> invented basketball in 1891.
2. <u>He</u> was a teacher in Springfield, Massachusetts.
3. <u>The head of the school</u> wanted a winter game.
4. <u>Naismith</u> tacked peach baskets to the walls of the gym.
5. <u>He</u> called the game "basket ball."
6. <u>The first players</u> used soccer balls.
7. <u>Each team</u> had nine players.
8. <u>The new players</u> scored only one basket in the first game.
9. <u>The members of the teams</u> loved the game anyway.
10. <u>A clever player</u> cut the bottoms out of the baskets fifteen years later.

The complete subject of each sentence is underlined. Write the simple subject.

Example: People all over the world play basketball. *People*

11. A high basket hangs at each end of the court.
12. A toss of the ball starts the game.
13. Players pass, dribble, and shoot the ball.
14. The team with the ball tries to put it into the basket.
15. The other team tries to stop them.
16. The five players on a team try to score points.
17. Michael Jordan scored a lot of points.
18. He was one of the best players in history.

19–28. The complete subject of each sentence is underlined in this online magazine article. Write the article, and circle the simple subjects.

Example: Modern baseball is fun. *Modern (baseball) is fun.*

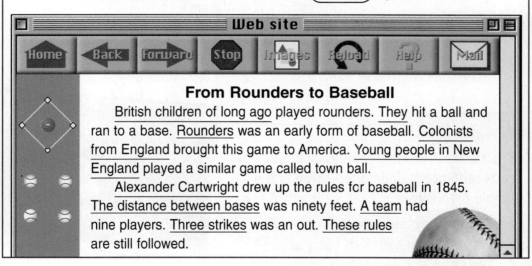

From Rounders to Baseball

British children of long ago played rounders. They hit a ball and ran to a base. Rounders was an early form of baseball. Colonists from England brought this game to America. Young people in New England played a similar game called town ball.

Alexander Cartwright drew up the rules for baseball in 1845. The distance between bases was ninety feet. A team had nine players. Three strikes was an out. These rules are still followed.

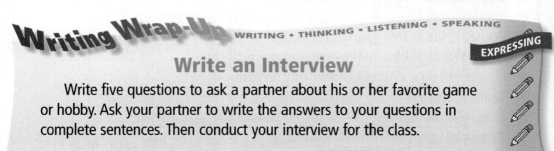

Writing Wrap-Up

WRITING • THINKING • LISTENING • SPEAKING

EXPRESSING

Write an Interview

Write five questions to ask a partner about his or her favorite game or hobby. Ask your partner to write the answers to your questions in complete sentences. Then conduct your interview for the class.

6 Simple Predicates

How many different ways can you complete this sentence?

The astronauts _____ amazing things in space!

The complete predicate includes all the words that tell what the subject does or is. In every complete predicate, there is one main word that is the simple predicate. **The simple predicate tells exactly what the subject does or is.** In each sentence below, the simple predicate is shown in yellow.

Complete Subjects	Complete Predicates
Some students	go to space camp.
The camp	is in Alabama.
Campers	build rockets.
They	wear real space suits.

Try It Out

Speak Up The complete predicate of each sentence is underlined. What is the simple predicate?

Space Camp in Huntsville, Alabama

1. Campers <u>are astronauts for a week</u>.
2. They <u>work in teams of ten</u>.
3. The members <u>name their teams after planets</u>.
4. Some of the teams <u>launch rockets into the air</u>.
5. Other teams <u>take a make-believe space flight</u>.
6. Campers <u>run a control center on the ground</u>.
7. Team members <u>work together to solve problems on the flight</u>.
8. They <u>use headphones to hear and talk to the astronauts</u>.
9. Teams <u>help the astronauts land safely</u>.

The complete predicate of each sentence is underlined. Write the simple predicate.

Example: Hundreds of boys and girls <u>attend space camp</u>. *attend*

10. One camp <u>is in Huntsville, Alabama</u>.
11. Trained leaders <u>help the campers</u>.
12. The campers <u>do different activities each day</u>.
13. These activities <u>teach them about an astronaut's job</u>.
14. Campers <u>visit the U.S. Space and Rocket Center</u>.
15. It <u>has special exhibits from the space program</u>.
16. Campers <u>taste freeze-dried space food</u>.
17. They <u>use spacecraft computers</u>.
18. Special equipment <u>imitates the feeling of a space walk</u>.

19–26. The complete predicate of each sentence is underlined in these tips. Write the tips, and circle the simple predicates.

Example: People <u>need advice for a trip</u>.   *People ⓝⓔⓔⓓ advice for a trip.*

These tips <u>are for new space travelers</u>.

- Most travelers <u>avoid crumbly foods</u>.
  The crumbs <u>float all over the spacecraft</u>.
- Muscles <u>lose strength in outer space</u>.
  Exercise <u>is very important</u>.
  Space travelers <u>use exercise machines to stay fit</u>.
- Some people <u>suffer from space sickness</u>.
  Light meals <u>help sometimes</u>.

Writing Wrap-Up

WRITING • THINKING • LISTENING • SPEAKING

INFORMING

Write a List

Write five helpful tips for new students in your school. Make sure each sentence has a subject and a predicate. Read your tips to a classmate. Have you left out anything important?

7 Correcting Run-on Sentences

Can you find two sentences in this sign? Where should an end mark and a capital letter be added?

This is a picture of a famous ship it is a whaling vessel.

- **When two sentences run into each other, they make a run-on sentence.** Do not use run-on sentences in your writing.

- A run-on sentence can be corrected by writing each complete thought as a separate sentence. Remember to use capital letters and end marks correctly. Do not separate the two sentences with a comma.

Incorrect:	Our class visited a museum we saw whaling ships.
Incorrect:	Our class visited a museum, we saw whaling ships.
Correct:	Our class visited a museum. We saw whaling ships.

Try It Out

Speak Up Which of the following sentences are run-on sentences, and which sentences are correct? What are the two complete thoughts in each run-on sentence?

Colonial Williamsburg in Virginia

1. History museums are fun they teach about the past.
2. A whaling museum is one kind of history museum.
3. A whole village can sometimes be a museum.
4. People dress in costumes, visitors can ask them questions.
5. Some famous people's homes become museums you can visit Paul Revere's house in Boston.
6. Natural history museums show animals and their habitats.
7. The Smithsonian Institution is the world's largest museum complex, it has fourteen museums and a zoo.

Rewrite each sentence correctly.

Example: Our class went to the museum it is at Science Park.
Our class went to the museum. It is at Science Park.

8. Nick had never been there he was eager to go.
9. There was a special show it was about China.
10. Jamie had read about China, she was prepared.
11. People were doing crafts we could watch them work.
12. There was a huge loom two men were weaving silk.
13. Kites are important in China we watched a kite maker.
14. He made a dragon kite it had a long tail.
15. Jamie bought a dragon kite Nick bought a book about China.

16–20. The information on this exhibit sign has five run-on sentences. Write the information correctly.

Example: Amber is a kind of fossil most amber is yellow.
Amber is a kind of fossil. Most amber is yellow.

Amber

Artists use amber to make jewelry some beads are amber. Amber is not a stone it is tree sap. The sap dripped from trees long ago, then it hardened.
Scientists use amber, it helps them study animals that lived long ago. Sometimes insects were trapped in the sap as it dripped down trees their bodies can still be seen today in the amber.

Writing Wrap-Up
WRITING • THINKING • LISTENING • SPEAKING

INFORMING

Write an Exhibit Sign

In the future, something of yours may be in a museum. Write several sentences about the object for an exhibit sign. Read your notes to a partner. Work together to check for run-on sentences.

Writing Good Sentences

Combining Sentences When two sentences run into each other, they make a run-on sentence. Good writers can fix run-on sentences by making two separate sentences. Another good way to fix run-on sentences is to add a comma (,) and the word *and* between the two sentences.

Incorrect: The potter pressed the clay with his thumbs a small bowl took shape.

Correct: The potter pressed the clay with his thumbs, and a small bowl took shape.

Apply It

1–6. Revise these captions for a poster. Correct each run-on sentence by adding a comma and the word *and* between the two sentences.

Revising

Making a Vase

1. The potter puts a ball of clay on the wheel he starts turning the wheel.

2. His hands shape the spinning clay it begins to look like a vase.

3. He fires the vase in a hot kiln the clay becomes dry and hard.

4. The potter decides on a color for the vase he glazes the vase.

5. The vase is fired again the glaze melts.

6. It forms a smooth, shiny surface it makes the vase waterproof.

Good writers use sentences of different lengths. Too many short sentences can make your writing sound boring and choppy. If two short sentences are about the same idea, sometimes you can join them to make a **compound sentence**. Use a comma and the word *and, but,* or *or* to join the sentences.

Most murals are wall paintings. } Most murals are wall paintings, and
Many are outdoors.   } many are outdoors.

Our mural is only half painted. } Our mural is only half painted, but
It already looks great!   } it already looks great!

Did one student paint the mural? } Did one student paint the mural, or
Did a group paint it?   } did a group paint it?

7–12. Rewrite this part of a letter. Combine each underlined pair of sentences into a compound sentence. Use the word in ( ).

Revising

Dear Mayor Stevens,

I am in fourth grade. I go to Washington School. My art teacher is Mr. Mori. (and) Last week Mr. Mori showed us slides of fantastic outdoor murals. Our neighborhood doesn't have a mural. We think it needs one. (but)

We would like to create a mural on the playground wall. Mr. Mori would design it for free. His students would paint it. (and) The mural would not cost the city anything. We would raise the money for supplies. Maybe a paint store would donate them. (or)

Will you support this project? People can see art in museums. Art should be part of their everyday lives too. (but) The students would be proud of their mural. Everyone would enjoy it! (and)

Enrichment

Sentences!

Rhyming Couplets

Write some two-line poems, called couplets. Use one compound sentence for each poem. Choose words that rhyme with each other for the two subjects. The two predicates should also rhyme with each other. Draw pictures to go with your couplets.

The train roars,
and the plane soars.

The dog flops,
and the frog hops.

Mixed-up Messages

Go to Pirate's Cove at sunset How beautiful the sky is
Stand on the beach facing the sun On your right is a
big tree Do you see its shadow The shadow falls over
a large rock The treasure is buried six feet below
the rock Do you have a shovel Start digging now
What a lot of work this is

Pirate Redbeard wrote this message. He forgot to use end marks. Write the message so that it makes sense. Add periods, question marks, and exclamation points.

Challenge Write your own message for a friend to solve.

1 What Is a Sentence? *(p. 32)*

If a group of words below is a sentence, copy it. If not, write *not a sentence.*

1. Many people visit parks.
2. The high mountains.
3. We slept in a tent.
4. Bears visit the campsites.
5. Looking for food.

2 Statements and Questions

(p. 36) Write *statement* or *question* to tell what kind of sentence each one is.

6. Airliners carry passengers, baggage, and mail.
7. Would you like to be a flight attendant?
8. My cousin is training to be an airplane pilot.
9. Have you ever flown in a plane?
10. Are you sending your package by air mail?

3 Commands and Exclamations

(p. 38) Write each command or exclamation correctly.

11. the buses in London are certainly wonderful
12. take a ride on one of these double-decker buses
13. what a strange bus this is
14. give your money to the collector
15. please sit in the top of the bus
16. how high we are

4 Subjects and Predicates

(p. 40) Write each sentence. Draw a line between the complete subject and the complete predicate.

17. My entire family entered the sandcastle contest.
18. I used my pail and my shovel.
19. We packed the pail with wet sand.
20. My brother shaped a tower at the top.
21. Many beautiful castles were in the contest.
22. Three judges chose the winner of the contest.
23. Our sandcastle won first prize.

5 Simple Subjects *(p. 42)*

The complete subject of each sentence is underlined. Write the simple subject.

24. <u>My older brother</u> plays in a wheelchair basketball league.
25. <u>His teammates</u> play the game in wheelchairs too.
26. <u>Their wheelchairs</u> move quickly and easily.
27. <u>The players on his team</u> practice twice a week.
28. <u>They</u> make some very difficult shots.
29. <u>The game on Friday</u> was quite exciting!
30. <u>That game</u> was the first game of the new season.

6 Simple Predicates *(p. 44)*
The complete predicate of each sentence below is underlined. Write the simple predicate.

31. A meteor is a bright streak of light in the sky.
32. Meteors travel through space at very great speeds.
33. A meteor leaves behind a trail of hot gas.
34. Meteors blaze in the sky for a few seconds.
35. Sometimes they explode into small pieces.
36. People hear the noise for miles.

7 Correcting Run-on Sentences *(p. 46)* Rewrite each of these run-on sentences correctly.

37. The museum had many old cars my friend liked that exhibit.
38. The whale looked huge Sara was amazed at the sharks.
39. The mummies were in a special room we wanted to see them.
40. The museum had an old airplane it looked small.
41. We saw a spacecraft it had two model astronauts.
42. There are fossils in this museum let's find the dinosaur bones.

Mixed Review 43–50. This announcement has three missing capital letters and five missing or incorrect end marks. Write the announcement correctly.

Proofreading Checklist
Did you write these correctly?
✔ capital letters
✔ end marks

Proofreading

Sign Up for the School Play!

Do you remember last year's school play. fifty students took part in *The Wizard of Oz*. What a success it was This year's play will be even better, we are putting on the musical *Cats*.

Can you act, sing, or dance? Come and try out for a part tryouts will be held on Friday in the cafeteria. Would you like to help with the scenery or costumes? Sign up for one of these jobs Plenty of jobs are left. We need you.

DRAMA CLUB

 See www.eduplace.com/kids/hme/ for an online quiz.

Test Practice

Write the numbers 1–8 on a sheet of paper. For items 1–4, read each sentence. Choose the underlined word that is the simple subject of the sentence. Write the letter for that answer.

1 A <u>major</u> <u>earthquake</u> <u>struck</u> the city around <u>midnight</u>.
      A   B   C   D

2 The <u>weary</u> <u>umpire</u> took a <u>rest</u> after the <u>game</u>.
        F   G   H   J

3 <u>That</u> <u>pumpkin</u> <u>weighs</u> three hundred <u>pounds</u>!
    A   B   C   D

4 <u>Ashley</u> <u>peeled</u> some <u>carrots</u> for the <u>salad</u>.
      F   G   H   J

For items 5–8, read each sentence. Choose the underlined word that is the simple predicate of the sentence. Write the letter for that answer.

5 The <u>ship</u> <u>moved</u> <u>quickly</u> through the <u>water</u>.
       A   B   C   D

6 A <u>castle</u> in a <u>forest</u> <u>is</u> the setting for the <u>play</u>.
      F   G H   J

7 The <u>driver</u> <u>honked</u> at his <u>friend</u> in the <u>truck</u>.
       A   B   C   D

8 The salesperson <u>sold</u> <u>Darius</u> some <u>laces</u> for his <u>boots</u>.
           F   G   H   J

Now write the numbers 9–18 on your paper. Choose the correct end mark for each sentence. Write the letter for that answer.

9 The airplane soared above the clouds

   A ?   **B** .   **C** !   **D** ,

10 What is your favorite summer sport

   F ?   **G** .   **H** !   **J** ,

11 Please put this letter in the mailbox

   A ?   **B** .   **C** !   **D** ,

12 What a dreadful movie that was

   F ?   **G** .   **H** !   **J** ,

13 Kirsten is making cocoa in the microwave

   A ?   **B** .   **C** !   **D** ,

14 Did the clown really juggle all of those balls

   F ?   **G** .   **H** !   **J** ,

15 Find the Amazon River on your map of South America

   A ?   **B** .   **C** !   **D** ,

16 How terrified the dog is of lightning

   F ?   **G** .   **H** !   **J** ,

17 Have you remembered to turn off the faucet

   A ?   **B** .   **C** !   **D** ,

18 Take those muddy shoes down to the basement

   F ?   **G** .   **H** !   **J** ,

Now write the numbers 19–24 on your paper. Read the passage and find the numbered, underlined parts. Choose the answer that shows the best way to capitalize and punctuate each part. Write the letter for that answer.

There are at least one million kinds of insects in the world. Some insects are <u>pests other</u> insects are
(19)
very helpful to people. A spider is not an insect. Do you know <u>why. Insects</u> have six <u>legs. Spiders</u>
(20)   (21)
have eight legs.

Have you heard about the time Derek decided to make himself a really special <u>sandwich. He</u> started
(22)
with two thick slices of rye bread. He spread strawberry jam on the <u>bread then</u> he put pepperoni on top
(23)
of the jam. He added some mustard. What a disgusting creation <u>it was?</u>
(24)

19 A Pests. Other

   B pests. other

   C pests. Other

   D Correct as it is

20 F why? Insects

   G why. insects

   H why? insects

   J Correct as it is

21 A legs? Spiders

   B legs! spiders

   C legs spiders

   D Correct as it is

22 F sandwich! he

   G sandwich? He

   H sandwich? he

   J Correct as it is

23 A bread Then

   B bread? Then

   C bread. Then

   D Correct as it is

24 F it was!

   G it was

   H it. Was

   J Correct as it is

Extra Practice

(pages 32–33)

Remember

1 What Is a Sentence?

- A sentence is a group of words that tells a complete thought.
- A sentence tells *who* or *what* and *what is* or *what happens.*

● Write *sentence* if the group of words is a sentence. Write *not a sentence* if it is not a sentence.

Example: Our camp was near a lake. *sentence*

1. My brother John.
2. We went fishing.
3. Caught a huge fish.
4. Dad cooked the fish.
5. The fish was very tasty.

▲ For each pair, write the group of words that is a sentence.

Example: Enjoyed driving to California.
The Lams drove to California.
The Lams drove to California.

6. They visited the national parks.
   Had very beautiful scenery.
7. Oldest and largest giant trees.
   Many giant trees are very old.
8. Wanted to see some of the giant trees.
   One giant tree is named General Grant.
9. Another tree is named General Lee.
   Were named for famous generals.

■ Write one sentence for each group of words.

Example: Saw wild animals. *Tim and Jasmine saw wild animals.*

10. A deer.
11. Hiked through the woods.
12. A small black bear.
13. Alone in the woods.
14. Strange sounds.
15. Swam in the cool lake.

(pages 36–37)

2 Statements and Questions

- A statement is a sentence that tells something.
  It ends with a period (.).
- A question is a sentence that asks something.
  It ends with a question mark (?).
- Every sentence begins with a capital letter.

Remember

● Write *statement* if the sentence is a statement. Write *question* if it is a question.

Example: How did the Wright brothers become famous? *question*

1. They began to build gliders in the early 1900s.
2. Where did they test the gliders?
3. Kitty Hawk, North Carolina, was a good place to test gliders.
4. When did they begin to build airplanes?
5. They built their first plane in 1903.

▲ Write each sentence correctly.

Example: did you read about the hot-air balloon
Did you read about the hot-air balloon?

6. two brothers in France invented the balloon
7. it carried a duck, a rooster, and a sheep
8. when was that flight
9. the flight took place in 1783
10. how long were the animals in the air
11. they landed safely after eight minutes

■ Change each statement to a question. Change each question to a statement. Write the new sentences correctly.

Example: was Richard Byrd in the United States Navy
Richard Byrd was in the United States Navy.

12. he was a pilot
13. was he also an explorer
14. He traveled to Antarctica in 1928
15. did Byrd set up a camp

(pages 38–39)

3 Commands and Exclamations

> **Remember**
>
> - A command is a sentence that tells someone to do something. It ends with a period.
> - An exclamation is a sentence that shows strong feeling. It ends with an exclamation point (!).
> - Every sentence begins with a capital letter.

● Write *command* if the sentence is a command. Write *exclamation* if it is an exclamation.

Example: Here comes the train at last! *exclamation*

1. Give your tickets to the conductor.
2. Let me show you to your seat.
3. What a loud noise the train makes!
4. I can't wait to eat in the dining car!
5. Please get me something to eat.
6. How fast we are moving!

▲ Write each command or exclamation correctly.

Example: be ready for the bike trip at eight o'clock
     Be ready for the bike trip at eight o'clock.

7. let me help you pump up your tires
8. be sure to bring a water bottle
9. don't forget your helmet
10. how tired I am
11. what a huge blister I have
12. this bike trip was so much fun

■ Write each sentence correctly.

Example: wait in line to board the ferry. *Wait in line to board the ferry.*

13. what a lot of cars there are
14. please come to the upper deck
15. why does the ferry open at both ends
16. it can be loaded from either end
17. it does not have to turn around
18. what a good idea that is

(pages 40–41)

4 Subjects and Predicates

Remember

- Every sentence has a subject and a predicate.
- The complete subject includes all the words that tell *whom* or *what* the sentence is about.
- The complete predicate includes all the words that tell what the subject *does* or *is.*

● For each sentence, write *subject* if the subject is underlined or *predicate* if the predicate is underlined.

Example: Ina <u>went swimming in the ocean.</u>   *predicate*

1. <u>Eric</u> stayed on the beach.
2. <u>Their mother</u> called Ina.
3. The waves <u>were too high.</u>
4. The sun <u>shone.</u>
5. The whole <u>family</u> enjoyed the beach.

▲ Write each sentence. Draw a line between the subject and the predicate.

Example: A fluffy white cloud drifted across the sky.
           A fluffy white cloud | drifted across the sky.

6. Luis watched the cloud.
7. It looked like a huge white elephant.
8. Then the cloud's shape changed.
9. An enormous white train was now in the sky.
10. The children enjoyed the clouds' shapes.

■ Add a subject to each predicate below. Add a predicate to each subject below. Write the complete sentences. Draw a line between the complete subject and the complete predicate.

Example: Streaks of lightning.   *Streaks of lightning | flashed across the sky.*

11. A strong wind.
12. Pounded on the rocks.
13. Towering waves.
14. The lifeguards.
15. Roared like a lion.
16. Small boats.

(pages 42–43)

5 Simple Subjects

Remember

- The simple subject is the main word in the complete subject. It tells exactly *whom* or *what* the sentence is about.

● Choose a simple subject from the box to complete each sentence. Write the sentence. Use each subject once.

Example: My favorite _____ is baseball.
My favorite sport is baseball.

name
Babe Ruth
games
sport
players
He
series

1. The most exciting _____ are the World Series.
2. This _____ is played in October.
3. Some baseball _____ become famous.
4. _____ was a famous player.
5. His real _____ was George.
6. _____ became a hero to many young people.

▲ The complete subject of each sentence is underlined. Write the simple subject.

Example: The game of baseball comes from an old English sport.   *game*

7. Children in colonial times played a game with two bases.
8. Abner Doubleday did not invent the game of baseball.
9. It developed from the English game of rounders.
10. The first professional baseball team was formed in 1869.
11. The name of the team was the Cincinnati Red Stockings.
12. Eight teams formed the National League in 1876.

■ Write the complete subject of each sentence. Then underline the simple subject.

Example: Outstanding athletes are honored in halls of fame.
Outstanding athletes

13. Baseball has its own Hall of Fame.
14. It opened in Cooperstown, New York, in 1939.
15. A candidate for the Hall of Fame must be retired.
16. Ten years in the major leagues is also necessary.
17. Many famous players are listed in the Hall of Fame.
18. Babe Ruth was elected to the Hall of Fame.

(pages 44–45)

6 Simple Predicates

Remember

- The simple predicate is the main word in the complete predicate. It tells exactly what the subject does or is.

● Choose a simple predicate from the box to complete each sentence. Write the sentence. Use each predicate once.

Example: Earth _____ a planet.   *Earth is a planet.*

1. Planets _____ around the sun.
2. The word *planet* _____ "wanderer."
3. Some planets _____ one or more moons.
4. Earth's moon _____ in the sky at night.
5. Astronauts _____ on our moon in 1969.
6. They _____ moon rocks and soil.
7. Scientists _____ more about the moon.

collected
have
learned
move
means
is
landed
shines

▲ The complete predicate of each sentence is underlined. Write the simple predicate.

Example: Comets <u>are balls of dust and ice.</u>   *are*

8. Early people <u>called them "hairy stars."</u>
9. A comet <u>has a tail.</u>
10. Comets <u>travel around the Sun.</u>
11. Halley's Comet <u>is a very brilliant comet.</u>
12. People saw this <u>comet long ago.</u>
13. Halley's Comet <u>appeared in 1985 and 1986.</u>

■ Write the complete predicate of each sentence. Then underline the simple predicate.

Example: Early people studied the sky.   *<u>studied</u> the sky*

14. They named groups of stars after heroes or animals.
15. We see these same star groups today.
16. The Big Dipper has seven stars.
17. It is part of the Great Bear group.
18. The handle of the dipper forms the tail of the bear.

(pages 46–47)

 Correcting Run-on Sentences

- A run-on sentence has two complete thoughts that run into each other. Correct a run-on sentence by writing each thought as a separate sentence.

● Write *run-on* if the group of words is a run-on sentence. Write *correct* if it is correct.

Example: The White House is in Washington it is the President's home.
run-on

1. It was not always white it was once gray.
2. Theodore Roosevelt had the walls painted white.
3. Roosevelt changed the name it became the White House.
4. Every President except George Washington has lived there.
5. The White House has more than 140 rooms you can visit five.

▲ Write each run-on sentence correctly.

Example: Mount Vernon is a famous house it was George Washington's home. *Mount Vernon is a famous house. It was George Washington's home.*

6. Washington's father built Mount Vernon it was a farm.
7. Mount Vernon is on a hill trees surround the house.
8. Washington planted trees many of them are still there.
9. Each year over a million people come they visit the graves of George and Martha Washington.
10. They see Washington's furniture his books are in the study.

■ 11–14. Rewrite the following paragraph. Correct each run-on sentence.

Example: Congress meets in the United States Capitol it is a building in Washington. *Congress meets in the United States Capitol. It is a building in Washington.*

The Capitol has two parts there is a huge dome over the center. One part is for the House of Representatives the other is for the Senate. There is a statue on top of the dome it is called the Statue of Freedom. Each year about ten million people visit the Capitol. People may watch a meeting of Congress these visitors need a special pass.

Nouns

Taking a shortcut through the coral, this squirrelfish dashes ahead of the diver.

1 What Is a Noun?

Read the sentence below. What words name persons, places, or things?

> In the fields, the horses pulled the plow up and down under the hot summer sun.

—from *Sarah, Plain and Tall,* by Patricia MacLachlan

A noun is a word that names a person, a place, or a thing.

Persons	Cheryl brother dentists	Cheryl and her brother are dentists.
Places	Waterville park zoo	Waterville has a park and a zoo.
Things	pears plums bag	Some pears and plums are in the bag.

Try It Out

Speak Up What are the two nouns in each sentence? Does each noun name a person, a place, or a thing?

1. Jeff lives on an island.
2. The house faces the dark blue ocean.
3. Fishing boats enter the harbor daily.
4. Many people catch lobsters.
5. Workers lift the heavy traps.
6. Gulls fly over the town.
7. Alicia stands on the shore.
8. The coast of Maine looks far away.
9. A ferry arrives from Portland.
10. Passengers step onto the dock.

Write the nouns in these sentences.

Example: Jamal and Lewis stepped off the airplane. *Jamal Lewis airplane*

11. The boys were excited about their vacation in Hawaii.
12. They stayed with their parents in a big hotel.
13. Their room opened onto a beautiful beach.
14. Some people rode surfboards over the waves.
15. Jamal found beautiful shells along the shore.
16. Lewis found a piece of pink coral.
17. The family traveled the twisting highways together.
18. Their car passed by valleys and mountains.
19. Jamal took many pictures with his new camera.

20–32. This part of a social studies report has thirteen nouns. Write the report. Underline the nouns.

Example: Many beautiful flowers grow in Hawaii.
Many beautiful <u>flowers</u> grow in <u>Hawaii</u>.

Hawaii

Hawaii is made up of many islands. The islands were formed by volcanoes. The state is famous for its beautiful scenery. Waikiki is a famous beach there. Swimmers enjoy the warm water. Tourists visit the many shops and big hotels.

Writing Wrap-Up

WRITING • THINKING • LISTENING • SPEAKING

INFORMING

Write a Fact Sheet

Write several sentences that describe your city, town, or state. Include any special features or interesting places to see. Use as many nouns as you can. Then read your sentences to a small group. Have the group list all of the nouns you used.

2 Common and Proper Nouns

One-Minute Warm-Up

Read the sentence below. Name the nouns. What nouns name special persons, places, or things?

Florida is a state in the southeastern corner of the United States.

—from *Florida*, by Dennis Brindell Fradin

- A noun that names any person, place, or thing is called a **common noun**. A noun that names a particular person, place, or thing is called a **proper noun**.

Common and Proper Nouns			
Common	**Proper**	**Common**	**Proper**
girl	Maria	bay	Bay of Fundy
uncle	Uncle George	park	Glacier National Park
queen	Queen Elizabeth	pet	Patches
state	Kansas	day	Saturday
country	Canada	holiday	Fourth of July

- Begin a proper noun with a capital letter. If a proper noun is more than one word, capitalize the first letter of each important word.

Try It Out

Speak Up Find the common noun and the proper noun in each sentence. Which nouns should begin with capital letters?

1. tanya is an explorer.
2. Her kitten magellan is too!
3. Their trips to florida are always exciting.
4. Do the alligators in everglades national park look scary?
5. The guides at cape canaveral are helpful.

List the common nouns and the proper nouns in these sentences. Begin the proper nouns with capital letters.

Example: The explorer christopher columbus made several voyages.
common: explorer   *proper: Christopher Columbus*

6. On tuesday timmy brought in a book about famous explorers.
7. The book told about brave sailors from europe.
8. Was columbus looking for gold and spices?
9. His ship got lost and landed off the coast of north america in 1492.
10. Now columbus day is celebrated in october.
11. Our class also learned about later explorers.
12. maria mitchell discovered a comet in 1847.
13. In 1969 neil armstrong walked on the moon.

14–20. This page from a biography has seven nouns that should have capital letters. Write the biography correctly.

Example: The explorer matthew henson made a daring journey.
The explorer Matthew Henson made a daring journey.

Proofreading

— Polar Explorer —

Matthew Henson was born in maryland in 1866. When he was a boy, Henson worked on a ship. Years later an explorer named robert peary hired Henson as an assistant. In 1909 the two men traveled northward on the arctic ocean. Their goal was to reach the north pole.

Writing Wrap-Up
WRITING • THINKING • LISTENING • SPEAKING

INFORMING

Write a Biographical Sketch
Find out some interesting things about a classmate. Take notes. Then write a paragraph about the person. Read the biography to some classmates. Have them identify proper nouns.

Writing with Nouns

Combining Sentences You know that too many short sentences can make your writing sound choppy. If two short sentences have the same predicate, you can combine them by joining the subjects with the word *and*. Your new sentence will have a **compound subject**.

Meriwether Lewis explored the West.
William Clark explored the West.

Compound Subject

Meriwether Lewis and William Clark explored the West.

Apply It

1–5. Revise these facts about the journey of Lewis and Clark. Combine each pair of underlined sentences.

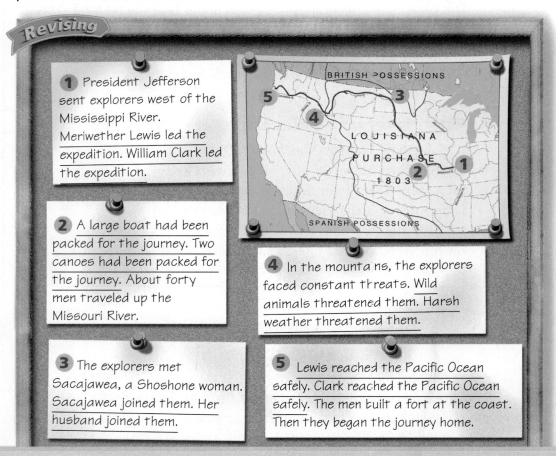

Revising

1 President Jefferson sent explorers west of the Mississippi River. Meriwether Lewis led the expedition. William Clark led the expedition.

2 A large boat had been packed for the journey. Two canoes had been packed for the journey. About forty men traveled up the Missouri River.

3 The explorers met Sacajawea, a Shoshone woman. Sacajawea joined them. Her husband joined them.

4 In the mountains, the explorers faced constant threats. Wild animals threatened them. Harsh weather threatened them.

5 Lewis reached the Pacific Ocean safely. Clark reached the Pacific Ocean safely. The men built a fort at the coast. Then they began the journey home.

BRITISH POSSESSIONS

LOUISIANA PURCHASE 1803

SPANISH POSSESSIONS

When one sentence gives details about a subject in a previous sentence, you can combine the two sentences. Put the details from one sentence directly after the noun in the other sentence.

The Omaha have lived in Nebraska since the 1600s.

They are a Native American people.

The Omaha, a Native American people, have lived in Nebraska since the 1600s.

Use commas to set apart the added words.

Apply It

6–10. Rewrite the underlined sentences in this first draft of a biography. The first pair of sentences has been done for you.

Revising

Second Draft
Susan La Flesche, an Omaha Indian, was a determined woman from Nebraska. La Flesche

First Draft
Susan La Flesche
Susan La Flesche was a determined woman from Nebraska. She was an Omaha Indian. La Flesche dreamed of becoming a medical doctor. She was a caring and smart woman.

Two people helped her with this goal. These people were her father and her friend. Her father made sure La Flesche had an excellent education. Her father sent her to a famous school in Virginia. Her father was an Omaha chief.

A friend helped La Flesche to enroll in medical school. The friend was Alice Cunningham Fletcher. The determined young woman was about to realize her childhood dream. La Flesche succeeded in her goal. She was an excellent student. She became the first Native American woman to graduate from medical school and practice medicine.

3 Singular and Plural Nouns

Look around the classroom. What objects do you see? Complete these sentences by filling in the blanks with different objects.

There is one _____.   There are several _____.

A noun can name one or more than one. **A noun that names only one person, place, or thing is called a singular noun. A noun that names more than one is called a plural noun.**

Singular Nouns	**Plural Nouns**
One goat is in the barn.	Many goats are in those barns.
This hen laid one egg.	These hens laid a dozen eggs.

How to Form Plurals		
Rules	**Singular**	**Plural**
Add -*s* to most singular nouns.	one boy one puddle a rose	two boys both puddles ten roses
Add -*es* to singular nouns that end with *s, x, ch,* or *sh.*	one bus this box one bunch a wish	three buses some boxes six bunches many wishes

Try It Out

Speak Up What is the plural form of each of the following singular nouns?

1. brush
2. gift
3. class
4. patch
5. prize
6. circus
7. inch
8. fox

Write the correct noun to complete each sentence. Label the noun *singular* or *plural*.

Example: My family works in many (business, businesses).
                businesses   plural

9. Cousin Woody makes many (toolbox, toolboxes).
10. Grandmother Hooper is a basketball (coaches, coach).
11. Uncle Sandy is a lifeguard at a (beach, beaches).
12. My sister grows bushels of (radishes, radish).
13. Grandpa Taylor makes some wedding (dress, dresses).
14. Aunt Fern owns a plant (store, stores).
15. I rest in the kitchen and eat lots of (sandwich, sandwiches)!

16–22. This list of tasks has seven incorrect plural nouns. Write the list correctly.

Example: Peel two bunchs of banana. *Peel two bunches of bananas.*

Proofreading

The Cozy Kitchen

ATTENTION WORKERS!

✔ Clean the three kitchen sinkes with scrub brushs.

✔ Mix a batch of dough. Shape it into a loaf six inchs long.

✔ Get two boxs of oniones from the cellar.

✔ Put four glass and a pair of candles on each table.

✔ Stack some menues near the cash register.

✔ Ask both of the bosses if you can leave early!

Writing Wrap-Up

WRITING • THINKING • LISTENING • SPEAKING

CREATING

Write a List

Years from now the chores you do at home might be very different. Write a list of chores for the year 2050. Use the plural form of four of these nouns: *box, house, dress, computer, batch, brush.* Read your list to a small group. Have them raise their hands when they hear a plural noun.

4 Nouns Ending with y

One-Minute Warm-Up

Read the sentences below. Can you name the plural noun?

In Europe the main area for drilling gas is the North Sea. The area is shared by several countries.

—from *Natural Resources*, by Damian Randle

You have already learned some rules for making nouns plural. Here are two special rules for making the plural forms of nouns that end with *y*.

How to Form Plurals

Rules	Singular	Plural
If the noun ends with a vowel and *y*, add -*s*.	one toy a monkey	many toys five monkeys
If the noun ends with a consonant and *y*, change the *y* to *i* and add -*es*.	one family this city a baby	some families six cities two babies

 HELP ? Tip

If you forget these rules, you can use a dictionary to find the plural spelling of a noun.

Try It Out

Speak Up What is the plural form of each noun?

1. berry
2. holiday
3. turkey
4. boy
5. pony
6. party
7. lady
8. donkey
9. puppy
10. sky
11. hobby
12. key
13. bluejay
14. bunny
15. firefly
16. ray

Write the plural form of the noun in ( ) to complete each sentence.

Example: People are finding _____ to save energy. (way) *ways*

17. Drivers save gas by driving slower on _____. (highway)
18. We save gas by taking buses or _____ to work. (subway)
19. In some _____, workers travel by boat. (city)
20. Many _____ help by turning off air conditioners. (company)
21. How can all the _____ in your town help? (family)
22. All _____ and girls can turn off extra lights. (boy)
23. People can make sure that their _____ are working properly. (chimney)

24–30. This speech has seven incorrect plural nouns. Write the speech correctly.

Example: Large bodies of water can be used to make energy.
Large bodies of water can be used to make energy.

Proofreading

We all worry about the energy wasted in American communitys. Supplys of oil and gas are being used up. We must use energy from the sun and from the waterfalls in our many valleyes. We must turn the garbage in alleyies into fuel for factorys. Leave your cars at home, ladys and gentlemen. Find other wayes to travel. Saving energy now will make a better future for everyone!

Writing Wrap-Up

WRITING • THINKING • LISTENING • SPEAKING

PERSUADING

Write a Speech

Your town is working on an ad campaign to discourage littering. Write a speech to give at a rally. Include reasons why people should dispose of trash properly. Use the plural form of *lady, highway, family, sky,* and *company.* Present your speech. Was it convincing?

5 More Plural Nouns

One-Minute Warm-Up

Can you make your own silly sentences using the words below?

foot goose mice feet mouse teeth geese tooth

Be careful when you peek at a crocodile's teeth!

- Some nouns have special plural forms. Since these words follow no spelling pattern, you must remember them.

Singular and Plural Nouns			
Singular	**Plural**	**Singular**	**Plural**
one child	two children	each tooth	five teeth
a man	many men	one goose	both geese
this woman	three women	an ox	nine oxen
that foot	these feet	a mouse	some mice

- Other nouns are the same in both the singular and the plural forms.

Singular Nouns	**Plural Nouns**
One deer nibbled the bark	Several deer ate quietly.
Did you see a moose?	Two moose crossed a stream.
I have a pet sheep.	These sheep have soft wool.

Try It Out

Speak Up Complete each sentence with the plural form of the underlined noun.

1. One <u>child</u> helped two smaller _____ tie their shoes.
2. That <u>man</u> sang while two other _____ played guitars.
3. This <u>sheep</u> is my pet, and those _____ belong to Dan.
4. Mai hopped on one <u>foot</u> and then jumped with both _____.
5. Ana saw one <u>moose</u> in Maine and four _____ in Canada.

Write each underlined noun. Label it *singular* or *plural*.

Example: The <u>child</u> and his grandfather stared out the window.
child   singular

6. Their train sped past many <u>sheep</u> grazing in a field.
7. Nearby, two <u>oxen</u> slowly pulled a plow.
8. A <u>woman</u> wearing overalls followed the animals.
9. In the distance, two <u>men</u> were cutting down trees.
10. The <u>teeth</u> of their saws gleamed in the sunlight.
11. Several <u>deer</u> watched from the edge of the forest.

12–18. This story beginning has seven incorrect plural nouns. Write the story beginning correctly.

Example: Papa whistled through his two front tooths.
Papa whistled through his two front teeth.

 LIFE ON THE FRONTIER

Papa tied the four oxes to the wagon. Several men and womans from nearby farms helped him load it. The five gooses would ride in the back of the wagon. All of the sheeps would walk beside the wagon. Our dog stood on his hind feets and looked longingly into the wagon. He would have to walk too. Both childs took a last peek into the house. It was empty except for a family of mouses.

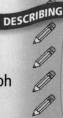

Writing Wrap-Up   WRITING • THINKING • LISTENING • SPEAKING

DESCRIBING

Write a Story Idea

Write a paragraph describing an idea for a story. Use the plural form of *child, man, woman, foot,* and *mouse.* Compare your paragraph with a partner's. How are your story ideas alike and different?

6 Singular Possessive Nouns

One-Minute Warm-Up

Read the sentences below. Which noun shows ownership? How do you know?

Matthew's room had pictures of great home run hitters of the past, like Babe Ruth, the Sultan of Swat.

—from *Yang the Youngest and His Terrible Ear*, by Lensey Namioka

Sometimes you may want to tell what someone or something has or owns. **A noun that shows ownership is called a possessive noun.** Add an apostrophe and an *-s* (*'s*) to a singular noun to make it possessive.

Singular Nouns	Singular Possessive Nouns
The football belongs to Bob.	This is Bob's football.
The bike the girl owns is new.	The girl's bike is new.
These poems by Wes are funny.	Wes's poems are funny.
The tail of the beaver is flat.	The beaver's tail is flat.

Try It Out

Speak Up What is another way to make each group of words show ownership? Use the possessive form of the underlined noun.

1. balloon of one <u>child</u>
2. nose of the <u>rabbit</u>
3. mask of <u>Carlos</u>
4. computer of this <u>man</u>
5. den of one <u>fox</u>
6. collar of our <u>puppy</u>
7. basketball of a <u>friend</u>
8. drawings by an <u>artist</u>

Write each phrase another way. Use the possessive form of each underlined noun.

Example: science projects of my <u>class</u> *my class's science projects*

9. eyes of the <u>dinosaur</u>
10. posters drawn by <u>Pervis</u>
11. magnets owned by <u>Marita</u>
12. rocks owned by <u>Chan</u>

13. telescope belonging to a <u>teacher</u>
14. hamsters owned by my <u>sister</u>
15. fur of one <u>hamster</u>
16. volcano made by <u>Chris</u>

17–24. This review for a school newspaper has eight incorrect singular possessive nouns. Write the review correctly.

Example: A monkeys tricks caused giggles.
  A monkey's tricks caused giggles.

Proofreading

𝕮𝖊𝖓𝖙𝖗𝖆𝖑 𝖘𝖈𝖍𝖔𝖔𝖑 𝕹𝖊𝖜𝖘   Volume 8, Number 4

Class's Circus Is a Hit

Mrs. Green class put on a circus show last week. Charles Owens was a clown. Charles jokes kept everyone laughing. He squirted one boys face with water from a fake flower and tickled the principal with a foxs tail. The audience also admired an elephant's dance and an acrobats skill. They cheered a lion tamer courage in handling a roaring lion (played by Josh Eng) and joined in the ringmasters song. The students made each performer's costume, with help from Sonia Perez mother.

Class Clown

Writing Wrap-Up
WRITING • THINKING • LISTENING • SPEAKING

EVALUATING

Write a Review

Think of a school event you have attended, such as a class play or a special assembly. Write a review of it for the school paper. Describe the event. Was anyone's performance particularly good or funny? Include singular possessive nouns. When you are done, read your review to a partner. Does your partner agree with your review?

7 Plural Possessive Nouns

One-Minute Warm-Up

This lost-and-found ad is missing an apostrophe. Where should the apostrophe go?

My kittens are lost. If you see them please call the kittens owner at 555-4072.

Sometimes you may want to show ownership by more than one person or thing.

- When a plural noun ends with -s, add an apostrophe (').

  pumpkins owned by the boys   the boys' pumpkins
  eyes of the puppies   the puppies' eyes

- When a plural noun does not end with -s, add an apostrophe and -s ('s).

  antlers of both deer   both deer's antlers
  reports by these men   these men's reports

Singular	Singular Possessive	Plural	Plural Possessive
animal	animal's	animals	animals'
pony	pony's	ponies	ponies'
class	class's	classes	classes'
mouse	mouse's	mice	mice's
deer	deer's	deer	deer's

Try It Out

Speak Up What is another way to make each group of words show ownership? Use the possessive form of the underlined noun.

1. canoe of two <u>women</u>
2. tails of some <u>deer</u>
3. poems by four <u>authors</u>
4. saddles of these <u>ponies</u>
5. cage of both <u>mice</u>
6. rules of many <u>coaches</u>

Write each phrase, using the possessive form of the underlined noun.

Example: reports by three <u>students</u>   *three students' reports*

7. horns of several <u>oxen</u>
8. duties of both <u>pilots</u>
9. trucks belonging to these <u>women</u>
10. reports by three <u>students</u>
11. antlers of some <u>moose</u>
12. tents owned by two <u>families</u>
13. awards of two <u>actresses</u>

14–18. This program for a pet show has five incorrect plural possessive nouns. Write the program correctly.

Example: The two judges tables faced the ring.
The two judges' tables faced the ring.

PET COMPETITION
Order of Events

2:00 The judges announce the finalists. Several childrens' pets will compete in each event.

2:15 Four dogs's barks are judged for the Most Annoying award.

2:30 Five mices' skills are tested in the Run the Maze contest.

2:45 Three canaries's songs are judged for the Most Musical award.

3:00 The winning pets' prizes are presented. Their owners pictures will be taken with their pets.

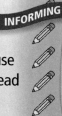

WRITING • THINKING • LISTENING • SPEAKING

INFORMING

Write a Program

List events for a contest, such as the Wild Animals' Olympics. Then use the list to write a program of events. Include plural possessive nouns. Read your program to a partner. Check the possessive nouns together.

Using Exact Nouns

When you write, it is important to use exact nouns. Using exact nouns will make your writing clearer and easier to understand.

Less exact noun: My pet likes to sit on my shoulder.

More exact noun: My frog likes to sit on my shoulder.

Apply It

1–8. Rewrite this journal entry. Change the underlined nouns to more exact nouns.

Revising

July 6

My aunt has a big place on top of a hill. My family and I went there for dinner to celebrate my cousin Jeff's birthday. The food was delicious. I got sauce on my clothes. My aunt brought out a birthday cake for Jeff. He cut pieces for everyone. I gave Jeff a great new toy.

Afterward, Jeff and I went outside to play with his three animals. They ran into the garden and ruined some of my aunt's flowers. They also knocked down my aunt's outdoor furniture. Boy, were we in trouble!

Enrichment

Nouns!

Plan Your Own Mall

Plan a new shopping mall for young people. First, write the name of the mall on a sheet of paper. Then list the names of the stores in alphabetical order. Use some singular and plural possessive nouns in the store names, such as Bob's Bikes or Girls' Sneakers. List some things that will be sold in each store. Finally, make a map of an imaginary town. Show where your mall will be located.

A Biographical Dictionary

A biographical dictionary lists famous people and tells what they are known for. Make your own biographical dictionary. Think of at least five famous people. List their names in alphabetical order as in the example below. Write a sentence explaining why each person is famous.

Jackie Robinson

Robinson, Jackie. He was an outstanding baseball player who opened up major-league baseball to African Americans.

Washington, George. He was the first president of the United States.

Challenge Find out more about one of the people in your dictionary who especially interests you. Write a paragraph about the person and add it to your dictionary as a special feature.

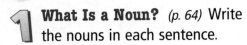

1 **What Is a Noun?** *(p. 64)* Write the nouns in each sentence.

1. Greenland is the largest island in the world.
2. One part is only ten miles from Canada.
3. The weather is usually cold on the island.
4. The people catch fish and seals for food.
5. Women wear traditional clothes on holidays.

2 **Common and Proper Nouns** *(p. 66)* Write the common nouns in these sentences in one list. Write the proper nouns in another list.

6. Pam and Robbie wrote a report about the Gulf of Mexico.
7. Kara went to the library to get some books.
8. Her class is learning about the Gulf Stream.
9. This stream was named by Benjamin Franklin.
10. The water in the Gulf Stream is warmed by the hot sun.

3 **Singular and Plural Nouns** *(p. 70)* Write the correct form of the noun in ( ) to complete each sentence. Label the noun *singular* or *plural*.

11. Mr. Graves is a forest _____. (ranger)
12. Reporting forest fires is one of the _____ of a ranger. (job)
13. Mr. Graves reports all forest _____ quickly. (fire)

14. Rangers clear away lots of dead _____. (branch)
15. Many bulldozers and _____ are used to clear forests. (ax)
16. People get a _____ to some special sights from the rangers. (pass)

4 **Nouns Ending with *y*** *(p. 72)* Write the plural form of the noun in ( ) to complete each sentence.

17. Acting is one of my favorite _____. (hobby)
18. I was in two school _____ last year. (play)
19. One play is made from three short _____. (story)
20. Two people in one story ride _____ to work. (trolley)
21. They talk during _____ on the trolley. (delay)

5 **More Plural Nouns** *(p. 74)* Write the plural form of the noun in ( ) to complete each sentence.

22. In 1850 some _____ were looking for gold. (man)
23. They walked until their _____ were very sore. (foot)
24. Sometimes _____ pulled the wagons. (ox)
25. Often they saw _____ in the distance. (deer)
26. Some field _____ nibbled the supplies of flour and cornmeal. (mouse)
27. Jake kept some _____ near his mine. (sheep)

28. The _____ shared the work. (woman)

29. The _____ played a simple game with a string and a button. (child)

6 Singular Possessive Nouns

(p. 76) Write each group of words another way. Use the possessive forms of each underlined noun.

30. brown horse belonging to <u>Sara</u>
31. shiny saddle on the <u>horse</u>
32. first horse show for <u>Mike</u>
33. cheers of my <u>brother</u>
34. voice of the <u>announcer</u>
35. horse the <u>rider</u> has
36. instructions of the <u>trainer</u>
37. starting point of the <u>jumper</u>
38. notebook of the <u>judge</u>
39. trophy belonging to the <u>winner</u>

Mixed Review 48–54. This newspaper article has two missing capital letters, three incorrect plural nouns, and two incorrect possessive nouns. Write the article correctly.

7 Plural Possessive Nouns

(p. 78) Write the possessive form of the plural noun in ( ) to complete each sentence.

40. Katie and Tyler enjoyed visiting my _____ farm. (grandparents)
41. Grandfather let us pat the _____ noses. (sheep)
42. The _____ coats are brushed every day. (horses)
43. The _____ chores take all day long. (workers)
44. The _____ lunch is hearty. (men)
45. Grandmother gathers the _____ eggs each morning. (chickens)
46. Some _____ nest is underneath the coop. (mice)
47. The _____ honking was heard all over the farm. (geese)

Proofreading Checklist

Did you write these words correctly?
- ✔ proper nouns
- ✔ plural nouns
- ✔ singular possessive nouns
- ✔ plural possessive nouns

Proofreading

Students' Plan Brings Cheer

This year a group of students in the town of waterville decided to make their thanksgiving more meaningful. Mrs. Brown fourth graders came up with a plan. The childrens' idea was to provide holiday meals for people in need.

The students collected twenty-five boxs of groceries from men and women in their neighborhoods. Local stores also donated twelve frozen turkies. All of the students' efforts made the holiday a happier one for many familys.

Test Practice

Write the numbers 1–8 on a sheet of paper. Choose the best way to write the underlined part of each sentence. Write the letter for that answer. If there is no mistake, write the letter for the last answer.

1 My little sister loves frilly <u>dressies</u>.

  A dresses

  B dresss

  C dress's

  D (No mistakes)

2 Uncle Kevin tells the best <u>storys</u>!

  F story

  G story's

  H stories

  J (No mistakes)

3 That <u>carpenter's</u> belt holds lots of tools.

  A carpenters

  B carpenteres

  C carpenters'

  D (No mistakes)

4 The dentist carefully checked all of Morgan's <u>tooth</u>.

  F tooths

  G teeth

  H teeths

  J (No mistakes)

5 All of the <u>actors'</u> costumes are too big for them.

  A actor's

  B actors

  C actor

  D (No mistakes)

6 You wouldn't want to swim in the icy waters of <u>crater lake</u>!

  F Crater lake

  G crater Lake

  H Crater Lake

  J (No mistakes)

7 The store sells <u>mattresses</u>.

  A mattress's

  B mattressies

  C mattress

  D (No mistakes)

8 Marcos stared at the <u>Statue of liberty</u>.

  F Statue of Liberty

  G statue of liberty

  H statue of Liberty

  J (No mistakes)

Now write the numbers 9–14 on your paper. Write the letter of the best way to write each sentence.

⁹Deer were becoming a real problem in our town. ¹⁰They wandered into peoples yards and ate the flowers. ¹¹One day aunt jane got an idea from a gardening magazine. ¹²She hung many bar of soap around her garden. ¹³Her plan worked the deer are staying away. ¹⁴Now mooses are her only problem.

9 **A** Deers were becoming a real problem in our town.

   B Deers was becoming a real problem in our town.

   C Deer was becoming a real problem in our town.

   D Best as it is

10 **F** They wandered into people's yards and ate the flowers.

   G They wandered into people yards and ate the flowers.

   H They wandered into peoples' yards and ate the flowers.

   J Best as it is

11 **A** One day Aunt jane got an idea from a gardening magazine.

   B One day Aunt Jane got an idea from a gardening magazine.

   C One day aunt Jane got an idea from a gardening magazine.

   D Best as it is

12 **F** She hung many bars of soap around her garden.

   G She hung many bar's of soap around her garden.

   H She hung many Bars of Soap around her garden.

   J Best as it is

13 **A** Her plan worked. the deer are staying away.

   B Her plan worked? The deer are staying away.

   C Her plan worked. The deer are staying away.

   D Best as it is

14 **F** Now meese are her only problem.

   G Now moose are her only problem.

   H Now moose is her only problem.

   J Best as it is

Unit 1: The Sentence

Sentences *(pp. 32, 36, 38)* If a group of words below is a sentence, copy it correctly. If not, write *not a sentence.* Label each sentence *statement, question, command,* or *exclamation.*

1. my family and I ski each winter
2. my skis, boots, and poles
3. cross-country skiing is hard work
4. how thirsty you get
5. have you ever skied downhill
6. what a thrill it is
7. near the trees
8. practice on the small hill
9. would you like some help
10. watch the instructor

Subjects and Predicates *(pp. 40, 42, 44)* Write each sentence. Draw a line between the complete subject and the complete predicate. Then underline each simple subject once. Underline each simple predicate twice.

11. This book is about insects.
12. Most bees are social insects.
13. They live in groups.
14. The bees live on food from plants.

15. Colorful flowers attract the bees.
16. Beekeepers raise bees for honey.

Run-on Sentences *(p. 46)* Rewrite each run-on sentence correctly.

17. Our class visited a museum it is on Oak Street.
18. The museum is in the heart of the city I had never been there.
19. Some teachers went to the museum they liked the Navajo art.
20. The paintings were very old we had learned about them in class.
21. The blankets were colorful Robin liked their beautiful patterns.

Unit 2: Nouns

Kinds of Nouns *(pp. 64, 66)* Write the fifteen nouns in these sentences. Label each noun *common* or *proper.*

22. Mr. Grasso and his family flew over the Rocky Mountains.
23. David and Jessica saw rivers, plains, and cities.
24. Their grandparents live in San Francisco.

25. Grandpa was at the airport.
26. The children and their parents enjoyed California.

Singular and Plural Nouns *(pp. 70, 72, 74)* Write the plural form of each singular noun.

27. joke
28. child
29. hunch
30. wax
31. journey
32. tooth
33. hobby
34. woman

Singular Possessive Nouns

(p. 76) Write the possessive form of the noun in ( ) for each sentence.

35. My _____ drama club put on a play. (sister)
36. _____ scenery was great. (Kim)
37. The _____ costumes were terrific. (cast)
38. The _____ helper collected the props. (director)
39. I laughed at the _____ entrance. (captain)
40. His voice sounded like a _____ roar. (lion)
41. That _____ song was the best in the show. (man)

Plural Possessive Nouns *(p. 78)*
Write the possessive form of the noun in ( ) for each sentence.

42. My twin _____ birthday party was yesterday. (brothers)
43. Everyone went to our _____ house to ride the ponies. (neighbors)
44. The _____ manes were tied with ribbons. (ponies)
45. The _____ games were fun! (children)
46. We made _____ tails out of colored paper. (donkeys)
47. Adam tied on the _____ blindfolds. (girls)
48. My _____ friend made the birthday cake. (parents)

(pages 64–65)

1 What Is a Noun?

Remember

• A noun is a word that names a person, a place, or a thing.

● One of the underlined words in each sentence is a noun. Write each underlined noun.

Example: <u>Justin</u> <u>learned</u> about underwater volcanoes. *Justin*

1. <u>First</u>, the <u>floor</u> of the ocean shakes.
2. Then a <u>long</u> <u>crack</u> appears.
3. Melted <u>rock</u> pushes <u>up</u> through the crack.
4. It comes from <u>deep</u> inside the <u>earth</u>.
5. The <u>volcano</u> gets <u>larger</u> and larger.
6. Finally, the <u>tip</u> <u>pushes</u> through the water.

▲ Write the two nouns in each sentence.

Example: The students are reading about Indonesia.
students   Indonesia

7. The country is located in Asia.
8. Its many islands are on the equator.
9. Many of its great mountains are volcanoes.
10. Tigers live in some of the dark, green jungles.
11. Rice is an important food.
12. Explorers once came searching for valuable spices.

■ Write the nouns in these sentences. Write *person, place,* or *thing* beside each noun.

Example: The Collinses flew to Bermuda in a jet.
Collinses—person   Bermuda—place   jet—thing

13. Then a taxi took the family to an inn.
14. Their room had a window facing the ocean.
15. Michael noticed that the beach had pink sand!
16. Sarah read from a magazine for tourists.
17. One story explained how some settlers came to the island.
18. Their ship crashed on the rocks during a bad storm.

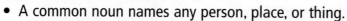

(pages 66–67)

2 Common and Proper Nouns

- A common noun names any person, place, or thing.
- A proper noun names a particular person, place, or thing.
- Capitalize proper nouns.

Remember

● Write each noun correctly. Next to it, write *common* or *proper*.

Example: aunt betty   *Aunt Betty—proper*

1. africa
2. maps
3. henry hudson
4. statue of liberty

5. sailor
6. forest
7. october
8. mississippi river

▲ List the common nouns and the proper nouns. Use capital letters correctly.

Example: Hikers follow trails through the grand canyon.
   common: Hikers   proper: Grand Canyon

9. Visitors from many states go there daily.
10. The spectacular canyon is located in arizona.
11. Its steep walls were formed by the colorado river.
12. Wind and water gradually wore away the rock.
13. Explorers from spain admired the spot long ago.
14. Now hikers climb down a trail called bright angel.
15. Some tourists ride mules instead.

■ Use one common noun and one proper noun to complete each sentence. Write the sentence correctly. You may add or remove words such as *a, an,* and *the.*

Example: _____ and his _____ are brave explorers!
   Henry and his sister are brave explorers!

16. They took a trip with _____ to explore the _____.
17. Henry carefully packed the _____ that _____ gave him.
18. On _____ they finally arrived at the _____.
19. According to their map, they had to cross _____ to reach _____.
20. They walked along _____ until they saw _____.
21. Henry quickly discovered _____ beside _____.
22. After climbing _____ they finally reached _____!

(pages 70–71)

3 Singular and Plural Nouns

- A singular noun names one person, place, or thing.
- A plural noun names more than one person, place, or thing.
- To form plural nouns, add -s to most singular nouns. Add -es to singular nouns that end with *s, x, ch,* or *sh.*

Remember

● Write each underlined noun. Beside it, write *singular* or *plural.*

Example: Mr. Okawa sells <u>peaches</u> at his farm. *peaches—plural*

1. He puts the peaches in large wooden <u>boxes</u>.
2. Mr. Okawa sells <u>pears</u> too.
3. My <u>bus</u> passes the farm stand every day.
4. We often see Mrs. Okawa out trimming her flower <u>bushes</u>.
5. She has a <u>basket</u> of beautiful pink roses beside her.
6. Once she gave two <u>bunches</u> of flowers to our bus driver.

▲ Write the plural form of the noun in ( ) to complete each sentence.

Example: Kayla went to work with her two _____. (uncle) *uncles*

7. They build _____ in the city. (skyscraper)
8. Kayla took two _____ and a pear for lunch. (sandwich)
9. Uncle Carl introduced Kayla to both of his _____. (boss)
10. Next, Kayla met several _____. (carpenter)
11. They explained how the tools in two _____ worked. (toolbox)
12. A woman hurried by with a box of _____. (paintbrush)

■ If the underlined noun is singular, make it plural. If it is plural, make it singular. Write the new sentence.

Example: Grandmother had her own clothing <u>store</u> in Italy.
Grandmother had her own clothing stores in Italy.

13. She made dresses for Italy's most famous <u>actresses</u>.
14. I hoped Grandmother would leave her <u>business</u> in Italy.
15. I wanted her to live with my <u>cousin</u> and me in New York.
16. My <u>wish</u> finally came true!
17. Grandmother arrived with her <u>boxes</u> of beautiful cloth.
18. Soon she opened her new dress <u>shop</u> downtown.

(pages 72–73)

Remember

4 Nouns Ending with *y*

- If a singular noun ends with a vowel and *y*, add *-s* to make the noun plural.
- If a singular noun ends with a consonant and *y*, make it plural by changing the *y* to *i* and adding *-es*.

● Write the plural nouns in these sentences.

Example: The libraries in our city are closed on holidays.
libraries   holidays

1. All the factories are closed as well.
2. Some companies remain open.
3. We can still buy groceries at the corner store.
4. The drugstores will not make any deliveries.
5. The subways do not run very often.
6. The airport runways are busier than usual.

▲ Write each sentence. Use the plural form of the noun in ( ).

Example: Two Presidents have _____ in February. (birthday)
Two Presidents have birthdays in February.

7. Our class performed two short _____ about them. (play)
8. Miss Moran read us _____ about both men. (story)
9. We learned many facts in just a few _____. (day)
10. Washington's army had very few _____. (supply)
11. Lincoln carried out his many _____ honestly. (duty)
12. He didn't want the northern and southern states to become _____. (enemy)

■ Find the noun in each sentence that should be plural. Write the noun correctly.

Example: Of all the holiday, Thanksgiving is my favorite. *holidays*

13. Dad gets up very early and puts two turkey in the oven.
14. I watch puffy smoke rise from all the chimney in town.
15. My sisters and both of their family arrive early.
16. Then Aunt Rita arrives with two large tray of fruit and cheese.
17. Uncle Nate tells long story of when he was a boy.
18. My favorite is about the time he lost his three pet donkey.

(pages 74–75)

5 More Plural Nouns

- Some nouns have special plural forms.
- Some nouns have the same singular and plural forms.

Remember

● Write each underlined noun. Beside it, write *singular* or *plural*.

Example: Some <u>deer</u> are good swimmers. *deer—plural*

1. The farmer uses two <u>oxen</u> to pull his cart.
2. Six <u>sheep</u> grazed quietly in the meadow.
3. The <u>men</u> drove tractors through the fields.
4. The <u>goose</u> honked loudly at some chickens.
5. Are the <u>children</u> awake yet?
6. My little pet <u>mouse</u> eats seeds and nuts.
7. A duck has webbed <u>feet</u> to help it swim.

▲ Write each sentence correctly. Use the plural form of the noun in ( ).

Example: Two _____ showed us the pioneer village. (woman)
           Two women showed us the pioneer village.

8. We saw some _____ working at spinning wheels. (child)
9. They made thread from the wool of many _____. (sheep)
10. Several _____ were repairing the roof of a barn. (man)
11. Some surprised _____ hurried across the barnyard. (mouse)
12. Two _____ pulled a wagon filled with hay. (ox)
13. A boy gathered eggs that all his _____ had laid. (goose)
14. A blacksmith put new shoes on a horse's front _____. (foot)

■ Write the correct form of the noun in ( ) for each sentence.

Example: A painting of a _____ was on the wall. (deer) *deer*

15. A picture of some _____ was next to it. (moose)
16. Two small _____ played by the fire. (child)
17. They sat on pillows stuffed with feathers from _____. (goose)
18. One child played with a pet white _____. (mouse)
19. Near the window, two _____ played fiddles. (woman)
20. They tapped their _____ to the music. (foot)

(pages 76–77)

6 Singular Possessive Nouns

- A possessive noun is a noun that shows ownership.
- To form the possessive of a singular noun, add an apostrophe and a *-s* (*'s*).

● Write the possessive form of each singular noun.

Example: brother   *brother's*

1. Monica
2. tiger
3. singer
4. Carlos
5. panda
6. Chris
7. mouse
8. principal
9. Kenny
10. coach
11. Jess
12. boy

▲ Write each group of words another way. Use the possessive form of the underlined noun.

Example: paintings by one <u>student</u>
        one student's paintings

13. picture painted by <u>Isabel</u>
14. paintbrushes belonging to <u>Li</u>
15. mask drawn by <u>Julio</u>
16. face of the <u>gorilla</u>
17. wings of the clay <u>dragon</u>
18. art show of the whole <u>class</u>

■ Write each sentence another way. Use a possessive noun to take the place of the underlined words.

Example: The club <u>of Jess</u> had a neighborhood circus.
        Jess's club had a neighborhood circus.

19. They held their circus in <u>the yard belonging to Mr. Wong</u>.
20. <u>Posters made by Chris</u> announced the circus.
21. Tickets were designed on <u>a computer owned by Marcus</u>.
22. Julia made <u>the nose of the elephant</u> from a hose.
23. <u>The roar of the lion</u> came from a tape recorder.
24. <u>The hat belonging to one clown</u> had tin cans on it.
25. <u>A goat owned by Marcy</u> pulled the circus wagon.

(pages 78–79)

7 Plural Possessive Nouns

Remember

- To form the possessive of a plural noun that ends with -s, add only an apostrophe (').
- To form the possessive of a plural noun that does not end with -s, add an apostrophe and -s ('s).

● For each pair, write the group of words that has a plural possessive noun.

Example: my teacher's dictionaries
my teachers' dictionaries   *my teachers' dictionaries*

1. the butterflies' wings
   the butterfly's wings
2. our bosses' notebook
   our boss's notebook
3. her brother's snowshoes
   her brothers' snowshoes
4. the woman's cameras
   the women's cameras

▲ Write the possessive form of the noun in ( ) for each sentence.

Example: The Young _____ Club meets after school. (Farmers)
Farmers'

5. Everyone learns a lot about _____ habits. (animals)
6. Each year the _____ entries win prizes at the fair. (children)
7. Their _____ eggs are the largest in the county! (geese)
8. People always admire the _____ dairy cows. (girls)
9. The _____ ponies win many ribbons. (boys)
10. Judges carefully check the _____ coats. (ponies)

■ Write the plural possessive form of the singular noun in ( ) to complete each sentence.

Example: Our _____ farm is next to ours. (neighbor)
Our neighbors' farm is next to ours.

11. Their _____ goats often wander onto our lawn. (son)
12. The goats have taken over my _____ job of cutting the grass. (sister)
13. Who would like my job of collecting the _____ eggs? (chicken)
14. Amy makes sweaters from the _____ wool. (sheep)
15. She makes all the _____ sweaters for the family. (child)

She raced to the ball, bent her knee, and kicked the ball solidly.

1 Action Verbs

One-Minute Warm-Up

Read the sentences below. Which word in each sentence shows action?

Diego sang. David tapped a rhythm on the side of the truck. . . .
The family drove through forests and through dry country.

—from *Radio Man/Don Radio*, by Arthur Dorros

You know that every sentence has a subject and a predicate. The main word in the predicate is the verb. **A verb is a word that can show action. When a verb tells what people or things do, it is called an action verb.**

Subjects	Predicates
Rita and Eric	dig slowly and carefully.
The students	helped the scientists.
Rita	uncovered some pottery.
The pieces of pottery	provide clues about the past.

Try It Out

Speak Up What is the action verb in each sentence?

1. Rita cleaned the pieces of pottery.
2. Two students stand in the water.
3. They hold a tub with a screen in the bottom.
4. Water fills the tub.
5. Eric pours dirt into the tub.
6. Light objects float in the water.
7. Dirt goes through the screen.
8. The students attach labels to the objects.
9. The scientists take the objects to their lab.
10. They learn many things about early people.

Write each action verb.

Example: Deserts cover a large part of the American Southwest. *cover*

11. Spanish explorers crossed these deserts long ago.
12. They noticed tall, steep rocks with flat tops.
13. The explorers named these rocks *mesas*.
14. They called smaller mesas *buttes*.
15. Early people settled on Mesa Verde in Colorado.
16. They built homes on the flat tops of the mesas.
17. These people disappeared long ago.
18. People tell stories about a famous mesa, Weaver's Needle.
19. Hundreds of people still search for a gold mine there.

20–30. This part of an online encyclopedia article has eleven action verbs. Write the article. Underline the verbs.

Example: Winds blow across the mesas. *Winds <u>blow</u> across the mesas.*

Web site

Mesas

Wind and water make a mesa. It takes millions of years. The wind and water carve the rock. The softer part of the rock disappears first. The harder part forms a mesa. The hot sun beats down on it. A few plants grow on mesas. Flowers open only at night. They protect themselves from the daytime sun. Only small animals live on mesas. Lizards and pack rats make their homes there.

Writing Wrap-Up

WRITING • THINKING • LISTENING • SPEAKING

EXPLAINING

Write Instructions

Think of a real rock, tree, building, or other object. Write instructions explaining how to get to the object from your school. Use action verbs in your sentences. Read your instructions to a partner. Have your partner identify the verbs.

2 Main Verbs and Helping Verbs

One-Minute Warm-Up

The verb in the sentence below is made up of two words. What are they? Which word shows the action?

Jim Thorpe had put the Olympics on the world map.

—from *The Story of the Olympics*, by Dave Anderson

A verb may be more than one word. **The main verb is the most important verb. The helping verb comes before it.**

Some Common Helping Verbs		
am	was	has
is	were	have
are	will	had

The main verbs below are in yellow. Helping verbs are in blue.

Alberto is training for a marathon.
He has run five miles each day.
His coach will help him next week.

Try It Out

Speak Up Find each helping verb and main verb.

1. Sara was racing in a wheelchair race.
2. She had joined the Wheelchair Athlete Club.
3. The racers were using special racing wheelchairs.
4. They are training several times a week.
5. They have lifted weights too.
6. Sara has raced for several years.
7. She will race many more times.
8. She is practicing for the Olympics.

Write the sentences. Underline helping verbs once and main verbs twice.

Example: I am reading about the Junior Olympics.
I am reading about the Junior Olympics.

9. The Junior Olympics were started in 1967.
10. The games are held every summer.
11. The annual event has included twenty-four sports.
12. Each young athlete was dreaming of a gold medal.
13. All of the competitors had won other contests.
14. They have earned a place in the Junior Olympics.
15. The athletes will remember the games all their lives.
16. I am practicing for the next Junior Olympics.

17–24. This announcement has eight verbs. Write the announcement. Underline each helping verb once and each main verb twice.

Example: The fans are holding their breath.
The fans are holding their breath.

The Murray School

The Murray School Olympic Games have started with a bang. The Red Team has claimed the gold for the sack relay. No one was expecting such a fast race. Last year's event had lasted twice as long. Now, which children will win the medals for the somersault race? A moment ago the teams were taking their places. The suspense is growing. Now they are rolling!

Writing Wrap-Up
WRITING • THINKING • LISTENING • SPEAKING

INFORMING

Write an Announcement

Write an announcement about an event for the Goofy Olympic Games. Use helping verbs. Read your announcement to a partner. Listen for the verbs. How many helping verbs did you use?

For Extra Practice see page 126.

3 Present, Past, and Future

OD TON
BRUTSID

Unscramble the label that goes with each group of words below.

repents: swoop, find, screech, land, hide
spat: ate, searched, collected, slept, soared
rufute: will clean, will go, will rest, will feed, will chase

A verb tells when something happens. **The tense of a verb lets you know whether something happens in the present, in the past, or in the future.**

Verb Tenses	
Rules	**Examples**
A verb in the **present tense** shows action that is happening now.	Bats hunt at night. Now the bat rests.
A verb in the **past tense** shows action that has already happened. Many verbs in the past tense end with -ed.	It hunted last night. The bats rested.
A verb in the **future tense** shows action that will happen. Verbs in the future tense use the helping verb will.	They will hunt tonight. The bat will rest.

Try It Out

Speak Up What is the verb in each sentence? Is it in the present tense, the past tense, or the future tense?

1. Michael likes many kinds of animals.
2. He collects facts about animals.
3. I finished a book about birds yesterday.
4. We will go to the library tomorrow.
5. Michael will look for books about bats.
6. The librarian will help him.

Write the verb in each sentence. Beside it write *present, past,* or *future.*

Example: Bats help people a great deal. *help* *present*

7. Most bats will eat insects.
8. They help gardeners a great deal.
9. A flying bat makes sounds.
10. The sounds send echoes to the bat's ears.
11. The echoes direct the bat.
12. One scientist studied bats.
13. Then he trained some of them.
14. The bats will fly to him on command.
15. Someday he will write a book about them.

16–24. This ad has nine verbs. Write each verb. Then write *past, present,* or *future* beside it.

Example: Every gardener needs a Cozy Bat House! *needs* *present*

> For years insects spoiled my flowers. They chewed every petal. Now I grow flowers with no trouble. I simply purchased a Cozy Bat House. Then I attached it to a tree. Bats sleep there during the day. At night they gobble up insects. A Cozy Bat House will keep your garden beautiful. You will thank your friends the bats.

Writing Wrap-Up

WRITING • THINKING • LISTENING • SPEAKING

EXPLAINING

Write a Cause-and-Effect Paragraph

Write a paragraph about what might happen if a bat got into your school. Use verbs in the past, present, and future tenses. Read your ideas to a partner. Can your partner add anything else?

Writing with Verbs

Keeping Verbs in the Same Tense You know that verb tense tells when an event happened. Verb tenses show past, present, and future time. When you write, use verb tenses carefully to make your meaning clear.

> Change tense only to show a change in time.

In the following paragraph, the writer switched from past to present tense for no reason. The result is confusing!

> In the 1800s, large herds of bison crossed railroad tracks in the Great Plains. They cause long delays for the trains. Railroad companies then encouraged bison hunting as a sport.

In the paragraph above, the verb *cause* should be changed to the past tense.

Apply It

1–5. Rewrite these two paragraphs from a social studies report so that every verb is in the same tense.

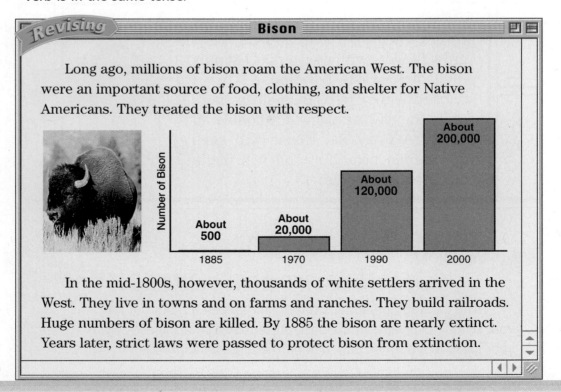

Revising

Bison

Long ago, millions of bison roam the American West. The bison were an important source of food, clothing, and shelter for Native Americans. They treated the bison with respect.

Number of Bison

About 500 — 1885
About 20,000 — 1970
About 120,000 — 1990
About 200,000 — 2000

In the mid-1800s, however, thousands of white settlers arrived in the West. They live in towns and on farms and ranches. They build railroads. Huge numbers of bison are killed. By 1885 the bison are nearly extinct. Years later, strict laws were passed to protect bison from extinction.

Combining Sentences Sometimes you can make your writing flow more smoothly by combining short sentences to form a longer sentence. If two short sentences have the same subject, you can combine them by joining the predicates with *and*. Your new sentence will have a **compound predicate**.

She was the smartest buffalo.
She had many friends.

She was the smartest buffalo
and had many friends.

6–10. Rewrite these paragraphs from part of a story. Combine each pair of underlined sentences.

Revising

Little Horn was a smart bison. She could teach the other bison. She could think of fun games. One summer she taught her brothers, sisters, and cousins how to swim. They swam fast. They raced each other.

One day a hungry cougar crept down a nearby mountain. It saw the herd. It hid in the grass. Little Horn spotted the cougar. She didn't want to scare the others, so she started a game.

Little Horn ran to the river. She began a race with everyone. They all swam across to safety. Meanwhile, the cougar came to a sudden stop at the riverbank. It couldn't swim. The big cat had been tricked. It looked silly. The bison cheered.

4 Subject-Verb Agreement

What is the subject of the sentence below? Is it singular or plural? What is the verb?

An internal modem fits into a special slot inside your computer.

—from *Why Doesn't My Floppy Disk Flop?*
by Peter Cook and Scott Manning

A verb in the present tense must **agree** with the subject of the sentence. This means that the subject and the verb must work together. They must both be singular or both be plural.

Subject-Verb Agreement	
Singular subjects	When the subject is a singular noun or *he, she,* or *it*, add -*s* to the verb.
	A <u>computer</u> helps people. <u>It</u> solves problems.
Plural subjects	When the subject is a plural noun or *I, we, you,* or *they*, do not add -*s* to the verb.
	<u>Computers</u> help people. <u>They</u> solve problems.

Try It Out

Speak Up Which verb correctly completes each sentence?

1. Marta (test, tests) her new computer program.
2. Marta (own, owns) a computer.
3. She (use, uses) it to do her homework.
4. The computer (help, helps) her parents too.
5. Her brothers (play, plays) games on it.
6. Computers (work, works) very rapidly.
7. Many people (use, uses) computers at work.
8. They (store, stores) a great deal of information.
9. I (want, wants) to learn more about computers.

Choose the verb that correctly completes each sentence. Write the sentence.

Example: Computers (produce, produces) pictures called graphics.
Computers produce pictures called graphics.

10. Computer pictures (help, helps) people in many ways.
11. They (assist, assists) pilots like my uncle.
12. Special graphics (imitate, imitates) a real flight.
13. People (send, sends) computers into space.
14. A camera (take, takes) a picture on Mars.
15. It (send, sends) signals to a computer on Earth.
16. Many other workers (use, uses) computers in their jobs.
17. A doctor (look, looks) deep inside the human body.
18. An engineer (design, designs) new cars.

19–26. This part of a note has eight incorrect verbs. Write the note correctly.

Example: The game get harder. *The game gets harder.*

Proofreading THANK YOU THANK YOU THANK YOU THANK YOU THANK YOU

Dear Grandpa,
    I loves my new computer game. You give the best gifts! The computer graphics looks so real. First, you follows a river through a tropical forest. A jungle animal ask you questions along the way. Correct answers brings you to the next level. Steven enjoy the game too. He stays on Level 2 all the time. It make him so angry! We all plays the game a lot.

Writing Wrap-Up
WRITING • THINKING • LISTENING • SPEAKING

EXPRESSING

Write a Thank-You Note

Write your name and the name of a gift on a piece of paper. Put the paper in a class "gift" bag. Pick a gift from the bag, and write a thank-you note to the person whose name you drew. Use present tense verbs. Read your note to a partner. Do subjects and verbs agree?

5 Spelling the Present Tense

What's wrong with this riddle? How can you fix it?

Question: Why does the baseball coach fix a pancake breakfast for his team?

Answer: His batter make a hit!

You add *-s* to most present tense verbs to make them agree with a singular subject. Some other verbs, however, add *-es* when they are used with a singular noun subject or with *he, she,* or *it.*

Present Tense with Singular Subjects		
1. For most verbs: Add *-s.*	sing + -s stay + -s	Corey sings. He stays.
2. For verbs that end with *s, x, z, ch,* or *sh*: Add *-es.*	pitch + -es buzz + -es	She pitches. A bee buzzes.
3. For a verb that ends with a consonant and *y*: Change the *y* to *i* and add *-es.*	study + -es fly + -es	Marisa studies. The bird flies.

Try It Out

Speak Up How should you spell the verb in the present tense to complete each sentence correctly?

1. Ben _____ tennis at the park. (play)
2. His friend Lin often _____ him. (watch)
3. Sometimes Ben _____ the ball. (miss)
4. Lin _____ his strokes carefully. (study)
5. Ben _____ his mistakes. (fix)
6. Ben _____ tennis. (enjoy)
7. He _____ to get better. (want)

Write each sentence with the correct verb.

Example: Nicole (love, loves) the game of softball.
Nicole loves the game of softball.

8. Every afternoon Nicole (hurry, hurries) to the field.
9. First, she (dress, dresses) in the locker room.
10. Then the players (toss, tosses) the ball around.
11. Nicole (throw, throws) the ball to Ashley.
12. The ball (fly, flies) high over her head.
13. Some more players (arrive, arrives) at the field.
14. The coach (teach, teaches) them some new plays.

15–22. This journal entry has eight incorrect verb forms. Write the entry correctly.

Example: My swing improve every day.
My swing improves every day.

Proofreading

July

Wednesday, July 25

I likes the mornings best at baseball camp. Our counselors practices with us every day after breakfast. One counselor pitchs extremely fast. The ball buzzies right past the batter! He showes us all his tricks. The other counselor watch us at bat. Sometimes he copys everyone's mistakes. We laugh at ourselves a lot. Then each camper tryes harder.

Writing Wrap-Up   WRITING • THINKING • LISTENING • SPEAKING

COMPARING / CONTRASTING

Write a Sports Report

Choose two sports that you like. Write one paragraph comparing the two sports and one paragraph contrasting them. Use verbs in the present tense. Find a partner, and read your reports to each other. Compare your choices.

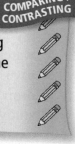

6 Spelling the Past Tense

This tongue twister doesn't match the picture. Fix it by moving one letter to a different word.

Molly mopped and mooed to be milked, but Marty merely moped.

The past tense is usually formed by adding -ed to the verb.

Rules for Spelling the Past Tense		
1. **Most verbs:** Add -ed.	play + -ed call + -ed	We played. Dad called us.
2. **Verbs ending with e:** Drop the e and add -ed.	graze + -ed rope + -ed	The cattle grazed. He roped a calf.
3. **Verbs ending with a single vowel and a consonant:** Double the consonant and add -ed.	stop + -ed tug + -ed	The horse stopped. I tugged the rope.
4. **Verbs ending with a consonant and y:** Change the y to i and add -ed.	carry + -ed hurry + -ed	Men carried ropes. They hurried out.

Try It Out

Speak Up What is the past tense of each verb?

1. splash
2. hum
3. bake
4. fry
5. watch
6. save
7. drop
8. study
9. slip
10. talk
11. divide
12. worry
13. hop
14. trip
15. spray
16. look

Use the past tense of the verb in ( ) to complete
each sentence. Write the sentence.

Example: Luis and Cristina _____ on a cattle drive. (help)
Luis and Cristina helped on a cattle drive.

17. Their grandparents _____ a cattle ranch. (own)
18. The whole family _____ the summer drive. (plan)
19. They _____ the cattle to new pastures. (move)
20. At night they _____ at a water hole. (stop)
21. The adults _____ dinner over a campfire. (cook)
22. Luis _____ buckets of water. (carry)
23. After dinner he _____ the dishes. (wash)
24. Cristina _____ them. (dry)

25–30. This part of an e-mail message has six misspelled verbs in
the past tense. Write the message correctly.

Example: I hoped onto the saddle.
I hopped onto the saddle.

Proofreading

e-mail

Dear Jarrod,
    We startted the third day of the cattle drive today.
It turnned exciting! One cow walked away from the
herd. Luis and I hurryed after the stray. Luis troted up
behind it on his horse. Then both of us guided the cow back. Mom
and Dad claped their hands. Grandpa praiseed us for our good work.

Writing Wrap-Up
WRITING · THINKING · LISTENING · SPEAKING

DESCRIBING

Write a Letter
    Write a letter to a pen pal in another country. Describe something
interesting, such as a town parade or a family event. Use verbs in the
past tense. Then read your letter to a partner. Did your partner
describe a similar experience?

7 The Past with Helping Verbs

One-Minute Warm-Up

Read the sentences below. Are the verbs in the present tense, the past tense, or the future tense? Which sentence has a helping verb?

> Aunt Molly worked for an airline. She had traveled all over the world.

—from *Cam Jansen and the Mystery of the Circus Clown*, by David A. Adler

You know that you can add *-ed* to most verbs to show action that happened in the past. There is another way to show that something has already happened.

- Use the helping verb *has, have,* or *had* with the past form of most verbs.
- The helping verb must agree with the subject of the sentence.

Agreement with Helping Verbs	
1. **With singular subjects:** Use *has.*	Jillian has joined a circus. She has traveled all over.
2. **With plural subjects and *I* or *you:*** Use *have.*	Horses have learned tricks. You have dropped your ticket.
3. **With either singular or plural subjects:** Use *had.*	Bears had danced. A clown had hurried into the ring.

Try It Out

Speak Up What are the helping verb and the main verb in each sentence?

1. We have watched the circus with Aunt Millie.
2. She had invited us two weeks ago.
3. Ray has hurried to the circus grounds.
4. The first act had started.
5. The ringmaster has stepped into the ring.

On Your Own

Write each sentence. Underline each helping verb once and each main verb twice.

Example: I have enjoyed the circus. *I have enjoyed the circus.*

6. You have liked it too.
7. The ringmaster has cracked her whip.
8. The elephants had paraded in a circle.
9. They have walked right in front of me.
10. One chimp has grinned at the audience.
11. We have clapped loudly for the performers.

12–18. This poem has seven incorrect helping verbs. Write the poem correctly.

Example: A dog have jumped through a hoop.
A dog has jumped through a hoop.

At the Circus

The acrobats has sailed through the air.
They has dangled on ropes without a care.
One clown have balanced a chair on his nose.
The others has sprayed the crowd with a hose.
A monkey have carried off the ringmaster's hat.
Nobody had planned on that.
The lions has settled down at last.
The show have ended much too fast!

Writing Wrap-Up WRITING • THINKING • LISTENING • SPEAKING

CREATING

Write a Poem

Can you fly a kite or do a handstand? Did you ever watch a fireworks show? Write a poem about something you like to do or see. Use verbs in the past with helping verbs. With a small group, take turns reading your poems aloud. Listen for any incorrect helping verbs.

8 Irregular Verbs

One of the verbs in the sentences below is incorrect.
Do you know how to fix it?

Someone has eaten my lunch! The sea gull has took it!

Verbs that do not add *-ed* to show past action are called irregular verbs. You must remember the spellings of irregular verbs.

I eat now.   I ate earlier.   I have eaten already.

Irregular Verbs		
Present	**Past**	**Past with helping verb**
begin	began	(has, have, had) begun
break	broke	(has, have, had) broken
bring	brought	(has, have, had) brought
come	came	(has, have, had) come
drive	drove	(has, have, had) driven
eat	ate	(has, have, had) eaten
give	gave	(has, have, had) given
grow	grew	(has, have, had) grown
know	knew	(has, have, had) known
make	made	(has, have, had) made
say	said	(has, have, had) said
sing	sang	(has, have, had) sung
take	took	(has, have, had) taken
tell	told	(has, have, had) told
throw	threw	(has, have, had) thrown
wear	wore	(has, have, had) worn

Try It Out

Speak Up What are the past tense and the past with a helping verb for each irregular verb below?

1. sing
2. begin
3. come
4. know
5. eat
6. tell

Write each sentence, using the correct form of the verb to show past action.

Example: His uncle had _____ Matthew sailing lessons. (give)
His uncle had given Matthew sailing lessons.

7. They had _____ many sailing trips together. (take)
8. Matthew _____ his friend Tyler to join them one day. (tell)
9. Tyler's father _____ him to the boat. (drive)
10. Tyler _____ good-bye to his father. (say)
11. Matthew's uncle _____ how to handle the boat. (know)
12. The boat had _____ to a pleasant island. (come)
13. Everyone _____ a big lunch on the island. (eat)

14–20. This part of an adventure story has seven incorrect irregular verb forms. Write the story. Correct the underlined verbs.

Example: Mr. Williams had taked Buster for a boat ride.
Mr. Williams had taken Buster for a boat ride.

Proofreading

Buster the Superdog

The trip had began calmly. Suddenly, the weather grown worse. Huge waves broked over the small boat. One wave pushed Mr. Williams overboard. Fortunately, he had wore a life jacket. Buster the Superdog had make a strict rule about that. Buster thrown Mr. Williams a rope. The clever pet bringed him safely back onboard.

Writing Wrap-Up

WRITING • THINKING • LISTENING • SPEAKING

NARRATING

Write a Story

Write the beginning of an adventure story. The setting might be the darkest jungle or the hottest desert or any place else you want. Use verbs from the chart on page 112. Then read your story to a partner. Ask your partner to listen for the verbs. Did you use the correct verb forms?

For Extra Practice see page 132.

9 The Special Verb *be*

One-Minute Warm-Up

Which word on the shirts will *not* complete the sentence below correctly?

Rigsy and Chuckles _____ glad they forgot their lunches.

The verb *be* has special forms for different subjects.

Subject	Present	Past
I	am	was
you	are	were
he, she, it	is	was
singular noun (Miguel)	is	was
we	are	were
they	are	were
plural noun (stories)	are	were

The verb *be* does not show action. It tells what someone or something is or is like.

I am a reporter.   You are a photographer.
That story was long.   Those cartoons were funny.

Try It Out

Speak Up Which verb correctly completes each sentence? Is it in the present tense or the past tense?

1. I (was, were) a cartoon writer last year.
2. Kayla (is, are) good at drawing.
3. We (is, are) a great team!
4. Two cartoons (was, were) about the cafeteria food.
5. The food (is, are) pretty bad!

Write the verb in each sentence. Then write *past* or *present* to tell the tense of the verb.

Example: The *Scoop* is our school newspaper. *is—present*

6. I am the editor of the *Scoop*.
7. William is a good writer.
8. He was the sports writer.
9. You are a good writer too.
10. I was happy with your last story.
11. All the reporters were busy.
12. The paper is ready for the printers.
13. We are proud of our work.

14–20. This part of a newspaper article has seven incorrect forms of the verb *be*. Write the article correctly.

Example: The fire were in an apartment building.
The fire was in an apartment building.

Proofreading

Smoky Blaze Alarms Residents

Chicago, April 12 — Mrs. Allen were at home with her husband when a fire began in the kitchen. "We was so afraid. The smoke were so thick and black," Mrs. Allen said. "The firefighters was there for us in minutes," she added. "They is heroes. I is very grateful."

"Your smoke detector batteries were dead," one firefighter told her later. "You was lucky this time," he warned. "Get new batteries right away."

Writing Wrap-Up
WRITING • THINKING • LISTENING • SPEAKING

EXPRESSING

Write an Opinion

Write a paragraph about fire safety in the home. In your opinion, what are the best ways to protect a home against fire? Use forms of the verb *be*. Then read your paragraph to a small group. Does the group share your opinion? Can anyone suggest other fire safety tips?

10 Contractions with *not*

Read the sentences below. Which word has an apostrophe? What two words make up this word?

"Shortcut?" asked Floyd. "I didn't know there were any good shortcuts to school."

—from *The Secret Shortcut*, by Mark Teague

Sometimes you can join a verb with the word *not*. **The shortened word is called a contraction.** An **apostrophe** (') takes the place of the letter *o* in each contraction with *not*.

Tim is not ready yet.   Tim isn't ready yet.

Contractions with *not*			
Word Pairs	**Contractions**	**Word Pairs**	**Contractions**
is not	isn't	has not	hasn't
are not	aren't	have not	haven't
was not	wasn't	had not	hadn't
were not	weren't	could not	couldn't
do not	don't	should not	shouldn't
does not	doesn't	would not	wouldn't
did not	didn't	will not	won't
cannot	can't		

Try It Out

Speak Up What is the contraction for each word or pair of words?

1. do not
2. could not
3. were not
4. have not
5. will not
6. has not
7. should not
8. cannot
9. is not

Please don't feed the birds!

Write the contraction for the underlined word or words.

Example: Tim <u>cannot</u> find his gloves. *can't*

10. They <u>are not</u> in his closet.
11. They <u>were not</u> anywhere he looked.
12. He <u>had not</u> started getting ready when I called.
13. Tim <u>should not</u> wait until the last minute.
14. I <u>did not</u> expect him to be ready on time.
15. This <u>was not</u> the first time.

16–22. This song has seven contractions that are misspelled or that have problems with apostrophes. Write the song correctly.

Example: My best friend did'nt call me. *My best friend didn't call me.*

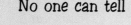

The Bad Day Blues

I have'nt done my homework. I cann't find my shoes.

No one can tell me that I dont have the blues.

Oh, why willn't this day ever end?

The TV isnt working. It hasn't worked all day.

My mom said I couldnt watch it anyway.

Oh, why doesn'nt this day ever end?

 WRITING • THINKING • LISTENING • SPEAKING

CREATING

Write a Song

Write your own song about a bad day. What went wrong? Use contractions from page 116. Then teach your song to a small group. Take turns performing one another's songs. Which song had the most contractions?

Using Exact Verbs

A verb is a word that can show action. Use exact verbs in your writing so the reader can imagine the actions you write about.

Less exact verb: Alicia said, "Watch out for the puddle!"

More exact verb: Alicia screamed, "Watch out for the puddle!"

Apply It

1–8. Use your Thesaurus Plus in the Tools and Tips section at the end of your book to find synonyms for each underlined verb. Then rewrite this story. Use a different, more exact verb in place of each underlined word.

Synonyms are words with almost the same meanings.

Revising

Enzo the Energetic Dog

Toby <u>saw</u> Enzo acting funny. Suddenly, Enzo <u>jumped</u> quickly to his feet and <u>jumped</u> the fence. Toby, who was sitting happily on the porch, <u>jumped</u> from his chair.

Toby got a pair of binoculars so he could <u>see</u> Enzo close up. He <u>saw</u> that Enzo wasn't wearing his collar. Just as Toby started to worry, Mimi came home. When she heard that Enzo was missing, she <u>shouted</u>, "Enzo, come home!" Then Enzo came <u>running</u> back.

Enrichment

Verbs!

Past, Present, and Future

Players: 2–4

Materials: For each player, 5 index cards with the word *past;* 5 index cards with the word *future;* 5 blank index cards. On each blank card, players write a sentence using a present tense verb.

To play: Players put all the sentence cards facedown in one stack. They put the *past* and *future* cards facedown in another. Players draw a card from each stack. If a player draws a *past* card, he or she changes the verb on the sentence card to the past tense. If a player draws a *future* card, he or she changes the verb on the sentence card to the future tense. Other players decide if the new sentence is correct.

Scoring: A correct sentence earns 1 point.

Challenge Use only the irregular verbs from page 112 in your sentences. Make *past* and *past with <u>had</u>* cards.

Change the Subject

Something unusual is happening. Draw pictures to tell the rest of the story, and write sentences about the action. Use *I* as the subject with present tense verbs. Then rewrite the sentences with someone else as the subject. Make subjects and verbs agree.

Knock, knock.

Who's there?

1 Action Verbs *(p. 96)* Write the action verbs in each sentence.

1. We played a terrific soccer game today.
2. Our team met the Pumas.
3. They scored a goal right away.
4. Our team tied the score with one minute left.
5. Coach Yin called time out.
6. She sent in a new player.
7. Anne made another goal.
8. We beat the champions!

2 Main Verbs and Helping Verbs *(p. 98)* Write the two verbs in each sentence. Draw one line under the helping verb and two lines under the main verb.

9. Manuel had wanted a guitar for months.
10. He was saving up for a new one.
11. He is taking lessons.
12. I am listening to Manuel.
13. He is becoming a good player.
14. I have heard this tune.
15. I will sing along.
16. Manuel's friend has joined us.

3 Present, Past, and Future *(p. 100)* Write the verbs in these sentences. Beside each verb, write *present, past,* or *future.*

17. The circus will arrive in town tonight.
18. The clowns are here now.
19. We saw the lion tamer.
20. He looks very brave.
21. The panther growled fiercely.

4 Subject-Verb Agreement *(p. 104)* Write the verb that correctly completes each sentence.

22. Spiders (spin, spins) silk threads.
23. The threads (form, forms) a web.
24. The web (trap, traps) food.
25. A water spider (make, makes) its web underwater.
26. It (eat, eats) tiny fish.

5 Spelling the Present Tense *(p. 106)* Write each sentence, using the correct present tense verb.

27. Ray (draw) funny cartoons.
28. Ben (copy) his pictures.
29. He (push) hard on the pen.
30. The pen (scratch) noisily.
31. The wet ink (dry) quickly.

6 Spelling the Past Tense *(p. 108)* Write each sentence. Use the past tense form of the verb in ( ).

32. Rosa (remember) a birthday.
33. She (want) to buy a gift.
34. She (work) to earn the money.
35. Rosa (hope) to find a sale.
36. The glass bowl (gleam).
37. Rosa (cry), "That's perfect!"
38. The clerk (wrap) the bowl.
39. Rosa's aunt (love) the bowl.

7 The Past with Helping Verbs *(p. 110)* Write each sentence. Use *have* or *has* and a past tense verb.

40. A busy Saturday (start).
41. Tyler (decide) to wash the car.
42. His friends (arrive) early to help.

 See www.eduplace.com/kids/hme/ for an online quiz.

43. Ali (attach) the hose.
44. Julie (drop) the heavy bucket of water.
45. Chip (hurry) to pick it up.
46. You (spray) them with the garden hose!

8 **Irregular Verbs** *(p. 112)* Write each sentence, using the correct past form of the verb.

47. I have (give) a report on my trip.
48. Our family had (drive) to Canada.
49. Alex and I had (bring) our skis.
50. We had (know) there would be snow.
51. We (eat) wonderful food.
52. We (take) a tour of Old Montreal.
53. A guide (tell) us about its history.

Mixed Review 64–72. This Web page has eight incorrect verb forms and one missing apostrophe. Write the page correctly.

9 **The Special Verb** *be* *(p. 114)* Write each sentence, using the correct form of the verb in ( ).

54. Our class play (is, are) a comedy.
55. The lines (is, are) very funny.
56. Kim (is, are) the star.
57. I (was, were) nervous on stage.
58. The play (was, were) a success.

10 **Contractions with** *not* *(p. 116)* Write the contraction for the underlined word or words.

59. Karl <u>will not</u> go to the movie.
60. He <u>does not</u> want to see it again.
61. I <u>have not</u> seen this film yet.
62. You <u>cannot</u> turn me down!
63. We <u>should not</u> arrive too late.

Proofreading Checklist
Did you write these words correctly?
✔ verbs in the present tense
✔ verbs in the past tense
✔ contractions

Proofreading

Web site

Welcome to the Boomerang Contest!

Most people dont know much about boomerangs. These sticks is twelve to thirty inches long. They moves through the air in amazing paths. People has used boomerangs in Australia, Africa, and North America since early times.

The contest has began! The spectators is quiet. Gavin Smith throw his boomerang. It hits the ground. Then it spins into the air. Now it fly in a circle. The boomerang droped right into Gavin's hand!

Test Practice

Write the numbers 1–8 on a sheet of paper. Choose the best way to write the underlined part of each sentence. Write the letter for that answer. If there is no mistake, write the letter for the last answer.

1 Robert <u>has broken</u> his leg.

  A has broke

  B has breaked

  C have broken

  D (No mistakes)

2 Yesterday you <u>was</u> late for school.

  F is

  G are

  H were

  J (No mistakes)

3 That woodpecker <u>hasnt</u> stopped making noise all morning.

  A hasn't

  B hasnt'

  C has'nt

  D (No mistakes)

4 I <u>is</u> a walrus in the school play this year.

  F are

  G be

  H am

  J (No mistakes)

5 Maria <u>worrys</u> too much.

  A worries

  B worry

  C worryes

  D (No mistakes)

6 Soon the zookeepers <u>will feed</u> the lions.

  F will fed

  G have fed

  H will feeds

  J (No mistakes)

7 The bus <u>stoped</u> at the train tracks.

  A stoppied

  B stopped

  C stop

  D (No mistakes)

8 The pig <u>wouldnt'</u> go back in its pen.

  F wouldn't

  G wouldnt

  H would'nt

  J (No mistakes)

Now write the numbers 9–16 on your paper. Read each paragraph. Choose the line that shows the mistake. Write the letter for that answer. If there is no mistake, write the letter for the last answer.

9   **A**   Noah began piano practice.

     B He didn't know the new song.

     C His next lesson was tuesday.

     D (No mistakes)

10 **F**   Nani took two eggs. She

     G broke them into a bowl.

     H Then she added some peachs.

     J (No mistakes)

11 **A**   I am on a soccer team. Last

     B week's game was the most

     C exciting of all. we won!

     D (No mistakes)

12 **F**   We watched a TV show

     G about foxes. These animals

     H can live in cities. they are
        very clever.

     J (No mistakes)

13 **A**   Soon the birds will hatch.

     B The mother birds life will be

     C hard. She must bring her
        babies food.

     D (No mistakes)

14 **F**   My feet are sore my shoes

     G are tight. I have grown a

     H lot since Grandma gave them
        to me.

     J (No mistakes)

15 **A**   The twins went to the

     B library. Two books were

     C overdue. Owed fifty cents.

     D (No mistakes)

16 **F**   We took a train to dallas.

     G What an exciting city it is!

     H We saw many tall buildings.

     J (No mistakes)

Now write the numbers 17–24 on your paper. Read each paragraph. Choose the line that shows the mistake. Write the letter for that answer. If there is no mistake, write the letter for the last answer.

17 A   Mice is cute in cartoons,

   B   but you don't want them in

   C   your home. Mom threw a shoe at one!

   D   (No mistakes)

18 F   Heather's dog had five

   G   puppys. She will keep one.

   H   She wants the one with the curly tail.

   J   (No mistakes)

19 A   Jamal jogged down the

   B   sidewalk someone turned on a

   C   sprinkler. How wet Jamal got!

   D   (No mistakes)

20 F   Jorge's family went to

   G   New York City. They skated

   H   in central park.

   J   (No mistakes)

21 A   I took a picture of my

   B   best friends. All the girls'

   C   faces had goofy smiles!

   D   (No mistakes)

22 F   Garth reads five books

   G   a week. He never watchs

   H   TV. He studies all the time.

   J   (No mistakes)

23 A   The grocery store has

   B   closed for the day. We need

   C   milk we will borrow some.

   D   (No mistakes)

24 F   The ground is dry. The

   G   plants are drooping. It hasnt

   H   rained in weeks.

   J   (No mistakes)

(pages 96–97)

1 Action Verbs

- An action verb is a word that tells what people or things do.

Remember

● The complete predicate of each sentence is underlined. Find the action verb in the predicate. Write the action verb.

Example: Our class <u>read about Mono Lake in California</u>. *read*

1. We <u>visited this unusual lake</u>.
2. A park ranger <u>guided us around the lake</u>.
3. The lake <u>covers a large area</u>.
4. It <u>contains unusual rocks</u>.
5. People <u>call these rocks *tufas*</u>.
6. Tufas <u>grow under the lake</u>.

▲ Write the action verb in each of the following sentences.

Example: No fish live in salty Mono Lake. *live*

7. Swimmers float easily in the lake.
8. The very salty water holds them up.
9. The water also stings the swimmers' eyes.
10. Freshwater springs bubble into the lake from the bottom.
11. The fresh water mixes with the salty lake water.
12. This mixture makes the strange-looking tufa rocks.

■ Use an action verb that makes sense to complete each sentence. Write the sentences.

Example: Many kinds of birds _____ Mono Lake.
Many kinds of birds visit Mono Lake.

13. The birds _____ in the spring and summer.
14. Some birds _____ for the whole summer.
15. Others just _____ for food and rest.
16. California gulls _____ their nests near the lake.
17. The eggs _____ sometime in June.
18. Birdwatchers _____ that Mono Lake is a great place for them.

 Remember

(pages 98–99)

2 Main Verbs and Helping Verbs

- A verb may be more than one word.
- The main verb is the most important verb.
- The helping verb comes before the main verb.

● Copy the underlined verbs in each sentence. Write *helping* or *main* beside each verb.

Example: I <u>am</u> <u>going</u> to soccer practice.   *am—helping   going—main*

1. Mrs. Martinez <u>has</u> <u>coached</u> our team for three years.
2. She <u>has</u> <u>started</u> a new job.
3. It <u>is</u> <u>keeping</u> her very busy.
4. We <u>will</u> <u>play</u> for Mr. Lewis this year.
5. He <u>was</u> <u>helping</u> Mrs. Martinez last year.

▲ Write each sentence. Draw one line under the helping verb and two lines under the main verb.

Example: Karla is signing up for soccer camp.
        Karla <u>is</u> <u>signing</u> up for soccer camp.

6. Cedric and Phong are thinking about it.
7. Susana has made her decision.
8. She will attend the camp for a week in July.
9. Her family had planned a vacation that week.
10. Now they have changed their plans.

■ Use a helping verb that makes sense to complete each sentence. Write the sentence.

Example: The students _____ talking about the games.
        The students are talking about the games.

11. The school Olympics _____ begin on Friday.
12. They _____ held at this time every year.
13. Each class _____ planned a game.
14. Last week the classes _____ divided into two teams.
15. Each team _____ play in every game.

(pages 100–101)

3 Present, Past, and Future

- A present tense verb shows action that is happening now.
- A past tense verb shows action that has already happened.
- A future tense verb shows action that will happen.

Remember

● Write *present, past,* or *future* to tell the tense of the underlined verb in each sentence.

Example: The birds <u>arrived</u> early last spring.   *past*

1. I <u>watched</u> them all summer from my window.
2. Then the air <u>grew</u> cold.
3. Winter <u>will come</u> soon.
4. The birds <u>will leave</u> for their winter homes.
5. Scientists <u>call</u> this migration.
6. Some birds <u>travel</u> many miles each year.

▲ Write the verbs in these sentences. Write *present, past,* or *future* to describe the verb in each sentence.

Example: I watch the birds in our yard.   *watch—present*

7. Last winter Dad and I built a birdhouse.
8. In the spring, some wrens made a nest in it.
9. Now a family of birds lives in the house.
10. The parent birds bring food to the babies.
11. Next spring a new family of birds will nest in our yard.

■ Write these sentences. Write each underlined verb in the tense shown at the end of the sentence.

Example: Jack <u>receive</u> a canary for his birthday. (past)
Jack received a canary for his birthday.

12. Rance <u>names</u> the bird Clarence. (past)
13. Clarence <u>sang</u> to Rance all day long. (present)
14. Rance <u>will read</u> a book about canaries. (past)
15. He <u>will give</u> Clarence fresh food and water. (present)
16. Clarence <u>stays</u> healthy with such good care. (future)

(pages 104–105)

4 Subject-Verb Agreement

Remember

- If the subject of a sentence is a singular noun or *he, she, they,* or *it,* add *-s* to a present tense verb.
- If the subject is a plural noun or *I, we, you,* or *they,* do not add *-s* to a present tense verb.

● For each sentence, write *correct* if the underlined verb agrees with the subject. Write *not correct* if it does not agree.

Example: Many schools <u>buys</u> computers.   *not correct*

1. A school <u>uses</u> computers in many different ways.
2. A teacher <u>keeps</u> records on a computer.
3. A computer <u>help</u> the school librarian.
4. Students <u>practices</u> math skills on a computer.
5. Some computers <u>make</u> writing fun and easy.
6. Sometimes we <u>play</u> games on the computer.

▲ Write each sentence with the correct verb.

Example: My sister Julie (work, works) with computers.
   My sister Julie works with computers.

7. She (write, writes) programs for computers.
8. The programs (tell, tells) the computer what to do.
9. Computers (change, changes) rapidly.
10. Julie (take, takes) classes to keep up with the changes.
11. I (plan, plans) to work with computers too.
12. I (read, reads) all the computer books I can find.

■ Use the correct form of the verb to complete each sentence. Write the sentences.

Example: Computers _____ people plan the Olympics. (help)
   Computers help people plan the Olympics.

13. They _____ the best route for carrying the torch. (show)
14. A computer _____ places for players to stay. (locate)
15. It _____ rooms for thousands of people. (find)
16. Computers _____ how much food will be needed. (figure)
17. A special computer _____ shoes for runners. (design)
18. Computers _____ the modern Olympics possible. (make)

Spelling the Present Tense

(pages 106–107)

For spelling present tense verbs used with singular subjects:

Remember

- Add -*es* to verbs that end with *s, x, ch,* or *sh.*
- If a verb ends with a consonant and *y,* change with the *y* to *i* and add -*es.*

● Choose the verb that correctly completes each sentence. Write the sentences.

Example: Jon (watch, watches) Keyshawn in a hockey game.
Jon watches Keyshawn in a hockey game.

1. Keyshawn (fix, fixes) his face mask.
2. A signal (buzzes, buzz) loudly.
3. Elsa (score, scores) first.
4. The crowd (cheer, cheers) for her.
5. The puck (flies, fly) toward the net.
6. The goalie (catch, catches) it in his glove.

▲ Use the correct present tense form of the verb to complete each sentence. Write the sentences.

Example: Jill's brother _____ hockey. (play)
Jill's brother plays hockey.

7. Jill _____ to play too. (want)
8. Mark _____ her all the rules. (teach)
9. Then Jill _____ out for the hockey team. (try)
10. Jill _____ the hockey stick well. (handle)
11. She _____ the puck well too. (pass)
12. Finally, the coach _____ her the good news. (give)

■ Write each sentence, spelling the present tense verb correctly.

Example: Jana love ice skating. *Jana loves ice skating.*

13. She wish for a new pair of skates.
14. She never miss a lesson.
15. Jana carry her skates to school every day.
16. She rush to the rink right after school.
17. She practice for three hours.
18. Her mother pick her up at six o'clock.

(pages 108–109)

6 Spelling the Past Tense

- Add -*ed* to most verbs to form the past tense.
- Remember the rules for spelling the past tense of verbs ending with *e*, with a single vowel and a consonant, and with a consonant and *y*.

Remember

● Write the verb in each pair that is in the past tense.

Example: grab—grabbed   *grabbed*

1. gulped—gulp
2. hemmed—hem
3. try—tried
4. trip—tripped
5. owed—owe
6. worried—worry

▲ Use the past tense of the verb to complete each sentence. Write the sentence.

Example: Susan _____ sandwiches for the trip. (prepare)
            Susan prepared sandwiches for the trip.

7. She _____ them in waxed paper. (wrap)
8. Tarika _____ up the backpacks. (zip)
9. Daryl _____ them to the car. (carry)
10. Dad _____ his list one more time. (check)
11. The children _____ into the back seat. (hop)
12. They all _____ their seat belts. (fasten)

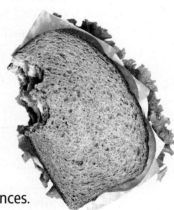

■ Change each present tense verb to past tense. Write the sentences.

Example: Jan's family explores a museum in the desert.
            Jan's family explored a museum in the desert.

13. A guide shows them around the outdoor museum.
14. Hats shade their faces from the hot sun.
15. Bobcats and beavers live in the area.
16. A new dam stops the river.
17. The streams dry up.
18. The animals move to other places.

The Past with Helping Verbs   (pages 110–111)

• The helping verbs *has, have,* and *had* can be used with the past form of a verb to show action that has already happened.

Remember

● Copy the underlined verbs in each sentence. Write *helping* or *main* beside each verb.

Example: Jim <u>had</u> <u>received</u> tickets to the ice show.
             had—helping   received—main

1. He <u>has</u> <u>offered</u> me a ticket.
2. I <u>have</u> <u>thanked</u> him for the ticket.
3. Jim and I <u>had</u> <u>hurried</u> to the show.
4. An usher <u>had</u> <u>guided</u> us to our seats.
5. Now the lights <u>have</u> <u>dimmed</u>.

▲ Write each sentence. Draw one line under the helping verb and two lines under the main verb.

Example: Posters had advertised the ice show.
             Posters <u>had</u> <u>advertised</u> the ice show.

6. Lin and Dan have hurried ahead for good seats.
7. I had arrived in time for the first act.
8. Ten skaters in mouse costumes had scurried onto the ice.
9. A skater in a cat costume has chased after them.
10. The crowd has clapped for the mice.

■ Rewrite each sentence. Use the helping verb *has, have,* or *had* and the past form of the verb.

Example: Two ice skaters dance in the spotlight.
             Two ice skaters have danced in the spotlight.

11. Their costumes sparkle in the golden light.
12. The man lifts the woman over his head.
13. They twirl like a top together.
14. The man trips on something.
15. The team tries the dance again.

(pages 112–113)

8 Irregular Verbs

- Irregular verbs are changed in special ways to show action that happened in the past. You must remember their spellings.

● Choose the correct verb to complete each sentence. Write the sentences.

Example: Pam's dad had (drove, driven) for three hours.
Pam's dad had driven for three hours.

1. The car radio had (break, broken) last week.
2. Pam and Joe (sang, sung) songs to pass the time.
3. Snow had (begin, begun) to fall.
4. Their mother (say, said) that the ski lodge was not far.
5. They (ate, eaten) supper at the lodge later.

▲ Write each sentence. Use the correct past form of the verb.

Example: Mary _____ the ski teacher a smile. (give)
Mary gave the ski teacher a smile.

6. She has _____ a V with her skis. (make)
7. Then she _____ to snowplow down the small hill. (begin)
8. The teacher _____ she was ready for a challenge. (say)
9. She _____ Mary to a bigger hill. (bring)
10. Mary _____ she could do it. (know)
11. Mary _____ down the hill without falling. (come)

■ Use the correct past form of the verb from the box to complete each sentence. Write the sentences.

Example: Kris had _____ about winter camping.
Kris had known about winter camping.

| break |
| know |
| give |
| come |
| make |
| say |

12. Eva had _____ that she wanted to learn.
13. The girls _____ to winter camping school.
14. An instructor _____ them directions for building a snow shelter.
15. Eva _____ the crust of the snow with a shovel.
16. Soon they had _____ a good snow shelter.

(pages 114–115)

9 The Special Verb *be*

- The special verb *be* does not show action. It tells what someone or something is or is like.
- Use *am* or *was* with the subject *I*.
- Use *is* or *was* with singular nouns and *he, she,* or *it*.
- Use *are* or *were* with plural nouns and *we, you,* or *they*.

● Write each sentence. Underline the form of the verb *be*.

Example: I am Jane's best friend.   *I <u>am</u> Jane's best friend.*

1. Jane is in my class.
2. I was at Jane's house yesterday.
3. Her mother was there too.
4. She is a sportswriter.
5. You are in her latest article.

▲ Choose the verb that correctly completes each sentence. Write the sentences.

Example: Kim Wang (is, are) a television reporter.
Kim Wang is a television reporter.

6. She (was, were) at our school last week.
7. You (was, were) not in school that day.
8. We (was, were) in the auditorium.
9. I (was, were) in the front row.
10. I (am, is) a big fan of Ms. Wang.

■ Write each sentence. Use the correct form of the verb *be*. The word in ( ) tells which tense to use.

Example: My father _____ a helicopter pilot. (present)
My father is a helicopter pilot.

11. He _____ also a traffic reporter. (present)
12. His reports _____ on the radio. (present)
13. Yesterday I _____ in his helicopter. (past)
14. It _____ very exciting. (past)
15. We _____ high above the ground. (past)

(pages 116–117)

10 Contractions with *not*

- A contraction is the combined form of two words. An apostrophe (') takes the place of any missing letters.

● Write the contraction in each sentence.

Example: I can't go out now.   *can't*

1. I haven't finished my homework.
2. It won't take long, though.
3. It isn't hard.
4. My sister hasn't come home yet.
5. I don't want to leave without her.

▲ Write each sentence. Use a contraction in place of the underlined words.

Example: We <u>were</u> <u>not</u> able to play softball today.
We weren't able to play softball today.

6. The rain <u>did</u> <u>not</u> stop all afternoon.
7. Our team <u>could</u> <u>not</u> have been luckier.
8. We <u>did</u> <u>not</u> have a chance against the Gorillas.
9. Now we <u>will</u> <u>not</u> have to play them this year.
10. There <u>is</u> <u>not</u> enough time left in the season.

■ Write a sentence to answer each question. Use a contraction made up of the underlined verb and the word *not* in each one.

Example: <u>Did</u> you try out for the school musical?
I didn't try out for the school musical.

11. <u>Were</u> Phil and Marita at the tryouts?
12. <u>Has</u> the school ever done a musical before?
13. <u>Do</u> you have a good singing voice?
14. <u>Does</u> Paul know how to dance?
15. <u>Can</u> Bob and Winona get the tickets printed?
16. <u>Will</u> Rico help build the scenery?

Adjectives

Although it's boldly dressed in bright reds, blues, greens, and yellows, the flashy toucan still blends with the forest colors.

1 What Is an Adjective?

How many describing words can you find in this sentence? What are they?

Through steep climbs and dangerous ascents, icy waters and confusing trails, Akiak always found the safest and fastest way.

—from *Akiak*, by Robert J. Blake

- **An adjective is a word that gives information about a noun.** A noun names a person, a place, a thing, or an idea. Some adjectives tell *what kind* or *how many*. They often appear right before the nouns they describe.

What Kind	How Many
We have a large dog.	Two dogs played in the yard.
The dog has a curly coat.	Many dogs like children.

- You can use more than one adjective to describe a noun.

  We have a large, friendly dog.   The brown and white puppy is sleeping.

  The dog has five tiny puppies.

Try It Out

Speak Up Find the adjectives that describe the underlined nouns. Does each adjective tell *what kind,* or does it tell *how many*?

1. Early <u>people</u> found that dogs made good <u>hunters</u>.
2. Strong <u>dogs</u> can pull sleds through deep <u>snow</u>.
3. One famous <u>dog</u> rescued forty lost <u>people</u> in the mountains.
4. Clever <u>sheepdogs</u> help farmers with large <u>herds</u> of sheep.
5. Some smart <u>dogs</u> help people who cannot see.

Write the adjectives that describe the underlined nouns. Write *what kind* or *how many* for each adjective.

Example: Linda Gunn has an interesting <u>job</u>.   *interesting–what kind*

6. Linda trains young <u>dogs</u>.
7. The dogs learn to help people with a hearing <u>problem</u>.
8. Two <u>people</u> in California found a lost <u>dog</u>.
9. They took the little white <u>dog</u> to a shelter.
10. One kind <u>worker</u> at the shelter named the dog Penny.
11. Linda found Penny at the shelter two <u>days</u> later.
12. She could see that Penny was an intelligent <u>dog</u>.
13. It took about four <u>months</u> to train Penny.

14–19. This lost-and-found ad has six adjectives that tell *what kind* or *how many*. Write the ad. Underline each adjective. Do not include *a*, *an*, and *the*.

Example: Trooper has a wonderful personality.
Trooper has a <u>wonderful</u> personality.

TROOPER IS MISSING!

Please help find Trooper. Trooper is a huge mutt with black spots. He has a large spot around one eye. He has a loud bark, but he does not bite. Trooper likes tasty snacks. Please return the dog to 120 Pleasant Street, and you will receive a reward.

Tim Baker
555-2894

Writing Wrap-Up WRITING • THINKING • LISTENING • SPEAKING

DESCRIBING

Write a Lost-and-Found Ad

Write a lost-and-found ad for something that you have lost. Use adjectives to describe the item clearly. Then read your ad to a partner. Have your partner name the adjectives you used.

Writing with Adjectives

Elaborating Sentences Adjectives add information about color, shape, size, and other details. Use adjectives to make your writing more interesting and to create pictures in your reader's mind.

> The dogs dressed for the fashion show.
>
> The four charming dogs dressed for the fashion show.

Apply It

1–8. Revise these cartoon captions about a fashion show for dogs. Each caption contains two sentences. Elaborate each one with adjectives.

Revising

This Dalmatian dreams of being a hero. She is wearing boots and a hat.

FooFoo is a designer. She is wearing jewels to a party with her friends.

Montie prepares for a hike. He is filling his backpack with gear and treats.

This Border collie is "the talk of Doggy town." Sheep obey this dog.

Combining Sentences Good writers try new ways to make their writing smooth and clear. You can experiment with your writing, too, by moving adjectives to combine sentences.

The two choppy sentences below are both about a rabbit. You can combine them to make one smooth sentence by placing the adjective *brown* before the noun *rabbit*.

A rabbit hops across the field.   } A brown rabbit hops across the field.
The rabbit is brown.

The two short sentences below each tell about rabbits' legs. The sentences can be combined by joining the adjectives *long* and *powerful* with the word *and*. Notice that both adjectives follow a form of the verb *be*.

Rabbits' hind legs are long.   } Rabbits' hind legs are long
Rabbits' hind legs are powerful.   and powerful.

Apply It

9–14. Read these paragraphs from a report. Rewrite each underlined pair of sentences by combining them.

Example: A rabbit's tail is short. Its tail is fluffy.
            A rabbit's tail is short and fluffy.

Revising

Rabbit Report

A rabbit's front teeth are long. The teeth are sharp. Rabbits use their teeth for gnawing plants. In warm weather, rabbits eat green, leafy plants. Rabbits like to nibble clover. Clover is sweet. During the winter a rabbit's diet changes. Rabbits eat twigs during the winter. During the winter rabbits also eat bark.

Rabbits are small. They are also weak. They have many enemies. Foxes are one enemy. Foxes are dangerous. When a fox is near, rabbits usually hide. They may hide in grass. The grass is tall.

2 Adjectives After *be*

Read the sentence below. How many adjectives can you find? What are they?

The next day was rainy and dark.

—from *Charlotte's Web*, by E. B. White

Adjectives describe nouns. They can also describe words like *I*, *it*, and *we*, which take the place of nouns. An adjective can come after the word it describes. This usually happens when an adjective follows a form of the verb *be*.

The project is ready.   I am excited.

Try It Out

Speak Up Find each adjective. What word does it describe?

1. The weather is beautiful.
2. The fair is exciting.
3. We were eager.
4. Jamie is proud.
5. The chicken is fat.
6. The eggs are large.

On Your Own

7–12. This checklist for an apple pie contest has six adjectives. Write each adjective and the word it describes.

Example: The crust is flaky. *flaky crust*

> **Apple Pie CONTEST Checklist**
> ☐ The pie is homemade.   ☐ The apples were fresh.
> ☐ It is moist.   ☐ They are juicy.
> ☐ The crust is delicate.   ☐ I am happy with the taste.

Writing Wrap-Up   WRITING • THINKING • LISTENING • SPEAKING

DESCRIBING

Write a Description

Use adjectives to describe your favorite food. Read your description to a partner. Do the descriptions make your mouth water?

                For Extra Practice see page 160.

3 Using *a, an,* and *the*

What mistake can you find in this ad?

For dads or moms a shovel makes a excellent gift!

The words *a, an,* and *the* are special adjectives called articles. Learn these rules for using articles.

With Singular Nouns:

Use *a* if the next word begins with a consonant sound.   a flower
Use *an* if the next word begins with a vowel sound.   an iris
Use *the* if the noun names a particular person, place, or thing.   the garden

With Plural Nouns:

Use *the*.   the flowers   the irises

Try It Out

Speak Up Which article or articles could be used before each word?

1. contest 2. award 3. orchids   4. students 5. prize

On Your Own

6–10. These tree labels for an Arbor Day poster have five incorrect articles. Write each label correctly. (Some labels can take more than one article.)

Example: a ash   *an ash, the ash*

Proofreading

- a dogwood
- an maples
- a aspen
- an weeping willow
- a oak
- a evergreens

Writing Wrap-Up   WRITING • THINKING • LISTENING • SPEAKING

INFORMING

Write Labels

Write labels for objects in the classroom. Use *a, an,* or *the*. Read your labels to a partner. Are the articles correct?

4 Making Comparisons

Look at the picture. How many sentences can you make to compare the sizes of the bears? Use words such as *tall, taller, tallest, fat, fatter, fattest*.

Sometimes you may want to tell how things are alike or how they are different. You can use adjectives to compare. You usually add *-er* to an adjective to compare two persons, places, or things, and *-est* to compare three or more.

One trip:	William took a long trip.
Two trips:	Jason's trip was longer than his.
Three or more:	I took the longest trip of all.

Rules for Adding *-er* and *-est*	
1. **Adjectives ending with *e*:** Drop the *e* before adding the ending.	wide wider widest
2. **Adjectives ending with a single vowel and a consonant:** Double the consonant and add the ending.	thin thinner thinnest
3. **Adjectives ending with a consonant and *y*:** Change the *y* to *i* before adding the ending.	tiny tinier tiniest

Try It Out

Speak Up What form of the adjective in ( ) completes each sentence correctly?

1. Alaska is not the _____ state. (new)
2. Every state except Hawaii is _____ than Alaska. (old)
3. Alaska is the _____ of all the states. (big)
4. However, Wyoming has the _____ population. (tiny)
5. _____ people live there than in my state. (few)

Alaska's State Flag

Write the correct form of the adjective in ( ) to complete each sentence.

Example: We will be visiting the _____ state of all. (large) *largest*

6. It is _____ to get to Alaska than it used to be. (easy)
7. We will see the _____ mountains in North America. (tall)
8. Mount McKinley is the _____ peak of all. (high)
9. Alaska is _____ than the last place we visited. (wild)
10. It is home to the _____ bears in the world. (big)
11. The Kodiak bear is even _____ than a grizzly bear. (large)
12. A Kodiak bear can also be _____ than a grizzly. (fierce)
13. The _____ thing of all is to keep away from these bears! (safe)
14. Don't make the bear any _____ than it already is! (angry)

15–20. This draft of an article for a Web site on Alaska has six incorrect forms of *-er* and *-est*. Write the article correctly.

Example: Northern Alaska has the colder climate in the United States.
Northern Alaska has the coldest climate in the United States.

Proofreading

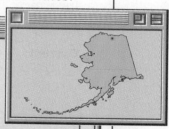

═══ Web site ═══

You Can Wear Shorts in Alaska!

Alaska's climate can be mild than many people think. The city of Anchorage can get hoter than seventy degrees. Southern Alaska has the warmer climate in the state. The south is also the wetter of all the regions. It has the higher average rainfall in Alaska. Northern Alaska is colder and dryer than the southern part of the state.

Writing Wrap-Up
WRITING • THINKING • LISTENING • SPEAKING

COMPARING / CONTRASTING

Write a Geography Report

How does your state compare with Alaska or another state? Does it have the same scenery, climate, or animals? Write a paragraph about how the two states are alike. Then write one about how they are different. Use adjectives with *-er* and *-est*. Find a partner and read your reports to each other. Did you make similar comparisons?

5 Comparing with *more* and *most*

What's wrong with this sentence? How can you fix it?
Did you know that cats are the most popularest pets in the United States?

- With long adjectives, use the words *more* and *most* to compare persons, places, or things. Use *more* to compare two. Use *most* to compare three or more.

One	Tiger is a playful cat.
Two	Ginger is a more playful cat than Tiger.
Three or More	Ike is the most playful cat of all.

- Never add *-er* and *more* or *-est* and *most* to the same adjective.

Incorrect: Tiger is <u>more smarter</u> than Ginger.
Tiger is the <u>most intelligentest</u> cat.

Correct: Tiger is smarter than Ginger.
Tiger is the most intelligent cat.

Try It Out

Speak Up What word should you add to the adjective in ( ) to complete each sentence correctly?

1. Cats and dogs are among the _____ of all pets. (common)
2. Cats are _____ than dogs, though. (independent)
3. One of the _____ of all breeds of cat is the Siamese. (popular)
4. Some people think that a Persian cat is _____ than any other cat. (beautiful)
5. However, a cat from an animal shelter can be the _____ of all. (lovable)

Add *more* or *most* to the adjective in ( ) to complete each sentence correctly. Write the sentence.

Example: Cats are _____ to train than kittens. (difficult) *more difficult*

6. A cat is one of the _____ kinds of pets. (independent)
7. Cats are among the _____ of all animals. (curious)
8. A cat's tricks can be _____ than a clown's. (amusing)
9. Cats are the _____ pets for keeping mice away. (useful)
10. Some cats are _____ hunters than others. (skillful)
11. Some people think that cats are _____ than any other pet. (intelligent)
12. Some cats seem to think that they are the _____ animals too. (intelligent)

13–18. This part of an article for a cat magazine has six missing or incorrect forms of *more* and *most*. Write the article correctly.

Example: The tabby's face is the most sweetest of all.
The tabby's face is the sweetest of all.

Proofreading

Tips Takes Top Honors

It was the excitingest moment of the annual cat show. The prize for the most beautiful cat went to Tips. His fur was even more sleeker than Moe's. His whiskers were even wonderful than Cleo's. His eyes were the most biggest I've ever seen. His tail was the more graceful of all. Never had I given the prize to a cat most deserving than Tips.

Writing Wrap-Up

WRITING • THINKING • LISTENING • SPEAKING

EXPRESSING

Write an Opinion

Write a paragraph explaining which animal you think is the most intelligent of all. Use adjectives with *more* and *most*. Read your paragraph to a partner. Does your partner agree with you?

6 Comparing with *good* and *bad*

One-Minute Warm-Up

I taste better than a lime!

Choose three foods to compare. How many ways can you compare two of them? How many ways can you compare all three? Use the adjectives *good, better, best* and *bad, worse, worst.*

Hey!

- Change the forms of the adjectives *good* and *bad* when you make comparisons. Change *good* to *better* when comparing two things. Change *good* to *best* when comparing three or more things.

One	I found a good book at the library.
Two	It is better than the last book I read.
Three or More	What is the best book you have ever read?

- Change *bad* to *worse* when comparing two things. Change *bad* to *worst* when comparing three or more things.

One	I read a bad story last night.
Two	It was worse than the story we read yesterday.
Three or More	It may be the worst story I ever read.

Try It Out

Speak Up What form of the adjective in ( ) completes each sentence correctly?

1. Danny thinks that the _____ thing of all on a rainy Saturday is to visit the library. (good)
2. Danny's sister had the _____ time ever at the library last Saturday. (bad)
3. She wanted a _____ book than her last one. (good)
4. Every book she looked at was _____ than the one before. (bad)
5. The one Danny chose for her was the _____ book of all. (bad)

Write the correct form of the adjective in ( ) to complete each sentence.

Example: This is the _____ weather of the week. (bad) *worst*

6. The rain today is much _____ than yesterday's. (bad)
7. Today would be the _____ day of the week to visit the library. (good)
8. I think that animal stories are _____ than science fiction. (good)
9. The _____ book I ever read was a science fiction book. (bad)
10. Pete thinks that this is the _____ library in all the city. (good)
11. It has a _____ set of Braille books than other libraries do. (good)
12. The _____ part of the trip will be carrying all the books home! (bad)

13–18. This book review has six incorrect forms of *good* and *bad*. Write the book review correctly.

Example: This is one of the worstest books ever published!
This is one of the worst books ever published!

Proofreading

Boring, Boring, Boring!

Book Review

I. M. Dull has published his fourth book, *How to Bore Anyone in Five Minutes*. It is his better book so far, but that isn't saying much. Dull's first work, *Boring Ways to Dress*, was the worstest book of 2001. His new book has better writing, but it's still a snoozer. *How to Bore Anyone in Five Minutes* is not a best book, but *Boring Ways to Dress* is worser. Will Dull ever write something really goodest? Maybe he needs a best name.

Writing Wrap-Up

WRITING • THINKING • LISTENING • SPEAKING

EVALUATING

Write a Book Review

Choose a book you have read and design a new cover for it. Write a review of the book for the back cover. Use forms of *good* and *bad*. Use other adjectives too. Share your work in a small group.

Using Exact Adjectives

Adjectives add important details about people, places, and things. Using exact adjectives in your writing will give your readers a clear picture of what you're writing about.

Less exact adjective: It is cold out today.

More exact adjective: It is chilly out today.

Apply It

1–6. Use your Thesaurus Plus in the Tools and Tips section at the back of your book to find synonyms for *wet*. Then rewrite this e-mail message. Use a different, more exact adjective in place of each underlined word.

Revising

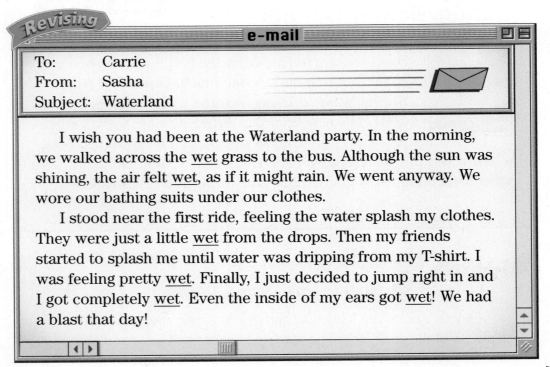

e-mail	

To: Carrie
From: Sasha
Subject: Waterland

   I wish you had been at the Waterland party. In the morning, we walked across the <u>wet</u> grass to the bus. Although the sun was shining, the air felt <u>wet</u>, as if it might rain. We went anyway. We wore our bathing suits under our clothes.

   I stood near the first ride, feeling the water splash my clothes. They were just a little <u>wet</u> from the drops. Then my friends started to splash me until water was dripping from my T-shirt. I was feeling pretty <u>wet</u>. Finally, I just decided to jump right in and I got completely <u>wet</u>. Even the inside of my ears got <u>wet</u>! We had a blast that day!

Enrichment

Adjectives!

Adjective Challenge

Players: 3 or more

Materials: Letter tiles or letter cards turned facedown; for each player, a grid with 4 with nouns written across the top

To play: One player draws a letter, and all players write it in the left column of their grid. Players fill each row with as many adjectives as they can in 3 minutes. The adjectives in the row must begin with that letter and must describe the noun in each column. Play as many rounds as there are players.

Scoring: Each different adjective on a player's grid earns 1 point.

	balloon	horse	lunchbox	jeans
B	beautiful blue bursting	bucking black	bursting banged-up bright	blue big
D		drowsy	dull	dirty dusty

Sneaky Poems

In small groups, list adjectives that describe sneakers. Then copy the poem on paper, leaving blanks where the adjectives belong.

Choose words from your list to complete the poem. Then read your group's poem aloud.

I like sneakers.
_____ sneakers,
_____ sneakers,
_____, _____, _____ sneakers,
Any kind of sneakers.
I like sneakers.

Challenge Write a poem about another object, leaving blanks where the adjectives belong. Have a partner complete your poem with adjectives that all begin with the same letter.

1 What Is an Adjective? (p. 136)
Write the adjectives that describe the underlined nouns. Write *what kind* or *how many* for each adjective.

1. Tara has an interesting <u>hobby</u>.
2. She collects beautiful <u>seashells</u>.
3. She has found thirty different <u>kinds</u> of shells.
4. She keeps them in glass <u>boxes</u>.
5. Liz is a clever <u>artist</u>.
6. She and Tara make lovely <u>jewelry</u> from the shells.
7. Tara and Liz go to sandy <u>beaches</u> to hunt for new <u>shells</u>.
8. Each day brings new <u>treasures</u>.
9. Calm <u>pools</u> are good <u>places</u> to find shells.
10. Most <u>snails</u> have a single, twisted shell.
11. Empty <u>shells</u> may be homes for tiny crabs.
12. Tara found three pink <u>stones</u>.
13. They have unusual <u>markings</u>.
14. Tara will begin a new <u>collection</u>.

2 Adjectives After be (p. 140)
Write each sentence. Draw a line under the adjective. Then draw an arrow to the word it describes.

15. Cal is eager to play the game.
16. The game is difficult.
17. It was new last year.
18. We are happy to play with Cal.
19. The questions are clever.
20. They were funny at first.
21. Now I am bored with them.

3 Using a, an, and the (p. 141)
Write the correct article to complete each sentence.

22. (A, An) trunk was in (a, an) corner of the attic.
23. It held (a, an) old white dress.
24. There was also (a, an) old album.
25. (A, The) pictures show (a, an) young woman.
26. There is (a, an) name on one of (a, the) photos.
27. (An, The) young woman is my grandmother!

4 Making Comparisons (p. 142)
Write each sentence, using the correct form of the adjective in ( ).

28. The sun is the (close) star of all to Earth.
29. However, the sun is not the (big) star of all.
30. The (hot) stars of all look blue.
31. A blue star is (hot) than a yellow star.
32. A red star is (cool) than the sun.
33. It is also (bright) than the sun.
34. Jupiter is (big) than the other planets.
35. Mercury is the (near) planet of all to the sun.
36. The moon is the (bright) object of all in our nighttime sky.
37. Earth's gravity is (strong) than the moon's.
38. This makes objects (heavy) on Earth than they are on the moon.

 Go to www.eduplace.com/tales/ for more fun with parts of speech.

5 Comparing with *more* and *most* (p. 144) Write each sentence, using the correct form of the adjective in ( ).

39. People think that bear cubs are (lovable) than grown bears.
40. However, all bears are (dangerous) than house pets.
41. The (common) bear of all is the black bear.
42. I think polar bears are (beautiful) than black bears.
43. They are (comfortable) in the cold weather than other bears.
44. Their thick white fur is their (valuable) protection of all.

6 Comparing with *good* and *bad* (p. 146) Write each sentence, using the correct form of the adjective in ( ).

45. I had a (good) time at summer camp this year than last year.
46. My cabin had the (good) view of all.
47. Insects are (bad) near the lake than in the woods.
48. That is the (bad) place in the whole camp to sleep.
49. The pool is a (good) place to swim than the chilly lake.
50. The weather was (bad) in July than in August.

Mixed Review 51–58. This entertainment report has two mistakes in using articles and six mistakes in comparing adjectives. Write the report correctly.

Proofreading Checklist

Did you write these correctly?
✔ the articles *a, an,* and *the*
✔ adjectives with *-er* and *-est*
✔ adjectives with *more* and *most*
✔ forms of *good* and *bad*

Proofreading

What's Hot?

Movies
Are you looking for an fun weekend activity? Try the movie at the Star Theater. It's much gooder than the last movie I saw there. It's about a monster. The hairy monster looks scary, but he is really more gentler than a kitten.

Museums
The dinosaur exhibit is the most excitingest at the museum. You can see the tinyest dinosaur ever found. You won't want to miss the big dinosaur bone in the world.

Music
Would you enjoy a evening of good music? Then I'd skip the concert at the library. The songs are worser than the ones they played last year.

Test Practice

Write the numbers 1–6 on a sheet of paper. Read each group of sentences. Choose the sentence that is written correctly. Write the letter for that answer.

1 A Was that an true statement?

 B Billy is the most honestest person in the world!

 C That was the sillyest excuse I've ever heard!

 D The truth is always better than a lie.

2 F My voice is hoarser today than it was yesterday.

 G Jillian's voice is the most beautifullest of all.

 H The first song on the CD is prettyer than the second song.

 J The chorus performed a old English ballad.

3 A This summer is the hotter of all the summers in this century.

 B Grandpa says the weather is badder than it used to be.

 C In some places the climate has become much weter.

 D Some scientists think the earth is getting warmer.

4 F The Johnsons grew the enormousest pumpkin!

 G These strawberries are riper than those.

 H Don't pick the cherries until they are reder.

 J Oscar is the goodest gardener we know.

5 A Kira's drawing of a dinosaur is gooder than Zack's.

 B Tyrannosaurus rex had the most tinyest hands!

 C Which is the most largerest dinosaur in the museum?

 D Dinosaurs had longer legs than other reptiles.

6 F The best thing to drink on a hot day is cold water.

 G This lemonade is more sweeter than that kind.

 H Dad whipped up an milkshake.

 J Kimiko added a ice cube to the juice.

Now write the numbers 7–12 on your paper. Look at each underlined part of the paragraph. Find the correct way to write the underlined part in each numbered line. Write the letter for that answer. If the part is already correct, write the letter for the last answer, "Correct as it is."

(7)   Nine planets <u>move</u> around our sun. Of these nine
(8) planets, the <u>larger</u> is Jupiter. It has 16 moons, and it is
(9) surrounded by a band of dust. Venus is the <u>hotest</u> of the
(10) nine. This <u>planets</u> temperature is about 896 degrees F.
(11) Spaceships <u>have took</u> pictures of many planets. Uranus
(12) and Neptune are both blue, but Neptune is <u>more darker</u>.

7 A moves
   B has moved
   C will move
   D Correct as it is

8 F more larger
   G large
   H largest
   J Correct as it is

9 A hottest
   B most hotest
   C hotter
   D Correct as it is

10 F planets'
   G planet's
   H planets's
   J Correct as it is

11 A has took
   B has taken
   C have taken
   D Correct as it is

12 F darker
   G more dark
   H darkest
   J Correct as it is

Now write the numbers 13–18 on your paper. Look at each underlined part of the paragraph. Find the correct way to write the underlined part in each numbered line. Write the letter for that answer. If the part is already correct, write the letter for the last answer, "Correct as it is."

(13)   For my birthday, Mom and Dad <u>gived</u> me a cute little

(14) hamster. I named it <u>chubby cheeks</u>. I saved my money

(15) to buy toys for the <u>hamsters</u> cage. I was for a time the

(16) <u>happyest</u> kid in the world! But now I have a problem.

(17) My pet makes noise all night. It chews on the cage <u>two</u>.

(18) Maybe I should trade it for some quiet little <u>mouses</u>!

13 A given

    B gives

    C gave

    D Correct as it is

14 F Chubby Cheeks

    G chubby Cheeks

    H Chubby cheeks

    J Correct as it is

15 A hamsters's

    B hamster's

    C hamsters'

    D Correct as it is

16 F most happiest

    G happiest

    H happier

    J Correct as it is

17 A too

    B to

    C tow

    D Correct as it is

18 F mousies

    G moose

    H mice

    J Correct as it is

Unit 1: The Sentence

The Sentence, Kinds of Sentences

(pp. 32, 36, 38) If a group of words below is a sentence, write it correctly. If not, write *not a sentence*.

1. do you know how to use the computer at school
2. it is a very useful tool
3. would you like to learn
4. stores large amounts of important information
5. the top row of keys
6. how quickly you learn
7. please turn the computer off now
8. makes corrections quickly and easily

Subjects and Predicates

(pp. 40, 42, 44) Write each sentence. Draw a line between the complete subject and the complete predicate. Draw one line under the simple subject and two lines under the simple predicate.

9. Mrs. Consuelo Greene has a solar house.
10. It has metal plates on the roof.
11. These metal plates are collectors.
12. They trap the sun's rays.
13. The heat of the sun warms a liquid inside the collectors.
14. The liquid heats a tank of water.
15. It is in the basement.
16. This water warms the whole solar house.

Run-on Sentences *(p. 46)* Write each run-on sentence correctly as two sentences.

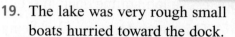

17. Jill and Ted were sailing a big storm suddenly came up.
18. A strong wind blew waves crashed onto the shore.
19. The lake was very rough small boats hurried toward the dock.
20. Then the thunder roared the downpour began.
21. Jill and Ted tied up the boat they had made it just in time.

Unit 2: Nouns

Common and Proper Nouns

(pp. 64, 66) Write each noun. Beside it, write *common* or *proper*. Begin each proper noun with a capital letter.

22. On friday uncle leo brought a newspaper to our house.
23. My mother read the news.
24. One story in the paper was about the fourth of july.
25. Our town will hold a celebration on that day.
26. A big parade will march right down main street.
27. The mayor will give a speech from the grandstand.
28. A band from middletown will play at goss park.
29. People will watch fireworks over the johnstown river.

 See www.eduplace.com/kids/hme/ for a tricky usage or spelling question.

Singular and Plural Nouns

(pp. 70, 72, 74) Write the plural form of each singular noun.

30. dish
31. mask
32. duty
33. sheep
34. compass
35. man

Singular and Plural Possessive Nouns *(pp. 76, 78)* Write the possessive form of the noun in ( ).

36. The (family) new house is being built rapidly.
37. The (carpenters) job will be done by the end of next week.
38. The (men) hammers are pounding away busily.
39. The (women) saws are noisy too.
40. Next week the (painters) work will start.
41. (Bert) room is in the back of the new house.
42. His (mother) office is next to it.
43. The other (children) rooms are upstairs.
44. (Dad) workshop will be in the basement.
45. The (animals) big new barn will be built next.
46. The (horses) stalls will be roomy and comfortable.
47. (Sport) new doghouse is not ready.
48. Bert is planning to build his (pet) house himself.

Unit 3: Verbs

Action Verbs, Main Verbs, and Helping Verbs *(pp. 96, 98)* Write the verbs in these sentences. Write *main* or *helping* beside each verb.

49. Heidi was making a collage.
50. She had found magazine pictures.
51. We were helping her.
52. She has glued them onto cardboard.
53. The glue is drying now.

Favorite Animals

Past, Present, and Future *(p. 100)* Write each verb, and label it *past*, *present*, or *future*.

54. Some trains carry passengers.
55. Other trains haul products.
56. The first railroads began in England in the 1820s.
57. Tomorrow's trains will be different.
58. Computers will steer those trains.

Agreement, Spelling the Present Tense (pp. 104, 106) Write the correct present tense form of each verb.

59. Candy (rub) the balloons on the wool rug.
60. Her brother (watch) curiously.
61. She (stick) them to the wall.
62. The balloons (stay) there!
63. Static electricity (make) them stick.

Spelling the Past Tense, The Past with Helping Verbs (pp. 108, 110) Write each sentence. Use *have* or *has* with the correct form of the verb.

64. Pete (enjoy) folk dancing.
65. This week he (try) a difficult new dance.
66. Everyone (practice) the steps.
67. The dancers (form) a circle.
68. They (step) to the music.

Irregular Verbs (p. 112) Write each sentence, using the correct past form of the verb.

69. The show (begin) at two o'clock.
70. One hundred people had (come).
71. The actors (wear) shiny costumes.
72. Jen and Terrance had (make) them.
73. We (take) our places on-stage.
74. I (grow) more and more nervous.
75. I had (know) my lines earlier!

The Special Verb *be* (p. 114) Write the verb that correctly completes each sentence.

76. My cousins (is, are) in Australia.
77. We (was, were) there last year.
78. Australia (is, are) both a country and a continent.
79. You (was, were) in Sydney for a month last winter.
80. It (is, are) the largest city.

Contractions with *not* (p. 116) Write the contractions for the following words.

81. is not
82. cannot
83. was not
84. would not
85. had not
86. do not
87. could not
88. did not

Unit 4: Adjectives

Adjectives (p. 136) Write each adjective and the noun it describes.

89. A giraffe is a tall animal that lives in dry areas of Africa.
90. It has a long, thin neck and four skinny legs.
91. The neck of a giraffe contains seven bones.
92. That is the same number that a human has.
93. Many people think that a giraffe cannot make a single sound.
94. However, most giraffes do make some low sounds.

Adjectives After *be* *(p. 140)* Write each adjective and the word it describes.

95. I am interested in quilting.
96. The art is old.
97. The stitches are tiny.
98. The patterns are different.
99. Mother said that Grandma was skillful at quilting.
100. Her quilts were beautiful.

Using *a, an,* and *the* *(p. 141)* Choose the correct article or articles in ( ) to complete each sentence. Write the sentences.

101. (A, The) names of many young animals are interesting.
102. (A, An) owl's baby is called (a, an) owlet.
103. (A, An) young eagle is called (a, an) eaglet.
104. We know that (a, an) baby cat is (a, an) kitten.
105. Does that mean that (a, an) infant bat is (a, an) bitten?

Comparing with Adjectives *(pp. 142, 144, 146)* Choose the correct word in ( ) to complete each sentence. Write the sentences.

106. *Stone Fox* is the (sadder, saddest) book I have read.
107. Is it (sadder, saddest) than *Annie and the Old One*?
108. What is the (better, best) mystery you have ever read?
109. Is *Charlotte's Web* (longer, longest) than *Stuart Little*?
110. I think it is a (better, best) story than *Stuart Little*.
111. Peg thinks that nonfiction books are the (more, most) useful kind of all.
112. Sometimes they are also the (harder, hardest) of all to read.

Extra Practice

1 What Is an Adjective?

- An adjective is a word that describes a noun. An adjective can tell *what kind* or *how many.*

● Write the adjective that describes each underlined noun.

Example: Carlo has a new <u>puppy</u>. *new*

1. Carlo takes good <u>care</u> of the puppy.
2. He gives it food in a clean <u>dish.</u>
3. The puppy always has fresh <u>water.</u>
4. Carlo gives the puppy four <u>meals</u> a day.
5. He is teaching the puppy to obey simple <u>commands.</u>

▲ Write each sentence. Underline each adjective. Then draw an arrow to the noun it describes.

Example: In cold places, many people travel by sled.

In <u>cold</u> places, <u>many</u> people travel by sled.

6. Huskies are strong, sturdy dogs.
7. A husky has two coats of thick fur.
8. Large, hairy feet keep it from sinking in soft snow.
9. There may be eight huskies in a team.
10. The team may travel forty miles in one day.

■ Write each sentence. Use one or two adjectives to replace each blank. Draw one line under adjectives that tell what kind and two lines under adjectives that tell how many.

Example: There were _____ dogs in the dog show.
There were <u>fifty</u> <u>excited</u> dogs in the dog show.

11. Jaime's _____ beagle Harry won a prize.
12. Rita's poodle Fifi won _____ ribbons.
13. The dog did _____ tricks.
14. _____ dogs pulled a _____ wagon.
15. We all laughed at the _____ sight.
16. LeShon's _____ collie was somewhat frightened by the _____ crowd.

(page 140)

2 Adjectives After *be*

- An adjective can follow the word it describes and a form of the verb *be*.

● Write the adjective that describes the underlined word in each sentence.

Example: The <u>streets</u> are crowded.   *crowded*

1. The <u>sun</u> is bright.
2. The <u>music</u> is loud.
3. The <u>people</u> are happy.
4. <u>Parades</u> are exciting.
5. The <u>food</u> was delicious.
6. The <u>speeches</u> were grand.

▲ Write each sentence. Underline the adjective. Then draw an arrow to the word that it describes.

Example: Dad is thrilled by the show.

Dad is <u>thrilled</u> by the show.

7. Before the show, the performers were nervous.
8. Under the lights, the costumes were beautiful.
9. Up on the stage, the tricks were dazzling.
10. I was amazed at one of the tricks.
11. It was unbelievable.
12. The children were speechless.

■ Write these sentences, supplying an adjective for each blank. Then write the word that the adjective describes.

Example: The dancers were _____.
The dancers were graceful.   dancers

13. The music was _____.
14. This morning's puppet show was _____.
15. The little puppet was _____.
16. His tricks were _____.
17. After the performance, I was _____.
18. The whole street fair was _____.

(page 141)

3 Using *a, an,* and *the*

- Use the articles *a* and *an* before singular nouns.
- Use the article *the* with both singular and plural nouns.

● Write each word. Before it, write *a* or *an*.

Example: _____ orange   *an orange*

1. _____ bulb		7. _____ eggplant
2. _____ onion		8. _____ vegetable
3. _____ root		9. _____ tomato
4. _____ stem		10. _____ apple
5. _____ edge		11. _____ inchworm
6. _____ carrot		12. _____ ice cube

▲ Write each sentence, using the correct article.

Example: Mushrooms grow in (an, the) woods.
          Mushrooms grow in the woods.

13. (A, An) mushroom is (a, an) kind of fungus.
14. It looks like (a, an) umbrella.
15. It does not grow from (a, an) seed.
16. (A, The) fungi grow from tiny cells called spores.
17. They may be blown by (an, the) wind.
18. (A, The) spores land on (an, the) warm, damp earth.

■ The following sentences have no articles. Rewrite the sentences, supplying the correct articles where they belong.

Example: Pitcher plant can eat insect.
          A pitcher plant can eat an insect.

19. Rainwater collects in plant's leaves.
20. Thick hairs grow at end of leaf.
21. Hairs point downward.
22. Sweet smell attracts insects.
23. Insect drowns in rainwater.
24. Then plant waits for new victim.

(pages 142–143)

4 Making Comparisons

Remember

- Add -*er* to most adjectives to compare two persons, places, or things.
- Add -*est* to compare three or more persons, places, or things.

● For each adjective, write the form for comparing two and the form for comparing three or more.

Example: pretty *prettier prettiest*

1. late
2. thick
3. safe
4. lucky
5. dark

6. hot
7. fine
8. shiny
9. wet
10. windy

▲ Use the correct form of the adjective in ( ) to complete each sentence. Write the sentences.

Example: The _____ bears of all live in Alaska. (big)
The biggest bears of all live in Alaska.

11. Polar bears live in the _____ part of the state. (cold)
12. The _____ bears of all can weigh 1,700 pounds. (heavy)
13. Bears are _____ in the fall than in the summer. (fat)
14. They eat _____ amounts of food in the fall than in the winter. (large)
15. Bears' food is the _____ of all in the winter. (scarce)

■ Write each incorrect sentence correctly. If a sentence is already correct, write *correct*.

Example: Bald eagles are America's mightier birds of all.
Bald eagles are America's mightiest birds of all.

16. A bald eagle is no baldest than any other bird.
17. In earlier times, *bald* meant "marked with white."
18. The eagle's body may be longest than three feet.
19. Its wingspan is greatest than six feet.
20. The largest eagle's nest ever found weighed two tons.

(pages 144–145)

5 Comparing with *more* and *most*

- With long adjectives, use *more* to compare two things and *most* to compare three or more.
- Never add *-er* and *more* or *-est* and *most* to the same adjective.

Remember

● Choose the correct word to complete each sentence. Write the sentences.

Example: What is the (more, most) popular zoo animal?
What is the most popular zoo animal?

1. The monkeys are the (more, most) amusing of all.
2. A big cat is (more, most) exciting than a monkey.
3. Leopards are the (more, most) graceful of all big cats.
4. They are also the (more, most) skillful climbers of all.
5. A leopard may be (more, most) dangerous than a lion.

▲ Use *more* or *most* to complete each sentence. Write the sentences.

Example: The lion is _____ social than any other cat.
The lion is more social than any other cat.

6. It is _____ likely than another cat to live in a group.
7. Lions are the _____ courageous of all animals.
8. The _____ beautiful part of a lion is its mane.
9. It makes the male lion _____ attractive than the female.
10. The female, however, is a _____ skillful hunter than the male.

■ Use the correct form of the adjective to complete each sentence. Write the sentences.

Example: The _____ of all cats is the tiger. (magnificent)
The most magnificent of all cats is the tiger.

11. A tiger's roar is the _____ of all sounds. (terrifying)
12. Tigers are _____ hunters than lions. (fierce)
13. Tigers are _____ in the water than any other cat. (comfortable)
14. Tigers hunt some of the _____ animals in the jungle. (big)
15. White tigers are one of the _____ animals of all. (rare)

(pages 146–147)

⑥ Comparing with *good* and *bad*

- When you use the adjectives *good* and *bad* to compare, you must change their forms.
- Use *better* or *worse* to compare two.
- Use *best* or *worst* to compare three or more.

● Write the adjective that correctly completes each sentence.

Example: I like mystery books (good, better) than any other kind. *better*

1. The (better, best) part of all is solving the mystery.
2. Michael's father won a special award for the (better, best) local writer.
3. I liked his last book (better, best) than his first.
4. The first one was not the (bad, worst) book I have read.
5. I have read a (worse, worst) book than that.

▲ Use the correct form of the adjective in ( ) to complete each sentence. Write the sentences.

Example: We were the _____ readers in the school. (bad)
We were the worst readers in the school.

6. We wanted to become _____ readers than we were. (good)
7. Ms. Lee gave us the _____ books in the library to read. (good)
8. Some of the books were _____ than we had expected. (bad)
9. Others were much _____. (good)
10. After a month, we reported on the _____ book we had read. (good)
11. The _____ part of all was choosing a favorite book. (bad)

■ Rewrite each sentence, using comparisons correctly.

Example: We wanted to be good writers than we were.
We wanted to be better writers than we were.

12. Mr. Diaz said that writing would be the better practice of all.
13. Our first paper had the worse mistakes of all.
14. The second paper was much good than the first.
15. My first story was not the better work I have done.
16. In fact, it was the bad thing I have ever written.

These ancient, mysterious statues stand on Easter Island in the South Pacific Ocean.

Capitalization and Punctuation

1 Correct Sentences

Read the sentences below. Which sentence is a statement? Which sentence is a question?

> He jabbed his hands into his pockets and sighed. Why couldn't he get his room straight?
>
> —from *Justin and the Best Biscuits in the World,* by Mildred Pitts Walter

- When you write, you must show where each sentence begins and ends. Use a capital letter to show where each sentence begins, and an end mark to show where it ends.

Run-on:	Something smells good are you baking bread?
Correct:	Something smells good. Are you baking bread?

- Statements and commands end with periods.
- Questions end with question marks.
- Exclamations end with exclamation points.

Statement:	We like warm bread.
Command:	Bake some bread, please.
Question:	Do you like warm bread?
Exclamation:	What wonderful bread this is!

Try It Out

Speak Up How would you write these sentences?

1. we are making dinner would you like to help
2. do you need an apron please find the large pot
3. pour in some ketchup
4. did you remember to add the peanut butter
5. i'll chop the cabbage what a great stew this will be
6. how surprised Mom and Dad will be
7. what should we have for dessert
8. do you like strawberries let's put some on the table

Write these sentences correctly. Add capital letters and end marks. Write each run-on sentence as two sentences.

Example: have you ever eaten soup made from a bird's nest

Have you ever eaten soup made from a bird's nest?

9. what a strange dish it must be
10. tell me how it is made
11. only the nests of swiftlets are used these birds are related to hummingbirds
12. the nests are made of saliva
13. that is amazing
14. where can I taste bird's-nest soup
15. try a Chinese restaurant
16. the soup has been a part of Chinese culture for hundreds of years
17. it is a special treat in Asia
18. does collecting the nests harm the birds
19. laws protect the birds the nests can be gathered only at certain times

20–26. This part of an interview has two missing capital letters and five missing end marks. Write the interview correctly.

Example: is bird's-nest soup expensive *Is bird's-nest soup expensive?*

Proofreading

Host:	Please welcome the author of *There's a Bird's Nest in My Soup.* What an amazing book this is Where do swiftlets live
Author:	They live high up on cliffs people climb to get the nests
Host:	What a dangerous job that must be
Author:	it is a traditional skill passed down from father to son.

Writing Wrap-Up WRITING • THINKING • LISTENING • SPEAKING

COMPARING / CONTRASTING

Write a Food Column

You are a reporter. Compare the best dish in the cafeteria with the worst. Include all four types of sentences. Read aloud your column to a partner. Does your partner agree with you?

Writing Good Sentences

Writing Different Types of Sentences You know how to write statements, questions, commands, and exclamations. Avoid using too many statements when you write. Make your writing livelier by turning some statements into questions, commands, or exclamations.

Compare the first paragraph below to the second paragraph. Notice how questions, commands, and exclamations make the writing more interesting.

My mom makes great burritos. I am learning how to make them myself. You can come over sometime and try them.

My mom makes great burritos! Can you believe that I am learning to make them myself? Come over sometime and try them.

Apply It

1–6. Rewrite this flier. Change each underlined statement to a question, a command, or an exclamation. The word in ( ) will tell you which kind of sentence to write.

Small World Picnic

Martin Luther King Jr. School
June 15, 12–2 P.M.

Admission: $3.00

A good meal and a good deed can go together. (question) You can come to our Small World Picnic at the King School. (command) Last year we raised more than two hundred dollars for our town's food bank. We all had a great meal too. (exclamation)

We need volunteers to bring food for the picnic. This is a great chance to make your favorite food. (exclamation) Come share your family traditions. You can bring one of your special dishes for others to try. (command)

You can join us on June 15. (question)

Combining Sentences You know that combining sentences can improve your writing. If two sentences have the same subject, you can combine them in two different ways. You can join the whole sentences with *and* to form a compound sentence.

He makes breakfast.   He serves his family.

Compound Sentence: He makes breakfast, and he serves his family.

You can also join just the predicates to form a sentence with a compound predicate.

Compound Predicate: He makes breakfast and serves his family.

> A compound sentence needs a comma. Do not use a comma with compound predicates.

Apply It

7–12. Rewrite each underlined pair of sentences in this comic strip in two ways. First, combine the two sentences to form a compound sentence. Then combine them to form a sentence with a compound predicate. The first pair has been done for you.

Revising

What happened in this kitchen? It is a mess. It has a hundred dirty dishes.

I made some biscuits. I saved one for you.

They are too dry! Blah! They taste awful.

Well, I love them. I make the best dog biscuits!

It is a mess, and it has a hundred dirty dishes.

It is a mess and has a hundred dirty dishes.

2 Names of People and Pets

One-Minute Warm-Up

What's wrong with this sentence? How can you fix it?

dr. belle e. ache cures stomach problems.

- A proper noun begins with a capital letter. Always capitalize the names of people and pets because they are proper nouns.

- When titles and initials are used with names, you should capitalize them too.

Mario Gomez	Miss Diane Dawson	Dr. Richard Cohen
U. R. Wright	Mrs. Carol M. Ling	Governor J. Bryant
Mr. Todd Rossi	Ms. E. S. Ryan	Sparky

- Capitalize family titles when they are used as names or as parts of names.

    Today Grandmother arrived.
    Did Uncle Harry bring worms?

- Do not capitalize family titles when the titles are not used as names.

    My grandmother took us fishing.
    Our uncle paddled the canoe.

Try It Out

Speak Up Where should you use capital letters?

1. Every morning mom and aunt helen read the newspaper.
2. Today a photo of mr. derek johnson is on the front page.
3. He and james p. mullen just ran a marathon.
4. Did governor garcia give them a special award?
5. On the next page is a story about miss rosa perez.
6. My aunt read about her amazing poodle named pinky.
7. That smart dog saved the life of mrs. betty bowman!
8. dr. samuel washington wrote a letter to the editor.

Write these sentences correctly. Add capital letters where they are needed.

Example: mr. nye runs the school newspaper.
Mr. Nye runs the school newspaper.

9. This year dillon, sonia, and I are reporters.
10. I wrote about the science fair that ms. chan organized.
11. One of the judges was the science writer dr. d. j. hillman.
12. According to principal schultz, the fair was a big success!
13. I told mom and my friend marcus barnes about my next article.
14. I want to interview grandma winkler.
15. She and granddad moved here many years ago.
16. They started a pet store with mrs. wilma katz.
17. I want to know how my grandma's parrot, cha cha, learned to talk.

18–24. This article from a town newspaper has seven missing or incorrect capital letters. Write the article correctly.

Example: Marie walks frisky for officer joe.
Marie walks Frisky for Officer Joe.

Proofreading

Issue 194 No. 40 — **Central Valley Newspaper** — Section 2 Page 11

Fourth-Grader Starts Business

Marie frasier has her own business. It all began when her neighbor Alex p. Sloan was planning a trip to visit his Aunt. He said, "Can I hire you to walk brownie while I visit aunt Rachel?"

Since then, miss Lena Chin has hired Marie to walk her dog. dr. Victor Ortiz also hired the girl to care for his cat.

Writing Wrap-Up
WRITING • THINKING • LISTENING • SPEAKING

PERSUADING

Write an Ad

Marie wants to expand her pet business. Write an ad to help her attract new customers. Include the names of people and pets she has worked with. Read your ad to a partner. Check capitalization of names.

3 Names of Places and Things

One-Minute Warm-Up

SADAKO
Eleanor Coerr · Ed Young

Read the sentence below. Name the common nouns and the proper nouns.

One morning in August 1954, Sadako Sasaki looked up at the blue sky over Hiroshima and saw not a cloud in the sky.

—from *Sadako*, by Eleanor Coerr

- Always capitalize the names of particular places and things.
- Whenever a proper noun is more than one word, remember to begin each important word with a capital letter.

Proper Nouns That Name Places and Things	

Places
street—Pebble Creek Road
city—Dallas
state—Colorado
country—Mexico
building—Museum of Science
mountain—Pikes Peak
park—Acadia National Park
water—Indian Ocean
	Things
	days—Monday
	        Thursday
	months—February
	        August
	holidays—Flag Day
	        Fourth of July
	groups—Avon Garden Club
	        New York Mets

Try It Out

Speak Up Which words need capital letters?

1. My pen pal from japan is coming to visit
2. He plans to arrive in ocean city next tuesday.
3. We'll visit the seaside museum if he isn't too tired.
4. Then we can go to pacific park or rocky road.
5. Afterward we can watch the miami dolphins play football.
6. I'm glad he's staying until columbus day!
7. Many exciting things happen here in september and october.

Write these sentences correctly. Add capital letters where they are needed.

Example: Last saturday Heather returned from her trip.
Last Saturday Heather returned from her trip.

8. On friday we saw the slides she took in june and july.
9. They showed highlights of her travels in canada.
10. Her trip began near the bay of fundy.
11. She drove north to forillon national park.
12. There were pictures of the st. lawrence river.
13. Heather was there for canada day!
14. She also visited the canadian museum of man.
15. I visited my uncle in montreal last year.
16. He works in a skyscraper on dorchester boulevard.

17–24. This part of an e-mail message has eight missing or incorrect capital letters. Write the message correctly.

Example: Will you climb Pikes peak?   *Will you climb Pikes Peak?*

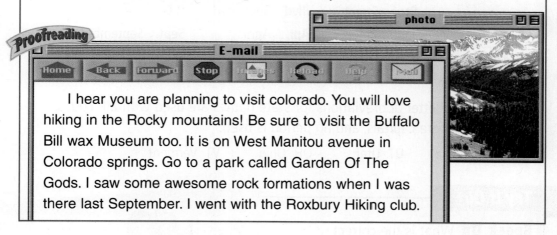

Proofreading

E-mail

Home   Back   Forward   Stop   Images   Reload   Help   Mail

I hear you are planning to visit colorado. You will love hiking in the Rocky mountains! Be sure to visit the Buffalo Bill wax Museum too. It is on West Manitou avenue in Colorado springs. Go to a park called Garden Of The Gods. I saw some awesome rock formations when I was there last September. I went with the Roxbury Hiking club.

photo

Writing Wrap-Up

WRITING • THINKING • LISTENING • SPEAKING

EXPRESSING

Write an Opinion

Write an e-mail message to a friend in another state. Tell about the best places to visit in your state. Include names of places and things. Read your message to a partner. Have your partner name the proper nouns.

4 Abbreviations

Which words can you shorten to make this sign fit on the truck better?

Mister Bucky Buckette's Cleaning Company

- **Some words have a shortened form called an abbreviation.** An abbreviation stands for a whole word. Most abbreviations begin with a capital letter and end with a period. Use them only in special kinds of writing, such as addresses and lists.

Some Common Abbreviations						
Titles	Mr.	Mister	Sr.	Senior	Mrs.	married woman
	Jr.	Junior	Dr.	Doctor	Ms.	any woman
Addresses	Rd.	Road	Ave.	Avenue	Co.	Company
	St.	Street	Blvd.	Boulevard	P. O.	Post Office
Months	Jan.	January	Apr.	April	Sept.	September
Days	Sun.	Sunday	Wed.	Wednesday	Thurs.	Thursday

- Special two-letter abbreviations for state names are used with ZIP codes. Both letters are capitals, and no period is used.

  AL Alabama   UT Utah   OH Ohio   VT Vermont

Try It Out

Speak Up What is the correct abbreviation for each underlined word?

1. Marina Boat <u>Company</u>
2. Monument Valley, <u>Utah</u>
3. A. V. Pyke <u>Junior</u>
4. <u>Tuesday</u>, April 5
5. <u>Doctor</u> Ramon
6. Grant <u>Road</u>

Monument Valley, Utah

Write these groups of words using correct abbreviations.

Example: Wednesday, November 4   *Wed., Nov. 4*

7. Doctor Ann Chang
8. Mister John Cliff Senior
9. May Lee, a married woman
10. Cooper Copper Company
11. Joseph L. Louis Junior

12. 19 Seneca Street
13. Tuesday, October 28
14. Post Office Box 6
15. El Monte Avenue
16. January 1, 1999

17–24. These addresses have eight incorrect abbreviations. Write the addresses correctly.

Example: 33 Forest ST   *33 Forest St.*

Proofreading

Mr. Aram Zakian
1875 Summit Rd
Columbus, OH. 43201

Wayne Hubbard Jun.
P O Box 300
Provo, UT 84603

RETURN TO SENDER

Dr Bonnie Buckman
1015 Timberlane Av.
Mobile, Al 36609

Pilgrim Paint Comp.
42 Brush Hill Blvd.
Stowe, VT 05672

Writing Wrap-Up

WRITING • THINKING • LISTENING • SPEAKING

CREATING

Write an Address Book

Make a booklet by folding several sheets of paper in half. Then make up some silly names and addresses to write in the booklet, such as *Mr. Rollin N. Dough, 50 Cash Lane, Richfield, PA.* Include a title and birth month for each person. Use correct abbreviations. Then read your address book to a partner. Check the abbreviations together.

5 Commas in a Series

Read the sentence aloud. When do you pause? Why?

His mother prepared warm flour tortillas, fried eggs, and fresh salsa for breakfast.

—from *Carlos and the Skunk/Carlos y el zorrillo*, by Jan Romero Stevens

- When you talk, you often pause briefly as you speak. When you write, you must use a comma (,) to tell your reader where to pause. Commas help make the meaning of your sentences clear.

    Incorrect: Alexa bought oatmeal bread cheese and nuts.
    Colin likes to ski swim or play tennis.

- How many things did Alexa buy? How many sports does Colin enjoy? Commas are needed to separate the items in each sentence. **When you list three or more words in a sentence, the list is called a series.** Use the word *and* or *or* before the last item in the series. Place a comma after each item except the last one.

    Correct: Alexa bought oatmeal, bread, cheese, and nuts.
    Alexa bought oatmeal bread, cheese, and nuts.
    Colin likes to ski, swim, or play tennis.

Try It Out

Speak Up Where are commas needed?

1. Gold is found in California Idaho and Georgia.
2. Tim Kara and David are learning to pan for gold.
3. Tim watches men women and children standing in a stream.
4. They scoop shovel or toss dirt into a pan.
5. Then they sift shake and slosh the gravel.
6. Pebbles sand and gold are left in the pan.
7. Panning for gold is muddy wet and tiring work.

Write these sentences correctly. Add commas where they are needed.

Example: Sarah Andy and Kristin learned about the Gold Rush.
Sarah, Andy, and Kristin learned about the Gold Rush.

8. They read studied and took notes.
9. Could anyone get rich with just a shovel a pan and a dream?
10. Farmers teachers and shopkeepers hoped so!
11. They headed west from Ohio Virginia and New York.
12. Many others came from Asia Europe and Australia.
13. The students wrote practiced and performed a play about the Gold Rush.
14. Their friends family and teachers watched the play.
15. They clapped cheered and whistled when it was over.

16–22. This part of an encyclopedia article has seven missing or incorrect commas. Write the article correctly.

Example: People left families friends, and jobs, to find gold.
People left families, friends, and jobs to find gold.

Proofreading

THE GOLD RUSH

Newspapers in Boston New York, and Philadelphia told amazing stories about the gold in California. People sailed, rode or walked to the region. They lived in tents, huts and shacks. Few became rich. Some suffered starved, and died. Others quit packed up, and left. However, many people stayed. They became storekeepers farmers, and, teachers.

Writing Wrap-Up   WRITING • THINKING • LISTENING • SPEAKING

NARRATING

Write a Story

Gold has been discovered on the moon. Write about joining the gold rush. Include sentences with a series of three or more words. Read your story to a group. Pause when you come to a comma. Work together to make sure all commas are in the right places.

Writing Good Sentences

Combining Sentences to Make a Series You know that a list of three or more words in a sentence is called a series. Sometimes you can combine short, choppy sentences by joining single words in a series.

Since ancient times, money has been earned.
It has been spent.
It has been saved.

Since ancient times, money has been earned, spent, and saved.

Remember to use a comma after each word in a series, except the last one.

Apply It

1–4. Rewrite the report on this poster. Combine each underlined set of sentences into one new sentence.

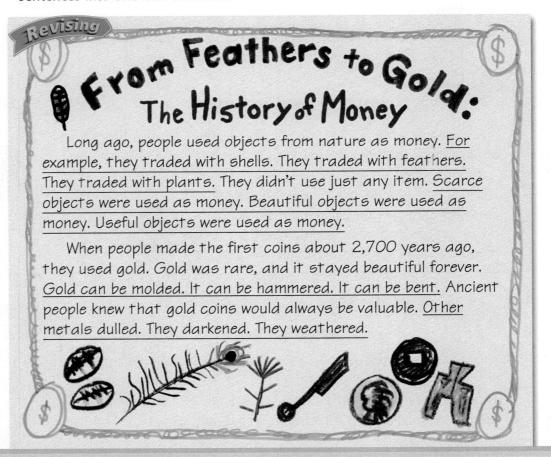

Revising

From Feathers to Gold: The History of Money

Long ago, people used objects from nature as money. For example, they traded with shells. They traded with feathers. They traded with plants. They didn't use just any item. Scarce objects were used as money. Beautiful objects were used as money. Useful objects were used as money.

When people made the first coins about 2,700 years ago, they used gold. Gold was rare, and it stayed beautiful forever. Gold can be molded. It can be hammered. It can be bent. Ancient people knew that gold coins would always be valuable. Other metals dulled. They darkened. They weathered.

You know how to combine sentences by joining single words in a series. You can also join groups of words, or phrases, in a series.

The United States Mint **collects worn-out coins**.
It **melts them down**.
It **makes new coins from the metal**.

} The United States Mint collects worn-out coins, melts them down, and makes new coins from the metal.

Apply It

5–8. Rewrite this part of a book report. Combine each set of underlined sentences into one sentence.

Revising

Money History answers just about every question you might ask about the subject. <u>The book is very interesting. It is easy to read. It is full of amazing facts. It</u> contains fun activities too. <u>The colorful pictures are great features of this book. The helpful charts are also great. The funny parts are great.</u>

One chapter shows how pennies are made. <u>They are cut from strips of metal. They are softened with heat. They are stamped with a design.</u>

Another chapter explains why ancient Romans used salt as money. Salt was hard to get and important. <u>It was needed for staying healthy. It was needed for seasoning food. It was needed for keeping food from spoiling.</u>

If you have any interest in money, read this book. It's fascinating!

6 More Uses for Commas

Read the riddle below. What punctuation mark should you add to the second sentence to make it correct?

Where did the horse get her wedding outfit, Allie?
Well I guess she got it at the bridle shop.

- When you speak, you pause briefly if you begin the answer to a question with *yes, no,* or *well.* Use a comma after these words to show the pause in your writing.

  Yes, I gave the horse some oats.
  No, I haven't brushed his coat.
  Well, you can clean his hoofs tomorrow.

- Sometimes you use a person's name when you address, or speak directly to, that person. When you write, use a comma or commas to set off the name of the person who is being addressed.

  Mariko, are you going riding with us?
  We wondered, Mariko, which trail we should take.
  We're really happy that you're joining us, Mariko!

Try It Out

Speak Up Where are commas needed?

1. Ryan have we always had horses in this country?
2. No explorers brought them in the 1500s.
3. They left some horses here Christopher.
4. Well did many people use the horses?
5. Yes the Plains Indians rode horses.
6. Later Eric horses pulled the pioneers' wagons.
7. Did you know Christopher, that wild mustangs are small, hardy, and smart?
8. No I didn't know that.
9. Well they are. They descended from tame horses of settlers and Plains Indians.

Write these sentences correctly. Add commas where they are needed.

Example: Have you heard of Chincoteague John?

Have you heard of Chincoteague, John?

10. Yes, it's an island off the coast of Virginia.
11. Well herds of wild horses live there.
12. Roberto have you read the book *Misty of Chincoteague*?
13. No I haven't read it.
14. The book Jillian tells about a pony from that island.
15. Joshua do you know where the ponies came from?
16. No where did they come from?
17. Well some people say a ship was wrecked in a storm.
18. The ship was carrying some ponies Marcos.
19. Each year Megan the ponies are rounded up.
20. Yes they swim to a nearby island.

21–28. This part of a script has eight missing commas. Write the script correctly.

Example: Dad the wild horses need help! *Dad the wild horses need help!*

Proofreading

document

Mark: You know Dad, about the wild horses out West. Well there isn't enough grass for them to eat.

Dad: That's a serious problem, Mark.

Mark: Yes I agree. Dad the government wants people to adopt these horses.

Dad: I know what's coming next Mark. No we can't have a horse in the city.

Mark: Wait Dad until I tell you my plan!

Writing Wrap-Up

WRITING • THINKING • LISTENING • SPEAKING

PERSUADING

Write a Persuasive Plan

Write a plan to convince Mark's father to adopt a horse. Include names and the words *well, yes,* and *no* in some sentences. Use commas correctly. Share your plan with a partner. Is it convincing?

7 Quotation Marks

One-Minute Warm-Up

Read the sentence below. What did the cat say? How can you tell?

"What a glorious supper!" said the Cat.

—from *Fables*, by Arnold Lobel

- Sometimes you may want to write a conversation between two or more people. **When you write the exact words that a speaker says, you are writing a direct quotation.**

- A direct quotation can come at the beginning or at the end of a sentence. Use **quotation marks** (" ") before and after a speaker's exact words. Do not place quotation marks around the words that explain who is talking.

  Ali asked, "Have you read about the fox and the grapes?"
  "That's my favorite fable!" I exclaimed.

- Do not use quotation marks unless you give the exact words of the speaker.

  Mr. Stuart said that we would write fables today.
  Mr. Stuart said, "Today we will write fables."

Try It Out

Speak Up Which sentences need quotation marks? Where should they be placed?

1. Ms. Diaz asked, Have you read Aesop's fables?
2. I've read them all! Nick exclaimed.
3. James explained that the characters are talking animals.
4. Melissa told us that each story teaches a lesson.
5. Aesop lived over two thousand years ago, Kelly added.
6. He was captured by pirates and taken to Greece, she said.
7. Kelly explained that Aesop worked in a court of law.
8. Many of his stories were used to make a point in court, she said.

On Your Own

Write each sentence. Add quotation marks where they are needed. Write *correct* for those sentences that do not need quotation marks.

Example: Who knows the fable of the crow? Kimi asked.
"Who knows the fable of the crow?" Kimi asked.

9. I remember that one! exclaimed Ashley.
10. Vanessa asked, Do you remember what the crow wanted?
11. The crow was thirsty and wanted water, answered Antonio.
12. Henry said, Some water was at the bottom of the jar.
13. Brandon explained that the crow couldn't push the jar over.
14. The crow filled the jar with pebbles, Ashley added.
15. Little by little the level of the water rose, Ben said.
16. Kimi asked if we knew what lesson the fable teaches.

17–24. This part of a fable has eight missing or incorrect quotation marks. Write the fable correctly.

Example: I'll try hard, said the tortoise.   *I'll try hard, said the tortoise.*

Proofreading

I'll win this race easily!" the hare bragged.

The tortoise replied, We shall see.

The crowd yelled "that the hare was way ahead."

Then the hare announced, "I think I will stop for a little snooze."

The tortoise kept going until he crossed the finish line. Where is the hare?" he asked.

The hare is still napping! yelled the crowd.

Writing Wrap-Up
WRITING • THINKING • LISTENING • SPEAKING

NARRATING

Write a Conversation

Write a conversation between your favorite story characters. Use quotation marks correctly. Then read your conversation to a partner. Check that you used quotation marks correctly.

8 Quotations

Read the sentence. What two punctuation marks should you switch to make the sentence correct?

"Does Polly want a cracker." Emily asked?

Quotation marks show a speaker's exact words. More punctuation marks, as well as capital letters, are needed to write quotations correctly.

- Always capitalize the first word of a quotation. When a quotation comes last in a sentence, use a comma to separate the quotation from the words that tell who is speaking. Put the end mark inside the last quotation marks.

  Brittany said, "All birds have feathers."
  Hideki asked, "Can all birds fly?"
  Lauren said, "Look at the tiny hummingbird."

- When a quotation that is a statement or a command comes first in a sentence, put a comma inside the last quotation marks. If the quotation is a question or an exclamation, put the question mark or the exclamation point inside the last quotation marks. A period always follows the last word in the sentence.

  "Say hello to Pauline," Renee suggested.
  "Pauline is a parrot!" I exclaimed.

Try It Out

Speak Up These sentences have quotations. How would you capitalize and punctuate each sentence?

1. Jay shouted there must be thirty birds here
2. Robin said I guess they like our bird feeder
3. Polly added they're eating all the sunflower seeds
4. what kind of bird is that I asked.
5. Look it up in our bird book Robin said
6. Jay exclaimed bird watching is a lot of fun

These sentences have quotations. Write them correctly.

Example: Lindsay asked how many kinds of birds are there
Lindsay asked, "How many kinds of birds are there?"

7. there are over nine thousand kinds Chan exclaimed
8. different birds live in different places Erin added
9. have you seen my list of birds Felipe asked
10. he explained I write down each kind of bird I see
11. Lindsay asked why do you put different seeds on the ground
12. all birds don't like the same food Erin explained
13. Chan said put out a pan of water too

14–22. These riddles have six missing or incorrect punctuation marks and three missing capital letters. Write the riddles correctly.

Example: Brian asked "is it an owl"? *Brian asked, "Is it an owl?"*

Proofreading

"what bird is always sad?" asked Heather

Brian replied, "It's the bluebird, of course".

"Name the bird that writes the best" said Heather.

Brian exclaimed "it must be the *penguin*"!

"What bird has an initial in its name"? Heather asked.

Brian responded, "could it be the blue jay?"

Writing Wrap-Up
WRITING • THINKING • LISTENING • SPEAKING

CREATING

Write Riddles

Write questions for two or three riddles about animals, plants, or food. Have a partner write the answers. Then write the riddles as conversations between you and your partner. Use correct punctuation. Then trade places. Read your conversations to the class.

9 Titles

Look at the picture. What do you think this book might be about? Make up an interesting title for the book.

- When you write the title of a book, a magazine, or a newspaper, capitalize the first, the last, and each important word. Capitalize words like *and, in, of, to, a,* and *the* only when they are the first or last word in the title.

Danger on Midnight River	*Children of the Midnight Sun*	*News and Views*
The Old Man and His Door	*Boys' Life*	*The Fun Times*

- In print the titles of books, magazines, and newspapers are set off by *italics*. Since you cannot write in italics, always underline the title of a book, a magazine, or a newspaper.

  Is <u>Tom Sawyer</u> your favorite book?   I am reading the magazine <u>Stone Soup</u>.

Try It Out

Speak Up How would you write these titles?

1. tracks in the wild
2. tales of a fourth grade nothing
3. the rooftop reporter
4. sports illustrated for kids
5. the real mcCoy
6. harbor town post
7. national geographic world
8. searching for velociraptor
9. harry potter and the sorcerer's stone
10. aladdin and the wonderful lamp

How would you write these sentences?

11. The chicago sun-times has great comics.
12. Is cricket a magazine?
13. Who wrote king of the wind?
14. Read a wrinkle in time.
15. Get walton weekly.
16. I read charlotte's web.

Write these sentences correctly.

Example: An article in this week's village herald praised the new library.
An article in this week's <u>Village Herald</u> praised the new library.

17. The library is giving away the magazine calliope.
18. My little sister is reading jalapeño bagels.
19. It was on a shelf next to tea with milk.
20. I found an article for my report in neighborhood news.
21. I'm also using the book boss of the plains.
22. Did you read a book called poppy and rye?
23. I thought the book by the shores of silver lake was better.
24. Is cobblestone your favorite history magazine?

25–32. This ad has eight errors in titles. Write the ad correctly.

Example: Perhaps you would enjoy Sarah, Plain And Tall.
Perhaps you would enjoy <u>Sarah, Plain and Tall</u>.

Proofreading

Would you like to read the Summer Of the Swans or The life and times of the Peanut? Maybe you'd prefer Arrow To the Sun or Orphan Train Rider. A New York Times report says that Wendy's Bookstore has books for everyone. You can also find magazines like highlights for children and Ranger Rick.

Wendy's Bookstore

Writing Wrap-Up
WRITING • THINKING • LISTENING • SPEAKING

SUMMARIZING

Write Summaries

On index cards, write the titles of books and magazines you like. Include a few sentences about each one. Then work with a partner to make sure your titles are written correctly. Next, decide what category each title belongs in, such as nature, mystery, or adventure, and arrange the cards by categories. File your cards in a class box.

Enrichment

Pet Hotel

You run a pet hotel. Fill out identification cards for five visiting animals. Make cards that include (1) the pet's name; (2) the owner's name, with a title such as *Mr.;* (3) the owner's address; (4) a description of the pet; and (5) the dates of the visit. Use correct abbreviations for titles, addresses, and months.

Pet's name:	Matilda
Owner's name:	Ms. Laura LaRue
Owner's address:	7 Purr St.
	Furball, MA 00001
Description of pet:	Matilda is an adorable, gray Siamese cat.
Dates of visit:	Sept. 30–Oct. 2

Talking Numbers

Imagine that numbers can talk. On index cards, write five quotations in which numbers give clues about themselves. Leave a blank for the number that is speaking.

Write the missing number on the back of each card. Then exchange cards with a partner. Does your partner know which numbers are speaking? Have you punctuated correctly?

Challenge Make your quotation into a math problem.

Example: "You will be left with four if you subtract eight from me," said number _____.

1 Correct Sentences *(p. 166)*
Write these sentences correctly.
Add capital letters and end marks.
Separate run-on sentences.

1. this is a lovely new aquarium
2. how long have you had it
3. some fish have unusual shapes other fish are brightly colored
4. how huge that angelfish is
5. can you see the tiny fish they are hiding among the rocks
6. do not give them too much food

2 Names of People and Pets
(p. 170) Write these sentences.
Add capital letters where they are needed.

7. My uncle has a dog named nomad.
8. He leaves uncle henry very early each morning.
9. First, nomad heads downtown.
10. He visits dr. sarah aaron.
11. Then he stops at central high.
12. My mother and mr. l. m. rowe are teachers there.

3 Names of Places and Things
(p. 172) Write these sentences.
Add capital letters where they are needed.

13. Cindy will go to cleveland in the middle of august.
14. She will return on labor day.
15. The terminal tower is the name of a tall building in cleveland.
16. Cindy wants to see the cleveland indians play baseball.

17. On monday the family will visit gates mills, a nearby village.
18. It is on the chagrin river.

4 Abbreviations *(p. 174)*
Write each group of words.
Use an abbreviation in place of each underlined word.

19. 98 South Main <u>Street</u>
20. <u>Doctor</u> James Asher
21. <u>Wednesday</u>, <u>November</u> 15, 2000
22. 86 Ripley <u>Road</u>
23. T. J. Lamont, <u>Junior</u>
24. <u>Post Office</u> Box 162

5 Commas in a Series *(p. 176)*
Write these sentences. Add commas where they are needed.

25. Cranberries blueberries and Concord grapes grow in the northern United States.
26. Cranberries grow in bogs where there are sand moss and water.
27. They grow in Massachusetts Wisconsin and Washington.
28. Josh Sarah and Liz are going to a bog to see the harvest.
29. Workers will pick inspect and pack the berries for sale.
30. Cranberries are used in sauce juice and baked goods.

6 More Uses for Commas
(p. 180) Write these sentences.
Use commas correctly.

31. Have you heard about the new contest Chris?
32. No I have not heard about it.

33. Well each person must design a stone carving.
34. Yes the best drawing will win.
35. What will you draw Lisa?
36. Damon what do you hope to win?
37. Well the winning design will be carved in stone.
38. It will be put on the roof Jon.

7 Quotations *(pp. 182, 184)* Write these sentences. Use capital letters and punctuation marks correctly. Write *correct* if a sentence is already correct.

39. I love to ice skate announced Jeff

40. Rebecca asked is the ice thick
41. Don't be afraid to fall said Don
42. Luke answered that he wouldn't.
43. Molly cried look out for the hole
44. I would much rather go in-line skating declared June

8 Titles *(p. 186)* Write these titles correctly.

45. a light in the attic
46. sports illustrated for kids
47. island of the blue dolphins
48. rocky mountain news
49. a very important day

Mixed Review 50–56. This story beginning has three capitalization errors and four punctuation errors. Write the story correctly.

Proofreading Checklist
Did you write these correctly?
✔ capital letters
✔ proper nouns
✔ punctuation marks
✔ abbreviations
✔ titles

Proofreading

It was a rainy july day. Eric's brother Nigel burst into the room. "Eric, look at this." said Nigel. He shoved a small ad from the magazine <u>Kids In Business</u> under Eric's nose.

Have you invented a game puzzle, or toy? You can get rich! Send for a free pamphlet.
Bright Ideas CO.
33 Lilac Blossom Ave
Canton, OH 44701

Bright Ideas Co.

Nigel announced, "I'm going to send for the pamphlet right away"

See www.eduplace.com/hme/ for an online quiz.

Test Practice

Write the numbers 1–6 on a sheet of paper. Read the passage and look at the numbered, underlined parts. Choose the answer that shows the best way to write each underlined part. Write the letter for that answer.

<u>Helen keller</u> was born in 1880 in <u>alabama. When</u> she was two years
(1)   (2)
old, she came down with a fever that left her deaf and blind. For the next

five years, Helen was <u>silent and unhappy</u> Then <u>miss anne sullivan</u> became
(3)   (4)
Helen's teacher. Sullivan taught Helen how to read words that were spelled

into her hand. Helen became a student at <u>Radcliffe College</u>. She even
(5)
wrote a famous book. It was called <u>the story of my life.</u>
(6)

1 A Helen Keller

  B helen keller

  C helen Keller

  D Correct as it is

2 F alabama, When

  G Alabama. When

  H Alabama. when

  J Correct as it is

3 A silent and unhappy?

  B silent and unhappy.

  C silent and, unhappy.

  D Correct as it is

4 F miss Anne Sullivan

  G miss anne Sullivan

  H Miss Anne Sullivan

  J Correct as it is

5 A radcliffe College

  B Radcliffe college

  C radcliffe college

  D Correct as it is

6 F <u>The story of my life</u>

  G <u>The Story of My Life</u>

  H <u>the Story of My Life</u>

  J Correct as it is

Test Practice *continued*

Now write the numbers 7–15 on your paper. Use the paragraphs to answer the questions. Write the letter for each answer.

⁷On Tuesday morning, Dorrie throwed on her new red shirt. ⁸Would people like it? ⁹In class mrs. Pierce stared. ¹⁰Then Dorrie's friend whispered, "Dorrie, your shirt is on backwards! ¹¹Dorrie felt like the sillyer person in the world.

7 Which is the best way to rewrite Sentence 7?

A On tuesday morning, Dorrie throw on her new red shirt.

B On Tuesday morning, Dorrie threw on her new red shirt.

C On Tuesday morning, Dorrie thrown on her new red shirt.

D Best as it is

8 Which is the best way to rewrite Sentence 8?

F Would people like it!

G would people like it?

H Would people like it.

J Best as it is

9 Which is the best way to rewrite Sentence 9?

A In class Mrs. Pierce stared.

B In class mrs. Pierce stared.

C In class Mrs. pierce stared.

D Best as it is

10 Which is the best way to rewrite Sentence 10?

F Then Dorries friend whispered, "Dorrie, your shirt is on backwards!"

G Then Dorries' friend whispered "Dorrie your shirt is on backwards!"

H Then Dorrie's friend whispered, "Dorrie, your shirt is on backwards!"

J Best as it is

11 Which is the best way to rewrite Sentence 11?

A Dorrie felt like the sillyest person in the world.

B Dorrie felt like the silliest person in the world.

C Dorrie felt like the most silliest person in the world.

D Best as it is

[12]Mariah went to the ashton public library. [13]She needed facts about swans ducks and geese. [14]The librarian showed Mariah a set of books called The Nature Encyclopedia. [15]"These books have the goodest pictures I have ever seen!" said Mariah.

12 Which is the best way to rewrite Sentence 12?

  F Mariah goed to the ashton public library.

  G Mariah went to the Ashton Public Library.

  H Mariah went to the Ashton public library.

  J Best as it is

13 Which is the best way to rewrite Sentence 13?

  A She needed facts about swans, ducks and geese.

  B She needed facts about swans, ducks, and geese.

  C She needed facts about swans, ducks, and, geese.

  D Best as it is

14 Which is the best way to rewrite Sentence 14?

  F The librarian showed Mariah a set of books called The nature Encyclopedia.

  G The librarian showed Mariah a set of books called The nature encyclopedia.

  H The librarian showed Mariah a set of books called The Nature Encyclopedia.

  J Best as it is

15 Which is the best way to rewrite Sentence 15?

  A "These books have the best pictures I have ever seen!" said Mariah.

  B "These books have the best pictures I have ever seen"! said Mariah.

  C "These books have the most bestest pictures I have ever seen!" said Mariah.

  D Best as it is

(pages 166–167)

1 Correct Sentences

- Begin every sentence with a capital letter.
- Use a period after a statement or a command.
- Use a question mark after a question.
- Use an exclamation point after an exclamation.

Remember

● Each sentence is missing a capital letter or an end mark. Write each sentence correctly.

Example: have you ever seen a dolphin? *Have you ever seen a dolphin?*

1. some scientists were diving near the Bahama Islands.
2. one scientist met a dolphin underwater.
3. How excited she was
4. What did the dolphin do
5. it poked her playfully with its snout.

▲ Write these sentences correctly. Add capital letters and end marks. Separate run-on sentences.

Example: dolphins breathe air how do they do it
        Dolphins breathe air. How do they do it?

6. a dolphin breathes through a blowhole
7. do you know where this is it is on top of the head
8. a dolphin can stay underwater for six minutes
9. that is a long time how long can you stay underwater
10. some scientists think that dolphins can learn to speak

■ Write these sentences correctly. Then label each sentence *statement, question, command,* or *exclamation.*

Example: can you name a very large animal
        Can you name a very large animal?   question

11. the blue whale is the world's largest animal
12. is it bigger than a dinosaur
13. this animal is as large as twenty-five elephants
14. they have no teeth they strain food from seawater
15. what interesting animals they are please tell me more

(pages 170–171)

2 Names of People and Pets

- Capitalize the names of people and pets.
- Capitalize titles and initials that are parts of names.
- Capitalize family titles when they are used as names or as parts of names.

Remember

● Write these names of people and pets correctly.

Example: aunt sally   *Aunt Sally*

1. uncle barry
2. fifi
3. queen elizabeth
4. dr. doris cortez
5. mr. joseph b. zaturka

6. betsy chun
7. miss w. r. lin
8. mayor santos
9. porky
10. p. j. levy

▲ Write these sentences. Use capital letters correctly.

Example: My aunt's cat scaredy was in the pet show.
My aunt's cat Scaredy was in the pet show.

11. Her cat's full name is lord summerfield.
12. I heard that dr. jessie jones was very disappointed.
13. The doctor's cat, harvey, climbed a tree and stayed there.
14. Even grandmother tried to get the cat out of the tree.
15. It was too late to enter harvey in the show.

■ Use a noun from the box to complete each sentence. Use each noun once. Write the sentences. Be sure to capitalize the proper nouns.

Example: Show this article to _____.   *Show this article to Aunt Jane.*

| dr. dan d. lyons | aunt jane | uncle |
| attorney m. dodd | grandmother | doctor |

16. It is about a veterinarian named _____.
17. The _____ has a new office.
18. It is above the law office of _____.
19. My aunt and _____ will take our cat to the vet.
20. _____ will take care of the other cats.

(pages 172–173)

3 Names of Places and Things

Remember

- Capitalize the names of streets, cities, states, countries, buildings, mountains, parks, and bodies of water.
- Capitalize the names of days, months, holidays, and groups.

● Write these names of places and things correctly.

Example: washington, d.c.   *Washington, D.C.*

1. monday
2. united states
3. potomac river
4. jefferson memorial
5. the white house
6. may 31
7. pennsylvania avenue
8. memorial day
9. rock creek park
10. capitol hill

▲ Write these sentences. Use capital letters correctly.

Example: The largest city in louisiana is new orleans.
The largest city in Louisiana is New Orleans.

11. This city lies along the mississippi river.
12. It is north of the gulf of mexico.
13. A holiday called mardi gras takes place every year.
14. Tourists come in february or march for this celebration.
15. Jazz fans hear great music at preservation hall.
16. One of the largest indoor stadiums is the louisiana superdome.
17. The new orleans saints play football there.

■ Invent a city. Write a sentence to answer each question about your city. Make up names to answer the questions.

Example: What is the name of your city?
The name of my city is Clowntown.

18. Who is the mayor?
19. What is the nearest body of water?
20. In what country is it located?
21. What big holiday is celebrated in your city?
22. When does it take place?

(pages 174–175)

4 Abbreviations

- An abbreviation is a short form of a word.
- Most abbreviations begin with a capital letter and end with a period.

● Write each group of words. Underline the abbreviation.

Example: Oct. 1, 1988   *Oct. 1, 1988*

1. Abbot Travel Co.
2. Sun., March 2, 1986
3. 3456 Fifth Ave.
4. Pots and Pans Co.
5. Ms. Maria Garcia
6. Marvin Hogan Jr.
7. Atlanta, GA 30043
8. Mrs. Monica Cohen
9. Leo Lyons Sr.
10. P. O. Box 567
11. Bennington, VT 05201
12. Jan. 4, 1989

▲ Write the words. Use an abbreviation in place of each underlined word.

Example: Douglas Food <u>Company</u>   *Douglas Food Co.*

13. <u>January</u> 12, 1874
14. Irving White <u>Senior</u>
15. <u>Mister</u> Howard Klein
16. <u>Doctor</u> Harriet Correlli
17. Cleveland, <u>Ohio</u> 44114
18. <u>Thursday</u>, July 4, 1776
19. <u>Post Office</u> Box 76
20. 6710 South Maple <u>Street</u>
21. Mobile, <u>Alabama</u> 36609
22. 5110 Clinton <u>Avenue</u>
23. Sporting Life <u>Company</u>
24. <u>Tuesday, November</u> 1, 2001

■ Write each group of words, using correct abbreviations. Add capital letters where they are needed.

Example: doctor ann mack   *Dr. Ann Mack*

25. thursday, january
26. apex shipping company
27. 678 goldrush road
28. post office box 89
29. mister michael burns
30. salt lake city, utah 84101
31. sunday, november 1
32. 450 milford avenue
33. doctor lorna cook
34. hunter boulevard
35. mister john chen senior
36. santora music company

(pages 176–177)

5 Commas in a Series

- A series is a list of three or more items.
- Use commas to separate the items in a series. Put a comma after each item in the series except the last one.

● Complete each sentence by adding words to form a series. Write the sentence.

Example: Rita's best friends are Kim, _____, and _____.
Rita's best friends are Kim, Tommy, and Ben.

1. They all like to swim, _____, and _____.
2. Rita likes to cook spaghetti, _____, and _____.
3. Last week she invited Kim, _____, and _____ for lunch.
4. She made salad, _____, and _____.
5. After lunch the friends talked, _____, and _____.

▲ Write these sentences. Use commas correctly.

Example: Farmers hunters and trappers became pioneers.
Farmers, hunters, and trappers became pioneers.

6. Pioneers settled in Kansas Nebraska and Minnesota.
7. Pioneer women spun wove and sewed cloth.
8. The pioneers built shelters wagons and boats.
9. At first men women and children lived in sod houses.
10. Sod houses were made of grass mud and dirt.

■ Write each sentence two different ways. The meaning of each sentence will change depending on where you use commas.

Example: Pioneers ate oatmeal bread and potatoes.
Pioneers ate oatmeal bread and potatoes.
Pioneers ate oatmeal, bread, and potatoes.

11. On the road, they ate cod stew pork and beans.
12. Cows gave them cream cheese and milk.
13. A good dinner included chicken soup and noodles.
14. They used cornmeal flour and eggs to make pancakes.
15. Their apple walnut and cherry breads were delicious.

(pages 180–181)

Remember

6 **More Uses for Commas**

• Use a comma to set off the words *yes, no,* and *well* when they are at the beginning of a sentence.

• Use a comma or commas to set off the names of people who are addressed directly.

● Write these sentences. Use commas correctly.

Example: Well have you heard about the wild horses?
Well, have you heard about the wild horses?

1. Yes I read that some people are adopting them.
2. No the horses are not still wild.
3. Carmen the horses have been tamed.
4. Well let's go to see them.
5. Bill have any wild horses become gentle pets?

▲ Write these sentences. Use commas correctly.

Example: Do you know how tall the first horses were Ann?
Do you know how tall the first horses were, Ann?

6. Yes this book says they were eleven inches tall.
7. Well today's horses are much taller.
8. Some horses grow to be seven feet tall Iris.
9. They are giants Paul compared to the early horses.
10. Frank did people always ride horses?
11. No the early horses were not tall or strong enough.

■ Write correctly the sentences that need commas. Write *correct* for each sentence that does not need commas.

Example: Can you tell me Marcos who the nomad people were?
Can you tell me, Marcos, who the nomad people were?

12. Nomads Jeff wandered from place to place.
13. Pete were they lost?
14. No the nomads were looking for food.
15. Nomads were the first people to ride horses.
16. They put animal skins on the horses' backs.

(pages 182–183)

7 Quotation Marks

- A direct quotation tells a speaker's exact words.
- Use quotation marks (" ") before and after a direct quotation.

● Copy each sentence. Underline the direct quotation.

Example: "I know a fable," said Alicia.   *"I know a fable," said Alicia.*

1. A fox said, "I will invite the stork for dinner."
2. The fox added, "I will serve soup in a shallow dish."
3. Then the stork said to the fox, "Have dinner with me."
4. "What did the stork serve for dinner?" asked Emily.
5. Alicia answered, "It was soup in a tall, narrow jar."
6. "Well, one bad turn deserved another!" laughed Carlos.

▲ Write each sentence correctly, using quotation marks.

Example: Let's hear another fable, begged Jon.
    "Let's hear another fable," begged Jon.

7. Carrie said, A crow found a piece of cheese.
8. A fox exclaimed, I want that crow's cheese!
9. You are a beautiful bird! the fox told the crow.
10. Then the fox asked the crow to sing, replied DeVona.
11. Ned said, It opened its beak and dropped the cheese.
12. Eric added, Do not be fooled by too much praise.

■ Write correctly each sentence that needs quotation marks. If a sentence is already correct, write *correct*.

Example: A lion caught a small mouse, said Joey.
    "A lion caught a small mouse," said Joey.

13. The mouse squeaked, Let me go, and I'll never forget it!
14. The lion declared that a mouse could never help a lion.
15. However, the lion let the mouse go, said Jason.
16. Hunters later tied the lion to a tree, added Leesa.
17. Nick said, The mouse chewed the rope and freed the lion.
18. May stated that little friends may prove great friends.

(pages 184–185)

8 Quotations

 Remember

- Begin a quotation with a capital letter.
- When a quotation comes at the end of a sentence, use a comma to separate the quotation from the words that tell who is speaking. Put end punctuation marks inside the last quotation marks.

● Each sentence is missing a comma or a capital letter. Write each sentence correctly.

Example: Don asked, "have you ever heard of a snipe?"
Don asked, "Have you ever heard of a snipe?"

1. "Please tell me about it" answered Flora.
2. Don said, "it is a kind of bird."
3. "The snipe is related to the gull" Ann continued.
4. Pat asked "What kind of bill does it have?"
5. "A snipe has a long, pointed bill" Phuong explained.

▲ Write each sentence correctly. Add capital letters, commas, and end marks where they are needed.

Example: Ellen exclaimed "what a funny-looking bird"
Ellen exclaimed, "What a funny-looking bird!"

6. Oscar explained "it is called an umbrella bird"
7. "it has a funny hat on its head" laughed Ellen.
8. "those are feathers" explained Lora.
9. Chan said "it has long feathers hanging from its neck"
10. "they look like an umbrella handle" added Al.

■ Write these sentences. Use capital letters and punctuation marks correctly.

Example: is that bird related to a woodpecker asked jo
"Is that bird related to a woodpecker?" asked Jo.

11. yes it is answered dan
12. please show me the picture begged les
13. its bill is almost as big as its body exclaimed kim
14. sue asked well what kind of bird is it
15. it is called a toucan, sue explained dan

(pages 186–187)

⑨ **Titles**

- Capitalize the first, the last, and each important word in the titles of books, magazines, or newspapers. Underline them.

● Write each sentence. Underline each title.

Example: This week's Brookland Bugle printed a list of books.
This week's <u>*Brookland Bugle*</u> *printed a list of books.*

1. A Cricket in Times Square was on the list.
2. Is Newsweek your dad's favorite magazine?
3. Did The Year of the Panda make you laugh?
4. How to Eat Fried Worms certainly did.
5. Did Kathleen Krull write Wilma Unlimited?
6. Yes, a Belview News critic wrote about that book.

▲ Write these sentences correctly.

Example: I lent stowaway to the mushroom planet to Jan.
I lent <u>*Stowaway to the Mushroom Planet*</u> *to Jan.*

7. She is reading the wind in the willows now.
8. There is a review of it in highlights for children.
9. I wrote a story about it for hale school news.
10. Another article was about the book runaway ralph.
11. Wasn't Ralph also in the mouse and the motorcycle?
12. The editor of lee times asked Jim to write a column.
13. This week's column discussed the book lou gehrig: The Luckiest man alive.

■ Make up a title to complete each sentence. Write the sentences correctly.

Example: _____ is a collection of scary stories. (book)
Terrifying Tales *is a collection of scary stories.*

14. _____ reports on scientific discoveries. (newspaper)
15. Read _____ to learn how to make a robot. (book)
16. Learn the latest news about musicians in _____. (magazine)
17. _____ is the story of a new pet. (book)
18. Buy a copy of _____ to learn about the zoo. (newspaper)

Picnic dinners are Grandpa's specialty. He packs our favorite summer foods in a basket and drives us to the park.

1 What Is a Pronoun?

Snails leave trails.
They drag their tails.

Make up your own silly rhyme. Begin the first sentence with a noun. Begin the second sentence with a word from the list that can replace the noun.

he   she   it   we   they

- A noun names a person, a place, or a thing. **A pronoun is a word that takes the place of one or more nouns.** When you write, you do not have to keep repeating nouns. Instead, you can replace some of the nouns with pronouns. Compare the two paragraphs below. What pronouns take the place of nouns?

> Sara asked Brett and Leah to go to the seashore with Sara. Sara, Brett, and Leah spoke to Ms. Lanski. Ms. Lanski gave Sara, Brett, and Leah a special book. The book was about sea life.

> Sara asked Brett and Leah to go to the seashore with her. They spoke to Ms. Lanski. She gave them a special book. It was about sea life.

- Like the nouns they replace, pronouns are singular or plural.

Singular Pronouns: I, me, you, he, him, she, her, it
Plural Pronouns: we, us, you, they, them

Try It Out

Speak Up Which words in these sentences are pronouns? Is each pronoun singular or plural?

1. Sara said, "Come with us to the seashore."
2. Leah carried a pail. She wanted to collect shells.
3. Brett took a notebook. Sara had asked him to take notes.
4. Leah saw a sea star. Brett wrote about it in the book.
5. "You are good scientists," Sara told Leah and Brett.

Write the pronoun in each sentence that takes the place of the underlined word or words.

Example: <u>Brett</u> said, "I see a large pink shell."   *I*

6. "Should we take this shell?" asked <u>Brett and Leah</u>.
7. Sara asked <u>Brett and Leah</u>, "What do you hear inside the shell?"
8. <u>Brett and Leah</u> listened. The noise reminded them of the ocean.
9. Sara told <u>Brett</u> that he had found a queen conch shell.
10. "I see that the shell is empty," said <u>Leah</u>.
11. "This book will tell us about the conch," said <u>Brett and Leah</u>.
12. <u>The conch</u> is a kind of snail. It lives in the sea.
13. Once there were many of these <u>snails</u>. Now they are rare.

14–20. Write the pronouns in this part of a newscast that take the place of the underlined word or words.

Example: Adam watches <u>conch eggs</u> and writes about them.   *them*

Marta Rivera is a young scientist. She is working to save the conch. <u>The job</u> is difficult, but it is rewarding. Marta collects <u>conch eggs</u> and puts them in tanks. <u>Adam Caldwell</u> assists <u>Marta</u>. He helps her to feed the young snails. When <u>the snails</u> are large enough, they will be returned to the sea. <u>Adam and Marta</u> believe the work they are doing is important.

Writing Wrap-Up
WRITING • THINKING • LISTENING • SPEAKING

INFORMING

Write Captions

Draw pictures of three or four things from nature, such as shells, plants, and animals. Then write a few sentences about each item below its picture. Use pronouns in each caption. Read your captions to a partner. Have your partner name the pronouns you used.

2 Subject Pronouns

Read the sentences below. What pronoun takes the place of the noun *earwigs*?

Imagine having thirty brothers and sisters to bug you! Some earwigs do. They also have a devoted mother.

—from *Creepy, Crawly Baby Bugs*, by Sandra Markle

- Like a noun, a pronoun can be used as the subject of a sentence. Remember that the subject tells whom or what the sentence is about.

Nouns
Aki did a project on insects.
Justin worked with Aki.
Aki and Justin gave a report.
Nakisha and I enjoyed the report.

Pronouns
She did a project on insects.
He worked with Aki.
They gave a report.
We enjoyed the report.

- Not all pronouns can be used as subjects. **Only the subject pronouns *I*, *you*, *he*, *she*, *it*, *we*, and *they* can be used as the subjects of sentences.**

Subject Pronouns	
Singular	**Plural**
I	we
you	you
he, she, it	they

Try It Out

Speak Up Which subject pronoun could take the place of the underlined word or words in each sentence?

1. Matt said to Selena, "Selena found a ladybug."
2. Matt and I know that ladybugs are helpful insects.
3. Ladybugs are not really bugs. Ladybugs are beetles.
4. This beetle eats insects that destroy plants.
5. Selena did not disturb the ladybug.
6. Selena said, "Selena should not hurt such a helpful insect."

Write each sentence. Use a subject pronoun in place of the underlined word or words.

Example: The book is about butterflies. *It is about butterflies.*

7. Holly and Henry read the book.
8. Henry learned that butterflies start out as eggs.
9. Then the eggs hatch into caterpillars.
10. Henry read that the third stage is the pupa.
11. Holly said that the caterpillar spins a hard shell.
12. When this shell cracks, a butterfly comes out.

13–18. Write these jokes. Use a subject pronoun in place of the underlined word or words.

Example: Nikki and Jason practice jokes with each other.
They practice jokes with each other.

Jason, why did the man keep wasps in the closet?

The man had a good reason. **The wasps** were yellow jackets! Now I will ask one. Can you guess why the fly landed on the toast?

The fly wanted to be a butterfly! I have another joke. Why did the woman call the insect expert?

The woman was sick with a bug! These jokes are funny. My father will love them!

Writing Wrap-Up WRITING • THINKING • LISTENING • SPEAKING

EXPRESSING

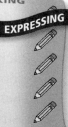

Write an Opinion

Write a paragraph on any kind of insect. Explain why the insect is harmful or helpful. Use as many subject pronouns as you can. Then read your paragraph to a group. Do they agree with you?

For Extra Practice see page 227.

3 Object Pronouns

Complete the sentence below with as many different pronouns as you can.

Frisky the pony gave a ride to _____.

- Subject pronouns can be used as the subjects of sentences. **The pronouns** *me, you, him, her, it, us,* **and** *them* **are called object pronouns.** Object pronouns follow action verbs and words such as *to, with, for,* and *at.*

Nouns

Mr. Rossi fed the horses.
James helped Mr. Rossi.
James showed a pony to Rachel and me.
Then James gave the pony a carrot.

Pronouns

Mr. Rossi fed them.
James helped him.
James showed a pony to us.
Then James gave it a carrot.

Object Pronouns	
Singular	**Plural**
me	us
you	you
him, her, it	them

- Never use the object pronouns *me, him, her, us,* and *them* as subjects. You can use the pronouns *you* and *it* as either subject or object pronouns.

Try It Out

Speak Up Which object pronoun could take the place of the underlined word or words in each sentence?

1. Rachel rides <u>horses</u> every day.
2. Cody said to Rachel, "Please teach <u>Cody</u>."
3. Rachel took Cody to the stable with <u>Rachel</u>.
4. Rachel told Cody, "I will teach <u>Cody</u> grooming first."
5. Then Rachel brushed <u>the horse</u>.
6. Cody said, "The horse likes <u>Rachel and Cody</u>."

Write each sentence. Use an object pronoun in place of the underlined word or words.

Example: Mr. Rossi handed <u>Ernesto and me</u> hard hats.
Mr. Rossi handed us hard hats.

7. He said, "You must wear <u>these hats</u>."
8. Kendra led a pony into the ring and patted <u>the pony</u>.
9. Mr. Rossi lifted <u>Kendra</u> onto the pony's back.
10. Pick up the reins and hold <u>the reins</u> like this.
11. Mr. Rossi gave <u>Ernesto, Kendra, and me</u> a riding lesson.
12. We thanked <u>Mr. Rossi</u> for the lesson.
13. We said that we had enjoyed <u>the lesson</u>.

14–20. Write this part of a story. Use an object pronoun in place of the underlined word or words.

Example: Tate and I hurried to <u>Cara</u>. *Tate and I hurried to her.*

Mystery on the Mountain

The horses carried <u>Cara, Tate, and me</u> slowly up the rocky trail. We had been searching since dawn for the missing ponies. My horse stumbled, and I spoke softly to <u>the horse</u>. Cara was far ahead of <u>Tate and me</u>. We couldn't see <u>Cara</u>. Suddenly, Tate heard Cara call excitedly to <u>Tate</u>. I told <u>Tate</u> to run ahead. He yelled that Cara had found the ponies. At last I reached the top of the trail. Then I too saw <u>the ponies</u>.

Writing Wrap-Up
WRITING · THINKING · LISTENING · SPEAKING

NARRATING

Write a Story
What may happen next in the story above? Write the next paragraph. Use three or four object pronouns. Then read your paragraph to a partner. Does your paragraph make sense?

Writing with Pronouns

Writing Clearly with Pronouns When you use pronouns, be sure their meanings are clear. This will help your reader understand your writing.

> Marja had never visited Aunt Shelby before. She ran a dairy farm in Vermont.

Did Marja or Aunt Shelby run a dairy farm? When a pronoun might confuse your reader, simply replace it with a noun.

> Marja had never visited Aunt Shelby before. Aunt Shelby ran a dairy farm in Vermont.

Apply It

1–4. Rewrite this journal entry. Replace the underlined pronouns with nouns. Make sure the sentences make sense.

Tuesday, May 4

Yesterday Aunt Shelby and Uncle Patel sheared the sheep with electric clippers. They were scared, but the clippers didn't hurt them. Uncle Patel struggled with one wiggly sheep named Albert. Later he looked so much cooler and happier!

Today I went to the hen house for eggs. The hens were sleeping inside. They woke up when I walked in. They started clucking, and they flew off their nests. They frightened me a little, but I stayed anyway. At last they ran out the door, and I collected six eggs!

Combining Sentences Sometimes you can combine two sentences by joining them with words such as *because, before, when, since,* and *after.* If the two sentences have the same subject, you can change one of the subjects to a pronoun. Your writing will be smoother and more interesting.

The cows are fed. The cows have been milked.

The cows are fed after they have been milked.

Apply It

5–8. Rewrite each picture caption below. Change the subject of the underlined sentence to a pronoun. Then use the word in ( ) to combine the two sentences.

Revising

Vermont Farm Life

Milking machines are used on most farms. Milking machines are faster and cleaner than hand milking. (because)

Sally had her first calf. Sally was about three years old. (when)

Ginger has kept invaders out of the barn. Ginger has been on mouse patrol. (since)

The milk is sent to a dairy to be bottled. The milk is sold in stores. (before)

4 Using *I* and *me*

What's wrong with this e-mail message?
How can you fix it?

> Please join Ethan and me for dinner. Mom and me will make tacos.

- When you talk or write about yourself, you use the pronoun *I* or *me*. Do you ever have trouble deciding whether to use *I* or *me* with another noun or pronoun? One way to check is to say the sentence to yourself with only *I* or *me*.

Kim and I study.	I study.
Mrs. Ling teaches Kim and me.	Mrs. Ling teaches me.
Aaron studies with Kim and me.	Aaron studies with me.

- Remember to use *I* as the subject of a sentence. Use *me* after action verbs and after words such as *to, with, for,* and *at.*

- When you talk about yourself and another person, always name yourself last.

  Incorrect: I and Kim help Aaron. Aaron thanks me and Kim.

  Correct: Kim and I help Aaron. Aaron thanks Kim and me.

Try It Out

Speak Up Which words complete each sentence correctly?

1. Reggie invited (me and Jen, Jen and me) to his house.
2. (I and Jen, Jen and I) walked home with Reggie.
3. Reggie talked to (Jen and me, me and Jen) about Barbados.
4. Jen and (I, me) were very interested.
5. Jen and (I, me) ate with Reggie's family.
6. The food tasted wonderful to Jen and (I, me).
7. (I and Jen, Jen and I) had never eaten a roti before.
8. A roti is a curried meat pie. Both (I and Jen, Jen and I) liked it immensely.

Write the words that correctly complete each sentence.

Example: (Scott and me, Scott and I) visited Japan. *Scott and I*

9. Scott came with (me and my family, my family and me).
10. (Scott and me, Scott and I) sat together on the plane.
11. (Scott and I, I and Scott) became friends with Michiko.
12. She took (Scott and me, Scott and I) on a tour.
13. (He and me, He and I) learned about the capital city, Tokyo.
14. Michiko taught (Scott and me, Scott and I) Japanese words.

15–20. This thank-you note has six mistakes in using *I* and *me*. Write the note correctly.

Example: Me and Becky love our kimonos. *Becky and I love our kimonos.*

Proofreading

Dear Mrs. Ono,

    Thanks for being a great host to my family and I in Japan. You showed my family and me a wonderful time! My family and me will never forget you. Dad is trying all your recipes. He made me and my sister some bean-curd soup. Me and Mom were talking about the Bunraku puppets today. They looked so real! Becky and me look at the photos from our trip every day. Will you write to Becky and I soon?

           Yours truly,

           Katie

Writing Wrap-Up

WRITING • THINKING • LISTENING • SPEAKING

EXPRESSING

Write a Thank-You Note

    Write a thank-you note to a friend or relative that you and your family visited recently. Use *I* and *me* in your sentences. Then read your thank-you note to a partner. Work together to make sure you used *I* and *me* correctly.

For Extra Practice see page 229.

5 Possessive Pronouns

Read the sentences below. Find the pronouns. Which pronouns show ownership?

"Llamas usually live in South America, in Peru," my mother said. "Their hair is used to make wool and they are good at carrying things."

—from *A Llama in the Family,* by Johanna Hurwitz

You have learned that possessive nouns show ownership. You can use pronouns in place of possessive nouns. **A pronoun that shows ownership is a possessive pronoun.**

Possessive Nouns

Pam feeds Pam's pet.
She fills the pet's dish.
The boys' gerbil is playful.

Possessive Pronouns

Pam feeds her pet.
She fills its dish.
Their gerbil is playful.

Possessive Pronouns	
Singular	**Plural**
my	our
your	your
her, his, its	their

Try It Out

Speak Up Which possessive pronoun should you use in place of the underlined word or words?

1. Max and I help Mr. Lee at <u>Mr. Lee's</u> pet shop.
2. Max gives the puppies <u>the puppies'</u> food.
3. Angela is saving <u>Angela's</u> money for a pet.
4. She will buy the parakeet and <u>the parakeet's</u> cage.
5. Angela, you and <u>Angela's</u> sister will love the parakeet.
6. Max watches the parakeet as it sits on <u>the parakeet's</u> perch.
7. Angela says, "One day this bird will be <u>Angela's</u> parakeet."

Write the possessive pronoun in each sentence.

Example: My favorite animal is the llama.   *My*

8. Its close relative is the camel.
9. People in Peru use llamas to carry their packs.
10. A llama will lie down if its pack is too heavy.
11. People in our country are using llamas too.
12. Sheep ranchers use llamas to guard their flocks.
13. One man in Nebraska raises llamas on his ranch.
14. A woman bought one as a pet for her grandchildren.

15–20. Write this letter. Use a possessive pronoun in place of each underlined word or words.

Example: Mr. Cook sold <u>Mr. Cook's</u> ranch.   *Mr. Cook sold his ranch.*

Dear Adriana,

   My uncle has two llamas on <u>my uncle's</u> ranch. If a coyote comes near, the llamas stamp <u>the llamas'</u> feet, bray, spit, chase, and kick. Coyotes decide to find <u>coyotes'</u> next meal elsewhere.

   The llamas will not let a coyote, wolf, or mountain lion near a lamb or <u>a lamb's</u> mother. In <u>Sam's</u> opinion, llamas are the best guards a rancher can have for <u>a rancher's</u> flock.

                                    Your frienc,
                                    Sam

Writing Wrap-Up

WRITING • THINKING • LISTENING • SPEAKING

EXPRESSING

Write an Interview

   You need to hire someone to take care of a pet. What skills will the person need? Write five questions to ask in an interview. Use possessive pronouns. Ask a partner to write answers to the questions. Conduct your interview for the class.

6 Contractions with Pronouns

Read the sentences below. Which word is a contraction?

As the sun set in the western sky, Steven turned to his grandfather. "Thanks, PaPa, I'll never forget this," he said.

—from *Clambake: A Wampanoag Tradition,* by Russell M. Peters

- **A contraction may be formed by combining a pronoun and a verb.** Use an apostrophe (') in place of the letter or letters that are left out.

Pronoun and Verb	Contraction	Pronoun and Verb	Contraction
I am	I'm	I have	I've
he is	he's	he has	he's
she is	she's	she has	she's
it is	it's	it has	it's
you are	you're	you have	you've
we are	we're	we have	we've
they are	they're	they have	they've
I will	I'll	I had	I'd
you will	you'll	you had	you'd
she will	she'll	he had	he'd
they will	they'll	we had	we'd

- Notice that *he's, she's,* and *it's* are listed twice. The contractions for the pronouns *he, she,* and *it* with the verbs *is* and *has* are the same.

Try It Out

Speak Up What is the contraction for each of the following pairs of words?

1. I had
2. she will
3. he had
4. we have
5. they will
6. she has
7. you have
8. it has

Write the contractions for the underlined words.

Example: <u>It is</u> time for our club's dinner. *It's*

9. <u>We are</u> going to have a potluck supper.
10. <u>We have</u> each planned to make something different.
11. We hope <u>you will</u> bring your famous apple pie.
12. The twins said <u>they will</u> bring chicken soup.
13. <u>They are</u> experts at making chicken soup.
14. Lori said <u>she will</u> come early to decorate the hall.
15. <u>She is</u> planning to bring vegetables and dip.

16–22. This cooking demonstration has seven incorrect contractions. Write the demonstration correctly.

Example: <u>Im</u> going to teach you how to prepare noodles.
I'm going to teach you how to prepare noodles.

Proofreading

The'yre easy to prepare and delicious too. Iv'e asked a volunteer to help me today. Hes never cooked before. First, sir, you're going to put water in the pot. When its' come to a boil, add the noodles. Separate them if they've stuck together. After youve done that, stir the noodles well. W'ell let them boil for eight minutes. Then, presto, theyre cooked!

Writing Wrap-Up

WRITING • THINKING • LISTENING • SPEAKING

EXPLAINING

Write Instructions

Write a paragraph explaining how to make a favorite food. Use at least five contractions. Then have a partner pantomime the instructions as you read them. Do your instructions make sense?

7 Pronouns and Homophones

What two words should you switch to make this sentence correct?

Your going to want this picture in you're photo album.

Homophones are words that sound alike but have different spellings and meanings. Writers often confuse some contractions and their homophones because these words sound alike. Study the chart below. Learn the spelling and the meaning of each homophone.

Homophone	Meaning	Sentence
it's	it is	It's a beautiful bird!
its	belonging to it; of it	Take its picture.
they're	they are	They're odd birds.
their	belonging to them	Their wings are big!
there	in that place	There is a black one.
you're	you are	You're very lucky.
your	belonging to you	Get your camera.

Try It Out

Speak Up Which word would you use to complete each sentence correctly?

1. I hear (you're, your) entering the photo contest.
2. Which of (you're, your) pictures will you enter?
3. (They're, There) all so good!
4. The puppies love having (they're, their) picture taken.
5. The picture (their, there) on your desk is interesting.
6. (It's, Its) colors are sharp and clear.
7. (It's, Its) hard to choose the best one!

Choose the word that completes each sentence correctly. Write the sentences.

Example: They've packed (their, they're) cameras.
They've packed their cameras.

8. (Their, They're) taking pictures in the park.
9. (You're, Your) invited to join them.
10. (There, They're) is a chipmunk.
11. (It's, Its) a member of the squirrel family.
12. You can take (it's, its) picture.
13. The squirrels over (they're, there) are noisy!
14. You should take (their, there) picture.
15. Is the chipmunk still sitting (their, there)?
16. (Your, You're) voice scared it.

17–22. This report has six incorrect pronouns. Write the report correctly.

Example: Squirrels use they're bushy tails like blankets.
Squirrels use their bushy tails like blankets.

Proofreading

Report, draft 2

Treetop Acrobats

Everyone has seen a gray squirrel making it's way through the trees. Their a familiar sight in cities and towns. Powerful jaws help squirrels remove seeds and nuts from there hard shells. Look out you're window. You might see a squirrel in your bird feeder!

The shy chipmunk is less common in the city. You probably won't find one they're. This little rodent makes it's home underground.

Writing Wrap-Up   WRITING • THINKING • LISTENING • SPEAKING

COMPARING / CONTRASTING

Write a Nature Report

Use the information on this page and what you already know to write a report about chipmunks and squirrels. Include homophones from the chart on page 218. Read your report out loud. After each sentence with a homophone, pause and ask your classmates to spell it.

Homophones

Words that sound alike but have different spellings and meanings are **homophones**. The words *it's* and *its* are homophones. When you write, make sure that you use the correct homophone. The chart below shows some homophones and their meanings.

Homophone	Meaning
our	belonging to us
hour	sixty minutes
weak	not strong
week	seven days

Homophone	Meaning
hear	listen to
here	at this place
blue	a color
blew	past tense of *blow*

Apply It

1–8. Rewrite this post card, using the correct homophones. Use the chart above to help you.

Austin, Texas

Hi, Asa!

It took only an our on the plane to get to Austin. We got hour luggage right away. We will be at our cousins' house for a weak. They have a blew house with a pool. It was stormy tonight and the wind almost blue over a tree. They are showing us all the neat places. My aunt stays home sometimes because she still feels week from the flu.

My little cousin is four, and she likes to here bedtime stories. It's really fun hear.

Your friend,

Ariel

Place
Stamp
Here

Enrichment

Pronouns!

Homophone Book

You're lucky to have your umbrella today.

Use four sheets of paper. On one page, write your name and *Homophone Book*. On the other pages, write a sentence using a set of homophones. Make pages for *it's, its; your, you're;* and *they're, their, there*. Underline the homophones. Then draw a picture for each sentence. Staple the pages together.

Challenge Think of other homophone sets, such as *sea, see* or *meat, meet*. Add these homophones to your book.

I or Me?

Will you sit beside ___?

Players: 3

Materials: A game board, 3 markers, and 30 index cards; on each of 10 index cards, each player writes a sentence, using *I* in 5 sentences and *me* in the other 5. Leave a blank where *I* or *me* should be.

Ryan and ___ ran one mile.

To play: Mix the cards. Put them facedown. One player picks a card and says *I* or *me* to complete the sentence. If correct with *I*, the player moves to the next space marked *I*. If correct with *me*, the player moves to the next space marked *me*. If incorrect, the player does not move. The first to reach *Finish* wins.

1 **What Is a Pronoun?** *(p. 204)*
Write the pronoun in each sentence that replaces the underlined word or words.

1. Gary and Ana went to the aquarium. They saw many fish.
2. A white shark was swimming in a tank. It is the most dangerous kind of shark.
3. Ana went to another tank. Gary followed her.
4. The penguins had a funny walk. Ana laughed at them.
5. A penguin has short wings. They look like flippers.
6. Gary and Ana said, "We can buy a poster of the penguins."
7. Ana asked Gary, "Do you have enough money for a poster?"

2 **Subject Pronouns** *(p. 206)*
Write each sentence. Use a subject pronoun in place of the underlined word or words.

8. Uncle Bill and Aunt Jenny joined a birdwatchers club.
9. Aunt Jenny takes pictures of birds.
10. The camera has a special lens.
11. Uncle Bill and Aunt Jenny bring the pictures to their club meetings.
12. The pictures help other members learn about different birds.
13. Aunt Jenny and I write the names of the birds in a notebook.
14. The notebook is very full now.

3 **Object Pronouns** *(p. 208)*
Write each sentence. Use object pronouns for the underlined words.

15. Mark took Megan and me riding.
16. Megan asked Mark for help.
17. Mark gave Megan a saddle.
18. She put a pad under the saddle.
19. The horse suddenly backed away from Megan and Mark.
20. Mark spoke softly to the horse.
21. The horse stood still for Mark.

4 **Using *I* and *me*** *(p. 212)*
Choose the word or words that complete each sentence correctly. Then write the sentences.

22. (Jeff and I, I and Jeff) visited Mr. Vega's kitchen.
23. The chef gave a lesson to (Jeff and me, me and Jeff).
24. He taught (him and me, me and him) how to make tortillas.
25. Jeff and (I, me) rolled the dough into pancakes.
26. It was hard for Jeff and (I, me).

5 **Possessive Pronouns** *(p. 214)*
Write each sentence. Use a possessive pronoun in place of the underlined word or words.

27. A llama looks like a small camel without the camel's hump.
28. For many years, people have made blankets from the llama's wool.
29. Peru's craft workers sell the workers' colorful woven goods.

30. My brother spent <u>my brother's</u> allowance on a scarf from Peru.
31. He gave the scarf to Alice for <u>Alice's</u> birthday.
32. My brother and sister collected pottery on <u>my brother and sister's</u> trip to Peru.

6 Contractions with Pronouns

(p. 216) Write the contraction for the underlined words in each sentence.

33. <u>We are</u> learning about foods.
34. <u>I am</u> cooking with new foods.
35. <u>I have</u> cooked corn and squash.
36. <u>You will</u> be surprised at what I did with them.
37. <u>I had</u> asked my mother for advice.
38. <u>They will</u> taste better that way.

Mixed Review 48–55. This letter has three mistakes in using *I* and *me,* four mistakes in using contractions and their homophones, and one other contraction mistake. Write the letter correctly.

7 Pronouns and Homophones

(p. 218) Write each sentence. Use the correct word for each sentence.

39. Parrots have many colors in (there, their) feathers.
40. (You're, Your) parrot is so pretty!
41. (It's, Its) name is Hector.
42. A parrot like Hector can repeat (you're, your) words.
43. (You're, Your) speaking like him!
44. Did you ever see parrots do (their, there) tricks?
45. (They're, There) very clever tricks.
46. (It's, Its) fun to talk to parrots.
47. (Their, There) is a sale on parrots at the pet store.

Proofreading Checklist

Did you write these words correctly?
✔ *I* and *me*
✔ pronouns and their homophones
✔ contractions

Proofreading

Dear Uncle Ricky,

Last week Mom took me and Carlos to Apple Acres. Its a huge orchard. You can pick your own apples their. There much crisper than the ones from the market. Carlos and I picked four big bagfuls. Were going to be eating apples for a long time!

Yesterday, Mom and me made an apple pie for Dad. I had never baked before. It was quite an experience for Mom and I.

How are you and you're family? I hope you're all fine.

Love,
Anita

Go to www.eduplace.com/tales/ for more fun with parts of speech.

Test Practice

Write the numbers 1–6 on a sheet of paper. Read each group of sentences. Choose the sentence that is written correctly. Write the letter for that answer.

1 **A** I'll send you a post card of a kangaroo from Australia!

  B Your going to have a great time on your trip to Kentucky.

  C Theyll stop and see the Grand Canyon.

  D He'ld better get me a gift from his vacation in Canada.

2 **F** I and Edgar will go skateboarding.

  G Their is a cool skateboard park in the center of town.

  H He's promised to teach me some new moves.

  J Mom is going to drive us their in a few minutes.

3 **A** Aunt Pamela gave Reta and I new necklaces.

  B Shes the nicest aunt in the world.

  C I put my necklace on right away.

  D Its a sparkling star on a thin silver chain.

4 **F** Is you're house really a log cabin?

  G The Wongs built they house in the side of a hill.

  H Im making a huge tree house with my cousin.

  J It's possible to build a house out of old tires!

5 **A** Jon and me will help clean the garage.

  B Dad will pay Jon and I five dollars for helping.

  C Me and Jon found my old tricycle behind a trunk.

  D Mom and Dad found their old snowshoes in a box.

6 **F** Isabel and Phil will bring they're pets to school.

  G His pet is a hairy spider.

  H She's pet is a big snake.

  J Im afraid to see these creatures up close!

Now write the numbers 7–10 on your paper. Read the passage all the way through once. Then look at the underlined parts. Decide if they need to be changed or if they are fine as they are. Choose the best answer from the choices given. Write the letter for each answer.

My grandmother was not born in the United States. She growed up in Mexico. She moved to this country when she was thirteen.

Her parents wanted a better life for their six children. At first

my grandmother missed her old home. She cried every night for a month. Then her mother said, "Maria, this is you're home now."

Over time my grandmother began to like her new home. She made new friends their. She learned English, and she did well in school.

7 A growed up in mexico
  B grow up in Mexico
  C grew up in Mexico
  D (No change)

8 F more better life for there six children
  G better life for their six childs
  H better life for they're six children
  J (No change)

9 A said "Maria this is your home now."
  B said, "Maria, this is you're home now."
  C said, "Maria, this is your home now."
  D (No change)

10 F She made new friends there.
   G She made new friends they're.
   H She made new friends theyre.
   J (No change)

(pages 204–205)

1 What Is a Pronoun?

- A pronoun is a word that replaces one or more nouns.
- A pronoun can be singular or plural.

Remember

● Write the pronoun in each sentence.

Example: Jan asked Dad to tell her about walruses.   *her*

1. "Daryl and I have never seen a walrus," Jan added.
2. "What would you like to know?" Dad asked.
3. "We want to know what a walrus weighs," said Jan.
4. "A big walrus can weigh a ton," he said.
5. "Please show us a picture," begged Jan.
6. Dad showed them a photograph of a walrus.
7. "It has big teeth called tusks," said Dad.

▲ Write each pronoun. Tell whether it is singular or plural.

Example: Rays are related to sharks, but they look different.   *they   plural*

8. Here is a picture of a ray. It has a flat body.
9. "Please show me that picture," said Marco.
10. Some rays are dangerous. People get stung by them.
11. "I once saw a stingray at the beach," Kate said.
12. "What do you know about stingrays?" Carlos asked Kate.
13. Kate said she knew that stingrays have poisonous tails.
14. "We would not want to get stung," Carlos and Marco said.
15. "Then you should be careful," Kate told Carlos and Marco.

■ 16–25. Write each pronoun and the word or words that it stands for.

Example: "Dolores and I know about sea horses," said Luis.   *I—Luis*

"Sea horses are strange-looking sea animals," he told Pete.

"A sea horse has a head like a horse's," Dolores said. "It has a pouch like a kangaroo's," she continued.

"Can you tell me how long a sea horse is?" Pete asked her.

"I can tell you," Dolores said to him. "It is about five inches."

(pages 206–207)

2 Subject Pronouns

- *I, you, he, she, it, we,* and *they* are subject pronouns.
- Use only subject pronouns as the subjects of sentences.

Remember

● Write the subject pronoun in each sentence.

Example: You must come and see the ant farm.   *You*

1. We set up the ant farm with Ms. Walton's help.
2. She has had ant farms before.
3. It is in the classroom near Nadeem's desk.
4. He takes care of the farm.
5. We study the ants every day.
6. They live inside the big plastic case.

▲ Write each sentence. Use a subject pronoun in place of the underlined word or words. Underline the subject pronoun.

Example: Ants live in nests that <u>the ants</u> build.
Ants live in nests that <u>they</u> build.

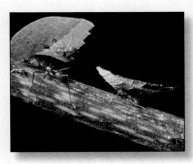

7. The nests may be above ground or underground.
8. <u>Eli and I</u> found an ant's nest.
9. <u>Eli</u> said that an ant's nest is called a colony.
10. <u>A colony</u> is a very orderly place.
11. Eli said to Peg, "<u>Peg</u> will be interested in the nest."
12. <u>Peg</u> was surprised at how many ants were in the colony.

■ Write each subject pronoun and tell whether it is singular or plural. Write the word or words that the pronoun stands for.

Example: Jay and Amy were walking. They disturbed some bees.
They   plural   Jay and Amy

13. "Amy, you almost stepped on a bee's nest," shouted Jay.
14. Amy and Jay said, "We should be more careful."
15. Later they talked about bees and bees' nests.
16. "I think bumblebees' nests are in trees," Amy said.
17. She had seen a movie about bumblebees.
18. It showed the bees making nests in tree holes.

(pages 208–209)

3 Object Pronouns

- *Me, you, him, her, it, us,* and *them* are object pronouns.
- Use object pronouns after action verbs and words such as *to, with, for,* and *at.*

● Write the object pronoun in each sentence.

Example: The Gaos bought the farm next door to us. *us*

1. Sally and Chip visited us yesterday.
2. Chip showed me a beautiful horse.
3. I fed it an apple.
4. The horse ate it in one bite.
5. Chip hitches it to a big sled in the winter.
6. Sally and Chip will take us for a ride sometime.

▲ Write each sentence. Use an object pronoun in place of the underlined word or words. Underline the object pronoun.

Example: Liz asked <u>Dan</u> about horses. *Liz asked <u>him</u> about horses.*

7. Dan knows a lot about <u>horses</u>.
8. He told <u>Liz</u> that there are about sixty kinds of horses.
9. Horses have long legs that help <u>the horses</u> run fast.
10. A horse will run if anything scares <u>the horse</u>.
11. Dan asked Liz, "What else can I tell <u>Liz</u> about horses?"
12. Liz told <u>Dan</u> that she wanted to know what horses eat.

■ Write each pronoun. Write *subject* if it is a subject pronoun and *object* if it is an object pronoun.

Example: Draft horses are very large. Farmers may use them. *them—object*

13. You can also see them in circuses and parades.
14. We went to a parade with draft horses in it.
15. People rode bareback and did tricks on them.
16. One huge horse had a woman on it.
17. It walked along very steadily for her.
18. "She stood on it and did somersaults," Yancy said.

(pages 212–213)

4 Using _I_ and _me_

- Use the pronoun _I_ as the subject of a sentence.
- Use the pronoun _me_ after action verbs and words such as _to, with, for,_ and _at._
- When you use the pronoun _I_ or _me_ with another noun or pronoun, always name yourself last.

● Copy the sentence that is correct in each pair.

Example: My sister and I have a pen pal.   I and my sister have a pen pal.
   My sister and I have a pen pal.

1. Ian writes to Kara and me.
   Ian writes to me and Kara.

2. Ian and I are the same age.
   I and Ian are the same age.

3. Ian and me both play soccer.
   Ian and I both play soccer.

▲ Use _I_ or _me_ to complete each sentence. Write the sentences.

Example: Kara and _____ visited our pen pal.
   Kara and I visited our pen pal.

4. Ian met Kara and _____ at the airport in Scotland.
5. He asked her and _____ what we wanted to do in Scotland.
6. Kara told Ian and _____ that she wanted to see Loch Ness.
7. She and _____ had read about this lake's famous monster.
8. Kara and _____ asked Ian where Loch Ness is.
9. Ian showed her and _____ a map.

■ Write each incorrect sentence correctly. Write _correct_ for each sentence that has no errors.

Example: Ian took I and Kara fishing on the lake.
   Ian took Kara and me fishing on the lake.

10. Kara caught a fish, but Ian and I did not.
11. Ian told Kara and I about a nearby castle.
12. I and Kara asked him to take us there.
13. My sister and me had never seen a real castle.
14. Kara and I learned that the castle is now a museum.

(pages 214–215)

5 Possessive Pronouns

- A possessive pronoun may be used in place of a possessive noun to show ownership.
- *My, your, her, his, its, our,* and *their* are possessive pronouns.

● Write the possessive pronoun in each sentence.

Example: Reggie enjoyed his book about llamas.   *his*

1. Their soft wool was black and brown.
2. My friend Alma saw a statue of a gold llama in a museum.
3. Her guide said that the Inca people had made the statue.
4. These people made their homes in what is now Peru.
5. Our teacher told Alma how these people used the llama.
6. The Inca people used its wool to make clothing.
7. Llamas carried their heavy loads across the mountains.

▲ Write each sentence. Use a possessive pronoun to take the place of the underlined word or words.

Example: Mark showed us <u>Mark's</u> new alpaca shirt.
 Mark showed us his new alpaca shirt.

8. <u>Mark's</u> brother Dom has one just like it.
9. <u>Cheryl's</u> sister said that alpacas are related to llamas.
10. People of ancient Peru wove <u>the alpaca's</u> wool.
11. Only <u>the people's</u> royal family could wear alpaca cloth.
12. <u>Mark and Dom's</u> uncle bought the shirts in Peru.
13. Uncle George spent <u>Uncle George's</u> vacation there.

■ 14–18. Copy the paragraph. Replace possessive nouns with possessive pronouns.

Example: Elena wrote Elena's report about the vicuña.
 Elena wrote her report about the vicuña.

   A vicuña looks like a llama. It is a llama's smaller relative.
The vicuña's home is in South America. Vicuñas' babies are able to run
soon after the babies' birth. The vicuña's wool is brownish-red. The
animals had almost disappeared from the countries of South America.
Then the countries' governments made a law protecting vicuñas.

(pages 216–217)

6 Contractions with Pronouns

- Pronouns and verbs may be combined to form contractions.
- Use an apostrophe (') in place of letters that are left out.

● Write the contraction in each sentence.

Example: I'm having a birthday next week. *I'm*

1. I've invited some friends for dinner.
2. You're invited to come too.
3. You'll love what my sister makes.
4. She's the best cook in our whole family.
5. I hope that she'll make her famous shrimp dish.
6. It's my favorite thing to eat.

▲ Write each sentence. Use a contraction in place of the underlined words.

Example: <u>We are</u> planning a special meal for our parents.
We're planning a special meal for our parents.

7. <u>They are</u> celebrating their fifteenth wedding anniversary.
8. Fran and I hope <u>they will</u> be surprised.
9. <u>I am</u> going shopping with Fran now.
10. <u>She is</u> taking a cooking course after school.
11. <u>It has</u> helped her learn how to shop for food.
12. <u>It is</u> going to be Mom and Dad's best anniversary ever!

■ Write each sentence. Use contractions whenever possible.

Example: You are sure to enjoy the farmers' market.
You're sure to enjoy the farmers' market.

13. It is the best place to buy fresh fruits and vegetables.
14. We are going with my parents.
15. They have been shopping there for years.
16. We will be able to buy fresh string beans.
17. I hope that you have brought your camera.
18. I am sure that you will get some good shots.

Remember

(pages 218–219)

7 Pronouns and Homophones

- Do not confuse the contractions *it's, they're,* and *you're* with their homophones *its, their, there,* and *your.*

● Write the words in each pair of sentences that sound the same but have different spellings and meanings.

Example: I picked up your pictures at the drugstore.
You're in for a real treat. *your   You're*

1. They're great pictures of our trip. There are some pictures of our hike in the woods.
2. Look! It's a red fox! How did you ever get its picture?
3. My sister says they're very shy. It is not easy to see them outside their dens.

▲ Write each sentence, using the correct word.

Example: Sean and Ike showed me (your, you're) pictures.
Sean and Ike showed me your pictures.

4. Today (their, they're) taking pictures of beavers.
5. (There, They're) are two beavers making a dam.
6. They use (there, their) sharp teeth to cut trees.
7. The dam is important. (Its, It's) a wall used to hold back water.
8. After a while, a deep pond forms (there, their).
9. A beaver will build (its, it's) home in the pond.

■ Write each incorrect sentence correctly. Write *correct* for each sentence that has no errors.

Example: Quick! Get you're camera.   *Quick! Get your camera.*

10. There is a cardinal perched on that branch.
11. It's feathers are a beautiful bright red color.
12. Your looking at the male bird.
13. It's more colorful than the female.
14. Cardinals once made their homes only in the Southeast.
15. Now its common to see them in the Northeast too.

Feet dance wildly in the air,
Hands stand firmly on the ground.
Will the kids break their old record
Or tumble and fall down?

Adverbs and Prepositions

1 What Is an Adverb?

Read the sentence below. Which two words tell *how*?
What are they?

Ernestine hugged everyone tightly, then slowly headed for bed.

—from *The Sunday Outing*, by Gloria Jean Pinkney

An adjective is a word that describes a noun or a pronoun. **An adverb is a word that describes a verb.** Adverbs give us more information about an action verb or a form of the verb *be*. They tell *how, when,* or *where*. Most adverbs telling *how* end with *-ly*.

How: Amanda typed the letter carefully.

When: Then I sealed the envelope.

Where: All the stamps were upstairs.

How	When	Where
angrily	always	downtown
carefully	finally	inside
fast	often	off
loudly	once	out
quickly	sometimes	there
sadly	then	upstairs

Try It Out

Speak Up Find the adverb that describes each underlined verb. Does the adverb tell *how, when,* or *where*?

1. Amanda and I waited inside.
2. The mail carrier finally arrived.
3. We ran out to get the mail.
4. I quickly opened the gold envelope.
5. Then Amanda read the letter.
6. "We won the contest!" she shouted proudly.

Write each adverb. Label it *how, when,* or *where.*

Example: Brandon always enjoys collecting stamps. *always   when*

7. He keeps his collection upstairs.
8. He works on it often.
9. Sometimes friends send Brandon new stamps.
10. He buys unusual stamps downtown.
11. Then Mark Miller trades with Brandon.
12. Brandon carefully soaks the used stamps.
13. He gently removes the wet paper.
14. Brandon arranges the stamps neatly.

15–22. This encyclopedia article has eight adverbs. Write each adverb and the verb it describes.

Example: Pony express riders once carried the mail. *once   carried*

The Pony Express

The Pony Express

These horseback riders bravely traveled a long route. They stopped briefly at small stations. There they received fresh horses. The pony express riders changed horses quickly. They continued ahead. The daring riders rode swiftly. People soon received their letters. Later the telegraph system replaced the pony express.

Writing Wrap-Up
WRITING • THINKING • LISTENING • SPEAKING

DESCRIBING

Write a Letter

You have decided to bury a time capsule. Write a letter to the people who will open your time capsule one hundred years from now. Describe ways people communicate with one another. Use adverbs in your letter. Then read your letter to a partner. Have your partner list the adverbs you used.

For Extra Practice see page 259.

What Is an Adverb?   **235**

Writing with Adverbs

Elaborating Sentences You know that adverbs tell *how*, *when*, and *where* something happens. You can make your writing clearer and more interesting by adding adverbs to your sentences.

The Collector Club had its meeting.

The Collector Club had its meeting yesterday.

She neatly arranged her posters on the wall.

She arranged her posters neatly on the wall.

Neatly she arranged her posters on the wall.

She arranged her posters on the wall neatly.

Adverbs usually can go in more than one place in a sentence.

Apply It

1–10. Rewrite this part of a letter to a travel agency. Elaborate each sentence with an adverb. Use adverbs from the box, or choose your own.

yesterday	before	sometimes	excitedly	now
badly	always	today	usually	soon

Revising

Dear Mr. Tikit T. Go,

   The posters of Asian countries arrived. I want to thank you for them. As I mentioned, I like to collect posters from different countries. I use them for school projects.

   I went to my friend's house. She showed me her new posters, and we traded our extra ones. This makes collecting much more fun.

   You have been a big help to me. I appreciate everything you've done. Because of your help, I have posters from many countries.

Combining Sentences You know that you can make your writing smoother by combining sentences. Sometimes you can combine them by moving an adverb from one sentence into another.

The first two choppy sentences below both tell about the same action. You can combine the two sentences by moving the adverb *eagerly* to the first sentence.

Our class is collecting one million popcorn kernels.
We collect eagerly .

}

Our class is eagerly collecting one million popcorn kernels.

Apply It

11–14. Rewrite this Web page. Combine each pair of sentences by moving an adverb from the second sentence into the first sentence.

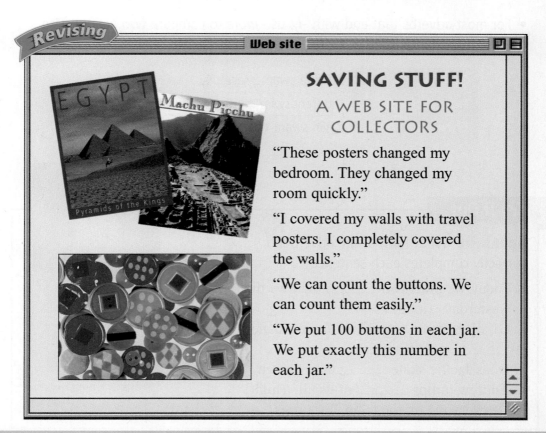

Revising

Web site

SAVING STUFF!
A WEB SITE FOR COLLECTORS

"These posters changed my bedroom. They changed my room quickly."

"I covered my walls with travel posters. I completely covered the walls."

"We can count the buttons. We can count them easily."

"We put 100 buttons in each jar. We put exactly this number in each jar."

2 Comparing with Adverbs

Goldstein runs more faster than Crawford!

What's wrong with this headline? How can you fix it?

- Adjectives are used to compare people, places, and things. You can also use adverbs to make comparisons. Add *-er* to short adverbs to compare two actions. Add *-est* to compare three or more actions.

One Action	Ken skis fast.
Two Actions	LaToya skis faster than Ken does.
Three or More	Katie skis fastest of the three.

- For most adverbs that end with *-ly,* use *more* to compare two actions. Use *most* to compare three or more actions.

One Action	Kristina swam gracefully.
Two Actions	Did Trent swim more gracefully than Kristina?
Three or More	Kevin swam most gracefully of all.

Try It Out

Speak Up What form of the adverb in ( ) correctly completes each sentence?

1. Today we practiced _____ than we did yesterday. (long)
2. Of all the team members, Fatima skated _____. (skillfully)
3. Does Jackie skate _____ than Shawn? (quickly)
4. Andrew jumps _____ of us all. (high)
5. Of everyone on the team, Tara tries _____! (hard)

Write each sentence. Use the correct form of the adverb in ( ).

Example: These Special Olympics lasted _____ than last year's. (long)
These Special Olympics lasted longer than last year's.

6. Richie's relay team ran _____ than my brother's team. (swiftly)
7. Meredith ran _____ of all the students. (fast)
8. I watched her _____ of all the runners. (closely)
9. She crossed the finish line _____ than the rest. (soon)
10. The runners moved _____ than the wheelchair racers. (slowly)
11. I cheered _____ of all the fans. (loudly)
12. The broad jump began _____ than the high jump. (late)
13. Roberto jumped _____ of all the boys. (high)

14–20. This part of a sportscast has seven incorrect adverb forms. Write the sportscast correctly.

Example: Paul swims more smoother than Jeremy.
Paul swims more smoothly than Jeremy.

Proofreading

Special Olympics

Nicholas swam skillfullier this year than last. Ross swam the faster of anyone. He had practiced longer and more harder than anyone else. He came nearer of all to setting a personal best. David swam only slightly slowest than Ross. Chris tried the most hardest of anyone in the diving event. He performed the backward somersault more expertlier of all.

Writing Wrap-Up

WRITING • THINKING • LISTENING • SPEAKING

COMPARING / CONTRASTING

Write a Sportscast

Write a sportscast about a sporting event at your school. Write about the different players, using adverbs to compare and contrast their performances. Then find a partner and read your sportscasts to each other. Work together to make sure you used the correct adverb forms.

Comparing with Adverbs   **239**

3 Using *good* and *well*

The words GOOD and WELL fell off this motel sign. Where would you put each word?

REST   HERE.

HAVE   A   NIGHT.

Sometimes it may be hard to decide whether to use *good* or *well*. How can you make sure that you use these words correctly? Remember, *good* is an adjective that describes nouns. *Well* is an adverb that describes verbs.

Marcia is a <u>good</u> guide.   She speaks <u>well</u>.

This photo album is <u>good</u>.   You chose the pictures <u>well</u>.

Try It Out

Speak Up Which word is correct?

1. Corey's trips are all (good, well).
2. He plans (good, well) for his adventures.
3. Corey's guidebook is (good, well).
4. His road maps are (good, well) too.
5. He has learned to read maps (good, well).
6. Corey speaks several languages (good, well).
7. Talking to people helps him learn (good, well) about other countries.
8. Corey is (good, well) at taking pictures.
9. Photos help him remember his trips (good, well).
10. Corey describes his travels (good, well).
11. Everyone listens (good, well) to his stories.
12. The presents that he brings to his family are always (good, well).
13. Corey is a (good, well) traveler.
14. He is polite to everyone and treats them (good, well).

Use *good* or *well* to complete each sentence correctly. Write the sentences.

Example: Erika's vacation didn't go _____. *Erika's vacation didn't go well.*

15. The train trip was not _____.
16. Her hotel room was not very _____ either.
17. She didn't sleep very _____ that night.
18. Erika discovered that she hadn't packed _____.
19. Erika learned her lesson _____.
20. This year she has prepared _____ for her vacation.
21. Her decision to stay home was _____.
22. It will be _____ to relax in the back yard.

23–28. This part of an online travel brochure has six mistakes in using *good* and *well*. Write the brochure correctly.

Example: You'll sleep good on our beds. *You'll sleep well on our beds.*

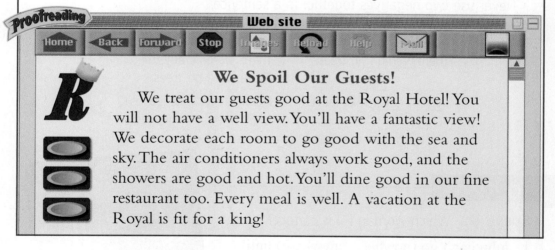

Proofreading

Web site

Home   Back   Forward   Stop   Images   Reload   Help   Mail

We Spoil Our Guests!

We treat our guests good at the Royal Hotel! You will not have a well view. You'll have a fantastic view! We decorate each room to go good with the sea and sky. The air conditioners always work good, and the showers are good and hot. You'll dine good in our fine restaurant too. Every meal is well. A vacation at the Royal is fit for a king!

Writing Wrap-Up WRITING • THINKING • LISTENING • SPEAKING

DESCRIBING

Write a Travel Brochure

Where would your "dream vacation" be? Write a travel brochure describing the place, what you eat, and what you do. Use *good* or *well* in each sentence. Then read your brochure to a partner. Have your partner check for the correct use of *good* and *well*.

4 Negatives

What's wrong with this riddle? How can you fix it?

Question: Why didn't the tree travel anywhere?

Answer: It couldn't never carry its trunk!

- Sometimes when you write sentences, you use the word *no* or words that mean "no." **A word that makes a sentence mean "no" is called a negative**.

   No one picked the beans.   I didn't water the garden.

- The words *no, no one, nobody, none, nothing, nowhere*, and *never* are negatives. The word *not* and contractions made with *not* are also negatives. Never use two negatives together in a sentence.

Incorrect	Correct
There weren't no trees.	There weren't any trees. There were no trees.
I won't never rake leaves!	I won't ever rake leaves! I will never rake leaves.

Try It Out

Speak Up Which word in ( ) is correct?

1. John can't go (nowhere, anywhere) until he has finished raking.
2. He never likes (anything, nothing) about yard work.
3. No one (never, ever) has time to help him.
4. Luckily there (are, aren't) no leaves left on the trees.
5. There won't be (no, any) more leaves to rake until next fall!

Write the correct word to complete each sentence.

Example: Aki (hadn't, had) never collected leaves before.   *had*

6. Now she never goes (nowhere, anywhere) without finding leaves.
7. Aki didn't find (anything, nothing) new today.
8. Jordan wouldn't show his collection to (no one, anyone).
9. He hasn't pressed (none, any) of his leaves in wax paper.
10. Jordan didn't know (no one, anyone) who could teach him how!
11. Nina couldn't find any red leaves (anywhere, nowhere).
12. She (hasn't, has) found no birch leaves today.
13. Didn't (anybody, nobody) find oak leaves?

14–20. These rules have seven mistakes in using negatives. Write the rules correctly.

Example: Don't never climb no trees.   *Don't ever climb any trees.*

Proofreading

Class Picnic Do's and Don'ts

- Don't never leave litter in the park.
- Bring food. You can't buy none there.
- Don't feed nothing to the ducks and geese.
- Use bug spray. The bugs never spare nobody.
- Never touch any poison ivy.
- Wear a hat. Sunburn isn't never good for anyone.
- Bring juice or water. There isn't none available.
- Never go nowhere without telling a teacher first.

Writing Wrap-Up

WRITING • THINKING • LISTENING • SPEAKING

INFORMING

Write Rules

Write five rules for your school. They can be silly or serious, such as *Don't do cartwheels on the desks!* Use a negative in each rule. Read your rules to a partner. Check that you used negatives correctly.

5 What Is a Preposition?

Look at the picture. Using complete sentences, tell where each item is located.

Little words can make a big difference in meaning.

The skate is **on** the table.   The skate is **under** the table.

- The words *on* and *under* show a different connection between the words *skate* and *table*. **A word that shows the connection between other words in a sentence is a preposition.**

Common Prepositions						
about	around	beside	for	near	outside	under
above	at	by	from	of	over	until
across	before	down	in	off	past	up
after	behind	during	inside	on	through	with
along	below	except	into	out	to	without

- **A prepositional phrase begins with a preposition and ends with a noun or pronoun.** All the words in between are part of the prepositional phrase.

Mike glided easily **across the frozen pond.**   His friends cheered **for him.**

Try It Out

Speak Up Find the preposition in each underlined prepositional phrase.

1. Jen had never skated <u>until last Tuesday</u>.
2. At first she wobbled <u>on her new skates</u>.
3. She clung <u>to the fence</u>.
4. Then Sofia skated <u>beside her</u>.
5. Together they moved <u>around the rink</u>.
6. Sometimes Jen glided <u>across the rink</u>.
7. At other times she stumbled ungracefully <u>along the ice</u>.

On Your Own

Write each sentence. Underline the prepositional phrase once and the preposition twice.

Example: Many talented skaters competed <u>for the championship</u>.

8. One skater fell during his performance.
9. Tina finished without a mistake.
10. Joe skated with her.
11. They performed to beautiful music.
12. A reporter wrote about them.
13. Joe flipped Tina over his shoulders.
14. She spun around him.
15. Then she leaped into the air.

16–22. This e-mail message has seven prepositional phrases. Write the message. Underline each prepositional phrase once and each preposition twice.

Example: Beth has skated <u>for years</u>.

---

e-mail

From: Joanne Olsen

To: Aaron Morris

Today I went ice-skating for the first time. I stayed near my friend Beth. We slowly skated across the pond. Then a little boy crashed into us. I lost my balance and slipped. Suddenly everyone was skating except me. I was sitting on the ice. My feet just wouldn't stay under me!

Writing Wrap-Up

WRITING • THINKING • LISTENING • SPEAKING

CREATING

Write a Comic Strip

Draw a comic strip about your first try at a sport. Write a one-sentence caption beneath each picture. Use a prepositional phrase in each sentence. Then read your comic strip to a partner. Which picture and caption did your partner like best?

Writing with Prepositions

Elaborating Sentences You can use prepositional phrases to add helpful and interesting information to your sentences.

My friend loves snow.

My friend from Florida loves snow.

We dug a long tunnel.

We dug a long tunnel through the snow.

Apply It

1–6. Rewrite the story, elaborating each line with a prepositional phrase. Use phrases from the box, or make up your own.

with one paw	on his nose
in the air	out the window
by the stove	to the house

Revising

When Snow Gets on Your Nose

The cat looks. What is swirling?

He scratches the front door.

The snow tickles.

The snow makes him sneeze.

He darts.

He sleeps.

Combining Sentences Sometimes you can combine two short, choppy sentences by moving a prepositional phrase from one sentence to the other. Because the two short sentences below both tell about Mia and her skiing, you can combine them by moving the phrase *across the park* from the second sentence to the first sentence.

Mia skied smoothly.

She skied across the park.   } Mia skied smoothly across the park.

Apply It

7–10. Rewrite this part of an essay. Combine each pair of underlined sentences by adding the highlighted phrase to the first sentence.

Revising

Downhill skiers race quickly. They race down steep slopes. Cross-country skiers glide more slowly. They glide along level ground. Both sports are fun and exciting.

I think, however, that cross-country skiing is better than downhill skiing. It provides better exercise. The exercise is better for the heart and the lungs. Cross-country skiing is also a safer and less complicated sport. These skiers have fewer risks. There are fewer risks of breaking an arm or a leg. Cross-country skiers can move at their own speed.

Changing Meaning with Adverbs

Adverbs are powerful words for a writer. Changing one adverb can change the meaning of an entire sentence. Read the sentences below. What do you picture when you read each sentence?

The hikers are climbing slowly and carefully.

The hikers are climbing quickly and excitedly.

Apply It

1–10. Write this paragraph. Fill in the blanks with adverbs from the box. Then change the meaning of the paragraph by using other adverbs from the box. You can use any adverb more than once.

happily	sadly	anywhere	carefully	easily
slowly	everywhere	late	loudly	eagerly
quietly	downtown	quickly	early	noisily

A New Day

The day began _____. As dawn grew near, the robins chattered _____. Subway cars ran _____. The city woke up _____ as the sun rose in the sky. Large buses carried workers _____. Kettles whistled _____ on kitchen stoves. People ate their breakfasts _____. Children slammed doors and walked _____ to school. The boys talked _____ as they waited for class to begin. A new student walked _____ into the classroom.

Enrichment

Adverbs!

From Story to Script

Choose a short scene from a favorite story. Write it as a play. Before each character's words, write the name of the character. After the name, write an adverb telling how the character says the lines. Have a narrator speak the lines that describe the scene or action. Practice your play, and perform it for the class.

Example:

Margarita (loudly):	The diamonds are missing!
Hernando (angrily):	Who could have done this?
Narrator (calmly):	They began searching for clues.

Preposition Poem

Write a poem about something that moves, such as a cat, a river, or a runner. Copy the form shown below. Then draw a picture to go with your poem.

The stream flows
<u>down</u> the mountain,
<u>across</u> the field,
<u>under</u> the bridge,
and <u>over</u> my feet.

(Subject) (verb)
   (prepositional phrase),
   (prepositional phrase),
   (prepositional phrase),
   and (prepositional phrase).

Challenge Write two more verses for your poem. How many prepositional phrases can you use?

1 **What Is an Adverb?** *(p. 234)*
Write each adverb and the verb that it describes.

1. Leo called Nick early.
2. "Let's go!" he said eagerly.
3. They both dressed quickly.
4. Then they got their fishing gear.
5. The boys met outside.
6. They found the boat quickly.
7. The boys rowed silently.
8. Finally, they found a good spot.
9. "Drop the anchor here," said Leo.
10. The boys baited their hooks carefully.
11. Nick and Leo sat patiently.
12. Suddenly Nick's line jerked.
13. A huge flounder had grabbed the worm greedily.
14. "I got one!" Nick cried excitedly.

2 **Comparing with Adverbs** *(p. 238)* Write each sentence. Use the correct form of the adverb in ( ).

15. This year plan your garden (carefully) than last year.
16. Order vegetable seeds (soon) than you order flowers.
17. You will work (hard) of all in the spring.
18. Plant the lettuce seeds (close) to the path.
19. Space the tomato plants (widely) apart than the rows of corn.
20. Of most spring crops, lettuce appears (soon).
21. You will find that weeds sprout (quickly) than vegetables.

22. Water the garden (long) of all in the hot weather.
23. Water the plants (heavily) in the morning than at night.

3 **Using** *good* **and** *well* *(p. 240)* Use *good* or *well* to complete each sentence.

24. The science program was _____.
25. Mr. Ray spoke _____ about animals.
26. The porcupine protects itself _____.
27. The porcupine is not _____ for other animals to eat.
28. The quills stick _____ into anything that touches them.
29. Mr. Ray also described _____ what a raccoon is like.
30. It is _____ at climbing trees.
31. Raccoons can handle objects _____ with their paws.
32. They can live _____ almost anywhere!

4 **Negatives** *(p. 242)* Each sentence has two negatives together. Write each sentence correctly.

33. Our school hasn't never had a band before.
34. Most students didn't know nothing about harmony.
35. Nobody never wanted to practice.
36. Now no one can't wait to learn the new songs.
37. Sam doesn't see nothing easy about this new piece.

38. At the concert, nobody could find a seat nowhere near the stage.
39. There wasn't no sound when Ms. Conti tapped her baton to begin the performance.
40. The band didn't make no mistakes.
41. "The Stars and Stripes Forever" hadn't never sounded so good!

43. We ran outside the house.
44. The snow was sticking to the sidewalks.
45. It covered the tops of the cars.
46. Patti tried catching snowflakes on her tongue.
47. The snowstorm continued during the night.
48. We heard the wind howling through the trees.
49. My sister and I snuggled deeper under our blankets.
50. Everything was white in the morning!

5 What Is a Preposition?

(p. 244) Write each sentence. Underline the prepositional phrase once and the preposition twice.

42. The snow began before noon.

Mixed Review 51–56. This part of a science report has four incorrect adverb forms, one mistake in using *good* and *well*, and one mistake in using negatives. Write the report correctly.

Proofreading Checklist

Did you use these words correctly?
✔ adverbs that compare
✔ *good* and *well*
✔ negatives

Proofreading

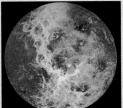

Venus, Lovely but Deadly

Venus is sometimes called Earth's sister. In size, it matches Earth most closely than any other planet. It's nearer to Earth than any other planet. A cloudless night is a good night to look for Venus. You'll see it more clearly than any star. It shines brighter of all the planets.

The ancient Romans thought Venus was the beautifulest star in the sky. They named the planet for their goddess of love and beauty. This name doesn't fit the planet very good. Human beings couldn't never live on Venus. Its temperature rises more higher than eight hundred degrees.

Go to www.eduplace.com/tales/ for more fun with parts of speech.

Test Practice

Write the numbers 1–8 on a sheet of paper. Read each paragraph. Choose the line that shows the mistake. Write the letter for that answer. If there is no mistake, write the letter for the last answer.

1 A Luis was playing catch
B with Antonio. Antonio threw
C the ball farther than Luis did.
D (No mistakes)

2 F The moon is shining
G brightlier tonight than it did
H last night. It looks like day!
J (No mistakes)

3 A Brittany was looking for
B deer tracks. She searched
C carefully in the snow.
D (No mistakes)

4 F There is a reason Keesha
G gets better grades than Mia.
H Keesha works more harder.
J (No mistakes)

5 A Nobody never puts
B anything away in this house.
C How messy it always is!
D (No mistakes)

6 F Of all the kids in the
G cabin, Sherilee snored the
H loudliest! She woke me up.
J (No mistakes)

7 A Eric makes funny
B pictures of weird creatures.
C He draws very good.
D (No mistakes)

8 F For vacation, Grandpa just
G sits on his front porch. He
H doesn't go anywhere!
J (No mistakes)

Now write the numbers 9–14 on your paper. Read the underlined sentences. Then find the answer that best combines them into one sentence.

9 The mayor ran in the race.
The doctor ran in the race.

  A The mayor ran in the race, and the doctor ran in the race.

  B The mayor ran and the doctor ran in the race.

  C The mayor and the doctor ran in the race.

  D The mayor ran in the race and the doctor also.

10 The car slid slowly.
The car slid down the hill.

  F The car slid slowly down the hill.

  G The car slid slowly and also slid down the hill.

  H The car slid, and down the hill.

  J The car slid down and slowly.

11 The bird gathered bits of string.
The bird made a nest.

  A The bird gathered bits of string and a nest.

  B The bird gathered bits of string and made a nest.

  C The bird gathered bits of string, and the bird made a nest.

  D The bird gathered and made a nest out of bits of string.

12 We will creep up the stairs.
We will creep up quietly.

  F We will creep up the stairs and creep quietly up the stairs.

  G We will creep quietly up the stairs.

  H We will creep quietly up.

  J We will creep up the stairs, and we will creep quietly.

13 LaToya collects buttons.
LaToya collects shells.

  A LaToya collects buttons and she also collects shells.

  B LaToya collects buttons and collects shells.

  C LaToya collects also buttons also shells.

  D LaToya collects buttons and shells.

14 Kevin skated fast.
His sister skated faster.

  F Kevin skated faster than his sister skated fast.

  G Kevin and his sister skated fast and faster.

  H Kevin skated fast and his sister faster.

  J Kevin skated fast, but his sister skated faster.

 **Test Practice** *continued*

Now write the numbers 15–20 on your paper. Read the underlined sentences. Then find the answer that best combines them into one.

15 Melissa wrote the class play.
Melissa made the costumes.

  A Melissa wrote and made the class play and the costumes.

  B Melissa wrote the class play, and the costumes.

  C Melissa wrote it and made the costumes too.

  D Melissa wrote the class play, and she made the costumes.

16 Andrew put air in the tires.
Then Andrew rode his bike.

  F Andrew put air in the tires, and then he rode his bike.

  G Andrew rode his bike with air in the tires.

  H Andrew rode his bike, and Andrew put air in the tires.

  J Andrew rode and put air in the tires of his bicycle.

17 The circus came to town.
The circus was famous.

  A The circus came to town that was famous.

  B The famous circus came to town.

  C The circus came to town and was famous.

  D The circus came to town, and the circus was famous.

18 Jamie built the sand castle.
Nick built the sand castle.

  F Jamie built the sand castle, and Nick built the sand castle.

  G Jamie built the sand castle, but Nick built the sand castle.

  H Jamie and Nick built the sand castle.

  J Jamie built the sand castle, and Nick.

19 The fox ran across the field.
The fox ran swiftly.

  A The fox ran and swiftly across the field.

  B The fox ran across the field and ran swiftly.

  C The fox ran swiftly while it ran across the field.

  D The fox ran swiftly across the field.

20 Mom does her sit-ups.
Mom watches TV.

  F Mom does and watches her sit-ups and TV.

  G Mom does her sit-ups while she watches TV.

  H Mom does her sit-ups, and Mom watches TV.

  J Mom does sit-ups and TV.

Unit 1: The Sentence

What Is a Sentence? Kinds of Sentences *(pp. 32, 36, 38)* If a group of words below is a sentence, write it correctly. If it is not, write *not a sentence*.

1. it was a rainy night
2. at the end of Nye Street
3. did you see the accident
4. please call the police
5. the driver of the car
6. went over the curb
7. how scary it was

Subjects and Predicates

(pp. 40, 42, 44) Write each sentence. Draw a line between the complete subject and the complete predicate. Underline each simple subject once, and each simple predicate twice.

8. Nellie Bly was a famous reporter.
9. Her news stories were daring.
10. Nellie read the book *Around the World in Eighty Days*.
11. Then she went around the world.
12. Her trip around the world took fewer than eighty days.
13. She made the trip by ship, train, cart, and donkey.

See www.eduplace.com/kids/hme/ for a tricky usage or spelling question.

Unit 2: Nouns

Common and Proper Nouns

(p. 64, 66) Write each noun. Then write *common* or *proper* beside each one.

14. Di and her family live in the city.
15. Her father is a salesperson.
16. Mr. Hall makes trips to Mexico.
17. Her mother, Betty, is a lawyer.
18. On Saturdays Di visits parks.

Singular and Plural Nouns *(pp. 70, 72, 74)* Write the plural of each noun.

19. ox
20. shark
21. bush
22. glass
23. berry
24. deer

Possessive Nouns *(pp. 76, 78)* Write the possessive form of each noun.

25. men
26. fox
27. Cindy
28. baby
29. families
30. nurses

Unit 3: Verbs

Action Verbs, Main and Helping Verbs *(pp. 96, 98)* Write each sentence. Draw one line under the main verb and two lines under the helping verb.

31. Mr. Largo is repairing his barn.
32. Fire had damaged it.
33. The animals were roaming around the barnyard.
34. Mrs. Largo has repainted the fence.
35. The neighbors will keep some of the animals for a while.

Present, Past, and Future *(p. 100)*
Write the verbs in these sentences. Label each verb *present*, *past*, or *future*.

36. Peter will tell the class about Eskimo houses.
37. The Eskimos built snow houses in the winter.
38. They called these houses *igloos*.
39. Peter will draw a picture of an igloo for his report.
40. Most of the Eskimos live in wooden houses today.

Using Verbs *(pp. 104, 106, 108, 110, 112, 114)* Write the verb that correctly completes each sentence.

41. Grandpa (play, plays) the violin.
42. He (try, tries) to practice daily.
43. His first concert (is, are) today.
44. I have (wore, worn) my new clothes.
45. We (has, have) found our seats.
46. Grandpa (hurry, hurried) onstage.
47. He has (took, taken) a bow.

Contractions with *not* *(p. 116)*
Write contractions for these words.

48. has not
49. does not
50. should not
51. will not

Unit 4: Adjectives

Adjectives *(pp. 136, 140)* Write each adjective and the word it describes.

52. Cobras and vipers are two kinds of harmful snakes.
53. Cobras are slender.
54. Long, fast cobras like to fight.
55. Heads of cobras are flat.
56. Many vipers have fat bodies.

Using *a, an,* and *the*
(p. 141) Write each correct article.

57. (a, an) alarm
58. (a, an) book
59. (a, the) trees
60. (a, an) owl
61. (a, an) pump
62. (an, the) oxen

Comparisons *(pp. 142, 144, 146)*
Write the correct word in ( ).

63. Texas is (larger, largest) than Delaware is.
64. Alaska is the (larger, largest) state of all.
65. Is Los Angeles the (more, most) exciting city in California?
66. Florida has a (better, best) climate than New England.
67. It's the (worse, worst) trip I've ever taken.
68. The Midwestern states have the (flatter, flattest) land of all.

Unit 5: Capitalization and Punctuation

Correct Sentences, Proper Nouns

(pp. 166, 170, 172) Write these sentences correctly.

69. have you ever seen a dolphin show
70. my aunt and I went to one near redondo beach in california
71. on friday aunt megan and mrs. feld took me my uncle met us
72. how intelligent the dolphins were
73. please get me the book dolphin adventure I'd love to read it

Abbreviations *(p. 174)* Write abbreviations for these words.

74. Doctor
75. Mister
76. Road
77. April
78. Ohio
79. Utah

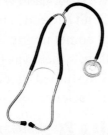

Commas *(pp. 176, 180)* Write these sentences correctly.

80. Deion tell me about storms.
81. Thunderstorms tornadoes and hurricanes are three kinds.
82. Thunderstorms Bob are common.
83. Yes most thunderstorms take place in spring and summer.
84. A thunderstorm brings lightning thunder and rain.

Quotations *(pp. 182, 184)* Write these sentences correctly.

85. Are we going to the fair asked Eva
86. Tad said I am working at a booth
87. I have entered a milking contest declared Ruben
88. How is the contest judged asked Tad
89. Ruben replied the judges will see how fast I can milk my cow

Unit 6: Pronouns

Subject and Object Pronouns

(pp. 204, 206, 208) Write each sentence. Use a pronoun in place of the underlined word or words.

90. Mr. Hayes played a record.
91. He questioned Amy and me.
92. Amy knew the answer.
93. Johann Bach wrote the music.
94. Amy likes music by Bach.

I and *me*, Homophones

(pp. 212, 218) Write each sentence. Use the word or words that complete each sentence correctly.

95. Luis and (I, me) are learning to skate.
96. (Its, It's) lots of fun.
97. Dad drives (me and Luis, Luis and me) to the park.
98. We have our lesson (their, there).
99. Bring (you're, your) inline skates.

Possessive Pronouns *(p. 214)* Write each sentence. Use a possessive pronoun in place of the underlined word or words.

100. Diane and <u>Diane's</u> brother Sam work in a pet store.
101. <u>Diane and Sam's</u> job is to feed the pets.
102. <u>Sam's</u> favorite pet is the parrot.
103. <u>The parrot's</u> feathers are yellow and blue.
104. The kittens snuggle with <u>the kittens'</u> mother.

Contractions with Pronouns *(p. 216)* Write the contractions for each of the following words.

105. you will
106. I have
107. he is
108. he has
109. we had
110. they are

Unit 7: Adverbs and Prepositions

What Is an Adverb? *(p. 234)* Write each adverb and the verb it describes.

111. Today Benita made a skirt.
112. She sewed the stitches neatly.
113. Benita left her machine here.
114. I quickly sewed a shirt.
115. Later I surprised Benita with it.

Comparing with Adverbs *(p. 238)* Write each sentence. Use the correct form of the adverb in ( ).

116. Of all the students, Beth studied (hard) for the spelling bee.
117. I lost my turn (quickly) than Steven did.
118. Beth spelled (correctly) of all.
119. She stayed in the contest (long) than any other student.
120. Our class cheered (loudly) than Mrs. Lopez's class.

Using *good* and *well*, Negatives *(pp. 240, 242)* Write the correct word to complete each sentence.

121. Pearl and Julian weren't going (nowhere, anywhere).
122. We (had, hadn't) nothing to do.
123. Can't (no one, anyone) think of something to do?
124. Pearl's idea was (good, well).
125. She studied (good, well) for her science test.

What Is a Preposition? *(p. 244)* Write each sentence. Draw one line under the prepositional phrase.

126. Ruth plays in a band.
127. She practices on Saturdays.
128. Sometimes she practices with a friend.
129. Her parents will come to her recital.
130. Ruth's younger brother will sit beside them.

(pages 234–235)

 What Is an Adverb?

- A word that describes a verb is an adverb.
- An adverb can tell *how, when,* or *where.*

Remember

● Write the adverb in each sentence.

Example: Nita always got mail. *always*

1. Erin wished that sometimes she would get letters.
2. Nita gladly told Erin about her pen pal.
3. They write letters frequently.
4. Erin then called World Pen Pals.
5. This company carefully matches pen pals.
6. They could find Erin a pen pal anywhere.

▲ Write each adverb. Then write the verb it describes.

Example: Tina carefully studied the catalog. *carefully studied*

7. Finally, Tina spotted the perfect gift for Paco.
8. She completed the order form neatly.
9. Then she checked the name and number of the item.
10. Paco once ordered a baseball glove.
11. He carelessly wrote the wrong item number.
12. He soon received a package containing boxing gloves.

■ Use an adverb to complete each sentence. Write the sentences. The clue tells what kind of adverb to use.

Example: My uncle Jerry delivers mail _____. (where)
My uncle Jerry delivers mail downtown.

13. He rises _____ each day and puts on his uniform. (when)
14. He greets everyone _____ as he delivers the mail. (how)
15. _____ bad weather forces businesses to close. (when)
16. Uncle Jerry dresses _____. (how)
17. He tramps _____ through snow and sleet. (how)
18. Uncle Jerry says, "I _____ deliver the mail." (when)

(pages 238–239)

2 Comparing with Adverbs

- Add *-er* to short adverbs to compare two actions.
  Add *-est* to compare three or more actions.
- For adverbs that end with *-ly,* use *more* to compare
  two actions. Use *most* to compare three or more actions.
- Never use *-er* with *more.* Never use *-est* with *most.*

Remember

● Choose the word that correctly completes each sentence. Write the sentences.

Example: Lena runs (faster, fastest) of all the runners.
Lena runs fastest of all the runners.

1. She warms up (more carefully, most carefully) than I do.
2. Lena holds her head (higher, highest) than Lee does.
3. Sam jogs (more evenly, most evenly) than Julio does.
4. Pilar runs (more gracefully, most gracefully) of all.
5. Chan reaches the finish line (sooner, soonest) of all.

▲ Use the correct form of the adverb in ( ) to complete each sentence. Write the sentences.

Example: My brother skis _____ than I do. (skillfully)
My brother skis more skillfully than I do.

6. I like to ski _____ than he does. (slowly)
7. Kay skis _____ of everyone in the family. (fast)
8. She started skiing _____ than Corliss. (soon)
9. Corliss falls _____ of the three of us. (frequently)

■ For each sentence below, write two sentences. Make one compare two actions and the other compare three or more actions.

Example: Connie swims expertly.   *Connie swims more expertly than Alison.*
Connie swims most expertly of all the team members.

10. She reaches the end of the pool soon.
11. Kiona cheers loudly for her.
12. Alex starts the race late.
13. He works hard to catch up.
14. Coach Okuda smiles proudly.

(pages 240–241)

3 Using *good* and *well*

- Use the adjective *good* to describe nouns.
- Use the adverb *well* to describe verbs.

Remember

● For each sentence, write *correct* if the sentence is correct. Write *not correct* if it is not.

Example: Jade gives directions good.   *not correct*

1. She gave us good directions to her house.
2. I listened good.
3. The trip went well.
4. Mario's sense of direction is well.
5. He and I followed Jade's directions good.
6. We had a good time walking along the country roads.

▲ Write each sentence, using *good* or *well* correctly.

Example: Mark and his older brother Joel get along _____.
Mark and his older brother Joel get along well.

7. The trips they take together are _____.
8. Joel is _____ at driving his car.
9. Mark can read road maps _____.
10. They are _____ as a team.
11. Joel keeps his car running _____.
12. The maps in his car are very _____.

■ Some sentences are incorrect. Write those sentences correctly. Write *correct* if a sentence has no errors.

Example: We asked Dr. Chu to speak about eating good.
We asked Dr. Chu to speak about eating well.

13. I needed a good way to help her find our school.
14. Then I had an idea that was well.
15. I knew I could make a good map.
16. First, I planned the map good on scrap paper.
17. Then I made the final drawing on good paper.
18. I know the map worked good because Dr. Chu found us!

(pages 242–243)

4 Negatives

- A negative is a word that means "no."
- Do not use two negative words together in a sentence.

Remember

● Write the word that makes each sentence mean *no.*

Example: Kevin hadn't met Aunt Ella until last month.   *hadn't*

1. Nobody had told him she lived on a farm.
2. At first there weren't many things he could do.
3. He had never milked a cow.
4. He went to collect eggs and came back with none.
5. His aunt told him there was no need to worry.
6. A person can't do everything right the first time.

▲ Each sentence has two negatives. Write the sentences correctly. There may be more than one way to correct a sentence.

Example: Sumi didn't know nothing about gardening.
          Sumi knew nothing about gardening.

7. Nobody never told her how much work it was.
8. She couldn't plant nothing until the soil was ready.
9. Nothing never grows well unless the soil is loose.
10. Sumi didn't have no experience preparing soil.
11. Nothing could be no harder than digging up rocks.
12. She thought she wouldn't never get to plant seeds.

■ Answer each question with a sentence that means *no.* Use a different negative in each sentence. There may be more than one correct answer.

Example: Have you ever planted a garden?   *I have never planted a garden.*

13. Do you have a good place to grow vegetables?
14. Will your plants get much sun?
15. Have you decided which vegetables to grow?
16. Can you start plants from seeds?
17. Is there somewhere you can buy small plants?
18. Do you know anyone who can help?

(pages 244–245)

5 What Is a Preposition?

- A preposition is a word that shows the connection between two other words.
- A prepositional phrase begins with a preposition and ends with a noun or a pronoun.

Remember

● The preposition is underlined in each sentence. Write the prepositional phrase.

Example: The Sanchez family camped <u>at</u> a state park.   *at a state park*

1. They climbed <u>up</u> the steep mountain.
2. A beautiful view spread <u>before</u> them.
3. They looked <u>across</u> a green valley.
4. A sparkling river wound <u>through</u> it.
5. Mr. Sanchez cooked <u>over</u> a glowing fire.

▲ Copy each sentence. Underline the prepositional phrase once and the preposition twice.

Example: A trail led to the lake.
         A trail led <u>to the lake</u>.

6. Anna ran down a sandy slope.
7. Carmen walked after her.
8. They gazed at the sparkling blue water.
9. Then they stepped into it.
10. Little minnows darted around their feet.

■ Use a preposition that makes sense to complete each sentence.

Example: The sun disappeared _____ the mountain.
         The sun disappeared behind the mountain.

11. Their sleeping bags lay _____ the soft ground.
12. The girls climbed _____ them.
13. They talked _____ their wonderful day.
14. The moon shone _____ the night.
15. Everyone slept _____ sunrise.
16. The sun rose _____ 4:30 A.M.

Part 2

Writing, Listening, Speaking, and Viewing

What You Will Find in This Part:

What You Will Find in This Section:

Getting Started

Listening to a Narrative

A **narrative** is a story about a real experience or an imagined one. Listening to a story is different from listening to a report. The general purpose for listening to a story is enjoyment. Use these guidelines to help you listen well.

Guidelines for Listening to a Story

▶ Listen for the one big idea. What is the story about?

▶ Listen for the main events. What happens? in what order?

▶ Listen to find out who the most important people or characters are and what they are like.

▶ Listen to find out where and when the story takes place.

▶ Listen for the author's purpose. Why is the author telling this story? Does the author want to make you laugh or cry? scare you? teach a lesson? share an experience?

Try It Out Listen as your teacher reads a true story, "Just a Sunday Drive in the Country," about an unusual experience that happened to the author, Pete Hendley. Listen for details that answer the questions below.

● What one big idea is the story about?

● When and where does the story take place?

● Who are the most important people in the story? What animal is important?

● Retell the story, telling the main events.

Writing a Narrative Paragraph

A group of sentences that tell about one main idea form a **paragraph**. The first line of a paragraph is **indented**. A paragraph has a topic and a main idea. The **topic** is the subject of the paragraph. The **main idea** is what the author wants to say about the subject.

A paragraph that tells a story is a **narrative paragraph**. What is the topic of the narrative paragraph below? What is the main idea?

Indent

Lead
sentence

Supporting
sentences

Closing
sentence

> My first try at making pizza was like a wrestling match. First, the dough attacked. It stuck to the rolling pin, to my fingers, and to the counter. Then the tomato sauce spilled under my feet and nearly made me slip. The cheese grater scraped my finger along with the mozzarella. Finally, I shoved the messy pizza into the oven. Twenty minutes later, I took my first bite. Mmmmmmmm. I knew I'd won the match!

Lead Sentence

Supporting Sentences

Closing Sentence

The topic of this paragraph is making pizza. The main idea is that making the pizza was difficult, like a wrestling match. Which sentence tells the topic and the main idea?

The labels show the three parts of a narrative paragraph.

- The **lead sentence** introduces the topic and gives a hint about the main idea of the story.
- The **supporting sentences** follow the lead sentence. They give details about what happens in the story.
- The **closing sentence** finishes the story.

Think and Discuss Reread the pizza paragraph.

- What details are given in the supporting sentences?

The Lead Sentence

You've learned that in a narrative paragraph, the **lead sentence** introduces the topic and may give a hint about the main idea of the story. The lead sentence should also get the reader interested in the story.

Topic   Main idea

Example: My first try at making pizza was like a wrestling match.

What do you think stories with these lead sentences might be about?

- "It will be impossible to choose only one," I thought when we walked into the animal shelter.
- When I heard the tire go *thumpety, thumpety, thumpety,* I knew this wasn't going to be the usual bus ride to school.

Try It Out Read the paragraphs below. Each is missing the topic sentence. On your own or with a partner, write the topic and the main idea of each paragraph. Then write two possible lead sentences for each.

1. _____Lead sentence_____. After breakfast, we tried cooling off in the sprinkler, but Dad squashed that plan. "You'll ruin the new grass!" he said. Then we tried reading in front of the fan, but we still felt sweaty. After lunch, LaToya invited us for a swim in her new pool. We swam until our lips turned blue! At least we couldn't complain about being too hot anymore.

2. _____Lead sentence_____. The score was 1–1 in the soccer game against the Rockets, and there was only one minute left. I sprinted down the field with the ball and booted it past the goalkeeper. Cheers exploded from the sidelines. "Goal!" I shouted, leaping into the air. When I saw my coach's face, I realized my mistake. I had kicked the ball into my own goal! I was the most valuable player, but for the wrong team.

Supporting Sentences

Supporting sentences follow the lead sentence. They support the main idea by telling details about it. They answer one or more of the questions *Who? What? Where? When? Why?* and *How?* In the pizza paragraph on page 269, the supporting sentences describe why making pizza was like a wrestling match.

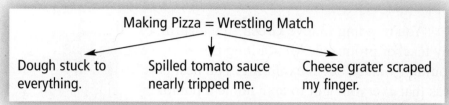

Making Pizza = Wrestling Match

| Dough stuck to everything. | Spilled tomato sauce nearly tripped me. | Cheese grater scraped my finger. |

Try It Out On your own or with a partner, choose one lead sentence below. List at least four details to support it. Then write at least three supporting sentences, using details from your list.

1. My day at the fair gave me a prize-winning stomachache.
2. Although the rides at the fair made me dizzy, I went on every one!

GRAMMAR TIP ▶ *Use an exclamation point (!) to end a sentence that shows strong feeling.*

Keeping to the Main Idea Be sure your supporting sentences give details only about the main idea. Do not include other details.

Think and Discuss Read the paragraph below. What is the main idea? Which sentence does not keep to the main idea?

> The minute the dentist clipped up my x-ray, I suspected trouble. First, Dr. Vargas squinted at it. Then she frowned. As she examined my x-ray more closely, she mumbled something about a retainer. My friend just got a retainer. Finally, Dr. Vargas snapped off the light and informed me, "You need braces."

Ordering Details Events in a narrative paragraph are usually told in the order they happened. **Time-clue words and phrases**, such as *first, next,* and *in the morning,* help signal when events take place.

 See page 18 for more time-clue words.

Think and Discuss Which sentence is out of order in the paragraph below? Why? Tell where it should go in the paragraph.

> "You're going to love Green Acres Farm!" my teacher promised. After a long bus ride, we couldn't wait to begin exploring. The best part was that everyone got to take home a pumpkin! We visited the horse stalls first. Then we learned how to milk a cow. Just before leaving, we took a hayride to a pumpkin patch. Nobody wanted to leave at the end of the day.

The Closing Sentence

The **closing sentence** in a narrative paragraph can tell the last event in the story, something learned from the story, or what the writer thought or felt about the experience. In the pizza paragraph on page 269, the concluding sentence tells how the "struggle" turned out.

Try It Out Read the paragraph below. It is missing the closing sentence. On your own or with a partner, write two different concluding sentences.

> We never know what's going to happen when we take our Labrador retriever, Rusty, on a trip. Last year Mom, Dad, my sister Bridget, and I were camping in a park. We set up our tent close by a stream so that we could hear the water gurgling over the rocks. In the middle of the night, I woke up and looked around for Rusty. He was gone! I woke up everybody else, and we crawled out of the tent and started calling for him. Splash, splash! Rusty was in the stream, soaking wet. _Concluding sentence_ .

Write Your Own Narrative Paragraph

Now it's time to write your own paragraph. Write about something that happened to you. First, think of a time when you felt happy, sad, scared, or embarrassed, or when something funny or unexpected happened. Then picture what happened, and make a list of details. After you have practiced telling your story to a partner, you are ready to write!

Checklist for My Paragraph

✔ My **lead sentence** introduces the main idea.
✔ Every **supporting sentence** tells details about the main idea.
✔ My **supporting sentences** tell what happened in order. Time-clue words and phrases make the order clear.
✔ My **closing sentence** sums up what happened or tells what I thought or felt.

Looking Ahead

Now that you know how to write a narrative paragraph, writing a longer narrative will be easy! The diagram below shows how the parts of a one-paragraph narrative do the same jobs as the parts of a longer narrative.

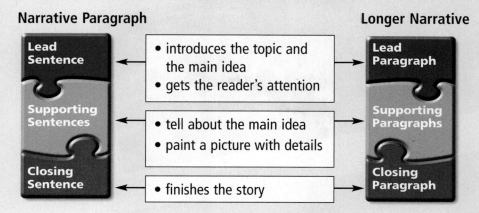

Narrative Paragraph

| Lead Sentence |
| Supporting Sentences |
| Closing Sentence |

- introduces the topic and the main idea
- gets the reader's attention

- tell about the main idea
- paint a picture with details

- finishes the story

Longer Narrative

| Lead Paragraph |
| Supporting Paragraphs |
| Closing Paragraph |

Writing a Personal Narrative

For weeks my sister had outplayed me on the home court. Finally, I figured out a way to outsmart her.

Eloise Greenfield wrote a personal narrative about something that happened to her in school. Can you understand how she felt?

A Play

from *Childtimes*, by Eloise Greenfield

When I was in the fifth grade, I was famous for a whole day, and all because of a play. The teacher had given me a big part, and I didn't want it. I liked to be in plays where I could be part of a group, like being one of the talking trees, or dancing, or singing in the glee club. But having to talk by myself—*uh uh!*

I used to slide down in my chair and stare at my desk while the teacher was giving out the parts, so she wouldn't pay any attention to me, but this time it didn't work. She called on me anyway. I told her I didn't want to do it, but she said I had to. I guess she thought it would be good for me.

On the day of the play, I didn't make any mistakes. I remembered all of my lines. Only— nobody in the audience heard me. I couldn't make my voice come out loud.

For the rest of the day, I was famous. Children passing by my classroom door, children on the playground at lunchtime, kept pointing at me saying, "That's that girl! That's the one who didn't talk loud enough!"

Go to www.eduplace.com/kids/ for information about Eloise Greenfield.

more ▶

A Published Model   275

I felt so bad, I wanted to go home. But one good thing came out of it all. The teacher was so angry, so upset, she told me that as long as I was in that school, I'd never have another chance to ruin one of her plays. And that was such good news, I could stand being famous for a day.

Reading As a Writer

Think About the Personal Narrative

- Who is the *I* in the story?
- What details help you understand how Eloise Greenfield felt when the teacher was handing out parts?
- What is the main part of the story?

Think About Writer's Craft

- How does Eloise Greenfield tie the beginning of her story to the ending?

Think About the Picture

- Why does the photo of Eloise Greenfield as a young girl help bring the story to life? Why might a photo be more effective than an illustration?

Responding

Write responses to these questions.

- **Personal Response** Think about a time you had to do something you didn't want to do. How was your experience similar to or different from Eloise Greenfield's?
- **Critical Thinking** Why does Eloise Greenfield decide that she "could stand being famous for a day"? Give examples from her narrative to support your answer.

What Makes a Great Personal Narrative?

A **personal narrative** is a true story about something that happened to the person who tells it.

Remember to follow these guidelines when you write a personal narrative.

▶ Grab your readers' attention at the beginning.

▶ Use the pronoun *I*.

▶ Include only the important events, and tell them in order.

▶ Use details that tell what you saw, heard, or felt. Include dialogue if appropriate.

▶ Write so that it sounds like you.

▶ Write an ending that tells how the story worked out or how you felt.

GRAMMAR CHECK

Use complete sentences. Begin each sentence with a capital letter, and end it with the correct mark.

WORKING DRAFT

Carolin Castillo had a shocking experience while on a family trip! She thought it would make a good topic for a personal narrative. Read Carolin's draft to find out what happened.

Carolin Castillo

This story is about my trip to Vernal Falls in Yosemite Valley with my family.

~~The drive was not the fifteen minutes my friend had told us about. It was more like an hour and a half, not including the wait for the bus.~~

Hiking to the waterfall was a mile UPHILL. We had lunch on the trail. Jonathan and I tossed pieces of bread to the ground squirrels, watching them nibble away.

> I like this detail. I can really picture the squirrels.

We were glad when we finally got to a huge slab of granite where we could lie and watch the waterfall. After a little rest, we ~~walked around~~ went exploring. All we saw was granite, granite, granite! Then we found a pool of water with water skeeters all over the surface. I was still hot from the hike, so I asked

Is this dialogue really important?

Dad if I could go swimming.

"Sure," he replied.

"Thanks," I said.

This is the most important part! Can you add more details?

Jumping into the melted mountain snow was not too smart. It was cold. I couldn't stay in the water long. Man, did that wake me up! When I got out of the water, the mountain air felt tropical.

Is this part important to the story?

On the way down the trail, we saw hundreds of ground squirrels. Jonathan thought they were all the same squirrel following us.

You told everything in order. Good!

At Yosemite Village we had ice cream. My Dad had vanilla. We got mint chocolate chip. That night I fell asleep thinking about my trip.

Reading As a Writer

- What did Sal like about Carolin's narrative? What questions did Sal have? What revisions could Carolin make to answer them?
- Why do you think Carolin crossed out some sentences?
- What questions would you like to ask Carolin about her experience?

Carolin revised her personal narrative after discussing it with classmates. Read Carolin's final version to see how she improved her story.

> *Your personality really comes through when you write!*

> *I can really hear Dad and Jonathan here.*

> *I like this comparison.*

Feeling Cool at Vernal Falls
by Carolin Castillo

I had been waiting for what seemed like forever for this time to come. My father, my younger brother, Jonathan, and I were finally going to Vernal Falls in Yosemite Valley. I could hardly wait!

Hiking to the waterfall was a mile UPHILL. We had lunch on the trail. Jonathan and I tossed pieces of bread to the ground squirrels, watching them nibble away.

We were glad when we finally got to a huge slab of granite where we could lie and watch the waterfall. After a little rest, we went exploring. All we saw was granite, granite, granite! Then we found a freezing pool of water with water skeeters all over the surface. I was still hot from the hike, so I asked Dad if I could go swimming.

He smiled and warned, "Sure, if you want to, but these mountain pools are not exactly warm."

Jonathan jumped up and down and said, "I've got to see this!"

Jumping into the melted mountain snow was not too smart. It was like jumping into a soft glacier and being able to surface again. The water was cold beyond belief, as cold as water can be without actually freezing. It was so cold that I could only stay in for about thirty seconds before my body forced me to get out. Man, did that wake me up! When I got out of the water, the mountain air felt tropical.

On the way down the trail, we saw hundreds of ground squirrels. Jonathan thought they were all the same squirrel following us.

Please take some advice from a girl who learned it the hard way. Unless you're a polar bear, DON'T go swimming at Vernal Falls!

You took out the part about the ice cream because it didn't keep to the topic. Good!

Reading As a Writer

- How did Carolin respond to Sal's questions?
- Compare the beginning and ending of Carolin's final copy with her working draft. Why are they better in the final copy?
- What details did Carolin add to tell how the water felt?

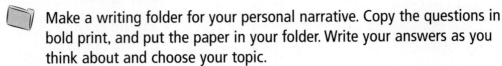
Write a Personal Narrative

▶ Start Thinking

📁 Make a writing folder for your personal narrative. Copy the questions in bold print, and put the paper in your folder. Write your answers as you think about and choose your topic.

- **Who will be my audience?** Will it be my classmates? a family member? a pen pal? a younger child?
- **What will be my purpose?** Do I want to make people laugh? to share a feeling or special time?
- **How will I publish or share my personal narrative?** Will I send it in a letter or an e-mail? read it aloud for my class? add pictures and make it into a book?

▶ Choose Your Story Idea

❶ List five experiences you could write about.

❷ Discuss your ideas with a partner.

- Which ones does your partner like? Why?
- Is any idea too big? Could you write about one part? Carolin broke one big idea, *camping in Yosemite*, into smaller parts. Each part could be a whole story.

> **HELP**
> **?** *Stuck for an Idea?*
> - What strange or funny thing happened to you?
> - What experience made you say *yuck* or *wow*?
> - When were you scared? proud? embarrassed?
>
> **See page 293 for more ideas.**

> camping in Yosemite
>
> hiked to Vernal Falls   visited giant sequoias in Mariposa Grove   watched rock climbers climb El Capitan

❸ Ask yourself these questions about each idea. Then circle the one you will write about.

- Can I remember enough details?
- Would this interest my audience?
- Would I enjoy writing about this?

Explore Your Story Idea

1 **Think** about your experience as a movie. Close your eyes, and watch it in your mind. You may want to draw a cartoon strip of the main events.

- List and underline the main events. Leave a lot of space between each one.

2 **Rewind** your movie. Zoom in on the most important part. Put a star next to it.

- A close-up shows details. Write a lot of details about this part. Use the Exploring Questions to help you.

Exploring Questions

What did I do and say?

What did other people do and say?

What did I see or hear?

What did I touch, taste, or smell?

How did I feel?

3 **List** any other details that your audience might need to know.

<u>went swimming</u>	<u>went exploring</u>
cold water	granite, granite, granite
woke me up	pool of water
air felt tropical	water skeeters
<u>hiked to Vernal Falls</u>	<u>got ice cream</u>
fed ground squirrels	vanilla
one mile uphill	mint chocolate chip

HELP ? **Stuck for Details?**

If you can't think of many details, try another topic.

▲ **Part of Carolin's list**

 See page 14 for other ideas for exploring your topic.

Focus Skill

Organizing Your Narrative

Tell the events in the order they happened. Be careful not to mention something in the middle that you should have told your audience at the beginning. Remember: they weren't there!

Keep to your topic. Take out any events or details that are not needed to understand the most important part.

Use time clues. Time clue words signal to your audience when events happened. What other time clue words can you add to this list?

Time Clue Words	Time Clue Phrases
first, second, third, before, after, next, later, finally, Monday, then, meanwhile, yesterday	by the time, later on, in the meantime, at last, at the same time, last summer, on Tuesday, this morning

Think and Discuss Look at Carolin's list on page 283.

- The events and details are not in the order they happened. What could she do to show the correct order without rewriting them?
- Which event and details are not important to the waterfall story?

▶ Plan Your Narrative

❶ **Number** the events of your narrative in the order they happened. Cross out events and details that are not needed.

❷ **Make a chart** that shows the events in order. Add the details that describe each event. Look at this chart as a model.

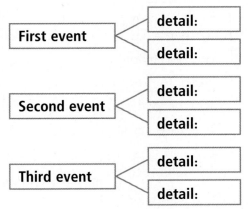

First event — detail: / detail:

Second event — detail: / detail:

Third event — detail: / detail:

 Go to www.eduplace.com/kids/hme/ for graphic organizers.

Focus Skill

Good Beginnings

Like a race, your story should begin with a BANG! A good beginning grabs your audience's attention and makes them want to keep reading. Here are three different ways to begin.

Ask a question. A question makes your readers want to know the answer.

Weak Beginning	Strong Beginning
Last Saturday we went to the grocery store and to the barber.	Have you ever gone to the barber and then wanted to hide for two months?

Make a surprising statement. Say something unexpected.

Weak Beginning	Strong Beginning
We went to Riverside Amusement Park for my birthday, and I rode on the roller coaster.	It looked as if I was going to drop into a hole as deep as the Grand Canyon, and there was nothing I could do about it.

Use dialogue. A person's exact words may be interesting.

Weak Beginning	Strong Beginning
One day my friend Ramón and I were walking home from school.	"I knew this was going to be an unlucky day," groaned my friend Ramón.

GRAMMAR TIP ▸ *Put a speaker's exact words in quotation marks.*

Try It Out

- With a partner, rewrite the first beginning as a surprising statement, the second as dialogue, and the third as a question.

▶ Draft Your Beginning

❶ **Write** three beginnings for your narrative, using a question, a surprising statement, and dialogue.

❷ **Choose** the beginning you like best.

Focus Skill

Writing with Voice

Your personal narrative is about you, and it should sound as if you wrote it. Writing with voice lets the audience hear the person behind the words. Writing without voice will sound flat. It won't grab the reader.

Compare the weak example below to the strong excerpt from Eloise Greenfield's narrative, "A Play."

Weak Voice	Strong Voice
I liked to be in plays if I was with other kids. I didn't like to talk by myself.	I liked to be in plays where I could be part of a group, like being one of the talking trees, or dancing, or singing in the glee club. But having to talk by myself—*uh uh!*

Think and Discuss Compare the weak and strong examples.

- Why does the weak voice sound flat?
- Why is the strong example better?

▶ Draft Your Narrative

❶ **Write** the rest of your narrative. Skip every other line to leave room for changes. Don't worry about mistakes. Just write.

❷ **Follow your chart**. Include the details. Add other details that you think of as you write. Use time clues.

❸ **Let your feelings show.** Allow your audience to hear your voice.

HELP

Paragraph Tip

Look for details that tell about the same idea. Group them together in one paragraph.

Focus Skill

Good Endings

A good ending makes your story feel finished. Just writing THE END is not enough.

Tell how the experience worked out. Compare these endings for a narrative about a terrible haircut.

Weak Ending	Strong Ending
I went home. After I got the haircut, I didn't want to go anywhere for a long time.	My Tigers cap stayed glued to my head for the next two months. Finally, my hair grew out enough for another haircut—with a different barber!

Share your thoughts or describe your feelings about the experience. If you end this way, don't just tell how you felt. Describe it! Compare these endings for a narrative about a baseball game.

Weak Ending	Strong Ending
The ball went over the wall. I ran around the bases and scored a home run.	The ball went over the wall! I ran around the bases, my heart pounding, and tagged home plate. I leaped into the air, yelling until I was hoarse. What a great day it was!

Think and Discuss

- Why are the strong endings better?
- What kind of ending does Carolin use in her final copy on page 281?

▶ Draft Your Ending

Write two endings for your narrative. Choose the one you like better.

Tech Tip
Cut and paste different endings on your story. Which ones do you like?

Evaluating Your Personal Narrative

▶ **Reread** your narrative. What do you need to do to make it better? Use this rubric to help you decide. Write the sentences that describe your narrative.

Rings the Bell!

- ■ The story starts with a question, a surprising statement, or dialogue.
- ■ Details and dialogue tell what I saw, heard, tasted, smelled, and felt.
- ■ All the events are important and in order.
- ■ I can hear my voice. My writing sounds like me.
- ■ The ending tells how the story worked out or what I thought or felt.
- ■ *There are almost no mistakes in capitalization, punctuation, or spelling.*

Getting Stronger

- ■ The beginning could be more interesting.
- ■ More details are needed to describe what happened more clearly.
- ■ Some sentences aren't important to the story.
- ■ In some places, my writing doesn't sound like me.
- ■ The ending needs more elaboration.
- ■ *There are a few mistakes.*

Try Harder

- ☐ The beginning is boring.
- ☐ Where are the details? It's hard to picture what happened.
- ☐ Most events are unimportant or out of order.
- ☐ My writing doesn't sound like me at all!
- ☐ The story just stops. How does it work out? What did I think or feel?
- ■ *There are a lot of mistakes.*

  Go to www.eduplace.com/kids/hme/ to interact with this rubric.

Revise Your Personal Narrative

1 Revise your narrative. Use the list of sentences you wrote from the rubric. Work on the parts that you described with sentences from "Getting Stronger" and "Try Harder."

2 Have a writing conference.

When You're the Writer Read your narrative to a partner. Discuss any questions or problems you're having with it. Take notes to remember what your partner says.

When You're the Listener Tell at least two things you like about the narrative. Ask questions about anything that is unclear.

HELP

Revising Tip

Write new paragraphs on strips of paper. Attach the strips where they belong in your narrative.

What should I say?

The Writing Conference

If you're thinking...	You could say...
The beginning isn't very interesting.	Could you start with a question? a surprising statement? dialogue?
I don't understand when things happened.	Can you add time clues?
I wonder what people said.	What did _____ say when that happened?
What does this part have to do with the main part of this story?	Is that part about _____ really important? Could you leave it out?
Your story is great, but it just stops.	I'd like to know how everything worked out.
This doesn't sound like you.	How did you feel when that happened?

3 Make more revisions to your personal narrative. Use your conference notes and the Revising Strategies on the next page.

Revising Strategies

Elaborating: Word Choice Use similes and metaphors to create pictures in the minds of your readers. A **simile** compares two different things, using the word *like* or *as*. A **metaphor** compares without using *like* or *as*.

Simile	The crash of the cymbals was as loud as thunder. The new students wandered the halls like mice in a maze.
Metaphor	Mom's new earrings are tinkling wind chimes.

▶ Find at least one place in your narrative where you can use a simile or a metaphor.   📖 See also page H11.

Elaborating: Details Insert details within a sentence or write more sentences.

Few details	When I crashed, I hurt my leg.
Elaborated with details	When I crashed, I got a gash in my leg about three inches long. I also had a big lump on my ankle.

▶ Find at least two places in your narrative where you can add details.

Sentence Fluency Try writing sentences different ways so that not all sentences are written the same way. Don't change the meaning when you rewrite.

Two sentences	I zipped down the hill. My bike slipped.
Combined with *and*	I zipped down the hill, and my bike slipped.
Combined with *as*	My bike slipped as I zipped down the hill.
Changed order	As I zipped down the hill my bike slipped.

▶ Write at least two sentences of your narrative a different way.

GRAMMAR LINK ▶ *See also page 49.*

▶ Proofread Your Personal Narrative

Proofread your narrative, using the Proofreading Checklist and the Grammar and Spelling Connections. Proofread for one skill at a time. Use a class dictionary to check spellings.

Proofreading Checklist

Did I
- ✔ indent all paragraphs?
- ✔ correct any run-on sentences?
- ✔ begin and end sentences correctly?
- ✔ use correct verb forms?
- ✔ correct any spelling errors?

📖 Use the Guide to Capitalization, Punctuation, and Usage on page H55.

Proofreading Marks
- ¶ Indent
- ∧ Add
- ℘ Delete
- ≡ Capital letter
- / Small letter

Tech Tip
The spelling tool on your computer cannot find words misspelled as other words.

Grammar and Spelling Connections

Past Tense Add *-ed* to most verbs to form the past tense.

Present tense	shout	holler	walk
Past tense	shouted	hollered	walked

 GRAMMAR LINK ▶ *See also page 108.*

Complete Sentences A sentence has both a subject and a predicate. It begins with a capital letter and ends with a period, a question mark, or an exclamation point.

Not a sentence	Up the steep mountain trail.
Sentence	The hikers carried backpacks.

GRAMMAR LINK ▶ *See also pages 32, 36, 38, and 166.*

Spelling Short Vowels A short vowel sound before a consonant is usually spelled with just one letter: *a, e, i, o,* or *u.*

staff, slept, mist, fond, bulb

📖 See the Spelling Guide on page H65.

▶ Publish Your Personal Narrative

❶ Make a neat final copy of your narrative. Be sure you fixed all mistakes.

❷ Write an interesting title for your narrative that will make your audience curious, such as "Goosebumps on the Trail" rather than "My Hiking Trip."

> **GRAMMAR TIP** ▶ *Capitalize the first, the last, and each important word in a title.*

❸ Publish or share your narrative in a way that suits your audience. See the Ideas for Sharing box.

Tips for Reading Aloud

- Read clearly, slowly, and loudly enough for everyone to hear.
- Read with expression. Pause at commas, and raise your voice at the end of questions. Say exclamations with feeling!
- Look at your audience from time to time.
- Let your face show your feelings.

Ideas for Sharing

Write It
- Send or e-mail your story to a magazine. See page H37 for tips.
- Send it with a greeting card.

Say It
- Read it aloud in the Author's Chair.
- Record it, adding sound effects.

Show It
- Display it with photos.

▶ Reflect

Write about your writing experience. Use these questions to get started.

- ● What was easy to do? What was hard to do?
- ● What are your goals for the next time you write?
- ● How does this paper compare with other papers you have written?

Writing Prompts

Use these prompts as ideas for personal narratives or to practice for a test. Some of them fit with other subjects you study. Decide who your audience will be, and write your narrative in a way that they will understand and enjoy.

1 Write about a time you learned how to do something new. Who taught you? How long did it take you to learn? Was it easier or more difficult than you had expected?

2 Going to a new place can be exciting. Write about a time you went somewhere you had never been before. What did you see? How did you feel? What did you learn?

3 Write about a time when you helped someone. Why did the person need help? What did you do to help?

4 Write about a special experience you had with a group of friends. Give details about the people, the places, what happened, and what was said.

Writing Across the Curriculum

 5 HEALTH
Write about a time when you should have been more careful. Write it for younger children to help them to learn to be safer.

 6 SOCIAL STUDIES
Many families and cultures have traditions for celebrating holidays or family events. Write about a tradition you have.

7 LITERATURE
Think about a book you have read. What happened to the main character? Write about an experience you had that was similar to that character's.

 8 PHYSICAL EDUCATION
Write about an experience you had while playing a game or a sport or about the first time you tried a particular game or sport.

✓ Test Practice

This prompt to write a personal narrative is like ones you might find on a writing test. Read the prompt.

> **Write about a special experience you had with a group of friends. Give details about the people, the places, what happened, and what was said.**

Here are some strategies to help you do a good job responding to a prompt like this.

Remember that a personal narrative is a true story about something that happened to the writer.

❶ Look for clue words that tell what to write about. What are the clue words in the prompt above?

❷ Choose a topic that fits the clue words. Write the clue words and your topic.

Clue Words	My Topic
a special experience you had with a group of friends	I will write about the day I went canoeing with my friends Jed and Tyrone.

❸ Plan your writing. Use a chart.

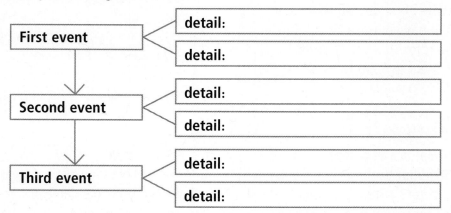

| First event | detail: |
| | detail: |

| Second event | detail: |
| | detail: |

| Third event | detail: |
| | detail: |

❹ You will get a good score if you remember the description of what kind of personal narrative rings the bell in the rubric on page 288.

Writing a Friendly Letter

A **friendly letter** is written to a person you know well. You can write a friendly letter to share news or to find out how someone is doing. Read Callie's letter.

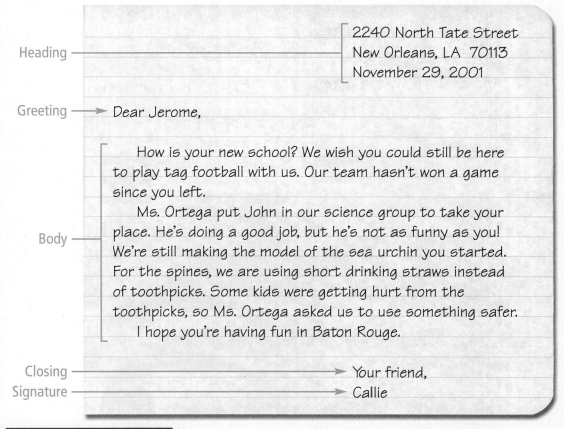

Heading

2240 North Tate Street
New Orleans, LA 70113
November 29, 2001

Greeting

Dear Jerome,

Body

How is your new school? We wish you could still be here to play tag football with us. Our team hasn't won a game since you left.

Ms. Ortega put John in our science group to take your place. He's doing a good job, but he's not as funny as you! We're still making the model of the sea urchin you started. For the spines, we are using short drinking straws instead of toothpicks. Some kids were getting hurt from the toothpicks, so Ms. Ortega asked us to use something safer.

I hope you're having fun in Baton Rouge.

Closing

Your friend,

Signature

Callie

Reading As a Writer

- The **heading** contains the writer's address and the date. *What information is on each line?*
- The **greeting** begins with *Dear* and gives the name of the person getting the letter, followed by a comma. Capitalize each word. *To whom is Callie writing?*
- The **body** is the main part of the letter. *What did Callie write about?*
- The **closing** finishes the letter. It is followed by a comma. *What closing did Callie use?*
- The **signature** is the writer's name. *Where is the signature written?*

more ▶

How to Write a Friendly Letter

❶ Think about what you want to say.

❷ Organize your information. You may want to make notes first.

❸ Write the letter. Include all five parts.

❹ Proofread for mistakes. Use the Proofreading Checklist on page 291. Use a dictionary to check spellings.

❺ Write a neat final copy of your letter.

❻ Address the envelope correctly. Stamp and mail your letter.

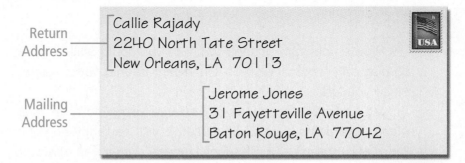

Return Address ⎯⎯ ⎡Callie Rajady
2240 North Tate Street
New Orleans, LA 70113⎦

Mailing Address ⎯⎯ ⎡Jerome Jones
31 Fayetteville Avenue
Baton Rouge, LA 77042⎦

Types of Friendly Letters

Thank-you Letter Writing a thank-you letter is a way for you to express your appreciation. You can elaborate using details about the gift or favor.

> Dear Roxanne,
>
> I love the 1,000–piece jigsaw puzzle of New York City that you gave me for my birthday. I have always wanted a hard puzzle with many different pieces. My whole family wants to work on it, which is good because it will probably take a lot of time!
>
> I'm so glad you could come to my party. Thanks again for the great present!

Invitation An invitation asks someone to come to an event, usually a party. Most invitations include the name of the event, the place, the date, the time, and any special information, such as what to wear or bring. Invitations often give a phone number that you can call to respond.

Writing a Story

Once upon a time, in their castle high on a rocky cliff, Princess Bright and her brother Prince Klever planned a surprise for the king and queen.

The story "Crows" is a legend told by members of the Seminole tribe in Florida. What does this legend teach us?

Crows

from *Legends of the Seminoles,* by Betty Mae Jumper

Once, among all the flying birds in the beautiful forest, were two special birds. They had very colorful feathers that shone brightly under the sun as they flew around. All the other birds admired and envied them. And the songs they sang were out of this world. When these birds sang, the others in the forest would quiet down and just listen to them.

One day, as these two birds were flying around, they saw a strange thing coming up in the air which was not a cloud. They looked and looked from up in the air, but they couldn't make out what it was. One said to the other, "Let us fly a little ways further and see what it is."

"I'm scared," said the other, but he followed his friend halfway to the strange thing. Then both stopped in a tree and looked and looked.

"What is that orange color below and that strange black color going in the air?" said the one bird, begging his friend to go closer. So, they flew right to the edge of where the forest was burning— something the birds had never seen before. They sat a long time watching it. Then one bird said, "Let us fly to that black tree and see the burning from the top."

The other said, "No. Let us go back. We have seen enough." But the other kept it up, wanting to fly to the top of the tall black tree. As usual, he won the argument and they flew to the top of the tree and tried to sit on a limb.

But the limb broke and the birds fell to the ground into the black soot, which burned their beautiful feathers into charcoal.

And their voices were gone. They couldn't get any sound out, until one day they learned to say "Caw. Caw." For this, they were ashamed and never returned to the beautiful forest they once knew.

Reading As a Writer

Think About the Story

- What lesson does this legend teach?
- What do you find out in the beginning about the characters and setting?
- What is the problem in the story? How do the birds deal with the problem?
- What happens to the birds at the end?

Think About Writer's Craft

- The author adds variety to her writing by making her sentences different lengths. Find at least three examples of this in the story.

Think About the Picture

- What is the main color in the picture? Why do you think the artist used so much of this color?

Responding

Write responses to these questions.

- **Personal Response** What did you like about the story? What didn't you like? Explain your answers.
- **Critical Thinking** How are the two birds alike and different?

What Makes a Great Story?

A **story** is a narrative
made up by the author.

Remember to follow these guidelines when you tell or write
a story.

▶ Develop a plot with a beginning, a middle, and an end.

▶ Introduce the main characters, the setting, and the problem in
the beginning in an interesting way.

▶ Show how the characters deal with the problem in the middle
and how the problem works out in the end.

▶ Describe the events in an order that
makes sense. Leave out events that
are not important to the story.

▶ Use details and dialogue to show
rather than tell about the characters,
events, and setting.

▶ Use details to make your story scary,
funny, serious, or sad.

GRAMMAR CHECK

Use singular verbs with
singular subjects. Use
plural verbs with plural
subjects.

WORKING DRAFT

Jessica Liu enjoys writing stories, especially funny stories. She decided to write this story about a pig in trouble to make her friends laugh. This is Jessica's first draft.

Jessica Liu

~~My story is about a pig that gets into trouble.~~

Once there was a pig. He was walking down the country road all by himself. He looked down and found a pretty flower. The flower had five petals and a long stem. It smelled really good.

This pig went on walking down the road ~~smelling~~ sniffing his flower. He wasn't paying very much attention to where he was going. All of a sudden, he slipped!

UP in the air he flew. DOWN to the ground he crashed!

When he finally landed, this young pink pig was sitting in a split. Oh, no! He couldn't get up! What would he do now?

> Can you tell more about the pig?

> Ouch! I can really picture what happened!

> I can't wait to find out what happens to the pig.

more

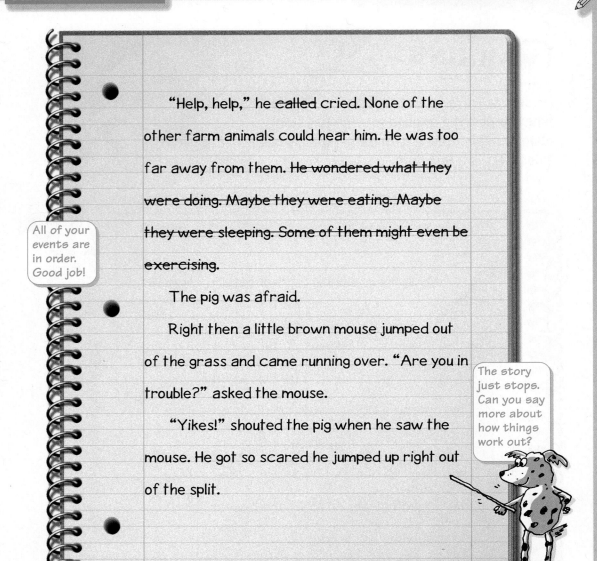

All of your events are in order. Good job!

"Help, help," he ~~called~~ cried. None of the other farm animals could hear him. He was too far away from them. ~~He wondered what they were doing. Maybe they were eating. Maybe they were sleeping. Some of them might even be exercising.~~

The pig was afraid.

Right then a little brown mouse jumped out of the grass and came running over. "Are you in trouble?" asked the mouse.

"Yikes!" shouted the pig when he saw the mouse. He got so scared he jumped up right out of the split.

The story just stops. Can you say more about how things work out?

Reading As a Writer

- What did Sal like about Jessica's story? What were Sal's questions? What revisions could Jessica make to answer them?
- What sentences should Jessica take out of the first paragraph on page 301? Why?
- Look at the first paragraph on this page. Why do you think Jessica crossed out some sentences?

FINAL COPY

Jessica revised her story after discussing it in a writing conference. Read her final copy to see what changes she made to improve her story.

There's More Than One Way to Scare a Pig

by Jessica Liu

Once there lived a roly-poly young pig. He was a lovely pink fellow. He lived on a farm with other farm animals. One morning he was walking down the country road all by himself. He looked down and found a pretty flower.

> These details help me picture the pig much better.

This young pink pig went on walking down the road, sniffing his flower. He wasn't paying very much attention to where he was going. All of a sudden, he stepped on a wet leaf and...slipped!

UP in the air he flew. DOWN to the ground he crashed!

When he finally landed, this young pink pig was sitting in a split. Oh, no! He couldn't get up! What would he do now?

> This story is really funny!

"Help, help," he cried. None of the other farm animals could hear him. He was too far away from them.

The pig was afraid. "Help, help," he called again. Now he was getting even more afraid because it was getting dark. "Oh, no! I can't stay here all night. It will be dark and cold."

more

Right then a little brown mouse jumped out of the grass and came running over. "Are you in trouble?" asked the mouse.

"Yikes!" shouted the pig when he saw the mouse. He got so scared he jumped up right out of the split. Then he ran back down the road right back to the farm.

The little mouse waved good-bye as the pig ran away. "I'm glad I could help you!" he said. "See you later!"

Good job! You told how everything worked out in the end. Now your story feels finished.

Reading As a Writer

- How did Jessica respond to Sal's questions?
- What details and dialogue did Jessica add to tell why the pig was afraid? What other details did she add?
- What other changes did Jessica make?

 See www.eduplace.com/kids/hme/ for more examples of student writing.

Write a Story

▶ Start Thinking

 Make a writing folder for your story. Copy the questions in bold print, and put the paper in your folder. Write your answers as you think about and choose your topic.

- **Who will be my audience?** Will I write this story for my classmates? younger students? my family?
- **What will be my purpose?** Do I want to make people laugh? scare them? take them on an adventure?
- **How will I publish or share my story?** Will I make a book with pictures? put on a radio play? act it out?

▶ Choose Your Story Idea

1 **List** five story ideas you could write about. Make a story chart like the one below.

Who?	Where?	What could happen?
pig	country road	an accident
boy	forest	lost in storm
cat	school	wants to win a contest

▲ **Part of Jessica's chart**

> **HELP**
> **?** **Stuck for Ideas?**
> Share your charts with a small group. Pick items from different charts, and combine them to create new story ideas.
>
> **See page 317 for more ideas.**

2 **Discuss** your ideas with a partner.

- Which idea is the most interesting to your partner? Why?
- Which idea has a good beginning, middle, and end?

3 **Ask** yourself these questions about each idea. Then circle the idea you will write about.

- Do I have enough ideas for my story?
- Will this interest my audience?
- Will I enjoy writing about this idea?

Focus Skill

Planning Characters

You are the casting director of your story. Do you need a computer genius or a mummy that sends e-mail in Egyptian picture language? Give your story at least one **main character** and as many **minor characters** as it needs.

Use details. Help your readers get to know your main character inside and out. Here are some ideas to get you started.

What does your character look like?
Describe your character's face, hair, clothes, and other features.

What is your character's personality?
Is he or she smart? funny? dreamy? loud?

What does your character say?
Does he or she recite poetry? make jokes?

What are your character's feelings?
Is she or he curious? lonely? brave? fearful?

How does your character act?
Does she or he whistle? shuffle? pout? blush?

What are your character's interests?
Does he or she collect posters? love sports?

Try It Out

● Work with a partner or a small group to describe the pictured character. Use the questions above. Make notes about your ideas. Then compare your ideas with those of other students.

▶ Explore Your Story

Think of two main characters that you might like to use in your story. Draw a picture of each character, and answer the questions above about each one. Describe each character's personality in one sentence.

 See page 14 for other ideas for exploring your topic.

Focus Skill

Planning Setting and Plot

The **setting** for a story is where and when the story takes place. The setting could be in a town like yours, on the moon, in a castle, on an island, or in a make-believe place. It could be long ago, today, or in the future.

A good story has a **plot** that focuses on a problem. The plot has three main parts: a beginning, a middle, and an end. This story map shows the three parts of "Crows."

Beginning ────────▶

- introduces the main characters
- introduces the setting
- introduces the problem

two beautiful birds sing in the forest; see something strange; try to find out what the strange thing is

Middle ────────▶

- tells how the characters deal with the problem

one bird wants to fly closer; other one doesn't	fly close; sit on branch over fire	tree burns; birds fall into fire

End ────────▶

- explains how the problem works out

feathers burned black; can't sing anymore

Try It Out

- With a partner, make a story map for Jessica's story on pages 303–304. Show the beginning, the middle, and the end.

▶ Plan Your Story

Make a story map for your story. Plan the beginning, the middle, and the end. Add notes about the characters, the setting, and the problem.

 Go to www.eduplace.com/kids/hme/ for graphic organizers.

Focus Skill

Developing Characters

Once you have planned what your characters are like, how can you help your readers imagine them?

Give details. Describe how your characters look, sound, and act.

> Will Trek slung a stuffed backpack over his shoulders, looped three cameras around his neck, grabbed two heavy suitcases, and slapped on his biggest smile before anyone could say, "Let's go!"

Show characters through their actions. Let the characters' actions reveal their personalities.

Telling	Showing
Mr. Trek told his family about the city's famous sites.	In his I-know-everything voice, Mr. Trek rattled off fifty zillion facts as he dragged his dazed family all over the city.

Show characters through dialogue. You can show your characters' thoughts, feelings, and personalities by what they say.

Telling, Without Dialogue	Showing, With Dialogue
Liane is always bragging.	"My family take trips all the time, and we see the best places. Pretty soon we'll start space traveling, I bet," Liane sighed.

Think and Discuss

● Look at your notes about the character shown on page 306. What might that character say that would show what he is like?

▶ Draft Some Dialogue

Write some dialogue for the main characters in your story. Use it to show what your characters are like.

> Remember to start a new paragraph each time the speaker changes.

Developing the Plot

The Beginning

Catch your audience's interest in the first sentence. Beginnings such as *My story is about . . .* are boring. A good beginning makes your readers wonder, *What is going to happen?* Here are some ideas for how to begin.

The beginning may be more than one paragraph.

Describe the setting.	Long vines looped around tree trunks and snaked along the ground in the thick rain forest.
Describe a character.	Sneaky Pete twisted the tips of his mustache and flashed a yellow-toothed grin at Clyde Clemhopper.
Describe an action.	The white horse pushed its hind legs against the ground and flew majestically into the clouds.

Think and Discuss

- What clues do the beginnings above give you about the stories?
- What catches your attention in each one?

The Middle

Include only the events that are important to the main idea. If your story is about a baseball game, include only important events related to the game. Don't include everything the characters did before, during, and after the game. Remember to begin a new paragraph for each new event.

Write the events in an order that makes sense. Use time clues, such as *before, after, later,* and *the next day,* to make the order clear.

Think and Discuss

- Choose one of the story beginnings above. What are some possible events for this beginning?

more ▶

Focus Skill continued

The Ending

A good ending makes sense of how the problem works out. Look again at this paragraph near the end of "Crows."

> But the limb broke and the birds fell to the ground into the black soot, which burned their beautiful feathers into charcoal.

If the story had ended there, you might have wondered, *Then what happened to the birds?* The last paragraph tells you. It finishes the story.

> And their voices were gone. They couldn't get any sound out, until one day they learned to say "Caw. Caw." For this, they were ashamed and never returned to the beautiful forest they once knew.

Try It Out

- Work with a small group of classmates to write another last paragraph for "Crows." Compare your ending with ones written by other groups.

▶ Draft Your Beginning

❶ Write three beginnings for your story.

❷ Choose the beginning you like best.

Tech Tip
You may want to write your draft on a computer.

Focus Skill

Writing with Voice

As the writer, you can give your characters a voice by letting your audience know your characters' thoughts, feelings, and personalities. You use another voice to tell the story. The details you write help to make the story sound sad, or funny, or scary. It's up to you!

Compare the weak examples below to the strong examples from Jessica's story.

HELP ?

Adding Voice

Does your story have more than one character? Use a different voice for each character.

Weak Voice	Strong Voice
Once there was a big pig. He was pink.	Once there lived a roly-poly young pig. He was a lovely pink fellow.
He went up in the air. He fell down.	UP in the air he flew. DOWN to the ground he crashed!

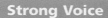

Think and Discuss Compare the weak and strong voices in each example.

- How does the voice sound in each weak example? each strong example?
- What details make each strong example sound the way it does?

▶ Draft Your Story

❶ **Decide** how you want your story to sound.

❷ **Write** the rest of your story. Use your story map and any dialogue and beginnings you have written.

❸ **Write** a good ending that wraps up your story. Skip every other line. Don't worry about mistakes until later.

Describe your characters and their actions in a lively, interesting way, so your audience will want to keep reading.

Evaluating Your Story

▶ **Reread** your story. What do you need to do to make it better? Use this rubric to help you decide. Write the sentences that describe your story.

Rings the Bell!

- ■ The beginning makes my audience want to read more. It introduces the characters, the setting, and the problem.
- ■ The middle shows how the characters deal with the problem.
- ■ All of the events are in order and are important to the story.
- ■ The ending shows how the problem works out.
- ■ Details and dialogue make the story come alive!
- ■ My characters have a voice, and the story sounds the way I wanted.
- ■ *There are almost no mistakes in capitalization, punctuation, or spelling.*

Getting Stronger

- ■ The beginning could be more interesting.
- ■ I haven't told how the characters deal with the problem.
- ■ I forgot to include some important events.
- ■ The story doesn't sound finished.
- ■ Details and dialogue need to show, not tell, about the characters, events, and setting.
- ■ My story doesn't sound the way I wanted.
- ■ *There are a few mistakes.*

Try Harder

- ☐ The beginning is boring.
- ☐ There is no clear problem.
- ☐ The story is confusing. Important events are left out.
- ☐ The ending just stops. How does the problem work out?
- ☐ Where can I add details and dialogue?
- ☐ My story is written in a dull, flat voice.
- ■ *There are a lot of mistakes.*

      See www.eduplace.com/kids/hme/ to interact with this rubric.

► Revise Your Story

1 **Revise** your story. Use the list of sentences you wrote from the rubric. Work on the parts that you described with sentences from "Getting Stronger" and "Try Harder."

2 **Have a writing conference.**

When You're the Writer Read your story to a partner. Discuss any questions or problems you are having with it. Take notes to remember what your partner says.

When You're the Listener Tell at least two things you like about the story. Ask questions about anything that is unclear.

Tech Tip
Always make a backup copy of your story when using a computer. Use the backup copy for revisions. Save the original version for reference.

What should I say?

The Writing Conference	
If you're thinking . . .	**You could say . . .**
I can't follow this story.	**What is the main idea of this story?**
The story is great, but the beginning doesn't catch my interest.	**Can you begin by describing an action, a character, or the setting?**
I can't picture these characters. The characters all have the same personality.	**What do the characters look like? How do they act? Can you give each character his or her own voice?**
I don't understand what the part about _____ has to do with the story.	**Why is the part about _____ in the story? Do you need it?**
The story just stops.	**Can you tell how the problem works out?**

3 **Make more revisions** to your story. Use your conference notes and the Revising Strategies on the next page.

Revising Strategies

Elaborating: Word Choice Exact words help your audience picture the characters, setting, and action in your story.

Without Exact Words	With Exact Words
Lindy's uncle completed the contest quickly while people watched.	Lindy's favorite uncle completed the skateboarding contest in record time while her friends watched.

▶ Find two places in your story where you can add exact nouns, verbs, adjectives, and adverbs.

📖 Use the Thesaurus Plus on page H79.

Elaborating: Details Insert prepositional phrases to add more information to a sentence.

Without Details	Elaborated with Details
Carlos wrote a story.	Carlos wrote a story with his friends for a class assignment.

▶ Add at least two prepositional phrases to your story.

GRAMMAR LINK ▶ *See also page 246.*

Sentence Fluency Avoid stringy sentences. Your audience may get lost if your sentence has too many *and*s. Rewrite your sentence to make it clearer.

Stringy Sentence	Smoother Sentences
Jessica had a lot of trading cards **and** one was old **and** a collector offered her fifty dollars for it.	Jessica had a lot of trading cards. One was old. A collector offered her fifty dollars for it.
	Jessica had a lot of trading cards. One was old, and a collector offered her fifty dollars for it.

▶ Look for stringy sentences in your story, and rewrite them to make them clearer.

▶ # Proofread Your Story

Proofread your story, using the Proofreading Checklist and the Grammar and Spelling Connections. Proofread for one skill at a time. Use a class dictionary to check spellings.

Proofreading Checklist

Did I
- ✔ indent each paragraph?
- ✔ begin and end sentences correctly?
- ✔ write dialogue correctly?
- ✔ make subjects and verbs agree?
- ✔ spell all words correctly?

📖 Use the Guide to Capitalization, Punctuation, and Usage on page H55.

Proofreading Marks

¶   Indent
∧   Add
⌐   Delete
≡   Capital letter
/   Small letter

HELP ?

Proofreading Tip

Read your story aloud to a friend. You may notice mistakes when you hear them.

Grammar and Spelling Connections

Writing Dialogue Put quotation marks around a speaker's exact words. Put the end punctuation inside the quotation marks.

"Watch out for the runaway horses!" warned Jake Johnson.
Theresa said slyly, "I know who can solve the mystery."

GRAMMAR LINK ▶ *See also pages 182 and 184.*

Subject-Verb Agreement
Use singular verbs with singular subjects. Use plural verbs with plural subjects.

Singular Subjects	Plural Subjects
The eagle scoops me up.	The eagles scoop me up.
It circles the sky.	They circle the sky.

GRAMMAR LINK ▶ *See also page 104.*

Spelling Long *i* The |ī| sound is often spelled *i, igh,* or *i*-consonant-*e*.

mild, slight, strike

📖 See the Spelling Guide on page H65.

▶ Publish Your Story

❶ Make a neat final copy of your story. Be sure you have fixed all mistakes.

❷ Title your story. Make your audience curious with a title that attracts their attention, such as "There's More Than One Way to Scare a Pig," rather than "A Scared Pig."

> **GRAMMAR TIP** Capitalize the first, last, and all important words in the title.

❸ Publish or share your story. Think about your audience to help you decide how to share. See the Ideas for Sharing box.

Ideas for Sharing

Write It
⭐ Make your story into a picture book for a young child.
• Write your story in the form of a comic strip.

Say It
• With a partner or small group, read your story aloud as though it is on the radio.

Show It
• Make puppets of the main characters.
• Act out your story with props. See page 324 for tips.

Tips for Making a Picture Book

• Plan what part of the story you will put on each page.
• Include interesting pictures to illustrate the story.
• Make an eye-catching cover with a title.

▶ Reflect

Write about your writing experience. Use these questions to get started.

• What did you enjoy most about writing your story? What was hard to do?
• How does this story compare with other papers you have written?

Writing Prompts

Use these prompts as story ideas or to practice for a test. Decide who your audience will be, and write your story in a way that they will understand and enjoy.

1 Write a fantasy story about an animal that becomes a hero. Where will the story take place? What problem does the animal solve? Will your story be silly? scary?

2 A character is walking through the woods and discovers a footprint that is eight feet long. Write a story that tells what happens next.

3 Write a story about a character who finds a jeweled box that has a secret message inside. Who finds the box? What does the secret message say? What does the character do next?

4 What would it be like to live on the moon? What would everyday life be like? What problems could happen? Write a story about a character living in a moon colony one hundred years from now.

Writing Across the Curriculum

5 FINE ART

Who is the girl in this picture? Where is she going, or where has she been on her bicycle? Does the dog belong to her? Write a story about the girl and the dog.

Oklahoma City Art Museum

Carri and Cocoa, by Robert Vickrey

✓ Test Practice

This prompt to write a story is like ones you might find on a writing test. Read the prompt.

> **Write a story about a character who finds a jeweled box that has a secret message inside. Who finds the box? What does the secret message say? What does the character do next?**

Here are some strategies to help you do a good job responding to a prompt like this.

Remember that a story is a narrative made up by the author.

❶ Look for clue words that tell what to write about. What are the clue words in the prompt above?

❷ Choose a topic that fits the clue words. Write the clue words and your topic.

Clue Words	My Topic
a character who finds a jeweled box that has a secret message inside	I will write about a detective who discovers a treasure map inside a jeweled box.

❸ Plan your writing. Use a story map.

Characters	Setting	Plot
		Beginning: Middle: End:

❹ You will get a good score if you remember the description of what kind of story rings the bell in the rubric on page 312.

Go to www.eduplace.com/kids/hme/ for graphic organizers.

Writing a Play

A **play** is a story written to be performed on a stage by actors. The author tells the story through the characters' words and actions. Read Jillian's play.

Burgers and Nuts

Characters

Props

NARRATOR
MR. DOE NUT
MS. HAM BURGER
CUSTOMER ONE
CUSTOMER TWO
CUSTOMER THREE

Two tables and six chairs
Paper plates
Cutouts of doughnuts and hamburgers
Tray for doughnut samples
Clear plastic bottle with red liquid
Clear plastic bottle with brown liquid

Scene ——————> **SCENE ONE**

Setting ——————> *(The setting is outside* MR. DOE NUT's *shop.)*

Stage directions *(*MS. HAM BURGER *is outside* MR. DOE NUT's *shop sprinkling red hot sauce onto doughnuts on a tray.)*

NARRATOR: Mr. Doe Nut and Ms. Ham Burger each own a food shop. The shops are next door to each other, and the shopkeepers have always competed for customers.

Dialogue

MS. HAM BURGER: Get your free doughnut sample here! Try Mr. Doe Nut's new flavor!

CUSTOMER ONE: *(Takes a sample and starts coughing, gagging)* Yuck! These doughnuts taste terrible. Who wants spicy doughnuts? I'm never coming here again!

(Two other CUSTOMERS *come along and sample the doughnuts. They cough, gag, and leave disgusted.)*

MS. HAM BURGER: Why don't you come next door for a hamburger?

more ▶

MR. DOE NUT: (*MR. DOE NUT sees* MS. HAM BURGER *taking his customers.*) Where's everyone going? What have you done to my doughnuts, Ms. Ham Burger?

SCENE TWO

(*The setting is* MS. HAM BURGER's *shop.*)

MR. DOE NUT: (*Walking into the shop and speaking in a sly voice*) Why, hello, Ms. Burger. I have something for you. (*He pulls a bottle of brown liquid out of his apron pocket.*) It's a new cooking oil. It will make your burgers taste terrific. It smells like syrup, but it works like cooking oil, and customers love it!

MS. HAM BURGER: Gee, that's great! Thanks!

(MS. HAM BURGER *takes the bottle, although she's a bit suspicious.*)

MR. DOE NUT: Have a nice day! (*He walks out giggling.*)

(MS. HAM BURGER *cooks a fresh batch of hamburgers with* MR. DOE NUT's *sauce and serves them to two customers who come in.*)

CUSTOMER TWO: (*Taking a bite*) Oh, gross! This tastes awful!

CUSTOMER THREE: Yuck! What is that terrible taste? I'm never coming here again!

(MS. HAM BURGER *looks at the bottle from* MR. DOE NUT *and storms out of her shop.*)

SCENE THREE

(*The setting is* MR. DOE NUT's *shop.*)

MS. HAM BURGER: (*Racing into* MR. DOE NUT's *shop*) You . . . you knew that wasn't cooking oil!

MR. DOE NUT: That's right. Just like you knew that awful hot sauce would ruin my doughnuts!

MS. HAM BURGER: *(Sighs)* This is crazy.

MR. DOE NUT: We should work this out. *(Holds out his hand)*

MS. HAM BURGER: *(Looking at the floor)* I guess so. *(Shaking hands with MR. DOE NUT)* You know, instead of fighting, maybe if we put our heads together, we could come up with some new ideas for a business together.

MR. DOE NUT: As a matter of fact, I have a great idea! I can use the syrup to make a new doughnut flavor and you can use the hot sauce on your hamburgers. *(The shopkeepers sit down and pretend to keep talking.)*

NARRATOR: Mr. Doe Nut and Ms. Ham Burger became best of friends. Two months later they opened a new shop called Burgers and Nuts. Business has never been better.

CURTAIN

Reading As a Writer

- The list of **characters** tells who is in the play. *Who are the characters in Jillian's play?*
- The **props** are the items the characters will use in the play. *What props are used in Jillian's play?*
- A **scene** presents the action that happens in one place at a certain time. *What happens in Scene One?*
- The **setting** tells where and when the action takes place. *What is the setting for Scene One?*
- The **stage directions** tell what the characters do, how they do it, and how they speak. *Which stage directions in Scene Two tell what the customers do?*
- The **dialogue** is what the characters say. It can reveal what they are thinking, seeing, and feeling. *What does Ms. Ham Burger say when she races into Mr. Doe Nut's shop at the beginning of Scene Three?*

more ▶

How to Write a Play

❶ Think about your audience. Choose a story idea for a short play that will interest or entertain them. You will need characters who do a lot of talking. Include only a few characters and one or two settings.

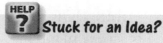

Stuck for an Idea?

Try one of these.
- a favorite story or scene from a book
- a story of your own
- an exciting, funny, or surprising experience that you or someone else had

You can use a T-chart to help you list details about your characters. Look at the sample T-chart below for Mr. Doe Nut and Ms. Ham Burger. Notice that the characters' names are across the top and details about each character are listed below his or her name.

Mr. Doe Nut	Ms. Ham Burger
• owns a food shop	• owns a food shop
• competes with Ms. Ham Burger for business	• competes with Mr. Doe Nut for business
• forgiving	• prankster

❷ Plan your play. Just like a story, a play has a beginning, a middle, and an end. Look at the story map below to help you plan your play. Add more details about your characters, setting, and plot as you plan.

Character	Setting	Plot
		Beginning
		Middle
		End

❸ Write your play.

- List your characters.
- Write stage directions telling what actions the characters will be taking at the beginning of the play.
- Write the dialogue. Write it the way you think the characters would talk. The dialogue should help tell the story.
- Write more stage directions throughout the play to tell how the characters talk and act.
- If the action moves from one place to another, divide your play into scenes. Describe each setting in stage directions.
- End your play in a way that wraps up the action. When you have finished, write BLACKOUT or CURTAIN.

❹ Revise your play. Ask yourself these questions.

- Is the plot clear?
- Does the characters' dialogue sound natural?
- Should any characters be taken out or added?
- Do the final events make the play feel finished?

❺ Proofread your play. Use a dictionary to check your spelling. Check that you have included punctuation such as exclamation points and question marks. These will help the actors read their lines with feeling.

❻ Make a neat final copy.

❼ Perform your play for an audience, such as your classmates or another class.

HELP ? See pages 324–325 for tips on dramatizing.

Ask some classmates to read the draft of your play aloud with you. Do they have any suggestions?

Dramatizing

Have you ever thought about being an actor? Actors dramatize, or act out, characters from stories, poems, or plays. They do this by speaking and moving the way they think the characters would.

Start Thinking

Read the example below. How do you think Annika feels? How might the sound of her voice change as she talks?

> "We played our hearts out, but we still lost the game. The most frustrating part is that we only lost by two points. I know we can play better next week if everyone keeps practicing. If we all put in some extra practice time this weekend, we could be great!"

Look at the photographs below. Can you figure out which face goes with which words or phrases from the example? If you were to act out the example, how and when would you change the look on your face? Would your expressions look like Annika's?

Here are some guides to help you dramatize a story, a poem, or a play.

Guides for Dramatizing

1. Put yourself in your character's shoes. What is the character like? How does the character feel?

2. Use your speaking voice. Change the volume, rate, pitch, and tone of your voice to show your character's feelings and mood. A shaky, high voice could show fear. A low, loud voice might show courage.

Using Your Voice	
volume	means loudness
rate	means speed
pitch	means how high or how low it sounds
tone	means mood

3. Use facial expressions. A wink might tell your audience that your character is up to something.

4. Use movements instead of words to show what you mean. A character might shrug his shoulders when he doesn't know how to answer a question.

5. Speak clearly but naturally. Think about your audience and the place in which you will be performing. Be sure everyone can hear you.

6. Practice reading your lines. Write key words or entire lines on note cards. Use these if you need a hint to remember your lines.

Apply It

Choose a poem or part of a story or play to dramatize. Follow the Guides for Dramatizing as you practice. Perform for another group or for the class.

- What was your character's mood? Did it change?
- In what ways did you show different feelings?
- What worked well? What would you do differently if you were to dramatize this character again?

Comparing Stories in Books and Movies

Movies are often made from stories that were first written in books. Often moviemakers change the stories. That's because books and movies tell stories in different ways.

The chart below shows some of the reasons why telling a story in a book is different from telling it in a movie.

Reading the Story	Watching the Story
Books use words to tell the story. The words describe the characters and the setting. Readers use the words to create pictures in their minds.	Movies use images and sounds to tell the story. The audience sees and hears the characters. Often, the action takes place in settings built by the moviemakers.
Readers can tell what a character is thinking or feeling from what the writer says about the character.	Actors show what the characters are thinking and feeling. They look, speak, and behave the way they think the characters would.
Readers can flip back and forth in a book to reread or to look ahead in the story. They can read the book as quickly or as slowly as they like.	People watching a movie in a theater cannot go back to watch something they have already seen. They also must wait to see what happens next and how the story ends.

Thinking Further

Written stories can be long or short, but most movies are about two hours long. When a story is too long for a movie, moviemakers may choose to leave out parts of it. They may add scenes when a story is too short.

Was a story you like changed when it became a movie? Use these guides to see how the movie version is different from the written story.

Guides for Comparing Stories in Books and Movies

1 Plot
- Are there events in the book that weren't in the movie? If so, why do you think they were left out?
- Are there events in the movie that weren't in the book? If so, why do you think they were added?
- Does the movie end the same way as the book?

2 Characters
- Are there any characters in the book who don't appear in the movie? Are there any characters in the movie who aren't in the book?
- Are the main characters the same in both versions? Are they different? In what ways?

3 Setting
- Is the setting in the book the same as in the movie?
- If the setting is different, how does it change the story?

Apply It

Choose a book you have read that has been made into a movie. After watching the movie, make a list of things that are the same and that are different between the two stories. Use the guides above and these questions to help you.

- Which did you like better, the book or the movie? Why?
- What were the biggest differences between the book and the movie? Why do you think these changes were made?

Books with Movie Versions
- Jumanji
- Harriet the Spy
- The Secret Garden
- Sarah, Plain and Tall
- James and the Giant Peach

Explaining and Informing

What You Will Find in This Section:

Listening for Information

When you listen to the news or to your teacher explaining a science lesson, you are **listening for information**, or facts. A **fact** can be proved true. Listening for information is different from listening to a story or a report. Use these guidelines to help you be a good listener.

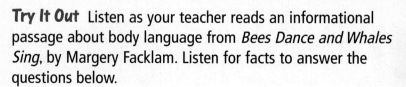

Guidelines for Listening for Information

▶ Listen for the topic. What is the author talking about?
▶ Listen for the main idea. What does the author have to say about the topic?
▶ Listen for details such as facts. How do they tell more about the main idea?
▶ Listen for the author's purpose. Why is the author telling about this topic?

Try It Out Listen as your teacher reads an informational passage about body language from *Bees Dance and Whales Sing*, by Margery Facklam. Listen for facts to answer the questions below.

- What is the topic?
- What is the main idea?
- What facts does the author use?
- Why do you think Margery Facklam wrote this piece?

See www.eduplace.com/kids/ for information about Margery Facklam.

Writing Informational Paragraphs

A paragraph that gives factual information is called an **informational paragraph.** The writer's purpose is to share information about a topic he or she knows well. An informational paragraph has a topic and a main idea. The **topic** is the subject of the paragraph. The **main idea** is what the writer wants to say about the topic. What is the topic of the informational paragraph below? What is the main idea?

Remember, the first line of a paragraph is indented.

Indent ——
Topic sentence ——

    The capybara is an unusual-looking animal. It has a large head with a blunt, square nose and jaw. Its front legs are

Supporting sentences ——

slightly shorter than its hind legs, and its toes are webbed. The capybara has a thick body that is covered with rough hair and ends in a short tail. It grows up to four feet long and may weigh more than one hundred

Closing sentence ——

pounds, about the size of a small pig. If animals had beauty contests, the capybara probably wouldn't win!

Topic Sentence

The topic is the capybara. The main idea is that the capybara is an unusual-looking animal. Which sentence states the topic and the main idea?

Supporting Sentences

The labels show the three parts of an informational paragraph.

Closing Sentence

- The **topic sentence** introduces the topic and states the writer's main idea.
- **Supporting sentences** usually follow the topic sentence and tell more about the main idea.
- The **closing sentence** finishes the paragraph.

Think and Discuss Reread the capybara paragraph above.

- What facts are given in the supporting sentences?

The Topic Sentence

You've learned that in an informational paragraph the **topic sentence** names the subject and tells what the writer wants to say about it. It is often the first sentence in the paragraph. A good topic sentence will also grab the reader's interest.

Topic   Main idea

Example: The capybara is an unusual-looking animal.

What are the topic and the main idea of these topic sentences?

- Even though they are no longer a major means of transportation, horses are still useful to people in many ways.
- The cotton gin, a machine that separates the seeds from cotton fibers, made it easier to manufacture cotton.

Try It Out Read each paragraph below. Each is missing the topic sentence. On your own or with a partner, write the topic and the main idea of each paragraph. Then write two possible topic sentences for each.

1. _____Topic sentence_____. The top layer is usually waxy or tough, which helps keep water inside the leaf. The middle layer is where a leaf makes its food. The bottom layer contains tiny holes, which allow water vapor, oxygen, and other gases to go in and out of the leaf. Together these layers work to make the leaf strong and healthy.

2. _____Topic sentence_____. The White House, where the President lives and works, is located in Washington, D.C. The city also has monuments to three American presidents—the Jefferson Memorial, the Washington Monument, and the Lincoln Memorial. Famous buildings there include the United States Capitol, the Supreme Court, and the museums of the Smithsonian Institution. You will need at least a week to see most of this city's historic spots.

Supporting Sentences

Supporting sentences usually follow the topic sentence. They contain details that explain the main idea. In informational writing, some details are facts, such as numbers. **Facts** can be proved true. Other details are **sensory words** that describe how things look, smell, feel, taste, and sound.

> Roller coasters are built to scare you. Some are 400 feet high and 5,000 feet long. A coaster's hair-raising speed can strike fear into a rider's heart. A California coaster, for example, zips around at 100 miles per hour. Scariest of all are the steep drops. On some coasters, the fall can be 200 feet. That's like dropping from a 10-story building! No wonder people scream!

Think and Discuss What facts do you find about roller coasters? What sensory words?

Ordering Details Supporting sentences are arranged in an order that makes sense. In the capybara paragraph on page 331, the details start at the animal's head and work backward. Details in the roller coaster paragraph above are arranged from least scary to scariest. **Transitional words**, such as *also, however, for example, more important,* and *finally,* help the reader see connections between sentences. How are details ordered in the paragraph below? What transitional words can you find?

> Visitors to a railroad museum discover just how different train travel was long ago. For example, the 1890 locomotive engine ran on steam. It was like a giant furnace fed by workers who shoveled chunks of dusty black coal into its firebox. Passenger cars, however, were dressed up in bright red paint, gold trim, and lacy curtains. The dining car seats were covered in soft velvet. Visitors can see how train travel was both dirtier and fancier than it is today.

HELP ? See page 16 for tips on ordering details. See page 18 for more transitional words.

more ▶

Try It Out Work on your own or with a partner. Use the diagram and the facts below to write some supporting sentences for the topic sentence. Link two of your sentences with a transitional word or phrase.

Topic sentence: The bald eagle has every tool it needs to be a fierce hunter.

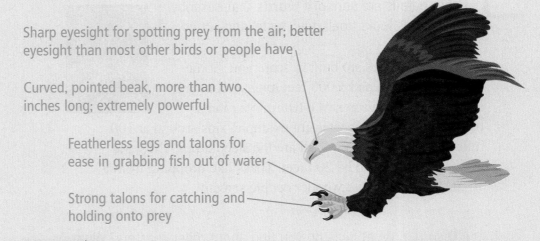

Sharp eyesight for spotting prey from the air; better eyesight than most other birds or people have

Curved, pointed beak, more than two inches long; extremely powerful

Featherless legs and talons for ease in grabbing fish out of water

Strong talons for catching and holding onto prey

GRAMMAR TIP ▶ Use a comma after most order words at the beginning of a sentence.

The Closing Sentence

The **closing sentence** wraps up the paragraph by repeating the main idea in different words or by adding one last comment. For example, the closing sentence makes a final comment in both the capybara paragraph and the roller coaster paragraph. In the railroad paragraph, the main idea is repeated, and more information is given.

Try It Out Read the paragraph below. It is missing the closing sentence. On your own or with a partner, write two possible closing sentences.

Exercise is a healthful activity. For one thing, it helps your circulatory system. As you exercise, your heart beats faster, and your heart muscle becomes stronger. Exercise also helps prevent your arteries from becoming clogged with fat. Finally, exercise helps you sleep better, so you wake up feeling ready to go. _Closing sentence_ .

Paragraphs That Compare and Contrast

One kind of informational paragraph compares and contrasts two subjects. When you tell how two subjects are alike, you **compare** them. When you show how two subjects are different, you **contrast** them.

A **paragraph that compares and contrasts** has a topic sentence, supporting sentences with details that show how the subjects are alike and different, and a closing sentence. Transitional words, such as *on the other hand* or *in contrast*, connect the supporting sentences and help the reader follow the details.

Notice which sentences compare and which contrast in the paragraph below. What transitional words and phrases do you find?

Topic sentence

Transitional word

Supporting sentences

Closing sentence

Although radio commercials and TV commercials have many things in common, they are not exactly alike. Both have the goal of selling products. In addition, they send their messages in just a few seconds. Radio is heard, however, while television is heard *and* seen. That means radio must use powerful words and sound effects to make the audience listen. Television, on the other hand, can use attractive pictures to carry part of its message. Another difference is that television and radio don't have the same audience. Because more children watch TV than listen to radio, there are more ads for toys and certain foods on television. TV and radio commercials are not exactly alike, but they are both important in the advertising world.

Try It Out Compare and contrast softball and soccer or two other sports. With a partner, list details that tell how the two subjects are alike and how they are different. Then use these details to write at least three supporting sentences. Use transitional words.

Paragraphs That Show Cause and Effect

An **informational paragraph that shows cause and effect** explains why or how one thing (cause) makes another thing (effect) happen. In this kind of paragraph, the topic sentence tells the cause, an effect, or both. The supporting sentences give more details about causes and effects. Transitional words, such as *first, then, later that day,* and *as a result,* help readers follow what happened. A closing sentence wraps up the paragraph.

Read the paragraph below. What is the cause? What are the effects?

Topic sentence — Supporting sentences — Closing sentence

> Our town has really grown! Three years ago a new store and a new factory were built. Then, because the store and the factory needed workers, new families moved into town. These families needed places to live, so builders constructed more homes and apartments. Soon we needed more schools and shops. Our town used to be small, but now it is big. It is finally catching up to its neighbors.

Try It Out On your own or with a partner, look at the picture below and read the topic sentence. Identify the cause stated in the topic sentence. Then write at least three supporting sentences that explain its effects.

Topic sentence: A power failure can cause lots of problems for a family.

Write Your Own Informational Paragraph

Now you're ready to write your own informational paragraph. You may choose to write a paragraph that compares and contrasts, one that shows cause and effect, or one that explains what something is or does.

First, think of a topic that interests you. Then make a list of details to include. After discussing your ideas with a partner, begin to write!

Checklist for My Paragraph

✔ My **topic sentence** introduces the subject and the main idea.
✔ Every **supporting sentence** gives facts and sensory details about the main idea.
✔ My **supporting sentences** are in a clear order. Transitional words make the meaning clear.
✔ My **closing sentence** repeats the main idea in different words or makes a final comment.

Looking Ahead

Once you know how to write an informational paragraph, writing a longer composition will be easy. The diagram below shows how the parts of an informational paragraph match the parts of a longer piece.

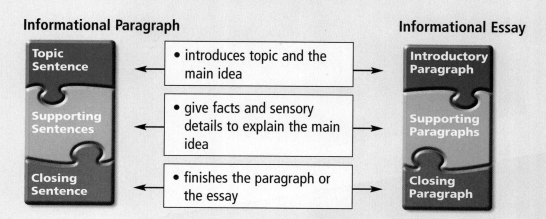

Informational Paragraph

Topic Sentence	• introduces topic and the main idea
Supporting Sentences	• give facts and sensory details to explain the main idea
Closing Sentence	• finishes the paragraph or the essay

Informational Essay

Introductory Paragraph

Supporting Paragraphs

Closing Paragraph

Writing Instructions

Now what do I do?

In "Knuckle Down That Taw!" Beth Kennedy gives instructions for a marble game called *ringer.* What steps does she describe for playing this game?

Highlights
for Children

JANUARY 1998

Fun with a Purpose

Knuckle Down That Taw!

by Beth Kennedy

The game of marbles dates back to ancient times. Historians think that children in Egypt, Rome, and North America may have played marbles thousands of years ago. In fact, signs of marble playing have been found in countries all over the world.

Marbles from long ago were not like those of today. People used stones, clay balls, nuts, and fruit pits as the first marbles. Later, people made marbles from materials such as glass, china, and real chips of marble. This gave the game its present name.

Adults as well as children enjoy marbles. Some people say that Presidents George Washington and Thomas Jefferson liked to play. Abraham Lincoln is thought to have been an expert at a marble game called *old bowler.*

How do you play marbles? Here are directions for *ringer,* a game that is popular today.

Getting Ready

Find a large flat surface where it's safe to play. It can be outside or inside. Use chalk or string to make a circle that is ten feet from one side to the other. Inside the circle, place thirteen marbles in the shape of a cross. Each marble should be three inches from the next one. These target marbles are sometimes called *mibs.*

How to Shoot

Turn your hand so that at least one knuckle rests on the ground. This is called "knuckling down." Hold your shooting marble between your curled index and middle fingers. Aim, then flick the shooter with your thumb. Shooters are also called *taws,* and they may be larger than the target marbles.

Let's Play!

From outside the circle, shoot at the marbles in the cross shape. Try to knock them out of the circle without having your shooter roll out. Shoot again from the spot where your shooter stopped. Your turn ends when you fail to knock a marble out of the circle or when your shooter rolls out.

Players take turns. The winner is the player who has knocked out the most marbles by the end of the game.

Ringer is just one kind of marble game. There are dozens of other marble games you can learn to play. So polish up those mibs and taws, call your friends, and knuckle down to an exciting and historic game.

Reading As a Writer

Think About the Instructions

- What are the steps for playing marbles? What would happen if the steps were out of order?
- In "Getting Ready," what details does the author give about the kind of surface to play on? What problem might a player have if the author left out these details?
- What information does the author put in the last paragraph? Why is this better than stopping with the last step?

Think About Writer's Craft

- Why are the headings in bold print helpful?

Think About the Picture

- What additional information about playing marbles is shown in the picture on page 340?

Responding

Write responses to these questions.

- **Personal Response** Explain why *ringer* does or does not seem like an interesting game to play.
- **Critical Thinking** Think of a game you know. How is the game like *ringer*? How is it different?

What Makes Great Instructions?

Instructions explain how to do something.

Remember to follow these guidelines when you write instructions.

▶ Begin with an interesting topic sentence that states the main idea.

▶ List all the materials that will be needed.

▶ Include all the steps. Leave out anything that doesn't belong.

▶ Put the steps in the correct order. Use order words.

▶ Include exact details that make each step clear.

▶ End with a closing sentence that wraps up the instructions.

GRAMMAR CHECK

Use commas to separate three or more items in a series. Put a comma after each item except the last one.

WORKING DRAFT

Colin McMillan enjoys building models. He made a papier-mâché model of a hot-air balloon and wrote down the instructions so his classmates could make one. Here is a working draft of his instructions.

Colin McMillan

> This is a great beginning!

Do you like high-flying adventure? Well, ~~get ready~~ strap on your safety belts. I'll show you how to make a model hot-air balloon.

First, make a papier-mâché balloon. Blow up the balloon and knot it. ~~I used a balloon left over from my last birthday party.~~ Take the newspaper and tear it up into strips. Put some papier-mâché paste into a bowl. You can also make papier-mâché

> Does this part belong in your instructions?

masks this way. Take a piece of paper and ~~put~~ dip it into the paste. Take the strip of paper and lay it on the balloon. Do that with lots of strips of newspaper until the whole balloon is covered. Leave a space at the bottom. Give it another four layers of newspaper dipped in the paste. Once the balloon is dry, it's time to pop the balloon and pull it out.

more

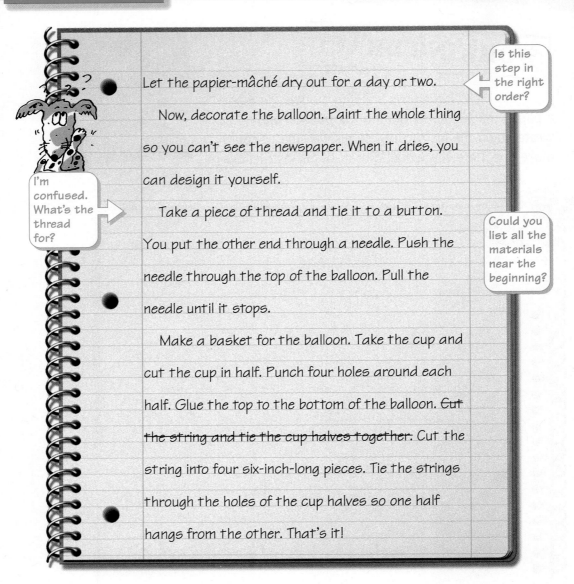

Is this step in the right order?

Let the papier-mâché dry out for a day or two.

Now, decorate the balloon. Paint the whole thing so you can't see the newspaper. When it dries, you can design it yourself.

I'm confused. What's the thread for?

Take a piece of thread and tie it to a button. You put the other end through a needle. Push the needle through the top of the balloon. Pull the needle until it stops.

Could you list all the materials near the beginning?

Make a basket for the balloon. Take the cup and cut the cup in half. Punch four holes around each half. Glue the top to the bottom of the balloon. ~~Cut the string and tie the cup halves together.~~ Cut the string into four six-inch-long pieces. Tie the strings through the holes of the cup halves so one half hangs from the other. That's it!

Reading As a Writer

- What did Sal like about Colin's instructions? What questions did he have? What changes could Colin make to answer Sal's questions?
- Look at the second paragraph on page 343. Why did Colin cross out a sentence?
- What questions would you like to ask Colin about his instructions?

FINAL COPY

Colin revised his instructions after discussing them with his classmates. Read his final version to see what changes he made.

How to Make a Model Hot-Air Balloon
by Colin McMillan

Do you like high-flying adventure? Well, strap on your safety belts. I'll show you how to make a model hot-air balloon.

Before you begin, you need to get your supplies. You will need newspaper, papier-mâché paste, a bowl, a rubber balloon, a paintbrush, poster paint, thread, a needle, a button, a large plastic cup, scissors, string, and glue. Don't worry, when you're done, you'll think it's worth it.

First, make a papier-mâché balloon. Blow up the balloon and knot it. Then take the newspaper and tear it up into one-inch-wide and six-inch-long strips. Next, put some papier-mâché paste into a bowl. Take a piece of paper and dip it into the paste. After that, take the strip of paper and lay it on the balloon. Do that with lots of strips of newspaper until the whole balloon is covered. Leave a space big enough for your fist at the bottom. Give it another four layers of newspaper dipped in the paste. Let the papier-mâché dry out for a day or two. Once the balloon is dry, it's time to pop the balloon and pull it out.

You've listed all the materials at the beginning. Good!

You took out the part about the masks. Good! It didn't keep to the topic.

You've added more order words. That's great!

more

Now, decorate the balloon. Paint the whole thing so you can't see the newspaper. When it dries, you can design it yourself.

Next, take a two-foot-long piece of thread and tie it to a button. You put the other end through a needle. From inside the balloon, push the needle through the top of the balloon. Pull the needle until it stops. The button keeps the thread secure. At the needle end, you tie a knot at the end of the thread so you can hang the balloon up.

Now I understand how to do this step—and why!

Finally, make a basket for the balloon. Take the cup and cut the cup in half. Then punch four holes around each half. Glue the top to the bottom of the balloon. Cut the string into four six-inch-long pieces. Tie the strings through the holes of the cup halves so one half hangs from the other. Now you can hang up your balloon and imagine yourself sailing away in it.

Reading As a Writer

- What changes did Colin make after thinking about Sal's questions? What else did Colin do that Sal liked?
- Look at the third paragraph on page 345. What detail did Colin add about the strips of newspapers? Why is this detail important?
- Compare the endings in Colin's working draft and final copy. Why is the ending in the final draft better?

 See www.eduplace.com/kids/hme/ for more examples of student writing.

Write Instructions

▶ Start Thinking

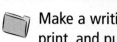

Make a writing folder for your instructions. Copy the questions in bold print, and put the paper in your folder. Write your answers as you think about and choose your topic.

- **Who will be my audience?** Will it be my classmates? a family member? a younger child?
- **What will be my purpose?** Do I want to explain how to do something? how to make something?
- **How will I publish or share my instructions?** Will I write a "How To" book? give a demonstration? make a poster?

HELP ? Stuck for a Topic?

Use these questions.
- What do I like to do in my free time?
- What could I make for someone?
- What am I good at doing?

See page 357 for more ideas.

▶ Choose Your Topic

❶ **List** five topics you could write instructions for. Colin made a list to help him think of topics.

Games I Know
checkers
dodge ball

Things I Can Make
paper airplane
model of a hot-air balloon
key rack

Work I Can Do
feed the cats

❷ **Discuss** each topic idea with a partner. Would your audience like to learn how to do this? Can you explain the topic in a few paragraphs?

❸ **Ask** yourself these questions about each topic. Circle the topic you will write about.
- Have I done this myself? Do I know all the steps?
- Would I enjoy explaining how to do this?

► Explore Your Topic

❶ Think about your "how-to" topic. Picture yourself doing it.

❷ Draw pictures or diagrams of the steps. Write notes about what is happening. Colin drew these pictures.

make basket

attach thread

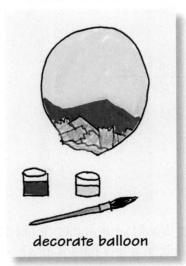

decorate balloon

make papier-mâché balloon

❸ Use your pictures or diagrams to explain the steps to a partner. Have your partner ask about anything that is not clear.

HELP? See page 14 for other ideas for exploring your topic.

Focus Skill

Organizing Your Instructions

Think of your instructions as stepping-stones across a brook. Your audience must follow the steps in order. Otherwise, they might fall in!

Put your steps in the right order. If the order doesn't make sense, your audience might be confused and make a mistake.

Use order words. Order words signal the sequence of steps. Use order words such as *first, second, next, finally, at the end, when, before, later, during, while*.

Colin numbered his pictures in order. Then he made a Step-by-Step Chart. Here is part of Colin's chart.

Steps	Materials Needed	Details
1. First, make a papier-mâché balloon.	rubber balloon newspaper bowl paste poster paint paintbrush	
2. Now, decorate the balloon.		

Think and Discuss Look back at Colin's pictures on page 348.

- What should steps 3 and 4 be on Colin's chart?
- What order words could he add to steps 3 and 4?

▶ Plan Your Instructions

❶ **Number** your pictures in the right order.

❷ **Use** the pictures to help you make a Step-by-Step Chart. List your steps with order words. Write the materials for each step.

Focus Skill

Using Details

Include exact details for each step so that your audience won't make a mistake. Be sure to include all the important details. Remember that your audience has never followed your instructions before.

Without Exact Details	**With Exact Details**
Cut the string and tie the cup halves together.	Cut the string into four six-inch-long pieces. Tie the strings through the holes of the cup halves so one half hangs from the other.

Think and Discuss Compare the examples above.

- Which example is clearer? Why?
- What might happen if the exact details were left out of the instructions?

▶ Draft Your Instructions

1 **Add** details to your Step-by-Step Chart. Here is an example from Colin's chart.

Steps	Materials Needed	Details
1. First, make a papier-mâché balloon.	rubber balloon newspaper bowl paste	blow up balloon tear newspaper put strips in paste

2 **Use your chart** to help you write your instructions. It's never too late to add more details if you need them.

3 **Skip** every other line. You can make corrections and changes later.

4 **Read** your instructions to a partner. Have your partner pantomime the steps.

HELP ? **Paragraph Tip**

Start a new paragraph when you begin a step that has many details.

Focus Skill

Good Beginnings and Endings

When you write instructions, think of yourself as a coach. Your beginning should get your team interested in the game, and your ending should leave them eager to play.

A good beginning includes a topic sentence that states the main idea. The beginning should also catch the interest of your audience.

Weak Beginning	Strong Beginning
This is how to grow carrots.	Here's how to have fun outdoors and grow the best carrots you've ever eaten.

A good ending wraps up your instructions. End with a closing sentence that makes your audience want to try out your instructions.

Weak Ending	Strong Ending
Now you can pick and eat your carrots.	After tasting your fresh, homegrown carrots, you'll never want to eat canned or frozen carrots again.

Try It Out With a partner compare the examples above.

- Write a different strong beginning.
- Write a different strong ending.

Draft Your Beginning and Ending

Don't just end with the last step.

❶ **Write** two beginnings and two endings for your instructions.

❷ **Choose** the beginning and ending you like better.

Evaluating Your Instructions

▶ **Reread** your instructions. What do you need to do to make them better? Use this rubric to help you decide. Write the sentences that describe your instructions.

Rings the Bell!

- ■ The beginning includes a topic sentence that tells what the instructions are about.
- ■ I included all the steps and listed the necessary materials.
- ■ All of the steps are in order, and I used order words.
- ■ Details make each step clear.
- ■ The ending wraps up the instructions in a fun or useful way.
- ■ *There are almost no mistakes in capitalization, punctuation, and spelling.*

Getting Stronger

- ■ The beginning could be more interesting.
- ■ A few steps are missing or out of order, or I forgot some materials.
- ■ I could use more order words.
- ■ A few steps need more details to make them clear.
- ■ The ending doesn't wrap up the instructions.
- ■ *There are a few mistakes.*

Try Harder

- ☐ The beginning doesn't say what my topic is.
- ☐ A lot of steps or materials that are needed are missing or in the wrong place.
- ☐ I forgot to include order words.
- ☐ Most of the steps have very few details.
- ☐ My instructions just end with the last step.
- ■ *There are a lot of mistakes.*

 See www.eduplace.com/kids/hme/ to interact with this rubric.

▶ Revise Your Instructions

1 **Revise** your instructions. Use the list of sentences you wrote from the rubric. Work on the parts that you described with sentences from "Getting Stronger" and "Try Harder."

2 **Discuss** your instructions in a writing conference.

When You're the Writer Read your instructions to a partner. Discuss any problems you're having. Take notes to remember what your partner says.

When You're the Listener Tell at least two things you like about the instructions. Ask questions about anything that is unclear. Use the chart below as a guide.

HELP
? **Revising Tip**

To add a step, write it on another piece of paper. Label it with a letter, such as *A*. Put a caret where the new step goes and write "Insert A."

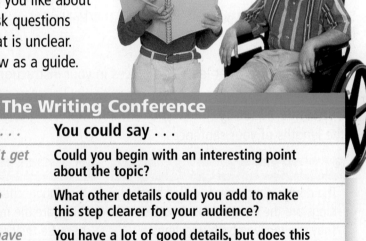

What should I say?

The Writing Conference	
If you're thinking . . .	**You could say . . .**
The beginning doesn't get me interested.	**Could you begin with an interesting point about the topic?**
I can't picture how to do this step.	**What other details could you add to make this step clearer for your audience?**
What does this part have to do with the topic?	**You have a lot of good details, but does this really belong in the instructions?**
I'm confused.	**Are the steps in the right order?**
The instructions just end with the last step.	**Can you add something to wrap up the instructions?**

3 **Make more revisions** to your instructions. Use your conference notes and the Revising Strategies on the next page.

Revising Strategies

Elaborating: Word Choice Use exact verbs to tell your audience exactly what to do.

Without Exact Verbs	With Exact Verbs
Make a row of holes in the paper. Then **put** the yarn through them.	Punch a row of holes in the paper. Then weave the yarn through them.

▶ Change at least two verbs in your instructions to be more exact.

📖 Use the Thesaurus Plus on page H79. See also page 118.

Elaborating: Details Insert adverbs to add details to help your audience picture the steps of your instructions more clearly.

Without Adverbs	With Adverbs
Open the lid. Hold the oars and pull.	Open the lid slightly. Hold the oars firmly and pull hard.

▶ Add adverbs in at least two places in your instructions.

Sentence Fluency Make your writing interesting to your readers by varying the lengths of your sentences.

All the Same Length	Different Lengths
The double checkers are called kings. Kings are the most useful checkers. They can move in both directions.	The double checkers are called kings. Kings are the most useful checkers because they can move in both directions.

▶ Find a group of at least three sentences in your instructions that are all short or all long. Rewrite them to vary their lengths.

GRAMMAR LINK ▶ *See also pages 49 and 211.*

Proofread Your Instructions

Proofread your instructions, using the Proofreading Checklist and the Grammar and Spelling Connections. Proofread for one skill at a time. Use a class dictionary to check spellings.

Proofreading Checklist

Did I
- ✔ indent all paragraphs?
- ✔ correct run-on sentences?
- ✔ use commas correctly?
- ✔ use negatives correctly?
- ✔ correct any spelling errors?

📖 Use the Guide to Capitalization, Punctuation, and Usage on page H55.

Proofreading Marks
¶ Indent
∧ Add
⤶ Delete
≡ Capital letter
/ Small letter

Tech Tip
Scroll down your instructions until just the top line shows. Then proofread your instructions one line at a time.

Grammar and Spelling Connections

Negatives Words that contain the meaning "no" or "not" are called negatives. Never use two negatives together in a sentence.

Incorrect: Play until there aren't no letters left.

Correct: Play until there aren't any letters left.

Correct: Play until there are no letters left.

GRAMMAR LINK *See also page 242.*

Commas in a Series Use commas to separate three or more items in a series. Put a comma after each item except the last one.

You need sand, food coloring, paper, a pencil, and glue.

GRAMMAR LINK *See also page 176.*

Spelling Long *o* The |ō| sound is often spelled *o, o*-consonant-*e, oa,* or *ow.*

no, note, float, grow   📖 See the Spelling Guide on page H65.

▶ Publish Your Instructions

❶ Make a neat final copy of your instructions. Check to make sure you corrected all mistakes.

❷ Write a title for your instructions. The title should make the topic clear and stir up interest in it. For example, "The Smart, Safe Way to Bike" is better than "How to Ride a Bike."

GRAMMAR TIP ▶ *Capitalize the first, the last, and each important word in a title.*

❸ Publish or share your instructions in a way that suits your audience. See the Ideas for Sharing box.

How to Stand on Your Head

1. Get into a kneeling position. Put your forehead and hands on the floor.

2. Raise your knees and rest them on your elbows.

3. Slowly raise your legs until they are straight.

Tips for Making a Poster

- Use color to make the main ideas stand out.
- Make separate sections for the materials and each main step.
- Number the steps.
- Include helpful photos or drawings.

Ideas for Sharing

Write It
- Make a class "How To" activity book.
- Make an instructions sheet. Use a computer to create a layout.

Say It
- Present the instructions to a group as you demonstrate.

Show It
- Make a poster.

▶ Reflect

Write about your writing experience. Use these questions to get started.

- What was challenging about writing instructions? What was easy?
- What will you do differently the next time you write instructions?
- How do your instructions compare with other papers you have written?

Writing Prompts

Use these prompts as ideas for writing instructions or to practice for a test. Some of them fit with other subjects you study. Decide who your audience will be, and write your instructions in a way that they will understand and enjoy.

1 Do you collect something, such as stamps, cards, or shells? Write instructions for how to start, build, or take care of a collection.

2 What do you do to help out at home? Write instructions for a chore you know how to do, such as setting the table or washing clothes.

3 Do you have your own special way of doing something? Have you discovered the perfect way to entertain a cat? get to sleep? eat a slice of pizza? Share your secret by writing instructions for it.

4 Imagine that you are entertaining a young child on a rainy day. What indoor game or activity do you know that the child could learn? Write the instructions for the game or activity.

Writing Across the Curriculum

5 SCIENCE
Write instructions for doing a science experiment. Include materials and safety information.

6 ART
Write instructions explaining how to do an art or crafts project. Can you make a necklace? paint a picture? Include a materials list.

7 MATH
Suppose you had a huge bank loaded with pennies, nickels, dimes, quarters, and half dollars. Write instructions for an easy way to count the money.

8 PHYSICAL EDUCATION
What athletic skill could you teach to a beginner? Can you hit a baseball? do a simple dive? skate without falling? Write instructions to help a beginner get started.

✓ Test Practice

Sometimes on a test you will be asked to write a paper in response to a picture prompt like this one.

Remember that instructions explain the steps for doing something.

These pictures show how to make a bookmark. Look carefully at each picture. Then **write instructions to go with the pictures that explain how to make the bookmark.**

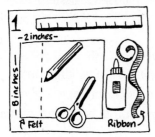
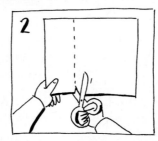

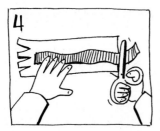
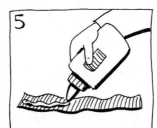

Here are some strategies to help you do a good job responding to a prompt like this one.

❶ Look at each picture and answer these questions.
- What materials are shown?
- What has been done with the materials in each picture?

❷ Plan your writing. Use the graphic organizer on page 349.

❸ You will get a good score if you remember the description of what kind of instructions ring the bell in the rubric on page 352.

Writing to Compare and Contrast

When you write to **compare**, you explain how two things are alike. When you write to **contrast**, you explain how two things are different. Read Jane's essay that explains ways in which ballet and football are different and alike.

Pointe Shoes and Cleats

Connecting words

Introduction —

Some people say ballet is just for girls, but it's not. Some say football is just for boys, but it's not. In fact, ballet and football have many things in common even though they seem very different.

Topic sentence —

It's easy to think of ways that ballet dancers and football players are different. In ballet, dancers can be short, tall, big, or small. It's not size that counts. It's flexibility. In football, though, the bigger the better, and speed helps, too. Some players need to be big to stop the other team. Some players need to run fast to carry the ball. Football players catch and throw footballs. In ballet, though, dancers catch and throw people—carefully! Finally, another difference is that ballet is danced on a stage, but football is played on a field.

Paragraph of contrast —

Topic sentence —

Ballet and football are also similar in some ways. They both take strength because practice sessions are long and hard. Both take concentration. Ballet dancers have to concentrate on all the dance steps, just as football players have to concentrate on all the plays. Also, the pointe shoes that dancers wear are as uncomfortable as football cleats. In fact, my sister who wears them says, "Pointe shoes hurt so badly I can't even say!" It takes guts to keep dancing or playing when your feet hurt.

Paragraph of comparison —

Conclusion —

The next time you see ballet dancers or football players, remember that they are more alike than you might think. They are all athletes who enjoy their sports, and we can too.

more ▶

Reading As a Writer

- The **introduction** presents the subjects being compared and contrasted. It also says something interesting about them to catch the attention of the reader.
  What does Jane say about ballet and football in her introduction that might surprise you?

- **Topic sentences** tell the main idea of each paragraph.
  What is the main idea of each topic sentence in Jane's essay?

- The **paragraph of contrast** gives details that tell how the two subjects are different.
  What differences does Jane describe?

- **Connecting words**, such as *of course, too,* and *also,* help readers move smoothly from one idea to the next.
  What connecting words does Jane use?

- The **paragraph of comparison** gives details about how the two subjects are alike.
  In what ways does Jane think that ballet and football are alike?

- The **conclusion** sums up the likenesses and differences.
  What does Jane want the reader to remember?

How to Write to Compare and Contrast

① **Choose** two subjects that are alike in some ways and different in other ways. You can pick people, places, animals, or objects. As you think about your subjects, ask yourself these questions.

- Are there at least two ways they are alike and two ways they are different?
- Will I be able to explain these likenesses and differences in writing?
- Are my choices too broad? Is there just too much to say about each subject?

Stuck for an Idea?

Here are some suggestions.

- penguins and eagles
- two places I have visited
- rock 'n' roll and hip-hop music
- my hand and my foot
- a cactus and a tree

② **List** details about each subject in a T-chart.

- Write details about one subject on the left. Write details about the other subject on the other side.
- Then find the likenesses and differences between your subjects. Draw lines to match the items in each column that are alike. See the T-chart on page 362.

Tech Tip
Make a two-column table. Use the Cut and Paste functions to line up likenesses and differences.

more ▶

Ballet	Football
Dancers can be short. They can also be tall, big, or small.	played on a field
takes strength	helps if players are big or fast
takes concentration	players catch and throw footballs
takes guts	uncomfortable shoes
for athletes	for athletes
uncomfortable shoes	takes strength
danced on a stage	takes concentration
	takes guts

▲ **Part of Jane's chart**

❸ **Organize** your details by putting them in a Venn diagram.

- Label your diagram with the names of your subjects, as shown below.
- Write what is different about each subject in the outside sections.
- Write how the subjects are alike in the inside section.

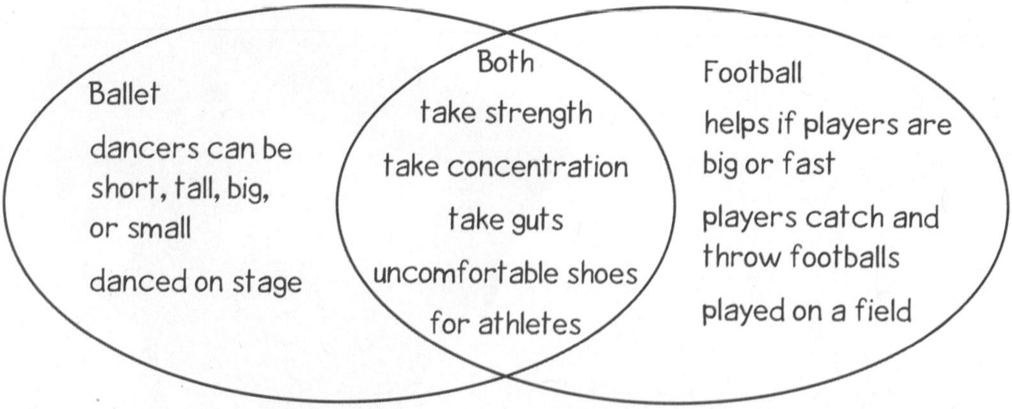

Are you having trouble finding enough details? Choose new subjects to compare and contrast.

Ballet

dancers can be short, tall, big, or small

danced on stage

Both

take strength

take concentration

take guts

uncomfortable shoes

for athletes

Football

helps if players are big or fast

players catch and throw footballs

played on a field

❹ **Introduce** your two subjects by telling something that will make your readers curious about them.

5 **Write** two paragraphs, one comparing and one contrasting your subjects.

- Write the paragraph that compares your subjects, using the details listed in the inside section of your Venn diagram.
- Write the paragraph that contrasts your subjects, using the differences listed in the outside sections.
- For each paragraph, write a clear topic sentence that gives the paragraph's main idea. Make sure all of the sentences that follow each topic sentence explain or tell more about the main idea.
- Use connecting words to help your readers pass easily from one idea to the next.

Connecting Words
To Show Likenesses and Differences in contrast   however   though   although   in fact   but
To Tell More another   also   in addition   too   finally

6 **Sum up** the likenesses and differences between your subjects in your conclusion. You could tell how you think or feel about these likenesses and differences.

7 **Revise** your essay, using the Revising Checklist.

Revising Checklist

✔ What information did I include in my introduction to get my readers' attention?

✔ Have I included at least two likenesses and two differences?

✔ Did I write all the likenesses in one paragraph and all the differences in another paragraph?

✔ Do my topic sentences clearly tell the main idea of each paragraph?

✔ Where can I add connecting words?

✔ Does my conclusion sum up the main points?

8 **Hold a writing conference.**
Take notes to remember your
partner's ideas, and then
decide whether you want to
make further changes to your
essay. These questions may
help during your conference.

The Writing Conference	
If you're thinking...	**You could say...**
This needs an introduction.	**Could you start with a question or a statement that will make your readers curious about your subjects?**
I can't tell how these subjects are different.	**Tell me more about how _____ is different from _____ .**
I can't tell how these subjects are alike.	**Tell me more about how _____ is like _____ .**
The likenesses are mixed up with the differences.	**Are you comparing or contrasting in this paragraph? Could you add a topic sentence that tells me that?**
That sentence seems out of place.	**What is this sentence telling more about? Does it tell more about the main idea of this paragraph?**
There's no conclusion.	**Can you sum up your main idea in a final paragraph?**

9 **Proofread** your essay, using the Proofreading
Checklist on page 355. Use a dictionary to
check spellings.

10 **Publish** or share a final copy
of your essay with your audience.
For example, on a long piece of
yarn you might string some
pictures showing how your
subjects are different and alike.

Giving and Following Instructions

When instructions are clear, the task or game is easier to figure out. Use these guides to give instructions.

Guides for Giving Instructions

1 Explain the purpose of the instructions.

2 Tell one step at a time. Use words such as *first, next,* and *finally* to show the order of the steps.

3 Include enough details to make each step clear. If you can, show how to do each step as you explain it.

4 Speak clearly. Adjust the volume of your voice to fit your audience and setting.

> Before you give your instructions, plan what you are going to say. Write down the steps first. Then try to follow them to see if they work.

If you follow instructions carefully, you will make fewer mistakes. These guides will help.

Guides for Following Instructions

1 Listen carefully to each step.

2 Listen to the order of the steps. Words like *first, then,* and *next* will help you.

3 Try to picture each step in your mind. If the person is showing you what to do, watch carefully.

4 Ask questions if you do not understand.

Apply It

Find or sketch a simple picture made up of different geometric shapes, including circles, triangles, and rectangles. Give instructions to your partner on how to draw the picture. Use words and phrases such as *above, on top of, to the right side,* and *below.* Switch roles and follow your partner's instructions.

- Does your partner's drawing look like the picture you described?
- How can you improve your instructions?

Comparing Visual Information

Information comes to you in many ways. Visual information is information that you see in pictures. A photograph, a diagram, a graph, a map, or a drawing can show ideas that may not be given in words.

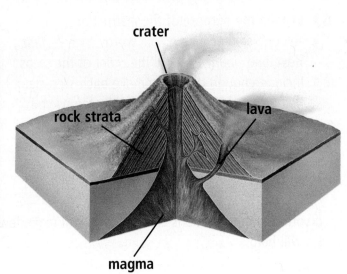

Photographs

Do photographs show things just the way they are? Not really. A photograph captures a single instant in time. Most things won't appear that way again.

Also, a camera shoots only what is in front of it. Photographers choose what to include and what to leave out in a photo. They decide on a center of interest. Their choices can make a difference in what you feel and think about when you look at a photograph.

Look at the photo of the volcano. What is the center of interest? How does the photographer bring out the idea of danger? Think about the information the photo gives about volcanoes.

Cut-away Diagrams

A cut-away diagram lets you see inside something. The artists who draw diagrams choose a center of interest for the picture. They may label different parts. Diagrams, though, often don't include as many details as a photograph.

Look at the cut-away diagram on page 366. Compare it to the photograph. What can you learn from each one? What information does the diagram give that the photograph doesn't?

Guides for Comparing Visuals

▶ Look for the center of interest in each picture, or visual. What do you think the artist or photographer is trying to show?

▶ Think about the kind of information the visuals show. Do the pictures include details? Which picture gives more information?

▶ Remember that photographers and artists leave out information in their work. Think about the kinds of information they left out of the visuals and why.

▶ Suppose that you have been given only one of the visuals to view. What information would you miss if one of them were gone?

Apply It

Use the guides above to compare the information in two different kinds of visuals. Then answer these questions.

- Did you learn more from one of the visuals than the other? Explain.
- Did either visual create a special feeling, such as enjoyment or tiredness? Why do you think this is so?
- What were the main differences between the two visuals?

Need ideas?

You can compare
- a photo and a cartoon of a famous person;
- a photo and a painting of a person, a place, or an event;
- a photo of a mountain and a relief map;
- a photo and a diagram from a news story.

NASA's *Voyager* explorations revealed more of Saturn's rings.

This report gives well-organized, detailed information about sea otters. What is the main idea of each paragraph?

What Do Sea Otters Look Like?

from *The Sea Otter*, by Alvin, Virginia, and Robert Silverstein

Sea otters have a streamlined appearance. They have a small round head, a long heavy body, and a thick, tapering tail that is flat on the bottom. Their eyes are dark, and their noses flat and diamond-shaped. Little pointed ears close when a sea otter dives underwater. The sea otter's whiskers, 4 inches long, point downward to act like feelers, helping the animal to find food as it swims along the bottom of the sea.

A sea otter's front paws look like mittens, but they are actually very useful hands. The backs of its front paws are covered with fur, but the palms have tough pads that help the otter to grip prey better. Its claws are retractable like those of a cat. The otter uses them to comb its fur and to snatch up clams from the sea bottom or mussels from a reef.

See www.eduplace.com/kids/ for information about Robert and Virgina Silverstein.

more ▶

The sea otter's hind feet are very different from its front paws. They are wide with long webbed toes, forming large flippers for swimming.

The average male southern sea otter is a little more than 4 feet long, including a tail about 12 inches long. He weighs about 65 pounds. The average female is a little shorter and weighs about 45 pounds. Northern sea otters are generally somewhat larger.

Reading As a Writer

Think About the Report

- What is the main idea of the first paragraph on page 369? Which sentence in this paragraph tells the main idea?
- What are the supporting details in the first paragraph?
- What facts did you learn about the size of the sea otter?

Think About Writer's Craft

- Look at the first two paragraphs. What comparisons help you picture the sea otter's whiskers and front paws?

Think About the Picture

- Look at the photo on page 369. Which details from the report are shown in the photo?

Responding

Write responses to these questions.

- **Personal Response** Which facts about the sea otter did you find surprising? Why?
- **Critical Thinking** What other animal does the sea otter make you think of? How is it the same? How is it different?

What Makes a Great Research Report?

A **research report** gives
factual information
found through research.

Remember to follow these guidelines when you write a research report.

▶ Research your topic. Organize your information carefully.

▶ Include facts, not opinions.

▶ Write an interesting opening that states the main idea.

▶ Write a paragraph for each main topic. Give supporting details.

▶ Use your own words. Don't copy!

▶ Write a closing that sums up your report.

▶ Include an accurate list of sources.

GRAMMAR CHECK

A proper noun
names a particular
person, place, or
thing. Capitalize
proper nouns.

James Lee

WORKING DRAFT

When James Lee read a story that took place in the Tropics, he decided that tropical rain forests would make a good topic for a research report. Here is his working draft.

Working Draft

Rain Forests

Tropical rain forests are a wonderful part of our environment. Many different species of plants and animals live there. Some are really strange-looking! Rain forests give us good things like food and medicine.

Your opening is great!

Tropical rain forests grow near the equator in an area called the Tropics. Brazil, Nigeria, and Thailand have rain forests. Most rain forests get at least 80 inches of rain every year. Usually they get rain all year round. It is always warm and humid, even in winter. Temperatures are between 68°F and 82°F all year.

You've done good research!

Many different kinds of plants and animals live in these forests. The rafflesia grows on the roots of vines. The smallest mammal in the world is a bat. It lives in the rain forests of Thailand. This bat is only about one inch long. Many of these plants and animals live only in the rain forest.

Can you tell more about the rafflesia? about this bat?

Things that we use every day come from the rain forest. We get rubber from the rubber tree to make tires for cars. Some medicines come from there too.

Some scientists estimate that 35 million acres of rain forest were destroyed each year in the 1990s. I think this is very bad. Well, that's everything I learned about rain forests.

> Can you give more facts about rain forests being destroyed, without stating your opinion?

Rafflesia Flower

Reading As a Writer

- What did Sal like about James's report? What suggestions does he make? What changes can James make to answer Sal's questions?
- Which sentence in the last paragraph states an opinion? What words tell you that it's an opinion?
- What else would you like to know about this topic?

James revised his report after discussing it with his classmates. Read his final copy to see what he changed.

The Wonders of the Rain Forest

by James Lee

Tropical rain forests are a wonderful part of our environment. Many different species of plants and animals live there. Some are really strange-looking! Rain forests give us good things like food and medicine.

Tropical rain forests grow near the equator in an area called the Tropics. Brazil, Nigeria, and Thailand have rain forests. Most rain forests get at least 80 inches of rain every year. Usually they get rain all year round. It is always warm and humid, even in winter. Temperatures are between 68°F and 82°F all year.

Many different kinds of plants and animals live in these forests. The rafflesia plant has the biggest flowers in the world. It grows on the roots of vines. One flower can be 3 feet wide and weigh 24 pounds. This flower actually smells like a rotting cheeseburger! The smallest mammal in the world is a bat. It is called the hog-nosed bat and lives in the rain forests of

Your information is well-organized.

Thailand. This bat is only about one inch long. Many of these plants and animals live only in the rain forest.

More Creatures of the Rain Forest

Animals	Plants
Leaf-cutter ants grow their own food. They raise funguses to eat.	**Pitcher plants** eat insects that fall into their tube-shaped leaves.
Three-toed sloths like to hang upside down from trees. They don't move much.	**Kapok trees** have huge trunks. The fruit fiber from the tree is used to fill mattresses.
Many kinds of **beetles** live in rain forests. Some can be 5 inches long.	**Lianas** are vines that climb up tall trees to reach the sunlight.
Monkeys use their tails to hold branches as they swing from tree to tree.	**Orchids** are beautiful flowers that grow on tree trunks in the forest.

Using a chart is a great idea!

Things that we use every day come from the rain forest, such as cinnamon, pineapples, bananas, sugar, and vanilla. We get rubber from the rubber tree to make tires for cars. Medicines are made from plants of the rain forest. Some medicines are used in heart and lung surgery.

These are strong supporting details.

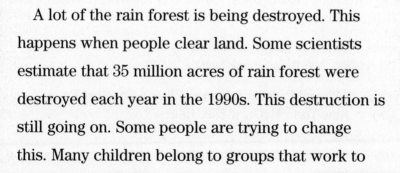

A lot of the rain forest is being destroyed. This happens when people clear land. Some scientists estimate that 35 million acres of rain forest were destroyed each year in the 1990s. This destruction is still going on. Some people are trying to change this. Many children belong to groups that work to protect these lands.

more

Scientists keep studying rain forests. They want to find cures for disease. They would like to learn more about the creatures that live there. Many people are working to preserve this part of nature.

> You've summarized like an expert!

Sources

Burton, John A. *Jungles and Rainforests*. San Diego, CA: Thunder Bay Press, 1996.

Losos, Elizabeth. "Rain Forest." *Microsoft Encarta Online Deluxe Encyclopedia*. 1997–99. 24 Nov. 2001.

Ricciuti, Edward R. *Rainforest*. Biomes of the World Series. Tarrytown, NY: Benchmark Books, 1996.

Silver, Donald, and Patricia J. Wynne (illus.). *Tropical Rain Forest*. New York: McGraw-Hill, 1998.

> This shows exactly where you found your information. That's great!

Reading As a Writer

- What did James do in response to Sal's suggestions?
- What comparison did James add to the third paragraph on page 374?
- What facts did James add about rain forests being destroyed?
- What did James do to improve his closing?

 See www.eduplace.com/kids/hme/ for more examples of student writing.

Write a Research Report

▶ Start Thinking

 Make a writing folder for your research report. Copy the questions in bold print, and put the paper in your folder. Write your answers as you think about and choose your topic.

- **Who will be my audience?** Will it be my classmates? a family member? a younger child?
- **What will be my purpose?** What do I want to learn? What do I want my readers to learn?
- **How will I publish or share my report?** Will I publish it as a magazine article? read it aloud as a news report? display it with visuals?

▶ Choose Your Topic

❶ List five possible topics by making an "I Wonder" list. Here is part of James's list.

> I Wonder
> _____
> Australia
> Wild West
> The Tropics
> Pandas

HELP ? *I Need Ideas!*

Use these questions.
- What TV shows or movies on real-life topics do you like? Which ones do you want to learn more about?
- What do you like to read about?
- Does something about the past interest you?

See page 393 for more ideas.

❷ Discuss your ideas with a partner. Which ones does your partner like? Why? Which ones do you like best?

❸ Narrow your list. Choose the top three topics you might write about. Ask yourself these questions about each one.

- Will it be interesting to research?
- Can I find information about it?
- Is it too large for a short report?

❹ Choose one topic and circle it. Keep your list of three topics in case you need them later.

▶ Explore Your Topic

❶ Narrow your topic. If it is too big, you can write about a part of it. Here is how James narrowed his topic to *tropical rain forests*.

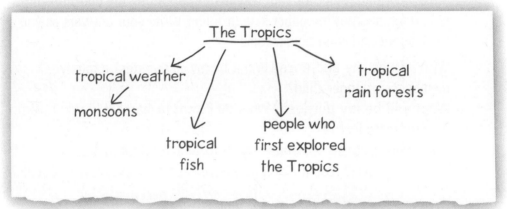

The Tropics

tropical weather

monsoons

tropical
fish

people who
first explored
the Tropics

tropical
rain forests

❷ Explore your topic by making a K-W-S chart. Write what you already know in the first column. Write your questions in the second column. Ask *Who? What? When? Where? Why? How?* Here is part of the chart that James made.

HELP
?
Read All About It!

To make sure that you're interested in your topic, read a short encyclopedia article about it.

What I Know	What I Want to Know	Possible Sources
Rain forests are wet.	What is the climate?	
They have many different plants and animals.	What are some of the interesting plants and animals?	
Rubber comes from there.	What other products come from rain forests?	
They are being destroyed.	Why are they being destroyed?	

Focus Skill

Finding the Best Information

Locating Sources

Now it's time to dig into your topic. To find information, you can talk to experts, use technology, and look in print sources.

Talk to people. Interview an expert to get inside information. You might speak to a high school biology teacher, a reporter at your local newspaper, an artist, or a person who was born in China. It all depends on your topic!

📖 See page H9 for information on interviewing.

Use technology. Surf the Internet to find online encyclopedias and Web sites related to your topic. Find out if your library has information on CD-ROM.

📖 See page H43 for more about using the Internet.

Look at print sources. Find sources in your library. Ask the librarian for help when you need it.

Your library is a gold mine of information!

Source	Examples	Tips
Encyclopedias have short entries about many topics.	*The World Book Encyclopedia*	• Get basic facts about your topic.
Nonfiction books give facts about real people, places, events, and things.	*The Wright Brothers* by Russell Freedman *Oceans* by Seymour Simon	• Find a book that tells all about your topic. • Find a book with one chapter on your topic.
Reference books are special nonfiction books. They are packed with different kinds of facts.	*Information Please Kids' Almanac* *Macmillan Color Atlas of the States*	• Find all kinds of facts in an almanac. Use a recent one. • Check maps in an atlas.
Magazines and **newspapers** give up-to-date information.	*National Geographic World* *Weekly Reader*	• Use these sources when you need the latest facts.

📖 See page H21 for more about using the library.

more ▶

Go to www.eduplace.com/kids/hme/ for topic links.

Focus Skill continued

Choosing the Best Sources

Sift through your sources. Which ones are the most valuable?

Test your sources. Use this checklist.

Is the Source...	How to Tell
_____ related to your topic?	Check the title and the headings. Read a few sentences.
_____ factual?	Look for facts, not opinions. Facts can be proved. Your report should give facts.
_____ dependable?	The writer should have experience or education in the topic you are researching.
_____ up-to-date?	Find out when the source was published. Use the most recent sources you can find.

WARNING: Web sites often have errors. You might want to check with your teacher before you use an Internet source.

Think and Discuss

- If you were doing research on George Washington, what sources would you explore first? Why?
- If you were doing research on a recent invention, what sources would you explore first? Why?

▶ Explore Your Topic

1 Find information. Look in your library for a variety of sources. Which ones answer the questions on your K-W-S chart? Write these sources in the third column of your chart.

If you can't find good sources, choose a different topic from your top three.

2 Test your sources. Choose the strongest ones. You should have at least three sources for your report. Only one should be an encyclopedia article.

▶ Research Your Topic

❶ Take notes to help you remember what you have heard or read. The questions on your K-W-S chart will guide you.

- Write the question you are answering at the top of the card. You may end up with more than one card for each question.
- Write facts that answer the question. Write just enough to help you remember the important ideas.
- Take notes in your own words.
- As you take notes, write the source on the bottom of each card. Here is a source that James used, along with one of his note cards.

Jungles and Rainforests

The main condition needed for a rainforest is—rain. In general, the average rainfall must be at least 80 inches each year, and this should be spread out over most of the year. This compares with the rainfall in London, which averages 23.3 inches each year, and New York, which has about 42.8 inches of rain yearly. Tropical rainforests have temperatures which are high and vary little, usually between 68°F and 82°F all year. Temperate rainforests are generally cooler, around 50°F in winter and up to 77°F in summer.

10

What is their climate?
—get a lot of rain
—at least 80 inches of rain a year
—between 68° F and 82° F all year
Jungles and Rainforests, by
John A. Burton, San Diego, CA:
Thunder Bay Press, 1996, p. 10.

Don't copy! Write in your own words.

❷ Focus on your topic. Don't write every fact you find. Ask yourself these questions.

- Does this fact answer one of my questions?
- Will it help my audience understand my topic?
- Is the fact interesting?

📖 See page H26 to find out more about taking notes.

❸ Review your K-W-S chart as you do research. Cross out questions that don't seem important anymore, and add questions about interesting information you want to use.

As he took notes from different sources, James added the question *What medicines come from the rain forest?* to his chart. Before working on his report, he didn't know that medicine was made from rain-forest plants. Here is part of his updated chart.

What I **K**now	What I **W**ant to Know	Possible **S**ources
Rain forests are wet.	What is the climate?	Burton, <u>Jungles and Rainforests</u>
They have many different plants and animals.	What are some of the interesting plants and animals?	Ricciuti, <u>Rainforest</u>
Rubber comes from there.	What other products come from rain forests?	
They are being destroyed.	Why are they being destroyed?	
	What medicines come from the rain forest?	

Plan Your Report

1 **Sort** your note cards.
- Make a stack for each question you answered. Put the cards in each stack in an order that makes sense.
- Remove cards that have repeated or unimportant information.
- Put the stacks in an order that makes sense.

2 **Make an outline** from your notes. Each question you answered will become a **main topic**. Each supporting detail will become a **subtopic**.
- List each main topic with a Roman numeral.
- List each subtopic with a capital letter.
- Give your outline a title.

Here are two of the note cards James wrote and part of his outline.

What is their climate?
—get a lot of rain
—at least 80 inches of rain a year
—between 68°F and 82°F all year
Jungles and Rainforests, by John A. Burton, San Diego, CA: Thunder Bay Press, 1996, p. 10.

What is their climate?
—very few dry periods or none at all
—always warm and humid
"Rain Forest" by Elizabeth Losos, Microsoft Encarta Online Deluxe Encyclopedia: 1997–99. 24 Nov. 2001

II. Climate in the rain forest
   A. Get a lot of rain
   B. At least 80 inches of rain a year
   C. Few dry periods
   D. Always warm and humid
   E. Between 68°F and 82°F all year

Your outline is a map that will guide you as you write your report.

📖 See page H28 for more about outlining.

Focus Skill

Writing from an Outline

Write topic sentences. For each main topic on your outline, write a topic sentence. It should tell what the paragraph is about.

Write paragraphs. Using the subtopics on your outline, write a paragraph for each topic sentence.

Here is part of an outline for a report on the career of Benjamin Franklin, along with the paragraph written from it.

II. Franklin's government jobs
  A. Ran the post office
  B. Provided army with gunpowder
  C. Directed printing of money
  D. Was ambassador to France

Ben Franklin did many jobs for the government of the United States. He ran the post office. He provided the army with gunpowder. In addition, he directed the printing of money and was ambassador to France.

Connect your ideas. Help your reader move smoothly through your report. Connect your thoughts with words such as *also, in addition, for example,* and *in conclusion.*

Think and Discuss Use the outline and paragraph to answer these questions.

- What is the topic sentence in the paragraph?
- What words did the writer use to connect ideas smoothly?
- Which sentence includes subtopic A? B? C? D?

▶ Draft Your Report

❶ **Write a topic sentence** for each main topic on your outline.

❷ **Write a paragraph** for each topic sentence. Include interesting details.

Write with voice! Show how interesting your topic is.

Focus Skill

Good Openings and Closings

Write an opening paragraph. Tell the main idea of your report in one sentence. Ask a question or state a surprising fact to catch the reader's interest.

Weak Opening	Strong Opening
The transcontinental railroad linked the East and the West in the United States. It took a lot of hard work.	What took seven years to build and linked the East to the West in the United States? The transcontinental railroad, begun in 1862, is the answer. With picks, shovels, and sledgehammers, workers built this historic railway.

Write a closing. A strong closing sums up the report and connects with the main idea in the opening.

Weak Closing	Strong Closing
The hard work was done. Now people could cross the United States by train. Most people would think this was important.	After the dangers of blasting through mountains and building bridges over deep gorges, the transcontinental railroad was complete. Passengers could now travel from New York to San Francisco by rail.

GRAMMAR TIP If you give an exact date, put a comma between the day and the year.

Think and Discuss Compare the weak and strong examples above.

- Why doesn't the weak opening above seem interesting?
- Why is the weak closing less interesting than the strong one?

▶ Draft Your Opening and Closing

1 **Draft** two openings for your report. Choose the one that fits better.

2 **Write** a closing that connects to your opening.

3 **Make** a list of sources as shown on page 376.

Evaluating Your Research Report

▶ **Reread** your report. What do you need to do to make it better? Use this rubric to help you decide. Write the sentences that describe your report.

Rings the Bell!

- The report has only facts and shows good research.
- My opening and closing are interesting and give the main idea.
- Each paragraph has a topic sentence supported by facts and details.
- I've written in my own words.
- My list of sources is complete and accurate.
- *There are almost no mistakes in capitalization, punctuation, and spelling.*

Getting Stronger

- I did some good research but not enough.
- My opening and closing give the main idea but are boring.
- I need topic sentences, facts, or details in a few places.
- I should check some sentences to make sure they're in my own words.
- I have a list of sources, but it is incomplete.
- *There are a few mistakes.*

Try Harder

- I did little research, and I mix facts with opinions.
- My report needs an opening and a closing.
- I need to write clear topic sentences and support them with details.
- I need to write in my own words.
- I forgot to include a list of sources.
- *There are a lot of mistakes.*

  See www.eduplace.com/kids/hme/ to interact with this rubric.

Revise Your Research Report

❶ **Revise** your report. Use the list of sentences you wrote from the rubric. Work on the parts that you described with sentences from "Getting Stronger" and "Try Harder."

HELP ?   **Revising Tip**

To add sentences, write them at the bottom of your paper, circle them, and draw an arrow to show where to add them.

❷ **Have a writing conference.**

When You're the Writer Read your report aloud to a partner. Discuss any questions or problems you have. Take notes to remember what your partner says. Then make the changes you want to make.

When You're the Listener Tell at least two things you like about the report. Ask questions about anything that seems unclear or boring. Use this chart to help you.

What should I say?

The Writing Conference

If you're thinking . . .	You could say . . .
Did you just make this up?	**Where did you find this information?**
The opening isn't very interesting.	**Can you start with a question or a surprising fact?**
Some facts aren't important.	**Does your reader really need to know this?**
The report is choppy. It's just one fact after another.	**Can you add words to connect your ideas?**
This part is hard to understand.	**It would help your readers if you could give details to make this part clearer.**
The report ends suddenly.	**Can you write a closing to sum up the report?**

❸ **Make more revisions** to your research report. Use your conference notes and the Revising Strategies on the next page.

Revising Strategies

Elaborating: Word Choice Definitions of special words will help your audience understand your report.

Without a Definition	With a Definition
Lava pours out of a volcano.	Lava, a flow of hot, melted rock, pours out of a volcano.
Some farmers **irrigate** their crops.	Some farmers irrigate their crops. This means they supply water to plants by using ditches, pipes, or canals.

▶ Find at least two places in your report where you can define special words.

Elaborating: Details Exact details such as dates, amounts, measurements, and locations help make the information clear.

Few Details	Elaborated with Details
Mount McKinley is the tallest peak in the United States.	Mount McKinley in Alaska is the tallest peak in the United States. It towers 20,320 feet above sea level.

▶ Find at least two places in your report where you can add exact details.

Sentence Fluency To keep your writing interesting for your readers, begin sentences in different ways.

> Death Valley in California has very high temperatures.
> In Death Valley, temperatures are very high.
> When summer arrives, temperatures climb high in Death Valley.

▶ Find at least two places in your report where you can vary the sentence beginnings.

GRAMMAR LINK ▶ *See also page 246.*

Adding Graphics and Visuals

Sometimes a visual can add interesting information to a report. Here are some ideas.

Pictures and Maps Draw or copy a picture to show something about your topic. Including a map can be helpful if you've written about a place or described a journey.

▶ Add a picture or a map if it fits your report.

Important Places in the California Gold Rush

Marysville
Sacramento
Sutter's Fort
Coloma (Sutters Mill)
Chinese Camp
San Francisco
Pacific Ocean

Charts and Graphs Using a chart or a graph is a good way to organize extra information.

Speedy Animals	
Animal	Speed
Cheetah	70 miles per hour
Pronghorn antelope	61 miles per hour
Wildebeest, lion, Thomson's gazelle	50 miles per hour
Quarter horse	47.5 miles per hour

▶ Add a chart or a graph to your report if you need to organize detailed information.

You can put visuals on your report cover or in the report.

Time Line If your report tells about a person's life or a series of events, you might show important dates on a time line.

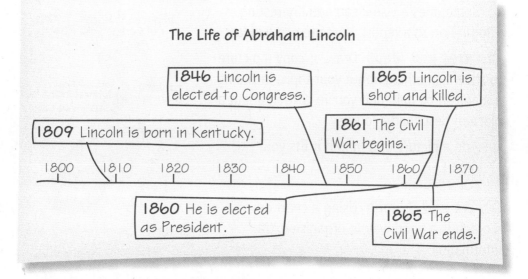

The Life of Abraham Lincoln

1846 Lincoln is elected to Congress.

1865 Lincoln is shot and killed.

1809 Lincoln is born in Kentucky.

1861 The Civil War begins.

| 1800 | 1810 | 1820 | 1830 | 1840 | 1850 | 1860 | 1870 |

1860 He is elected as President.

1865 The Civil War ends.

▶ Create a time line if it fits your report.

Diagrams Draw a diagram to show the parts of something in your report.

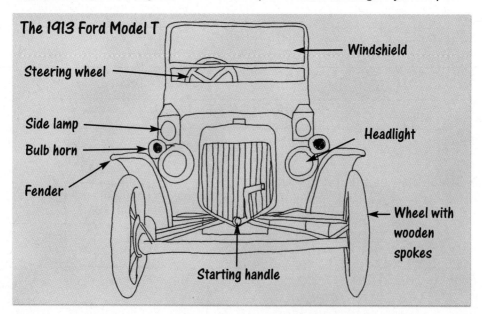

The 1913 Ford Model T

Windshield

Steering wheel

Side lamp

Headlight

Bulb horn

Fender

Wheel with wooden spokes

Starting handle

▶ Add a diagram to your report if it will help your readers.

Proofread Your Research Report

Proofread your report, using the Proofreading Checklist and the Grammar and Spelling Connections. Proofread for one skill at a time. Use a class dictionary to check spellings.

Proofreading Checklist

Did I
- ✔ indent all paragraphs?
- ✔ correct any run-on sentences?
- ✔ begin proper nouns with capital letters?
- ✔ use comparisons with *-er* and *-est* correctly?
- ✔ correct all spelling errors?

📖 Use the Guide to Capitalization, Punctuation, and Usage on page H55.

Proofreading Marks
¶ Indent
∧ Add
⌒ Delete
≡ Capital letter
/ Small letter

Tech Tip
The spelling tool will not catch every capitalization mistake.

Grammar and Spelling Connections

Proper Nouns The names of particular people, places, and things are called **proper nouns**. Capitalize every important word in a proper noun.

Common Nouns	Proper Nouns
scientist	Marie Curie
park	Yellowstone National Park
city, state	Tampa, Florida
holiday	Fourth of July

GRAMMAR LINK ➤ *See also pages 66, 170, and 172.*

Spelling final |ər| The final |ər| sounds in two-syllable words are often spelled *ar, or,* or *er.*

cell**ar**	sail**or**	ladd**er**
sug**ar**	harb**or**	prop**er**

📖 See the Spelling Guide on page H65.

Publish Your Research Report

1 **Make a neat final copy** of your report. Be sure you fixed all mistakes.

2 **Write** an interesting title for your report that will make your audience curious, such as "Ford's Tin Lizzie" rather than "An Old Car."

3 **Publish** or share your report in a way that suits your audience. See the Ideas for Sharing box.

Ideas for Sharing

Write It
• Put your report in a homemade booklet.

Say It
• Present your report orally.
  See page 400 for tips.
• With other classmates, form a panel of experts. Record your reports on videotape.

Show It
• Make a multimedia presentation. See page H45 for tips.
  Create a visual display for your report.

Tips for Creating a Visual Display

• Make large visuals to go with your report. Use nice lettering.
• Find objects related to your report, make a cardboard or clay model, or create a mural or a collage. Add helpful labels.
• Put your visuals on poster board, or arrange them on a table. Display your report with them.

📖 See page H24 for more tips.

Reflect

Write about your writing experience. Use these questions to get started.

● What was hard about writing a research report? What was easy?
● What else would you like to learn about your topic?
 ● How does this paper compare with other papers that you have written?

Writing Prompts

Use these prompts as ideas for writing research reports. Think about who your audience will be, and write your report in a way that they will enjoy and understand.

Writing Across the Curriculum

1 CAREER EDUCATION

What career interests you most? Would you like to be a computer programmer? a cook at a fancy restaurant? a singer? a doctor? Write a report on the career. Try to interview someone who works in that area.

2 MATH

People have invented many things to help them keep track of numbers and amounts. Research the history of the calendar, the abacus, early units of measure, or an instrument such as the barometer. Include diagrams or pictures if you'd like.

3 HEALTH

What does exercise do for health? Would you like to know more about vitamins or nutrition? Write a report on a health topic that interests you. Report facts without giving your opinion. Use up-to-date sources.

4 PHYSICAL EDUCATION

Who first played soccer? Who made up the rules for tennis? Who designed golf clubs? Report on the history of your favorite sport or pastime. You might include diagrams of special equipment.

5 FINE ART

The Mexican artist Rufino Tamayo was important in modern art. Research the man and his career, and write a report. Which artists did he learn from? What is his style of painting? Tell about some of his major works of art.

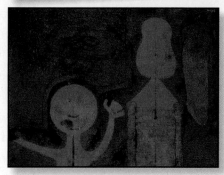

Niño En Rojo, by Rufino Tamayo

Writing to Solve a Problem

When you write to **solve a problem**, you tell what your problem is, find and use resources to help you solve it, and then explain your solution. Read how this student did research to solve her problem.

Problem ⟶ Problem: How do I start a stamp collection?

- Where do I get stamps?
- What kinds of stamps are there to collect?
- How much does it cost to collect stamps?
- Where do I keep my stamps?

Possible Sources ⟵ Resources
of Information

- the Internet
- the United States Post Office
- books about stamp collecting

Summary —

My problem was finding out how to start a stamp collection. I decided that a good place to look for information was the Internet. I found the United States Postal Service Web site. It answered a lot of my questions, such as how to organize and keep my stamps in albums or notebooks. I learned that stamp collecting doesn't have to cost very much, especially if I take stamps from letters my friends and family get.

There are many different kinds of stamps to collect, such as stamps of animals and famous people, stamps from other countries, and airmail stamps.

Next, I went to the post office in my town. The clerk gave me a catalog showing stamps that I could order.

Finally, I went to the library. The librarian helped me find books that showed old and new stamps from around the world. I decided to start my collection with stamps

Solution — from my friends' and family's mail. I'll keep them in a notebook.

- The **problem** is a question or a situation that needs to be solved. *What is this student's problem?*
- **Resources** are people, places, and materials that might give you information to solve the problem. *What possible sources are listed?*
- The **summary** retells the problem and explains the actions taken to solve the problem. *Which paragraph retells the problem?*
- The **solution** is the decision you make. *What decision does this student make?*

How to Write to Solve a Problem

1 **State** your problem in one clear sentence.

2 **Write** a list of questions you want to answer, or make notes about parts of the problem.

3 **Find** sources of information to help you. Then do the research you need to do. Organize your questions, information, and sources in a chart.

Question	Information	Source
Where do I get stamps?	from mailed envelopes or from a catalog	the U.S. Postal Service Web site and a postal clerk
What kinds of stamps are there to collect?	many different kinds, like stamps from other countries or that show famous people	the U.S. Postal Service Web site, a postal clerk, and library books
How much does it cost to collect stamps?	not much if I start with used ones	the U.S. Postal Service Web site
Where do I keep my stamps?	in albums or notebooks	the U.S. Postal Service Web site

4 **Solve** the problem using the information you collected. Write a summary paragraph explaining what you learned and what you decided.

Writing a News Article

A **news article** tells about a recent event. It reports facts about what happened. Read Jeremy's news article below about a sporting event.

Headline

Bulldogs Beat Cougars

Lead paragraph

At the Beechmont Civic Arena Friday night, the Beechmont Bulldogs beat the Cannonstown Cougars in the Junior Varsity basketball playoffs.

Supporting details

The scores were close up to the very end. With four minutes left on the clock, one of the Beechmont players raced with the ball to the basket. A Cougar caught up with him and stole the ball to make a two-point lay-up. Then the Cougars fouled the Beechmont Bulldogs. Joey Wong, Beechmont's best free thrower, went to the line and made the two baskets.

With two minutes to go, the crowd cheered wildly for each team. Bulldog Michael Hernandez made a slam dunk. The score was tied. Cougar Tim Jackson bounced the ball under his leg and shot a terrific basket. The score then was 42 to 40. Then, Wong shot a dramatic three-pointer on the buzzer and won the game for the Bulldogs!

Conclusion

Asked about the game, Wong said, "This was really a team effort. Everyone deserves credit."

- The **headline** gets the reader's attention and tells the main idea of the news article. *What is the main idea of Jeremy's article?*
- The **lead paragraph** tells the most important facts about the event. It answers the questions *Who? What? Where? When? Why?* and *How? Where and when did the event in Jeremy's article take place?*
- The **supporting details** give more information about the facts. *How did Joey Wong win the game for the Bulldogs?*
- The **conclusion** ends the article. The writer may quote someone or give some final details about the event. *How does Jeremy end his article?*

How to Write a News Article

❶ Choose a recent event to write about. Think about what your audience would want to know.

❷ Outline your news article, using a pyramid like the one shown.

❸ Research your subject. Take careful notes to answer each of the six questions. If possible, interview people who were at the event, or know about it, for quotations.

❹ Write your article. Remember to write only the facts, not your opinions. Start with a lead paragraph that tells about the event. Quote people who were there. End with a conclusion that wraps up the story.

Who?
What?
Where?
When? Why? How?

Supporting details

Other, less important, details

❺ Think of a short, attention-getting headline for your news article.

❻ Revise and proofread your article. Check to be sure that the names you've used are spelled correctly.

❼ Make a final copy. Work with classmates and make a class newspaper.

Completing a Form

One way to supply information to another person, to an organization, or to a business is to **complete a form**. Forms are sometimes needed to register a bicycle, to order from a catalog, to get a dog license, or to join a book club. Read this form.

APPLICATION   **Public Library Card**

Directions —— *Fill in the information. Print one letter or number in each box.*
If something does not apply to you, leave those boxes blank.

First Name   **Middle Initial**
| M | i | c | h | a | e | l | | | | | → | S | ←

——→ *Boxes for letters and numbers*

Last Name
| B | a | k | e | r | | | | | | | | | | | | | ←

Date of Birth (month/day/year) (sample: 03/16/1991)
| 0 | 7 | | 2 | 3 | | 1 | 9 | 9 | 2 |

Information about you

Street Address   **Apt. #**
| 3 | 2 | 5 | | W. | | P | a | l | m | | D | r | i | v | e | | | | | | |

City
| A | n | y | t | o | w | n | | | | | | | | | |

County   **State**   **Zip Code**
| M | a | n | a | t | e | e | | | | F | L | | 3 | 4 | 2 | 0 | 5 |

Area Code   **Home Phone**
| 9 | 4 | 1 | | 5 | 5 | 5 | | 9 | 8 | 7 | 6 |

I agree to be responsible for the materials I check out with this card. I will return all materials, including books, tapes, and videos, in good condition and on time. I agree to pay any fines charged to me.

Signature —— *Michael S. Baker*   *January 16, 2001* ←— *Date*
Signature of Applicant   **Date**

- The **directions** tell you how to fill out the form.
  What should Michael do if something does not apply to him?
- Some forms have **boxes for letters and numbers**. Only one letter or number is written in each box.
  How many letters or numbers did Michael write in each box?
- The **information about you** is often your name, address, and phone number. *Where does Michael live?*
- Some forms ask for your **signature**, which is your name written in cursive. Your signature means that you understand and agree with everything on the form. *What did Michael agree to do?*
- The **date** gives the month, day, and year on which you fill out the form. Sometimes a zero is needed before the digit, as in 01, 02, 03, and so on. *When did Michael fill out this form?*

How to Complete a Form

① **Read** the directions carefully.

② **Complete** the form by filling in the boxes. Put only one letter or number in each box. For any information you don't know, ask a family member to help you.

③ **Sign** the form.

④ **Date** the form.

⑤ **Proofread** your form for mistakes. Check to see that the information is correct and that you have filled in all of the information.

Giving an Oral Report

The research you do for an oral report can include finding different kinds of media to present, such as photographs or videos. These help make your topic more interesting for your audience. You might make visual aids of your own, such as models, charts, or slides, to support your spoken ideas.

Which Media?

Models Models give a sense of size. They show subjects in three dimensions. Would your listeners better understand your topic if you made a model?	Dioramas, clay models, and papier-mâché objects
Photographs Photographs can show hard-to-explain events or details. Would your report be clearer if you used pictures to explain what you mean?	Posters, slides, and pictures from newspapers, magazines, or books
Illustrations Can you present data from your report? Information presented in charts and drawings can help explain your ideas.	Charts, graphs, diagrams, and tables 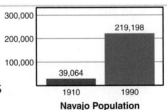
Technology Can you present your ideas through music? Could you show part of a video on your topic to interest your audience?	Videotapes, CDs, cassette tapes, the Internet, CD-ROMs, and digital photography 

 See also pages H45–H47 in the Tools and Tips Handbook.

Getting Ready

Prepare your materials ahead of time. If you plan to show photographs from books, use bookmarks so that you can easily turn to the right pages. If you are using cassettes or videos, be sure the equipment is set up and that it works. Here are some guides to help you give your report.

Before the Talk

- Write notes, or key words and phrases, on cards.
- Practice your talk using the cards.
- Add more notes if you need to.
- Practice saying words that are hard to pronounce.

Guides for Giving an Oral Report

▶ Stand up straight.

▶ Speak clearly and loudly enough to be heard by everyone in the room.

▶ Don't fidget or rock back and forth. Keep your hands out of your pockets.

▶ Be sure not to say *ah, well,* and *um.*

▶ Make eye contact with your audience.

▶ Be sure everyone in the audience can see or hear the media you are using.

▶ Sound interested in what you are saying. Vary the tone of your voice to keep your listeners interested.

Apply It

Choose a report you have already written and prepare media to use in presenting it orally. Make sure the topic would interest your audience. Use the guides above as you give your report. Then answer the following questions.

- Which media did you choose for your report? Why?
- Did your presentation hold the attention and interest of your audience? How do you know?
- If you could present your report again, what would you do differently?

Looking at the News

What is news? It is information about current events. To get the day's news, your family may watch a television news program. News is also found on the radio, in newspapers, and on the Internet.

You probably expect the news to be true and fair. Is it? When you watch the evening news on TV, what are you actually seeing and hearing?

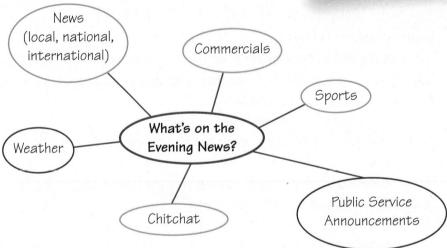

Behind the News

Television is a business. That means that most TV networks must make money. They do this by selling time during their programs for companies to play commercials. Even news programs have commercials.

Look at the word web above. Many topics are part of an evening news program. Stories about weather and sports are included along with the national news. Think of a reason to explain why so many topics are included.

Thinking Further

News people make decisions about what you see on TV. They select stories for a purpose. Some news people cover issues they believe are important. Others choose stories that will entertain their audience. Use the guides below to think about the news.

Guides for Looking at the News

▶ Notice the first story. Why do you think that story was chosen to lead or begin the news? Count how many are meant to inform. Count how many are meant to catch the interest of the audience.

▶ Notice which stories take more time than the others. What information do you think is left out of the shorter stories? Do you think information has been left out of the longer stories too? Why or why not?

▶ Notice how much time is given to sports and weather. Why do you think these subjects receive this much coverage?

▶ Pay attention to the commercials. Can you tell who the audience of the news program is? Are the commercials aimed at voters? teenagers? workers? or retired people?

▶ Listen to the chitchat among the news people. Why do you think they talk like that?

Apply It

Watch an evening news program on television. Use the guides above and take notes. Answer these questions.

- What businesses paid to have their commercials played during the news?
- Do you think the news stories you watched gave the whole picture about what happened that day? Explain why or why not.
- Why do you think the news people picked the stories they ran?
- What part of the news did you like to watch?

Section 3

Expressing and Influencing

What You Will Find in This Section:

Listening to an Opinion

An **opinion** tells a person's thoughts or beliefs about a topic. Two general purposes for listening to an opinion are to learn what someone else thinks and to help yourself make up your own mind. Listening to an opinion is different from listening to a story or a report. Use these guidelines to help you be a good listener.

Guidelines for Listening to an Opinion

▶ Listen for the topic. What subject is the author discussing?

▶ Listen for the main idea. What is the author's opinion?

▶ Listen for reasons. Does the author explain why he or she holds this opinion?

▶ Listen for details. What facts or examples explain the reasons?

▶ Listen for the author's purpose. Why does the author want you to know what he or she thinks?

Try It Out Listen carefully as your teacher reads an opinion essay by Alma Flor Ada. Then answer the questions below.

- What is the topic?
- What is Alma Flor Ada's main idea?
- What reasons does the author give?
- What are some details that the author gives to explain her reasons?
- Why do you think Alma Flor Ada wrote this piece?

Alma Flor Ada

See www.eduplace.com/kids/ for information about Alma Flor Ada.

Writing an Opinion Paragraph

A paragraph that tells what someone thinks or feels about a topic is an **opinion paragraph**. An opinion paragraph has a topic and a main idea. The **topic** is the subject of the paragraph. The **main idea** is the writer's opinion about the topic. What is the topic of the opinion paragraph below? What is the main idea?

Remember, the first line of a paragraph is indented.

Indent ——

Opinion statement —

Supporting sentences —

Closing sentence —

My neighborhood is a great place for kids. First of all, there are lots of people my age, so I always have someone to play with. A second reason is that we have a huge park with a baseball field. I can play there every day. The best reason is the neighbors. They are always organizing ball games and picnics. My neighborhood is definitely kid-friendly.

Opinion Statement

The topic is the writer's neighborhood. The main idea, the writer's opinion, is that this neighborhood is a great place to live. Which sentence states the topic and the main idea?

Supporting Sentences

The labels show the three parts of an opinion paragraph.

- The **opinion statement** tells what the writer thinks or feels about the topic.

Closing Sentence

- **Supporting sentences** state clear reasons and give details that explain the reasons.
- The **closing sentence** completes the paragraph.

Think and Discuss Reread the neighborhood paragraph above.

- What are the three reasons why the writer likes the neighborhood?

The Opinion Statement

You know that a well-written paragraph usually begins with a sentence that states the topic and tells the main idea. In an opinion paragraph, this sentence is called the **opinion statement**. It tells what the writer thinks or feels about the topic.

        Topic   Main idea

Example: My neighborhood is a great place for kids.

What opinions can you think of for these topics?

- performing in plays
- vegetables
- a book you've just finished

Try It Out Each paragraph below is missing its opinion statement. On your own or with a partner, write the topic and the main idea of each paragraph. Then write two possible opinion statements for each paragraph.

1.   <u>   Opinion statement   </u>. That's why when I see someone looking a little bit sad or lonely, I'll tell them a joke or a funny story. Laughing can make people forget their problems for a while. My mom tells me she hopes I have a silly story for her after a hard day at work. Laughing is also healthy, according to some doctors. They say it is good for the lungs. I say that laughing every day is as important as eating.

2.   <u>   Opinion statement   </u>. For every chore that they finish and do well, they receive money. This teaches them that money can be a reward for work well done. An allowance also helps kids learn to budget their money so that they can buy some of the things that they want. At the same time, it teaches them to save money for things they may want to buy later. Keeping track of their money might even help kids with their math! An allowance is an excellent learning opportunity.

Supporting Sentences

Supporting sentences usually follow the opinion statement. They give reasons that answer the question *Why?* about the opinion. Details, such as facts and examples, explain the reasons. In the neighborhood paragraph on page 407, the supporting sentences explain why the writer thinks the neighborhood is great for kids.

Reason: lots of people my age

Detail: always have someone to play with

Read the paragraph below. Look for reasons and details that support the writer's opinion.

Our town has an excellent summer recreation program. First, it teaches kids new skills. It offers classes in arts and crafts, math puzzles, and golf. It also helps kids discover new interests. Every summer many children try hiking, bird watching, or drama for the first time. Most important, the program gives children a place to make new friends. Four hundred excited kids take part in the program every summer. This program helps make summer fun here!

Think and Discuss What reasons and details are in the paragraph above?

Ordering Reasons and Details The supporting sentences in an opinion paragraph are often arranged from most important to least important or from least important to most important. **Transitional words**, such as *first, also, another reason, the best, for example,* and *finally,* help the reader see the connections between reasons and details. Which reason is most important to the writer of the paragraph above? What transitional words can you find?

 See page 18 for more transitional words.

more ▶

Try It Out Look at the picture of the summer outdoor scene. On your own or with a partner, use the opinion statement and the picture to write at least three sentences that support the opinion. Include reasons and details such as facts and examples. Link at least two of your sentences with a transitional word or phrase.

Opinion statement: Summer is the best season of all.

GRAMMAR TIP ▶ Watch out for run-on sentences!

The Closing Sentence

The **closing sentence** finishes the opinion paragraph. It can repeat the writer's opinion in an interesting way or make a final comment. In the summer-program paragraph on page 409, the closing sentence makes a final comment.

Try It Out The paragraph below is missing its closing sentence. On your own or with a partner, write two different closing sentences for it.

I'm lucky because I know how to read. Reading helps me many times each day. Because I can read, I know whether a store is open or closed or whether to wait or walk at a crosswalk. Reading also helps me find out how to build and fix things. For example, reading the directions helped me build a birdhouse last summer. Best of all, reading introduces me to new people and carries me to faraway lands. I have met Abraham Lincoln and traveled to Antarctica through books. _____*Closing sentence*_____.

Write Your Own Opinion Paragraph

Now it's your turn to write a paragraph. What do you have an opinion about? It might be something that is happening at school. It might be something you like or do not like. Write reasons for your opinion. Include details, such as facts and examples, to support your reasons. Share your opinion and reasons with a partner. Then go ahead and write!

Checklist for My Paragraph

✔ I wrote an **opinion statement** that introduces the topic and main idea.
✔ My **supporting sentences** give reasons for my opinion and details that elaborate the reasons.
✔ I wrote a **closing sentence** that restates the main idea or makes a final comment.

Looking Ahead

Now that you know how to write an opinion paragraph, writing a longer composition will be a snap! The diagram below shows how the parts of an opinion paragraph do the same jobs as the parts of an opinion essay.

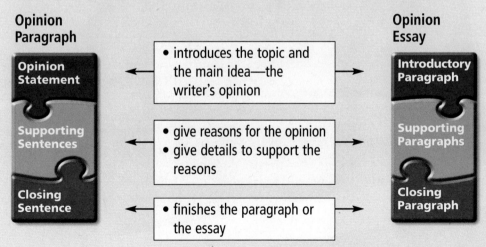

Opinion Paragraph

- Opinion Statement
- Supporting Sentences
- Closing Sentence

- introduces the topic and the main idea—the writer's opinion
- give reasons for the opinion
- give details to support the reasons
- finishes the paragraph or the essay

Opinion Essay

- Introductory Paragraph
- Supporting Paragraphs
- Closing Paragraph

Unit 12

Writing to Express an Opinion

Everyone needs someone or something special to love. For me it's Jamie, my pet dog.

George Ancona is a freelance photographer, and he wrote this essay to explain why he enjoys taking pictures. What reasons does he give to support his opinion?

Why I Like to Take Pictures

by George Ancona

A long time ago, I began to take pictures with my father's camera. We lived on Coney Island, and I would wander the empty streets in winter taking pictures of the snow-covered clowns. I found that I really enjoyed taking pictures.

What I liked most was to take pictures of my family. After high school I went to Mexico to meet my grandparents, aunts, uncles, and cousins. I took pictures of them, and with these pictures I began my family album.

more ▶

See www.eduplace.com/kids/ for information about George Ancona.

I also like to take pictures because it gives me a chance to travel. When I returned from Mexico, I became a freelance professional photographer. This has allowed me to go to many wonderful places around the world, including Iceland, Tunisia, France, Brazil, Japan, Cuba, and many other countries.

One of my favorite reasons for taking pictures is to meet people. In countries where I do not speak the language, I will meet a person who sees me as a stranger. I look him or her in the eyes and smile. Usually the response is a twinkle in the eyes, and then I take a picture. If it's a frown, I move on.

Once, in a small village in Mexico, I saw a man loading his ox cart with corn stalks. I asked if I could take a picture of his ox. He said no. As I moved on down the street I wondered why, so I turned

back and asked him. He had no answer, but he said I could take the picture. Then I asked him to stand next to the ox, and he did. Soon his whole family came to have their picture taken.

Once I took my granddaughter with me, and she would complain, "Poppi, you are always talking to people. You don't even know that man." "Yes, Sweetie," was my answer, "but now I do!"

Today, when I look through my photographs, my thoughts go beyond them to the fond memories of the people I have met, of meals shared with strangers that became friends, of long walks and long talks, of music and dances and festivals, and of how alike we all are—the peoples of the world.

Reading As a Writer

Think About the Opinion Essay

- What reasons does the author give to support his opinion?
- In which paragraph does the author state his opinion?
- In the first paragraph on page 414, what details does the author give to support his reason?
- In which paragraph does the author sum up why he likes photography?

Think About Writer's Craft

- Reread the third paragraph on page 414. What story does the author tell? Which reason does this story help explain?

Think About the Pictures

- What do the photos show that helps you understand why the author enjoys taking pictures?

Responding

Write responses to these questions.

- **Personal Response** Think of something you like to do. Are your reasons for liking it similar to the author's reasons for liking photography? In what ways are they different?
- **Critical Thinking** After reading this essay, how would you describe the kind of person George Ancona is?

What Makes a Great Opinion Essay?

An **opinion essay** tells what the writer thinks or feels about a topic.

Remember to follow these guidelines when you write an opinion essay.

► Introduce your topic in the opening. Say something that will hook your audience right away.

► For each paragraph, write a topic sentence that tells the main idea.

► Include strong reasons to support your opinion.

► Use details, such as examples, to explain each reason.

► Write in a way that sounds like you.

► Sum up the important points in the closing.

GRAMMAR CHECK

Use singular pronouns to take the place of singular nouns. Use plural pronouns to take the place of plural nouns.

WORKING DRAFT

Asa Horvitz likes to play soccer. He wanted to tell other students who didn't play what he liked and what he didn't like about the game. Asa wrote this draft of his opinion.

Asa Horvitz

I'm going to talk about soccer.

~~You can use any part of your body except the hands to hit the ball. Each time you score you get one point. Games last one hour.~~

> Can you say something in your opening that will make your readers curious?

I like soccer a lot. One reason is that I can play fullback. ~~In soccer there are ten positions.~~ The fullback kicks the ball hard so that it goes down the field. All my practice has made me an expert kicker. Another reason is that soccer is fast moving and never stops. Another reason I like soccer is that it can be played anywhere by groups of any size. Soccer is played all over the world. Anywhere I go I'll be able to play with other people. I can play with

> I can really hear your voice when you write about soccer!

> This reason has strong details. Good!

two people or as many as twenty. Sometimes
I just kick the ball around the yard with
my family or with my friends at the
park. Another reason is that the coach
gives me a ride to all of the games.

> Is this reason really important?

There are some things I don't like.
I don't like soccer because goalie is a
dumb position. When I play goalie, I
don't ~~play much~~ see much action. I usually
just stand around and watch the other
players having fun. Another reason I don't
always like soccer is that you have to work
with the team, and sometimes that can be
hard. I might have to sit out for a long
time. This can happen if there are twelve
people on a team because only eleven play at
a time.

> This isn't a good reason. Can you be more exact?

Reading As a Writer

- What did Sal like about Asa's essay? What were Sal's questions? What revisions could Asa make to answer them?
- Why did Asa cross out the second paragraph?
- Look at the paragraph that tells why Asa likes soccer. Which reason needs details?
- What questions would you like to ask Asa about his opinion?

FINAL COPY

Asa revised his essay after discussing it with a partner.
Read Asa's final paper to see what changes he made.

The Ups and Downs of Soccer
by Asa Horvitz

Whenever I can run and have fun, I'm happy. That's why I play soccer.

I like soccer a lot. The most important reason is that I can play fullback. The fullback kicks the ball hard so that it goes down the field. All my practice has made me an expert kicker. A second reason is that soccer is fast moving and never stops. Two teams are always running back and forth across a huge field to make a goal. The players never seem to stop running during the four fifteen-minute quarters. Time flies! The last reason I like soccer is that it can be played anywhere by groups of any size. Soccer is played all over the world. Anywhere I go I'll be able to play with other people. I can play with two people or as many as twenty. Sometimes I just kick the ball around the yard with my family or with my friends at the park.

> This opening is much more interesting!

> These examples make your second reason much stronger.

Soccer isn't always a dream sport, and there are some things I don't like. The worst part about soccer is that the goalie position can be lonely. When I play goalie, I don't see much action. I usually just stand around and watch the other players having fun. Another reason I don't always like soccer is that you have to work with the team, and sometimes that can be hard. I might have to sit out for a long time. This can happen if there are twelve people on a team because only eleven play at a time. Then there is the weather. We play under the hottest sun, the wettest rain, and the coldest snow. The cold weather is the hardest to play in because the ball hurts if it hits me.

The cheers from the crowd make me feel good. I forget about being cold or sitting out. I know I'll get to run and play fullback again in the next game.

> This reason is more exact now. Good!

> These details help me understand how you feel about the weather. I feel the same way!

Reading As a Writer

- How did Asa respond to Sal's questions?
- Asa added a closing to his final copy. Why does this make his essay better?
- What words did Asa add to the beginning of each reason? Why does adding these words make his paper easier to read?

Write an Opinion Essay

▶ Start Thinking

 Make a writing folder for your opinion essay. Copy the questions in bold print, and put your paper in your folder. Write your answers as you think about and choose your topic.

- **Who will be my audience?** Will it be my classmates? a family member? the school principal?
- **What will be my purpose?** Do I want to tell my audience about a place I like to visit? Do I want to help myself make a decision?
- **How will I publish or share my opinion essay?** Will I send it as a letter to a newspaper? make a tape recording? make a collage?

▶ Choose Your Topic

❶ **List** five topics that you have a strong opinion about. There should be things you like and dislike about each one. (Don't list people.) Look at part of Asa's list.

> chores—earn money, but less
> time for fun
> soccer—can play fullback, but
> goalie position dumb
> television—can learn a lot, but
> watch too much

HELP ? **Stuck for a Topic?**

Here are some ideas.
I like/I don't like . . .
- playing computer games
- studying math
- owning a pet
- playing an instrument

See page 433 for more ideas.

❷ **Discuss** your topics with a partner. What are your reasons for liking and not liking each one?

❸ **Ask** yourself these questions about each topic. Circle the topic you will write about.

- Do I feel strongly about this topic?
- Do I have several good reasons for why I like it? why I dislike it?

An opinion essay can also be about what you like about a topic or about what you dislike.

Focus Skill

Choosing Strong Reasons

Reasons tell why you feel or think a certain way. To help you think of reasons, ask *Why?* about your opinion. Compare the weak and strong reasons below.

I like _____ because _____

I don't like _____ because _____

Opinion: I like walking the dog.

Weak Reasons	Strong Reasons
general reason: have fun	**exact reason:** playing outside together
unimportant reason: get to wear new sneakers	**important reason:** make friends with other dog walkers

Think and Discuss Compare the examples above.

- Why is the exact reason better? Why is the important reason better?

▶ Explore Your Reasons

Make a T-Chart. Write three or four reasons why you like the topic and three or four reasons why you don't like it. Cross out any reasons that are not important.

If you can't think of three strong reasons, try another topic.

I like soccer.	I don't like soccer.
fast-moving game	goalie a dumb position
play anywhere	~~early games on weekends~~
~~great snacks~~	work with the team
fullback position	

▲ **Part of Asa's chart**

HELP? See page 14 for other ideas for exploring your topic.

 Go to www.eduplace.com/kids/hme/ for graphic organizers.

Elaborating Your Reasons

Reasons are like the wheels on a bike. Wheels support a bike, and reasons support your opinion. Details are like the spokes that make the wheels strong.

Use details to elaborate, or explain, your reasons. Give examples. Include enough details to make your reasons exact and clear. Suppose your opinion is *I like Saturdays*. Compare the weak and strong details below.

Reason: I see my best friends.

Weak Details	Strong Details
do fun things	get to play outdoors
have a good time	have a good time riding our bikes down the dirt path

Think and Discuss Compare the examples above.

- Why are the strong details better?
- Suggest other ways to make the weak details stronger.

▶ Explore and Plan Your Essay

❶ Make two clusters. Label one main circle *I like* _____. Label the second main circle *I don't like* _____. Write your reasons from your T-Chart, circle them, and connect them to the main circles. Add details in circles for each reason. Here's an example from one of Asa's clusters.

I like soccer. — play anywhere
- all over the world
- play with two people or twenty
- kick ball with family and friends

❷ Number the reasons in the order you will write about them.

 Go to www.eduplace.com/kids/hme/ for graphic organizers.

Writing with Voice

When you write something as personal as an opinion, you should tell your audience how you really feel. Let your audience hear your voice.

Look at one student's working draft and final copy.

Working Draft

> Dogs can be annoying. They can wake you up. If you're not looking, they chew things. They bark at everything. Sometimes they bark really loudly for a long time.

Final Copy

> Dogs don't always have the best habits. Before the sun is up, they dive into your bed. Oh, no! If you're not looking, they'll chew your shoes to a pulp. When the phone rings or someone comes over—yap, yap, yap—they bark forever.

Dogs are people too.

Think and Discuss Compare the examples above.

- What is the weak example about? the strong example?
- What words and details make the strong example better than the weak example?

more ▶

▶ Draft Your Essay

❶ Write your draft. Leave some space so that you can write an opening later. Make your writing sound like you.

> Skip every other line, and don't worry about mistakes. You can fix them later.

❷ Write two paragraphs. In the first paragraph, tell what you like about your topic. In the second paragraph, tell what you don't like. Use the reasons and details from your clusters.

- Write a topic sentence for each paragraph that states the main idea.
- Write the reasons that tell more about the main idea.
- Use the details to write supporting sentences for each reason.

❸ Use transitional words or phrases. Help your reader move smoothly from reason to reason.

Transitional Words	Transitional Phrases
also	the first reason
then	the most important reason
next	
besides	for example
finally	worst of all
	another reason

Tech Tip
You might want to use a computer to draft your essay.

Focus Skill

Openings and Closings

Good Openings

A good opening gives a clue, or preview, of what the topic is about and hooks the reader right away. Avoid dull openings. Compare these examples.

Weak Opening	Strong Opening
Here are some reasons why I like Saturdays.	One day a week I hop out of bed as soon as my eyes pop open. It's Saturday!

Good Closings

A good closing sums up the important points. Don't just stop after your last reason. End in a way that your reader will remember.

Weak Closing	Strong Closing
So that's why I like Saturdays.	Saturdays just aren't long enough. My friends, family, sports, and games keep me extra busy. Next week I'm getting up even earlier and doing more!

Think and Discuss Compare the examples above.

- What makes the strong opening better than the weak one?
- What makes the strong closing better than the weak one?

▶ Draft Your Opening and Closing

❶ Write two openings and two closings for your opinion essay.

❷ Choose the opening and the closing you like better.

Evaluating Your Opinion Essay

▶ **Reread** your opinion essay. What do you need to do to make it better? Use this rubric to help you decide. Write the sentences that describe your essay.

Rings the Bell!

- The opening tells what my topic is and gets my audience curious.
- Each paragraph has a topic sentence that states the main idea.
- My reasons are exact and important and are supported with details.
- My writing sounds like me.
- My closing sums up the main points.
- *There are almost no mistakes in capitalization, punctuation, and spelling.*

Getting Stronger

- My opening could be more interesting.
- One paragraph that tells reasons needs a topic sentence.
- Some reasons are not exact or important. A few reasons need more details.
- In some places, my writing doesn't sound like me.
- My closing does not sum up the important points.
- *There are a few mistakes.*

Try Harder

- My opening is boring.
- None of my paragraphs have topic sentences.
- My reasons aren't strong. Each reason needs more details.
- My writing doesn't sound like me at all!
- My essay just stops with my last reason.
- *There are a lot of mistakes.*

  See www.eduplace.com/kids/hme/ to interact with this rubric.

Revise Your Opinion Essay

1 **Revise** your essay. Use the list of sentences you wrote from the rubric. Work on the parts that you described with sentences from "Getting Stronger" and "Try Harder."

2 **Have a writing conference.**

When You're the Writer Read your essay to a partner. Discuss the parts that are giving you trouble. Take notes to remember what your partner says. Make any other changes you want.

When You're the Listener Tell at least two things you like about the essay. Ask questions about anything you don't understand. Use this chart to help you.

Tech Tip
Insert your partner's comments in bold print so that you can think about which changes you want to make.

What should I say?

The Writing Conference

If you're thinking . . .	You could say . . .
The opening doesn't tell what the essay is about.	Could you give your audience a clue about your topic?
This reason isn't important.	Are you sure you want to include this reason?
I don't understand some reasons.	Can you include more details to explain your reasons?
I can't tell when one reason stops and the next one starts.	Can you add transitional words to connect your reasons?
The paper just stops after the last reason.	Can you sum up the important points?

3 **Make more revisions** to your essay. Use your conference notes and the Revising Strategies on the next page.

Revising Strategies

Elaborating: Word Choice **Synonyms** are words that have the same or almost the same meaning. Choosing the best synonym will help make your writing more interesting and exact.

Without Synonyms	With Synonyms
The **cold** lemonade tastes **good** on **hot** summer days.	The icy lemonade tastes delicious on scorching summer days.

▶ Replace at least three words in your essay with synonyms.

📖 Use the Thesaurus Plus on page H79. See also page H13.

Elaborating: Details Insert details within a sentence, or write more sentences.

Without Details	Elaborated with Details
I enjoy playing in the water.	I enjoy splashing and throwing a ball in the water. The best part is wearing my new goggles.

▶ Add details in at least two places in your essay.

Sentence Fluency Your sentences won't be choppy if you make them different lengths.

Choppy Sentences	Smoother Sentences
I like summer vacation. My friends stop over. I get to stay up late.	I like summer vacation. My friends stop over, and I get to stay up late.
	I like summer vacation. When my friends stop over, I get to stay up late.

▶ Change at least two sentences in your essay to make them different lengths.

GRAMMAR LINK ▶ *See also pages 49 and 169.*

Proofread Your Opinion Essay

Proofread your opinion essay, using the Proofreading Checklist and the Grammar and Spelling Connections. Proofread for one skill at a time. Use a class dictionary to check spellings.

Proofreading Checklist

Did I

✔ indent all paragraphs?

✔ correct any run-on sentences?

✔ use pronouns correctly?

✔ write contractions correctly?

✔ correct any spelling errors?

📖 Use the Guide to Capitalization, Punctuation, and Usage on page H55.

Proofreading Marks

¶   Indent

∧   Add

⌒   Delete

≡   Capital letter

/   Small letter

HELP ? **Proofreading Tip**

Read one line at a time. Hold a ruler or a piece of paper under each line to help you focus on each word.

Grammar and Spelling Connections

Pronouns Use singular pronouns to take the place of singular nouns. Use plural pronouns to take the place of plural nouns.

Singular noun	Fishing is important to me.
Singular pronoun	It is important to me.
Plural noun	The waves splash over the boat.
Plural pronoun	They splash over the boat.

GRAMMAR LINK *See also pages 204 and 206.*

Contractions Use an apostrophe to take the place of letters left out.

Two Words	Contraction
is not	isn't
I am	I'm

GRAMMAR LINK *See also pages 116 and 216.*

Spelling Suffixes A **suffix** is a word part added to the end of a base word. kindly, peaceful, hopeless   📖 See the Spelling Guide on page H65.

Publish Your Opinion Essay

❶ **Make a neat final copy** of your essay. Be sure you fixed all mistakes.

❷ **Write a title** to make your reader curious, such as "The Ups and Downs of Soccer" rather than "Playing Soccer."

GRAMMAR TIP Capitalize the first, the last, and each important word in the title.

❸ **Publish** or share your essay in a way that suits your audience. See the Ideas for Sharing box.

Ideas for Sharing

Write It
Write a letter to the editor of your school or town newspaper.

Say It
• Make a tape recording of your opinion essay.

Show It
• Make a collage with pictures or drawings. Show what you like on one side and what you don't like on the other side.

Tips for Sending a Letter to the Editor

• If you are sending the letter to your town newspaper, include the name and address of the newspaper in the inside address.
• Include your name and phone number so that the paper can verify who wrote the essay.
• Address the envelope *Letter to the Editor.* Most newspapers also accept letters by e-mail and by fax.

Reflect

Write about your writing experience. Use these questions to get started.

● What did you learn about writing an opinion essay?
● What was the easiest part? What was most difficult?
● How does this paper compare with other papers you have written?

Writing Prompts

Use these prompts as ideas for opinion essays or to practice for a test.
Decide who your audience will be. Write your essay in a way that they will enjoy.

1 Your teacher asks your opinion about places your class might go for a field trip. Write your opinion about a special place you have visited. Tell what you liked about it.

2 Write about a ride at an amusement park. What did you like about the ride? What didn't you like? Would you recommend it to a friend?

3 Write about an animal that interests you. Tell why you would like to have it for a pet, and why you would not.

4 Think about a book or story you have read recently. Write a review of it. Tell what you liked about the book or what you didn't like. Support your opinions with strong reasons.

Writing Across the Curriculum

5 FINE ART

Have you ever seen a camel like this one? Did the artist want to show what a real camel looks like, or was he trying to be funny? Write your opinion about this sculpture.

National Gallery of Art, Washington, D.C.

Black Camel with Blue Head and Red Tongue,
by Alexander Calder (1898–1976)

See www.eduplace.com/kids/hme/ for more prompts.

✓ Test Practice

This prompt to write an opinion essay is like ones you might find on a writing test. Read the prompt.

> **Write about an animal that interests you. Tell why you would like to have it for a pet, and why you would not.**

Here are some strategies to help you do a good job responding to a prompt like this.

Remember that an opinion essay tells what the writer thinks or feels about a topic.

❶ Look for clue words that tell you what to write about. What are the clue words in the prompt above?

❷ Choose a topic that fits the clue words. Write the clue words and your topic.

Clue Words	My Topic
why you would like to have it for a pet, and why you would not	I will write about the iguana I saw on television last week.

❸ Plan your writing. Use two clusters.

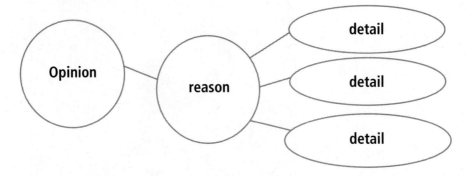

❹ You will get a good score if you remember the description of what kind of opinion essay rings the bell in the rubric on page 428.

 Go to www.eduplace.com/kids/hme/ for graphic organizers.

Writing a Book Report

Writing a **book report** is a way to share information and opinions about a book you have read. Read Aimee's report on *Little House on the Prairie*, which is a story of fiction that is set in the past.

Title → Little House on the Prairie
Author → by Laura Ingalls Wilder

LAURA INGALLS WILDER
Little House
on the Prairie

Introduction —
    Have you ever wondered what it would be like to leave your home and travel in a covered wagon to a new place? Well, that's exactly what the Ingalls family does in the book Little House on the Prairie.

Description —
    The story begins when the family moves from Wisconsin to Kansas. On their journey they see many new animals and have exciting adventures. Early in the story the family crosses a flooding creek. They reach the other side, but Jack, the dog, is missing. Later, after the family builds a house, the chimney catches fire. Ma and Laura try to put it out. What happens to Jack? Do Ma and Laura put out the fire? Read the book to find out.

Opinion —
    I really liked this book because you feel like you're on the prairie as you read. The author also makes you feel like you actually know the Ingalls family. If you enjoy reading stories full of excitement and adventure, Little House on the Prairie is the book for you.

See www.eduplace.com/kids/hme/ for more examples of book reports.

more ▶

Reading As a Writer

- The **title** gives the name of the book.
  What is the title of this book?
- The **author** is the person who wrote the book.
  Who is the author?
- The **introduction** presents the subject of the report and captures the interest of the reader.
  How did Aimee begin her report?
- The **description** tells what the book is about.
  What is this book about? What did Aimee tell about the book she read?
- The **opinion** explains what the writer thought about the book.
  Why did Aimee like this book?

How to Write a Book Report

1 **List** the title of the book and the author's name.

2 **Introduce** your book by making your reader curious about it. You might ask a question, give a startling piece of information, or use a quotation from the book.

3 **Describe** the book. Include at least one event from the story in your summary.

4 **Give** your opinion. Tell what you thought about this book and why. Did the picture on the book's cover or the illustrations in the book help bring the story to life?

5 **Revise and proofread** your book report. Use the Proofreading Checklist on page 431. Use a dictionary to check your spelling.

6 **Display** a neat final copy of your book report in your classroom's reading center, or place it in the school library for others to read.

? **Need help?**

Ask yourself these questions to help you decide what to write.

- Is the book nonfiction (a real story) or fiction (a made-up story)?
- Is the story funny, exciting, scary, or sad?
- What is the setting?
- Who are the main characters?
- How do the photos or illustrations help tell the story?

Writing a Poem

Poets put words into interesting patterns. One kind is **rhythm**, a pattern of beats that you can tap out with your finger as you read the words. Some poems have the same number of beats in every line.

Another kind of pattern is **rhyme**. Words rhyme when they have the same ending sound, such as *moose, goose,* and *caboose.* In lots of poems, the rhyme comes at the ends of lines.

Read these poems to see how the writers used rhythm and rhyme.

Keziah

I have a secret place to go.
Not anyone may know.

And sometimes when the wind is rough
I cannot get there fast enough.

And sometimes when my mother
Is scolding my big brother,

My secret place, it seems to me,
Is quite the only place to be.

Gwendolyn Brooks

A MATTER OF TASTE

What does your tongue like the most?
Chewy meat or crunchy toast?

A lumpy bumpy pickle or tickly pop?
A soft marshmallow or a hard lime drop?

Hot pancakes or a sherbet freeze?
Celery noise or quiet cheese?

Or do you like pizza
More than any of these?

Eve Merriam

more ▶

Penguin

O Penguin, do you ever try
To flap your flipper wings and fly?
How do you feel, a bird by birth
And yet for life tied down to earth?
A feathered creature, born with wings
Yet never wingborne. All your kings
And emperors must wonder why
Their realm is sea instead of sky.

Mary Ann Hoberman

I'm Hungry

My dish is empty. They're all in bed.
Don't they know I need to be fed?

I start to meow to get them awake.
I am so hungry, I could eat a steak!

I jump on their bed and lick their ears.
My stomach is growling. I am close to tears!

Finally Jack gets up and gets my dish.
He feeds me my favorite, tunafish.

My tummy is full, my eyes start to close,
and I start to dream as off I doze.

Elizabeth Allen,
Student Writer

Reading As a Writer

- Most of the lines in the poem "Keziah" have four beats. How many beats are in lines 2, 5, and 6?
- In "A Matter of Taste," how do lines 7 and 8 change the way the poem rhymes?
- How many beats are in each line of "Penguin"? What words rhyme?

How to Write a Poem in Couplets

1 **Choose** a topic. You can write a poem about almost anything—an experience you had, or a favorite place, person, or activity.

2 **Make** an idea tree to explore your topic.

- Write your topic under the trunk.
- On each branch, write an idea you'd like to include in the poem. It may be a thought, a feeling, or something that happens.
- Add some twigs to each branch. Put exact words, details, and rhyming words on the twigs.

Here is Elizabeth Allen's idea tree ▶

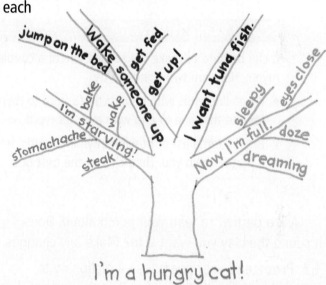

jump on the bed   Wake someone up.   get fed   get up!   I want tuna fish.   sleepy   eyes close

bake   wake   Now I'm full.   doze

I'm starving!

stomachache   steak   dreaming

I'm a hungry cat!

Here are more ideas.

- Write as if you were speaking as a different girl or boy, as Gwendolyn Brooks did in "Keziah."

- Write to an animal, as in the poem "Penguin." What would you like to ask your dog? a porcupine in the woods? a lion at the zoo?

- Write as if you were an animal, as in "I'm Hungry." What might your parakeet say about the room it lives in?

---

3 **Write** your poem in **couplets**. A couplet is made of two lines (a *couple* of lines). Both lines should have the same or almost the same number of beats. The words at the end of each line should rhyme.

Don't worry if your poem doesn't come out perfectly the first time!

more ▶

❹ Reread your poem.

- Have you said everything you want to say?
- Check the rhythm of your poem. Does each line have the right number of beats? Most lines should follow the pattern you have chosen.
- Check your rhymes. Does each pair of lines end with rhyming words?

Reread your favorite poem in this lesson. Feel the rhythm of the lines. Then put that rhythm in your poem.

I Can't Make It Rhyme!

It can be hard to make the second line of a couplet rhyme. Here are two things to try.

- If one line ends with a word that's hard to rhyme, rewrite that line to end with a better word.
- Brainstorm a list of possible rhyming words. Have a partner help you. Then choose the best one.

Mat? Flat? Acrobat?

Ask a partner to read your poem aloud. Does it sound the way you want it to? Make any changes.

❺ Proofread your poem. Use a dictionary to check spellings. Remember that the ends of rhyming words may be spelled differently, even though they sound the same, as in *crews, choose,* and *use.*

❻ Publish your poem. Make a neat final copy of your poem to include in a class booklet. You can also display your poems on a bulletin board.

Draw a picture for your poem, if you wish. Here are more ideas.

- Have a class poetry fair. Take turns reading your poems. Select one or two poems for a group to dramatize for your class.
- Make a tape recording of class poems. Share it with a younger class.

Writing a Nonsense Poem

Writing a nonsense poem about yourself is like dressing in a silly costume or drawing a cartoon portrait of yourself. It's also a way to play with words. Read these two examples.

As I Was Going Out One Day

As I was going out one day
My head fell off and rolled away.
But when I saw that it was gone,
I picked it up and put it on.

And when I got into the street
A fellow cried: "Look at your feet!"
I looked at them and sadly said:
"I've left them both asleep in bed!"

Anonymous

My Name Is . . .

My name is Sluggery-wuggery
My name is Worms-for-tea
My name is Swallow-the-table-leg
My name is Drink-the-Sea.

My name is I-eat-saucepans
My name is I-like-snails
My name is Grand-piano-George
My name is I-ride-whales.

My name is Jump-the-chimney
My name is Bite-my-knee
My name is Jiggery-pokery
And Riddle-me-ree, and ME.

Pauline Clarke

Reading As a Writer

- What makes each of these poems funny?
- What patterns of rhymes and beats can you find in the poems?

How to Write a Nonsense Poem

1. **Choose** an idea for a nonsense poem about yourself. It could be about funny names for yourself, odd things you collect, or silly things you'd like to do. List the things you'll put in your poem.

2. **Write** your poem. You might try using a pattern of rhymes and beats.

3. **Revise** your poem to make it as humorous as you can. Use exact words to paint clear pictures in your reader's mind, and try to find words with interesting sounds. If you wish, make up some words!

Use the Thesaurus Plus on page H79 to find words with pizzazz.

Having a Panel Discussion

In a panel discussion, a group of people talk about a topic in front of an audience. Each member of the group is called a panelist. Panelists take turns sharing their information and ideas. Look at the chart below to see one way a classroom panel discussion can work.

The moderator	• tells the audience the topic • introduces the panelists
Panelist 1	• speaks on the topic for three minutes
Panelist 2	• speaks on the topic for three minutes
Panelist 3	• speaks on the topic for three minutes
The moderator	• announces that the panelists can now discuss the topic together for ten minutes
The panelists	• talk and disagree politely
The audience	• asks questions of any or all of the panelists for ten minutes; panelists respond

When you take part in a panel discussion, you are both a speaker and a listener. Be sure that you understand the other speakers' opinions and reasons before you agree or disagree.

The guides below can help you be a good panelist.

Guides for Being a Panelist

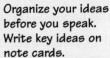

Organize your ideas before you speak. Write key ideas on note cards.

When You Are Speaking

▶ Clearly state your opinion about the topic.

▶ Give reasons for your opinions. Support your reasons with facts.

▶ Speak loudly enough so that everyone can hear you.

▶ Be polite when you disagree with others.

When You Are Listening

▶ Pay close attention to the person who is speaking. Try to block out sounds that make your mind wander away from the discussion.

▶ Try to understand each speaker's point of view. Listen to the reasons the speaker gives for his or her views. Are the reasons based on facts or opinions? Do they make sense?

▶ Don't interrupt another panelist. Ask questions after the speaker has finished.

▶ Be sure that you understand a speaker's opinions and reasons before you agree or disagree.

Apply It

Plan a panel discussion. Choose a topic and decide on time limits for the panelists. Research the topic. Write your opinion about it. Follow the guides above during the discussion. After the discussion, answer these questions.

● Which guides were difficult to follow? Why do you think so?

● What kinds of topics do you think would work well for a panel discussion? Explain why.

HELP
? **Need a Topic?**

Try one of these.
- favorite kinds of music
- the best way to spend free time
- peer tutors

Finding Points of View in Visuals

The visuals that you see in the media have many different purposes. The people who make the visuals give them a certain message about a subject. The message can tell you what those people think about the subject.

A way of thinking about a subject is called a point of view, or viewpoint. The photographs below show two different viewpoints.

Visuals do not always tell the whole story. They may leave out information that could greatly change the message. Further, when you change the focus of a visual, you can also change the viewpoint.

. . . .

Think and Discuss

- What is shown in the photo on the left?
- What is its focus, or center of attention?
- How is that focus different from the focus in the photograph on the right?
- Did you notice that the photo on the left is a part of the photo on the right?

Use the guides below to help you look at visuals.

Guides for Finding Points of View in Visuals

1 Focus
- Look for the main subject of the visual. What captures your attention?

2 Purpose
- Look at the details. What do you think is the purpose of the visual?

> Visuals have many purposes! These include:
> - to persuade
> - to sell
> - to express an opinion
> - to inform
> - to mislead
> - to entertain
> - to influence

3 Audience
- If you know who the audience is, you can tell a great deal about the purpose of a visual. Who does the visual appeal to?

4 Message
- Look for the message. What is the visual telling you? Ask yourself whether you are seeing all of the information. Could important details be missing?

5 Viewpoint
- The person or persons who made the visual have a way of thinking about the subject. What do you think it is?

Apply It

Use the guides above to help you show different points of view with visuals.

- Find a newspaper photograph, magazine advertisement, or other visual. Think about the point of view of the image. Then change the image to give a different point of view. You might cut the image apart, cover up parts, or add details.
- Draw, photograph, or videotape the same subject to create two visuals. Design each visual for a different audience. Each visual should show a different point of view or send a different message.

Writing to Persuade

Why spend time on games you played last year? Move up to a game that will really test your strategy skills.

Betsy Maestro believes that bats can help people. What does she want her readers to do?

Bats

from *Bats: Night Fliers,* by Betsy Maestro

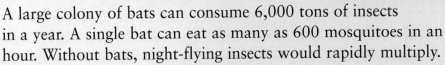

No one knows exactly how many bats there are on Earth. But we do know that Earth would not be the same without bats. A large colony of bats can consume 6,000 tons of insects in a year. A single bat can eat as many as 600 mosquitoes in an hour. Without bats, night-flying insects would rapidly multiply.

Tropical bats are like the bees of the night. They are the only pollinators of some night-opening flowers. And in the rain forests, where too much timber is being cut, seed dispersal aids in new tree growth. In these areas, over 300 kinds of trees and plants depend on fruit-eating bats for their survival.

 See www.eduplace.com/kids/ for information about Betsy Maestro.

Bats can live for 25 to 30 years. But many are eaten by natural enemies like owls, snakes, raccoons, and hawks. Spring floods can wash out caves and destroy whole colonies of bats. But the most harmful enemies of bats are human beings. Sadly, many bats are killed by humans, accidentally or on purpose.

The use of insecticides and poisons in the environment can also cause the death of many bats. Farmers kill bats for eating their fruit. However, bats only eat fruit that is too ripe to be sold. Cave explorers and vandals often disturb or destroy hibernating bats, resulting in the death of thousands of bats.

Some people believe bats attack and bite humans. They also mistakenly think all bats carry the disease *rabies*. But bats are very gentle creatures that rarely bite except when caught and frightened. They don't carry rabies any more often than other mammals. Bats are helpful, not harmful.

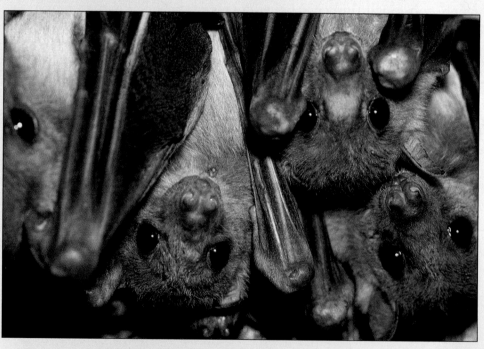

By protecting bats, people also help themselves. The Chinese have always believed that bats bring good luck. And they probably do. Places where bats live are usually healthy places where all life exists together in the right balance. Humans must learn to be kind to bats. They are nature's helpers and true friends of the earth.

Reading As a Writer

Think About the Persuasive Essay

- What does the author want her audience to do?
- Look at the second paragraph on page 447. What reason does the author give to support her goal?
- Some people believe that bats harm humans. What facts does the author use to show that this isn't true?

Think About Writer's Craft

- In the second paragraph on page 447, the author compares bats to bees. In what ways does she think bats and bees are alike?

Think About the Pictures

- Look at the photos of bats on pages 447 and 448. Which photo gives you a closer view? What does the photo with the more distant view let you see that the close-up photo does not?

Responding

Write responses to these questions.

- **Personal Response** What was your opinion of bats before you read this excerpt? after you read this excerpt?
- **Critical Thinking** Why might it be difficult to persuade people not to be afraid of bats?

What Makes a Great Persuasive Essay?

In a persuasive essay, a writer tries to persuade an audience to do something.

Remember to follow these guidelines when you write a persuasive essay.

▶ Start by telling your goal. Your goal is what you want your audience to do.

▶ Write a paragraph for each reason. State the reason in a topic sentence.

▶ Give strong reasons that support your goal. Back up your reasons with facts and examples.

▶ Tell your reasons from most important to least important.

▶ Use a confident voice.

▶ Write an ending that sums up your goal and your reasons.

GRAMMAR CHECK

Add an apostrophe and s ('s) to a singular noun to make it possessive. When a plural noun ends in s, add an apostrophe (') to make it possessive.

WORKING DRAFT

Andrea Zawoyski wants a dog, and she has many good reasons why. She wrote this draft to persuade her parents to get her one.

Andrea Zawoyski

Working Draft

A Dog for a Pet

A friendly puppy can make you as happy as a clam!

I could teach our dog to be a loyal watchdog. We worry so much about James wandering off. "Where's James?" someone asks a dozen times a day. Well, if we got a dog, that wouldn't be a worry for us any longer. A faithful dog would bark as loudly as an alarm if James walked out of our cozy, warm house. It would also bark if any strangers came to the door.

A dog would teach responsibility. That is one of the most important skills to learn.

A dog would be a fantastic furry friend. If you play with it as much as you can, it'll grow up to be a great loving dog. A puppy is like a pal. It would be fun to teach it new tricks too.

> What is your goal?

> This reason supports your goal. Well done!

> What facts and examples support this reason?

more →

Working Draft

> **Will this reason convince your parents?**

We would buy all sorts of stuff for our puppy. We would buy a tiny collar, a colored leash, and a little bed. We would also have to buy dog food every week. A cute, puppy-sized food bowl would be nice.

> **Why? Could you remind me?**

I've wanted a dog for as long as I can remember. I hope you understand why I want a dog so much.

THE END

Reading As a Writer

- What questions did Sal ask? What revisions might Andrea make?
- Find the reason about buying things for the puppy. Why might this reason not be convincing to Andrea's parents?
- Think of some reasons for buying a dog that Andrea didn't use. Which of these reasons might help convince her parents?

FINAL COPY

Andrea revised her persuasive essay after discussing it with a classmate. Read her final version to see how she improved it.

My Furry Wish

by Andrea Zawoyski

> Your opening states your goal clearly.

What do you think I've wanted for the longest time? I want a furry, friendly dog for a pet! Yes, I would love to get a small puppy.

> Your reasons are clearly ordered.

My first reason for getting a dog is that I could teach it to be a loyal watchdog. We worry so much about James wandering off. "Where's James?" someone asks a dozen times a day. Well, if we got a dog, that wouldn't be a worry for us any longer. A faithful dog would bark as loudly as an alarm if James walked out of our cozy, warm house. It would also bark if any strangers came to the door.

> You sound so confident!

My second reason is that a dog would teach responsibility. That is one of the most important skills to learn. James and I would be the ones feeding, bathing, and playing with it. We would brush it so its fur would be as soft as silky cotton. I wouldn't be able to walk it because I am not old enough, and it would probably pull me to Poland. However, I would be responsible for many other things.

> You support this reason well now.

My final reason is that a puppy would be a fantastic furry friend. A friendly puppy can make you as happy as a clam! If you play with it as much as you can, it'll grow up to be a great loving dog.

more

You sum up your goal and reasons nicely.

A puppy is like a pal. It would be fun to teach it new tricks too.

I've wanted a dog for as long as I can remember. I hope you understand why I want a dog so much. Dogs are very lovable animals. They teach responsibility. They can become good watchdogs. I know as soon as we get one, you'll feel the same way I do!

Reading As a Writer

- How did Andrea respond to Sal's questions?
- What facts and examples did Andrea give to support her reason that a dog teaches responsibility?
- Which reason do you think will be most convincing to Andrea's parents? Why?

 See www.eduplace.com/kids/hme/ for more examples of student writing.

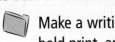
Write a Persuasive Essay

▶ Start Thinking

📁 Make a writing folder for your persuasive essay. Copy the questions in bold print, and put the paper in your folder. Write your answers as you think about and choose your topic.

- **What is my purpose or goal?** What do I want to persuade someone to do? Why do I care about this?
- **Who is my audience?** Do I want to persuade my parents? my friends? the principal of my school?
- **How will I publish or share my essay?** Will I reach my audience through a newspaper editorial? in a flier? in a speech?

HELP ? Stuck for an Idea?

Try these goal-starters.
- My school should have a _____.
- Our class should take a trip to _____.
- Everyone should learn to _____.

See page 467 for more ideas.

▶ Choose a Goal

❶ **List** five goals on a chart. Write what should be done (your goal) and who should do it (your audience). Part of Andrea's chart is shown below.

What Should Be Done?	Who Should Do It?
join the games club at school	my friends
get a dog	my parents

❷ **Discuss** each goal with a partner. Is any goal too large? Can you write about only one part? What reasons will you use? Will these reasons convince your audience?

❸ **Ask** yourself these questions about each goal. Then circle the goal you will write about.

- Do I really care about this goal? Will it interest my audience?
- Can I think of enough facts and examples to support my reasons?

▶ Explore Your Goal

❶ Start a web. Complete the sentence shown to tell your goal.

Goal: I want (name your audience) to (name your goal).

❷ Imagine yourself talking to your audience.

Mom, I really want a dog.

We don't need a dog.

A dog could watch out for James.

Taking care of a dog will teach me responsibility.

❸ Add reasons to your web. Each reason should explain why your audience should do what you want.

Stuck for a Reason?

If you can't think of at least three reasons, try another goal.

Goal: I want my parents to get me a dog.

- It would be a loyal watchdog.
- I would have a happy, furry friend.
- We'd get to buy a lot of stuff.
- It would teach me responsibility.

▲ **Part of Andrea's web**

See page 14 for other ideas about exploring your topic.

Focus Skill

Supporting Your Reasons

Pillars are strong posts that hold up a building. Facts and examples are the pillars that support your reasons and your goal.

Goal

reason   reason   reason

Fact Example Fact Example Fact Example

Elaborate reasons with facts and examples. Don't use opinions to support your reasons. An opinion tells feelings or thoughts. A fact can be proved. An example tells what has happened to you or someone you know.

Reason: *You should join the swim team because we have a good coach.*

Weak Support	Strong Support
Opinion: I think Coach Roth is the nicest guy!	**Fact:** For the last three years, Coach Roth's teams have all won the championships.
Opinion: I think Coach Roth is a good teacher.	**Example:** Coach Roth helped improve my backstroke by taking time to teach me after practice.

Think and Discuss Look at the published model on pages 447–449.

- Find three facts or examples that the writer uses to support her reasons.

▶ ## Explore Your Reasons

Add facts and examples to support each reason on your web.

It would be a loyal watchdog.

would bark if James left the house

would bark if a stranger came to the door

▲ **Part of Andrea's web**

Focus Skill

Evaluating Your Reasons

Be sure each reason is right for your audience. Different reasons work for different people. Think about what matters to your audience.

Goal: *Our class should take a trip to the computer museum.*

Reason for Teacher	Reason for Classmates
We will learn how new inventions can change our lives.	We will get to try new computer games.

Check your support for each reason. Do not exaggerate. Choose reasons that you can explain simply and honestly.

Goal: *Our class should take a trip to the computer museum.*

Weak: Unconvincing Reason	Strong: Convincing Reason
We will learn everything about computers.	We will get an introduction to how computers work. We will learn how software programs are written.

Try It Out

- With a partner, think of two strong reasons to persuade your friends not to watch any television for a week.

▶ Explore Your Reasons

❶ **Reread** your web. Which reasons will matter most to your audience? Which reasons are supported by the most facts and examples?

❷ **Choose** your most convincing reasons. You need at least three. Star them.

Focus Skill

Organizing Your Essay

Order your reasons from most important to least important. Tell your most convincing reason first. Tell your least convincing reason last.

Make each of your reasons a paragraph. The reason itself will be your topic sentence. The facts and examples will be the supporting details.

Keep to your topic. Leave out reasons that do not support your goal. Leave out facts and examples that do not support your reasons.

Use transitional words. Transitional words help your readers move smoothly from paragraph to paragraph. What other words can you add to this list?

First Reason	Second Reason	Third Reason
first, in the first place, my first reason	also, too, another, next, my second reason	in the third place, lastly, last of all, finally

Think and Discuss Look at Andrea's web below and her final copy on pages 453-454.

- Which reason does she tell first? Why?
- Which reason does she leave out of her final copy? Why?

▶ Plan Your Essay

Reread your web. Cross out reasons, facts, or examples that don't keep to your topic. Number your reasons from most to least convincing.

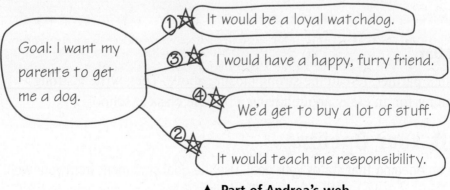

Goal: I want my parents to get me a dog.

① It would be a loyal watchdog.

③ I would have a happy, furry friend.

④ We'd get to buy a lot of stuff.

② It would teach me responsibility.

▲ **Part of Andrea's web**

 Go to www.eduplace.com/kids/hme/ for graphic organizers.

Focus Skill

Openings and Closings

Reasons, supported by facts and examples, are the meat of a good persuasive essay. The opening and closing are like the slices of bread that hold the whole sandwich together.

An opening clearly states your goal. Start by telling your audience exactly what you want them to do. You should also try to grab their attention.

Weak Opening	Strong Opening
Different flowers bloom at different times. This means you can plant a garden that will bloom and bloom. Wouldn't that be nice?	How often have you smiled at a flower? We should plant a flower garden at the senior center. All the blooms will make everyone smile.

A closing makes a call to action. Remind your audience of what you want. Sum up your reasons. Then get them excited about doing what you ask!

Weak Closing	Strong Closing
Once my friend was on his bike, and he didn't stop at a corner. He got hit by a car. Now do you see that we need a bicycle-safety class?	A bicycle-safety class will make biking safer, cut down on stolen bikes, and help us have more fun. This class is one more way school can make our lives better.

Try It Out

- With a partner, reread the strong closing above. Then write a strong opening for an essay about having a bicycle class at school.

▶ Draft Your Opening

Write an opening that states your goal. Use the goal statement from your web. Try to think of ways to make your audience interested in reading your essay.

Writing with Voice

Writing with voice means writing so that your thoughts and feelings come through clearly. Your own voice can make your essay more persuasive.

Show that you care. Choose words and phrases that show your goal is important to you. Try to sound positive, however. Don't sound angry.

Weak: Negative Voice	Strong: Positive Voice
Some people are too careless to recycle. Haven't these lazy people heard that we're running out of places to put all our trash?	What if all our fields and forests became garbage dumps? Recycling can prevent such a sorrowful disaster.

Write with a confident tone. Say "Follow me!" to your audience. Use persuasive words such as *certainly, clearly, definitely, obviously,* and *really.*

Weak: Not Confident Voice	Strong: Confident Voice
Let's get a second computer, okay? Maybe that will mean fewer arguments about whose turn it is.	Obviously, a second computer means less time waiting. This will really help our whole family, and clearly it will mean fewer arguments.

Think and Discuss Compare the examples of weak and strong voices.

- What words and phrases make the writer sound angry in the example of negative voice?
- Find the persuasive words in the example of confident voice.

▶ Draft Your Essay

❶ **Write** the rest of your essay. Follow your web. Skip every other line.

❷ **Write** a closing that sums up your goal and your reasons.

❸ **Use** a confident voice.

Evaluating Your Persuasive Essay

▶ **Reread** your persuasive essay. What do you need to do to make it better? Use this rubric to help you decide. Write the sentences that describe your essay.

Rings the Bell!

- ■ The opening tells my goal simply and clearly.
- ■ Each paragraph has a strong reason backed up by facts and examples.
- ■ I put my most important reason first.
- ■ A confident voice supports my goal and reasons.
- ■ My closing sums up my reasons and calls my audience to action.
- ■ *There are almost no mistakes in capitalization, punctuation, and spelling.*

Getting Stronger

- ■ The opening tells my goal, but it is unclear.
- ■ Some reasons don't support my goal. I need more facts and examples.
- ■ My first reason isn't the most important one.
- ■ My voice sounds angry or not confident.
- ■ My closing doesn't remind my audience of my reasons or my goal.
- ■ *There are a few mistakes.*

Try Harder

- ☐ The opening does not tell my goal.
- ☐ I haven't made my reasons clear. Every reason needs more facts and examples.
- ☐ My reasons are in no particular order.
- ☐ I don't sound as if I care at all about this goal.
- ☐ I forgot to write a closing.
- ■ *There are a lot of mistakes.*

  See www.eduplace.com/kids/hme/ to interact with this rubric.

▶ Revise Your Persuasive Essay

❶ Revise your essay. Use the list of sentences you wrote from the rubric. Work on the parts that you described with sentences from "Getting Stronger" and "Try Harder."

❷ Have a writing conference.

When You're the Writer Read your essay aloud to a partner. Ask questions about any problems you are having. Take notes to remember what your partner says.

When You're the Listener Say at least two things you like about the essay. Ask questions about parts that are unclear. Use the chart for help.

Revising Tip

If you reorder your reasons, don't forget to change the transition words also.

What should I say?

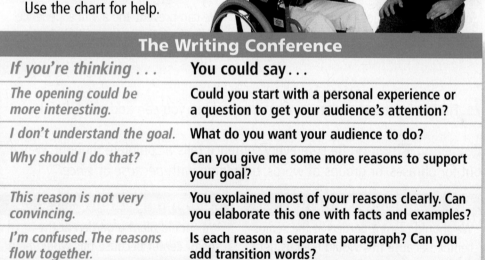

The Writing Conference

If you're thinking . . .	You could say . . .
The opening could be more interesting.	Could you start with a personal experience or a question to get your audience's attention?
I don't understand the goal.	What do you want your audience to do?
Why should I do that?	Can you give me some more reasons to support your goal?
This reason is not very convincing.	You explained most of your reasons clearly. Can you elaborate this one with facts and examples?
I'm confused. The reasons flow together.	Is each reason a separate paragraph? Can you add transition words?
The writer sounds uncertain.	Where can you use persuasive words?

❸ Make more revisions to your persuasive essay. Use your conference notes and the Revising Strategies on the next page.

Revising Strategies

Elaborating: Word Choice Choose words that support your goal and reasons. A word that is right for one goal can be wrong for another.

Wrong Word	Right Word
Your store should replace my computer monitor. It cracked when I **smashed** it against a table.	Your store should replace my computer monitor. It cracked when I bumped it against a table.

▶ Find at least two places in your essay where you can use a better word to support your goal and reasons.

📖 Use the Thesaurus Plus on page H79. See also page H13.

Elaborating: Details Make your facts and examples come alive for your audience. Use vivid, descriptive details.

Few Details	Elaborated with Details
We can prevent kids from getting their bikes stolen.	We can prevent the awful experience of finding only an empty hole in the bicycle rack.

▶ Find at least two places in your essay where you can add vivid details.

Sentence Fluency Be sure every sentence tells a complete thought. Watch out for phrases, or groups of words, beginning with *because* or *since*.

Not a Complete Sentence	Complete Sentence
We should plant a garden at the senior center. Because this would help us get to know senior citizens.	We should plant a garden at the senior center because this would help us get to know senior citizens.

Find and fix any incomplete sentences in your essay.

GRAMMAR LINK *See page 34.*

Proofread Your Persuasive Essay

Proofread your essay, using the Proofreading Checklist and the Grammar and Spelling Connections. Proofread for one skill at a time. Use a class dictionary to check spellings.

Proofreading Checklist

Did I
- ✔ indent all paragraphs?
- ✔ use complete sentences?
- ✔ use correct adverb forms?
- ✔ use apostrophes correctly?
- ✔ correct any spelling errors?

📖 Use the Guide to Capitalization, Punctuation, and Usage on page H55.

Proofreading Marks
¶ Indent
∧ Add
⌿ Delete
≡ Capital letter
/ Small letter

Tech Tip
Use the Find function to locate words you may have overused, such as *really* or *very*.

Grammar and Spelling Connections

Adverbs Add *-er* to short adverbs to compare two actions. Add *-est* to short adverbs to compare three or more actions.

Juan ran faster than Charles. Of all the runners, Juan ran fastest.

GRAMMAR LINK > *See also page 238.*

Possessive Nouns Add an apostrophe and *s* ('s) to a singular noun to make it possessive. When a plural noun ends with *s*, add an apostrophe (') to make it possessive.

the student's speech   the students' speeches

GRAMMAR LINK > *See also pages 76 and 78.*

Spelling |ôr| The |ôr| sounds are often spelled *or, ore,* or *oar.*

horse, more, soar   📖 See the Spelling Guide on page H65.

Publish Your Persuasive Essay

① **Make a neat final copy** of your essay. Be sure you fixed all mistakes.

② **Title** your essay. Choose an attention-grabbing title, such as "Send Your Dog to College" rather than "Obedience School."

> **GRAMMAR TIP** *Capitalize the first, the last, and each important word in a title.*

③ **Publish** or share your essay in a way that fits both your goal and your audience. See the Ideas for Sharing box.

Tips for Giving a Speech

- Practice your speech beforehand.
- Speak with expression. Use a persuasive tone.
- Use your face and hands to express your feelings.
- Speak loudly and slowly enough for your audience to hear and understand you.

📖 See page H5 for more tips.

Ideas for Sharing

Write It
- Post your essay on your school's Internet site.

Say It
- Present your essay as a speech.

Show It
- Make a flier and pass out copies. Include pictures that illustrate your reasons.

Reflect

Write about your writing experience. Use these questions to get started.

- What have you learned about writing persuasively?
- What was most difficult about writing a persuasive essay? What was easiest?
- How does this paper compare with other papers you have written?

Writing Prompts

Use these prompts as ideas for persuasive essays or to practice for a test. Some of them will work well for other subjects you study. Decide who your audience will be, and write your essay to convince them.

1 Choose a place you have visited recently, such as a park or a museum. Write a letter persuading a friend to visit it also.

2 All dog owners should take their pet to obedience classes. Write an essay agreeing or disagreeing with this idea.

3 What does your school need? It could be a playing field or more computers. Write a letter persuading your principal that your school needs it.

4 Kids should be allowed to watch as much television as they want. Persuade parents to agree with this statement, or persuade kids to disagree with it.

Writing Across the Curriculum

5 **LITERATURE**

Choose a book you really care about. Persuade your friends to read it too. Use details from the book to support your reasons.

6 **HEALTH**

Persuade both your classmates and your teachers to eat a good breakfast before coming to school.

7 **SOCIAL STUDIES**

What can be changed in your town to make bicycling safer? Write a persuasive letter to a local newspaper suggesting these changes.

8 **MATHEMATICS**

Persuade your classmates to join a math club. Use facts and examples from your own experience with mathematics to support your reasons.

Test Practice

This prompt to write a persuasive essay is like ones you might find on a writing test. Read the prompt.

> **What does your school need?** It could be a playing field or more computers. Write **a letter persuading your principal that your school needs it.**

Here are some strategies to help you do a good job responding to a prompt like this.

❶ Look for clue words that tell what to write about. What are the clue words in the prompt above?

❷ Choose a topic that fits the clue words. Write the clue words and your topic.

> Remember that in a persuasive essay a writer tries to persuade an audience to do something.

Clue Words	My Topic
What does your school need? a letter persuading your principal that your school needs it.	I will write a letter persuading our principal to buy more computers for our school.

❸ Plan your writing. Use a web.

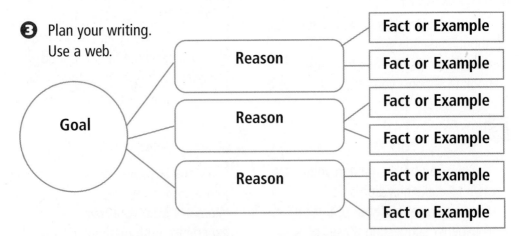

❹ You will get a good score if you remember the description of what kind of persuasive essay rings the bell in the rubric on page 462.

Writing a Business Letter

A **business letter** is usually written to someone you do not know. It may ask for information, order a product, give an opinion, or persuade someone to do something. Read Wesley's business letter.

Heading

> 1138 Reserve Avenue
> Glenview, IL 60025
>
> March 7, 2001

Inside address

> Wisconsin Department of Natural Resources
> Bureau of Fisheries Management
> 101 S. Webster Street
> Madison, WI 53717

Greeting → Dear Sir or Madam:

Body

> My aunt, my uncle, and I are planning a fishing trip this summer, and we would like to visit Wisconsin. We are interested in bass fishing there and would like to know the best lakes for catching bass.
>
> Do you have a map that shows where to fish for largemouth and smallmouth bass? Also, how much does a fishing license cost?
>
> I would appreciate your sending me any information you have about bass. I hope to catch one of Wisconsin's biggest fish! Thank you for your help.

Closing → Yours truly,

Signature → *Wesley Crane*

> Wesley Crane

Reading As a Writer

- The **heading** contains the writer's address and the date.
  Where is the date?
- The **inside address** is the name and address of the person, business, or agency to whom you are writing.
  In what city is the Wisconsin Department of Natural Resources?
- The **greeting** usually begins with *Dear* and includes the title and the last name of the person receiving the letter. A colon follows the name.
  Why didn't Wesley use a person's name?
- The **body** is the main part of the letter. It has one or more paragraphs.
  What did Wesley request?
- The **closing** finishes the letter, and it is followed by a comma. Common closings are *Sincerely* and *Yours truly*. *What closing did Wesley use?*
- The **signature** is the writer's name written in cursive.
  What is Wesley's full name?

How to Write a Business Letter

1 **Think** about the purpose of your letter and your reader. What do you want your reader to know or do?

2 **Organize** your thoughts. Jot down notes about what you want to say.

3 **Write** the letter. Include all six parts of a business letter.

4 **Use** polite, formal language. Make your point and include all necessary details. You can be friendly without being chatty.

5 **Revise** your business letter. Reorder sentences or change wording.

6 **Proofread** for mistakes. Use the Proofreading Checklist on page 465. Use a dictionary to check spellings.

7 **Write or type** a neat, correct final copy of your letter.

8 **Address** the envelope correctly and put a stamp on it. Make sure the addresses in the letter match those on the envelope. Mail the letter.

Return address

Wesley Crane
1138 Reserve Avenue
Glenview, IL 60025

USA

Mailing
address

Wisconsin Department of Natural Resources
Bureau of Fisheries Management
101 S. Webster Street
Madison, WI 53717

Listening for Persuasive Tactics

When a speaker is trying to persuade you, he or she wants you to do something. Listen for the reasons the speaker gives. Then ask yourself why you should take the action the speaker wants. Watch out for persuasive tactics that can tug on your feelings and keep you from thinking clearly.

Look at the tactics shown below.

Promise

Flattery

Other Tactics

Sometimes a speaker may use the fact that he or she is older than you to convince you to do something. Other times, a speaker may use taunts or dares, claiming that you can't do something, just so you will try to prove that you can. What other tactics are familiar to you?

more ▶

Decide for Yourself

Think about what you hear. Then decide for yourself what to do.

- **Think about the goal.** What does the speaker want you to do? Why is this goal important to him or her?

- **Think about the reasons.** Why does the speaker think you should do this? Does each reason make sense to you?

- **Think about the support.** How does the speaker explain each reason? Does the speaker just repeat an opinion or does he or she give facts and examples?

Guides for Listening for Persuasive Tactics

1 Listen for promises. Is the speaker saying that you'll get something good if you do this? Will this promise really be kept? How?

2 Listen for flattery. Is the speaker saying good things about you? Does this person really mean it? Has the speaker given you a good reason for doing what he or she asks?

3 Listen for taunts or dares. Is the speaker telling you that you're afraid to do something or that you don't really know how? Is the speaker asking you to prove something about yourself that you already know? Is the speaker trying to scare you into doing this? Is what the speaker saying true? Is it fair?

Apply It

For the next week, listen carefully every time someone asks you to do something. Take notes on what you hear.

- What did each speaker want you to do?
- What reasons did each speaker give? What facts and examples did each speaker give?
- Were persuasive tactics used? Did you notice them at the time?

Watching for Persuasive Tactics

Mass media are used to get information to large numbers of people. Television, billboards, and magazines are types of mass media.

Advertising is a big part of many forms of mass media. Companies pay to place ads so that they can be seen by large audiences. These ads are meant to persuade you that you need the products or services that they show.

Tactics You've Seen

The people who make ads use tactics, or ways, to get people to buy products. Some tactics are meant to play on your feelings. Look at the examples below. You've probably seen these used on television or in magazines.

Persuasive Tactics	
Bandwagon Everyone else has one, so you should too. You'll feel left out if you don't.	
Superstars A sports star or a movie star says the product is good.	
Friendly Face Someone who seems trustworthy says you should use the product.	
Flattery You are wonderful. You deserve this product.	
Before and After The plant looks bad. Use the product and—wow! The plant looks great.	

more ▶

Stop and Think

When you look at an advertisement, remember that you are seeing only what the people who made it want you to see. Because an advertiser's goal is to sell the product, important information about the product may be left out of the ad.

Most advertisers want you to feel before you think. If you act on your feelings, you might buy the product. If you think about it first, you might find reasons not to buy the product.

The billboard above uses the bandwagon tactic. It makes it seem as if "everyone else" is riding the roller coaster. It wants you to believe that if you don't go to the amusement park, you won't get to take part in something special.

Sometimes a star athlete sells a product. The people who make this kind of ad hope that you will buy the product because you admire famous sports figures. Ads like this often suggest that if you use the product, you will become strong or famous too.

When you look at an ad or a commercial, notice how it tries to persuade you. Here are some guides to follow.

Guides for Looking at Media Advertising

▶ Look carefully at the advertisement. Who made it? What does it want you to do?

▶ Think about how the ad is trying to make you feel.

▶ Check the ad to see whether it uses facts or opinions. Does it tell you all there is to know about the product or service? Does it make something seem too easy?

▶ Study the ad to see if any persuasive tactics were used. If so, which?

▶ Ask yourself if the ad is fair. Do you think it is truthful?

▶ Ask yourself what the ad is trying to make you believe. Make up your own mind about what you see.

Apply It

Watch the commercials that air during a television show you like. Videotape them if you can. Following the guides above, take notes on one. Then answer these questions.

● What product or service is being advertised?

● Is the commercial fun and entertaining? What do you like about it?

● If you could talk to the people who made it, what questions would you ask?

Look through several children's magazines. Find an ad that uses one of the persuasive tactics described in this lesson. Share the ad with your classmates and talk about the messages it uses. Then create an ad of your own, using the same tactic.

3

Tools
and
Tips

What You Will Find in This Part:

Taking and Leaving Messages

People keep in touch by using the telephone. If you answer a call for someone else, take a message. If you make a call and no one answers, you can leave a message on an answering machine. Read this conversation and Keisha's message. What information did she write?

MR. BAY: Hello, Keisha. This is Mr. Bay. May I speak to your father?

KEISHA: I'm sorry, he can't come to the phone right now. May I take a message?

MR. BAY: Yes, please ask him to call me at 555-2197.

KEISHA: I'll tell him to call Mr. Bay at 555-2197.

Saturday, 10:15 a.m.

Dad, please call Mr. Bay at 555–2197.

Keisha

Keisha included all of the information that her father would need in her message. When you take or leave messages, follow these guidelines.

Guidelines for Taking and Leaving Messages

1. When you take a message, write the caller's name, the telephone number, and the message. Ask questions if any part of the message is not clear, and retell the message to be sure you have taken it correctly. Include the day and time that you take the call.

2. When you leave a message, give your name, your telephone number, and a brief message, including the day and time you called.

3. Be polite. Speak slowly and clearly.

Apply It

A. Follow the guidelines and practice taking notes as your teacher reads a telephone message.

B. Role-play giving and taking telephone messages with a classmate.

Giving a Talk

When you give a talk, you speak about a certain topic. You need to plan, prepare, and practice your talk before you present it. Follow these guidelines when you give a talk.

Guidelines for Giving a Talk

1 **Plan** your talk.

- Decide if the purpose of your talk will be to inform, to persuade, or to entertain. The tone of your talk, such as humorous or serious, should match your purpose.

- Think about your audience. Should you use formal or informal language? How much do the listeners know about your topic?

2 **Prepare** your talk.

- Find the information you need. Gather any graphics or visuals, such as maps, pictures, or objects, that you want to show.

- Jot down notes or key words on note cards. Be sure to use words that are appropriate for your audience.

> Kennedy Space Center
> - full name: John F. Kennedy Space Center of the National Aeronautics and Space Administration (NASA)
> - location: Merritt Island, Florida, near Cape Canaveral (show map)
> - what they do: test, repair, and launch all manned U.S. space missions

- Be sure your talk has a beginning, a middle, and an end. Put notes in the order you will talk about them. You might want to highlight key words.

more ▶

Giving a Talk *continued*

❸ Practice your talk.

● Give your talk to a friend or family member, using your notes and your visual aids. Revise your talk after listening to their comments.

Tips for Using Visual Aids
• Make sure any lettering is large enough for your audience to read. • Practice using any machines, such as an overhead projector or a slide projector, before you give your talk. • Don't block the visuals from the view of the audience.

● Practice how you say your words. Think about the rate, volume, pitch, and tone of your voice.

Speaking Tips
• Don't talk too fast or too slowly. • Talk loudly enough to be heard, and remember to talk more loudly in a big room than in a small space. • Speak with expression.

HELP ? **Talk About Talk**

Rate: how fast or slowly you talk

Volume: how loud or soft your voice is

Pitch: how high or low your voice is

Tone: how happy, sad, funny, or angry you sound

● Practice until you have almost memorized your talk.

❹ Present your talk.

● Remember to use your voice and visual aids in the same way you practiced.

● Project your voice. Avoid saying *um, ah,* and *well.*

● Make eye contact with people in your audience.

Apply It

Give a talk about a funny experience, an opinion you have, or another topic that interests you. Then follow the guidelines as you **plan, prepare, practice,** and then **present** your talk.

Understanding Nonverbal Cues

Look at the students pictured below. Imagine they are talking about having to take part in a new school sport—tennis. How do you think each one feels about it?

Just like words, your face and body movements or positions can let others know what you think or how you feel. This "body language" is known as **nonverbal cues**.

Using Nonverbal Cues

You can use nonverbal cues to support what you are saying. Here are some examples.

- Use facial expressions to match your message.
- Use hand motions to stress a point when persuading.
- Use your hands to show sizes and shapes.
- Point to show a direction or an object. (Don't point to people!)
- Make eye contact to show you're aware of your listeners.

more ▶

You can use nonverbal cues to send a message without words. Here are some examples.

- Smile and nod your head to show interest and understanding. Look puzzled when something is not clear.
- Put your arm around a family member to show affection or around a friend to show comfort.
- Give a thumbs up to show support.
- Give a high-five to show friendship.
- Smile to show friendliness. Frown to show unhappiness.
- Sit back to show you're relaxed. Lean forward to show special interest.

Warning! Nonverbal cues can give away your true feelings or send the wrong message!

Observing Nonverbal Cues

Watch others' nonverbal cues. A pained look on someone's face may show that you said something that hurt. Someone looking at the ground while talking may be shy or embarrassed. Someone slouching or staring into space may be bored. If you are aware of a person's nonverbal cues, you will know better how to react appropriately.

Guidelines for Nonverbal Cues

1. Always have good eye contact when speaking.

2. Use nonverbal cues to support your words.

3. Use nonverbal cues to show what you think or feel without words.

4. Watch others' nonverbal cues as clues to their thoughts and feelings, and respond appropriately.

Apply It

With your class or in a small group, take turns demonstrating different nonverbal cues. Discuss what message each nonverbal cue sends.

Interviewing

One way to get facts for a report or a news article is to **interview** someone who knows that information. An interview is a kind of conversation. One person asks questions and the other person answers them. The **interviewer** is the person who asks the questions.

To get all the facts you want during an interview takes careful planning. The guidelines below will help you.

Guidelines for Interviewing

1. Decide what you want to know.

2. Think of questions that will help you get the information you want to know. Try to think of questions that begin with *Who, What, Where, When, Why,* or *How*. Do not ask questions that can be answered *yes* or *no*.

3. Write your questions in an order that makes sense. Leave space after each question for writing notes during the interview.

4. Before you ask your first question, tell the person the reason for your interview.

5. Ask your questions clearly and politely. Pay close attention to the answers.

6. Take notes to help you remember the answers. You may want to write the person's exact words if it is an important piece of information. Write these words as a quotation and use quotation marks.

7. If you don't understand something, ask more questions about it.

more ▶

Interviewing *continued*

The following notes were taken during an interview with a person who plays the steel drums.

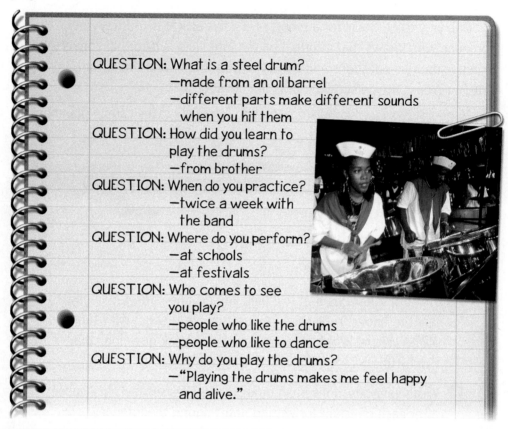

QUESTION: What is a steel drum?
 —made from an oil barrel
 —different parts make different sounds
  when you hit them
QUESTION: How did you learn to
  play the drums?
 —from brother
QUESTION: When do you practice?
 —twice a week with
  the band
QUESTION: Where do you perform?
 —at schools
 —at festivals
QUESTION: Who comes to see
  you play?
 —people who like the drums
 —people who like to dance
QUESTION: Why do you play the drums?
 —"Playing the drums makes me feel happy
  and alive."

Think and Discuss

- What kinds of questions did the interviewer ask?
- Do any of the questions call for *yes* or *no* answers? Why not?
- Work with a partner. Make up three more questions you could ask during the interview with the person who plays the steel drums.

Apply It

A. Pair up with a classmate. Tell each other a topic that you know about. Then interview each other, using questions each of you has written about the other person's topic. Follow the guidelines.

B. Interview a parent, a relative, or a neighbor about that person's job, hobby, or other interest. Use the guidelines. Share your questions and what you learned with your class.

Similes and Metaphors

Writers often try to describe something by using a comparison to create a picture in your mind. One way they do this is by using similes. **A simile compares two different things using the word *like* or *as*.** What two things are being compared in each sentence below?

The circling helicopter was as annoying as a giant mosquito.

The hose looked like a coiled green snake ready to strike.

The night sky was like black velvet sprinkled with glitter.

Sometimes writers use a different kind of comparison. **A metaphor is a comparison of two things without using *like* or *as*.** What two things are being compared in each of these sentences?

The broken window was a ragged web of cracks and holes.

The shirts on the clothesline were colorful banners flapping in the wind.

The dog was a detective investigating every corner of the yard.

Why do the similes and metaphors above help you better picture what the writer is describing?

Building Vocabulary

Apply It

Complete each sentence with a simile or a metaphor. Use the kind of comparison shown in ( ).

1. The bike seat felt like _____. (simile)
2. The clouds were _____. (metaphor)
3. The thunder sounded like _____. (simile)
4. The cat was _____. (metaphor)
5. The dog's eyes were as _____. (simile)

Idioms

An **idiom** is a phrase with a special meaning. The meaning of an idiom is completely different from the meaning of its separate words added together. Did anyone ever offer to sell you something for a song? The salesperson probably wasn't really asking you to sing. He or she was just telling you that the item cost very little. The expression *for a song* is an idiom. Here are some more examples.

Idiom: The lesson was over my head.

Meaning: The lesson was too hard for me to understand.

Idiom: What are you driving at?

Meaning: What are you trying to say?

Apply It

Write each sentence. Replace the underlined idiom with a meaning from the word box. Be sure that the answer makes sense in the sentence.

agree	became afraid
better than	exactly
hurry	immediately
listening carefully	teasing you
told me about	trouble

1. We'll have to step on it to get home in time.
2. I was just pulling your leg about going to school on Saturday.
3. Max was all ears when the teacher talked about space travel.
4. Karen filled me in on the swim meet.
5. Dan was going to dive, but he got cold feet.
6. Please wash the dishes right away.
7. This book is a cut above other books by that author.
8. My teacher and I don't see eye to eye about homework.
9. Tia was in hot water for being late again.
10. Theodore guessed the price on the nose.

Synonyms

Words that have nearly the same meaning are called synonyms.
Notice how this writer uses two different words for *happy.*

The family was glad to have a picnic.
The family was pleased to have a picnic.

glad   pleased

Here are some more synonyms for *happy.*

delighted   thrilled   overjoyed

Your writing will be more interesting if you do not use the same words over and over again. You can vary your writing by using synonyms. Use a thesaurus to find synonyms.

Apply It

Rewrite these sentences. Replace each underlined word with a synonym from the word box.

drowsy	blazed	hurried
frosty	sack	tasks
scraps	tossed	

1. Madeline awoke on a <u>cold</u> winter morning.
2. She <u>threw</u> off her warm covers.
3. Then she <u>rushed</u> over to the wood-burning stove.
4. Madeline grabbed the <u>bag</u> filled with kindling.
5. She stacked a few <u>pieces</u> of wood in the stove.
6. Soon the fire <u>burned</u> cheerfully.
7. The warmth made her <u>sleepy</u>.
8. However, she had many more <u>jobs</u> to do.

Antonyms

Antonyms are words that have opposite meanings. You can use antonyms to show how people, places, or things are different. Here are some antonyms for common words.

Antonyms			
stop—start	left—right	shiny—dull	sharp—dull
lost—found	good—bad	love—hate	hard—easy
dark—light	heavy—light	top—bottom	under—over

Apply It

Complete each sentence with the word from the word box that is an antonym for the underlined word. Write the sentences. You may use a dictionary for help.

long	enjoyed
important	eagerly
interesting	ancient
frequently	strange
rural	bought

1. Karen never reads <u>dull</u> books because she can always find _____ ones.
2. Sometimes she reads about <u>familiar</u> places, but more often she reads about _____ places.
3. She read one book about <u>modern</u> Greece, but she preferred a book about _____ Greece.
4. She <u>disliked</u> one book about Iceland, but she _____ another book about that country.
5. Karen <u>rarely</u> travels, but she _____ visits other lands in her imagination.

Prefixes

A **prefix** is a word part added to the beginning of a word. This word is called the **base word**.

Add the meaning of the prefix and the meaning of the base word to get the meaning of the new word.

Prefix	Base Word	New Word	Meaning
un-	lucky	unlucky	not lucky
re-	paint	repaint	paint again
mis-	place	misplace	put in the wrong place

paint

repaint

Apply It

Write each sentence. Replace the underlined words with a single word that begins with the prefix *un-*, *re-*, or *mis-*.

1. Ty <u>spelled</u> a word <u>wrong</u>.
2. The baby is <u>not happy</u>.
3. I <u>understood</u> you <u>wrong</u>.
4. Lu was <u>not kind</u> to me.
5. <u>Fill</u> the glass <u>again</u>.
6. I'll <u>write</u> the list <u>again</u>.
7. He is <u>not able</u> to sing.
8. <u>Heat</u> the stew <u>again</u>.

Suffixes

A suffix is a word part added to the end of a base word. Like a prefix, a suffix is a word part that has meaning. A suffix added to a base word makes a new word with a different meaning.

You can usually figure out the meaning of a word that has a suffix. Just add together the meaning of the base word and the meaning of the suffix.

fearful   **fearless**

Base Word	Suffix	New Word	Meaning
pitch	-er	pitcher	one who pitches
fear	-ful	fearful	full of fear
hope	-less	hopeless	without hope

Apply It

Add the suffix *-er, -ful,* or *-less* to the word in parentheses to make a new word that makes sense in the sentence. Write the sentences.

1. The _____ set up her easel by the lake. (paint)
2. An umbrella is _____ in the rain. (use)
3. The lion tamer was brave and _____. (fear)
4. Sandy was _____ and spilled the juice. (care)
5. The nurse was gentle, but the shot was _____. (pain)
6. Mr. Lopez is a _____ for the *Daily Sun*. (report)
7. Jenny Lind was a famous _____. (sing)
8. Nick was tired after a _____ night. (sleep)

Regional and Cultural Vocabulary

Which word or words do you use to name this insect? Depending on where you live, you might call it a darning needle, a mosquito hawk, a dragonfly, or a snake feeder. People in different regions of the country sometimes use different words for the same thing. Here are more examples of words that reflect regional differences.

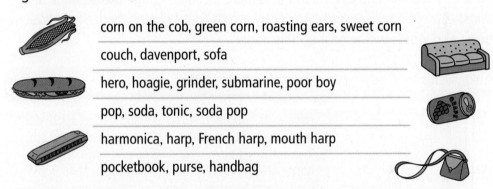

corn on the cob, green corn, roasting ears, sweet corn

couch, davenport, sofa

hero, hoagie, grinder, submarine, poor boy

pop, soda, tonic, soda pop

harmonica, harp, French harp, mouth harp

pocketbook, purse, handbag

People of different cultures and in other countries might also use different words to name the same thing. The game of soccer in the United States is called football by people in other countries, such as Great Britain. In Great Britain, a baby carriage is called a pram, and French fries are called chips. Friends are called mates in Australia and amigos in Hispanic cultures. In Hawaii, people say aloha to greet one another, but in Hebrew, the greeting is shalom.

Apply It

Choose a word from the examples above to complete each sentence. Use the word that comes most naturally to you. Discuss your choices with classmates.

1. Mom keeps money, keys, and stamps in her _____.
2. A _____ is a sandwich made from deli meats served on a long roll.
3. We were thirsty, so Dad bought us each a can of fizzy _____.
4. The butter melted on the hot _____.
5. The two _____ traded baseball cards.

Using a Dictionary

Entry Words and Guide Words

Entry Words Each main word listed in your dictionary is called an **entry word**. It is printed in heavy, dark type.

Guide Words At the top of each page in a dictionary are **guide words**. The guide word on the left tells the first entry word on the page. The one on the right tells the last entry word. In the sample dictionary page below, *mine* and *minstrel* are the guide words. Any entry words that fall alphabetically between these two words will appear on this page.

Guide words ———— **mine² ▸ minstrel**

Entry word ————
mineral *noun* **1.** A natural substance, such as a diamond, that is not of plant or animal origin. **2.** A natural substance, such as ore, coal, or petroleum, that is mined for human use. ◊ *adjective* Containing minerals: *Mineral water is good for the health.*
min·er·al (mĭn′ər əl) ◊ *noun, plural* **minerals** ◊ *adjective*

Other Forms of Words Entry words are usually listed in their simple forms, without endings such as *-ed, -ing, -s, -er,* and *-est.* Suppose you are looking for the word *mingled* on the sample dictionary page. The basic form of *mingled* is *mingle.* Find *mingle* as an entry word. Another form of the word, *mingling,* is also listed in the entry.

mingle *verb* **1.** To mix or become mixed; combine: *The sound of chimes mingled with the ringing of the doorbell.* —See Synonyms at **mix. 2.** To join in company with others: *We mingled with the crowd during the play's intermission.*
min·gle (mĭng′gəl) ◊ *verb* **mingled, mingling**

Other forms ————

Definitions

When you come across an unfamiliar word in your reading, first use the context of the sentence to figure out its meaning. If these words do not help you, look up the word in a dictionary.

Words with More Than One Meaning Many words have more than one meaning. Read the meanings for *harbor*.

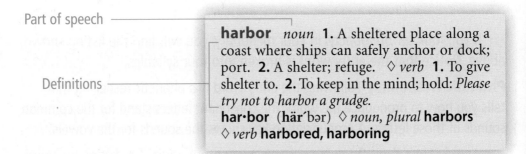

Part of speech

Definitions

> **harbor** *noun* **1.** A sheltered place along a coast where ships can safely anchor or dock; port. **2.** A shelter; refuge. ◇ *verb* **1.** To give shelter to. **2.** To keep in the mind; hold: *Please try not to harbor a grudge.*
> **har·bor** (här′bər) ◇ *noun, plural* **harbors** ◇ *verb* **harbored, harboring**

Parts of Speech Some words can be used as more than one part of speech. The entry above gives two meanings for *harbor* used as a noun and two meanings for *harbor* used as a verb.

Homographs Two or more different words that have the same spelling but different meanings are called **homographs**. Homographs come from different word roots, or sources. In the entries for *mint,* each homograph is marked with a raised number.

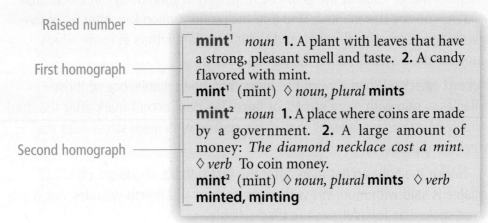

Raised number

First homograph

Second homograph

> **mint¹** *noun* **1.** A plant with leaves that have a strong, pleasant smell and taste. **2.** A candy flavored with mint.
> **mint¹** (mĭnt) ◇ *noun, plural* **mints**
>
> **mint²** *noun* **1.** A place where coins are made by a government. **2.** A large amount of money: *The diamond necklace cost a mint.* ◇ *verb* To coin money.
> **mint²** (mĭnt) ◇ *noun, plural* **mints** ◇ *verb* **minted, minting**

more ▶

Research and Study Strategies

Using a Dictionary *continued*

Pronunciations

Look at this picture of a flying reptile that lived during the dinosaur age. Can you pronounce the creature's name?

Syllables   Accent marks

pter·o·dac·tyl (tĕr′ə **dăk′** təl)

Phonetic respelling

If you look up *pterodactyl* in your dictionary, you will find the listing shown above. Notice that the entry word is broken into four syllables.

Phonetic Respelling Following the entry word is a phonetic respelling that tells you how to pronounce the word. The consonant letters stand for the common sounds of those letters. A pronunciation key shows the sounds for the vowels.

Pronunciation Key On every page or every other page of a dictionary, there is a pronunciation key. One is shown below.

ă	pat	ĭ	pit	oi	**oil**	th	bath
ā	pay	ī	ride	ŏŏ	book	*th*	bathe
â	care	î	fierce	ōō	boot	ə	ago,
ä	father	ŏ	pot	ou	**out**		item
ĕ	pet	ō	go	ŭ	cut		pencil
ē	be	ô	paw, for	û	fur		atom
							circus

Schwa Sound Look at the phonetic respelling of *pterodactyl*. In the second syllable, you see this mark: ə. Find it in the pronunciation key. After ə are five words: **ago, item, pencil, atom,** and **circus.** The dark letters in those words stand for the ə sound, called the **schwa sound.**

Accent Marks When a word has more than one syllable, one of those syllables is said with more **stress,** or force. The dark accent mark after the third syllable of *pterodactyl* means that *dăk* is spoken with more stress than the other word parts.

Notice the light accent mark after the first syllable of *pterodactyl*. That syllable is said with more stress than the second and fourth syllables, but it is not spoken as forcefully as the third syllable.

Research and Study Strategies

Using the Library

How Libraries Arrange Books

Libraries arrange books into two main categories, fiction and nonfiction.

Fiction books are stories made up by the author. They are arranged alphabetically by the author's last name in one section of the library.

Nonfiction books contain factual information. They are in a separate section and are grouped by subject, such as government, music, or travel. Each subject has its own range of call numbers, which tell where a book is located on the shelves. A specific call number is printed on the spine of each book.

Searching for Books

Using an electronic or traditional card catalog will enable you to find any book a library owns when you know the title or author. It will also help you find a selection of books when you just have a subject in mind.

Using an Electronic Catalog There are many different electronic catalogs, but all are easy to use if you follow the directions on the computer screen. Enter the book's title, the author's name, or the subject of the book. Don't enter the words *A, An,* or *The* at the beginning of a title.

The computer will search its database of materials in the library's system for your request. When you make an author entry, you will get a list of all the books the author has written. When you make a subject entry, you will get a list of all books related to that subject. To see an information screen about a particular book, choose an item from the list.

Electronic input screen

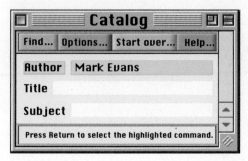

Author information list

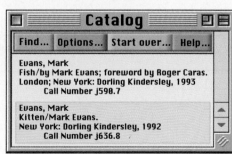

more ▶

Using the Library *continued*

When you enter a book title, you will automatically receive an information screen if the library owns the book. An information screen will give you a book's title and author. If the book is nonfiction, the screen may also display a call number.

Book information screen ——

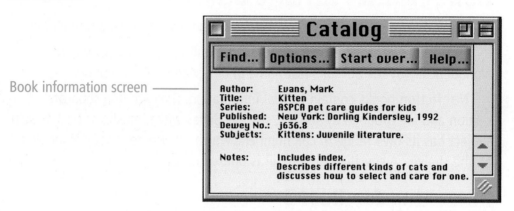

Using a Card Catalog A traditional card catalog can also help you to find a book. This type of catalog lists an author card and title card for every book. Some books have a subject card too. The cards are filed alphabetically in long wooden drawers. To help you find the book, write the title, the author, and the call number. Here is a set of author, title, and subject cards for one book.

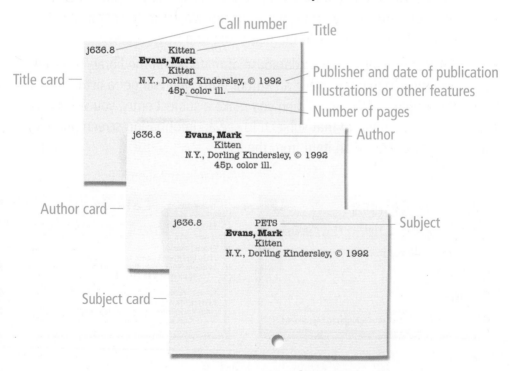

Research and Study Strategies

Reference Materials

The library can provide information on almost any subject. Here is a list of nonfiction reference materials in print that can help you. Most of these materials can also be found as electronic versions on CD-ROMs or on electronic databases in your library. (See "The Internet" on pages H43–H44 for more about using computers to find information.)

Encyclopedia An encyclopedia is a set of books that have articles about people, places, things, and events. The articles are arranged in alphabetical order in volumes. Each volume is lettered with the beginning letter or letters of the topics in that book. Guide words at the tops of pages help locate key words related to a topic.

Atlas An atlas is a book of maps. The atlas index provides the page number of each map and also gives the exact location of cities and towns.

Almanac An almanac is published once a year and has facts and other information on important people, places, and events. The index in the front lists every subject covered in the almanac. The most current almanac has the most accurate information.

Thesaurus Like dictionaries, most thesauruses list entry words in alphabetical order. In a thesaurus, however, these words are followed by lists of synonyms and antonyms. Writers use a thesaurus to find words that will make their writing more interesting.

More Dictionaries There are many special dictionaries that deal with specific topics. For example, there are dictionaries of geography or biographies that you can use to search for detailed information.

Periodicals Most libraries subscribe to magazines and newspapers from all over the country. Recent issues are usually available for use, but back issues are often bound into books and stored. Use the *Reader's Guide to Periodical Literature* to find an article on a specific topic in a back issue of any magazine.

Using Visuals

Tables

Facts can be shown on tables, or charts, that make it easy to see how different kinds of information fit together. The table below shows the typical temperatures of some cities in the United States.

Temperatures in U.S. Cities		
	January	**July**
Denver, Colorado	30°F (−1°C)	73°F (23°C)
Fairbanks, Alaska	−12°F (−24°C)	61°F (16°C)
Honolulu, Hawaii	72°F (22°C)	80°F (27°C)
New York, New York	32°F (0°C)	77°F (25°C)

This table has captions across the top and along the left side. The top captions are *January* and *July*. The side captions name five cities.

The lines that go across are called **rows**. The lines that go up and down are called **columns**. To use the table, trace across the row and down the column that you are interested in. The entry where the row and column meet will give you the information you need.

Bar Graphs

The bar graph below shows how long certain zoo animals usually live. Like the table above, this graph has captions. Notice that ages in years are shown by lines that cross the entire length of the graph. To figure out how long an animal lives, look where a bar meets a number line.

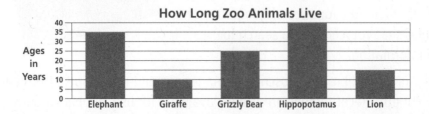

A bar graph shows how different things compare to one another at the same time. The bars can go up and down or sideways.

Maps

A map is a drawing or chart of all or part of the earth's surface, including features such as mountains, rivers, boundaries, and cities.

Legend Every map has a legend, which usually appears in a box near the map. The legend explains the map's **symbols,** the marks that stand for various things. For example, a star is a symbol for a state capital.

Distance Scale A distance scale is usually shown below the legend. It shows how a particular distance on the map relates to real distance in miles or kilometers.

Compass Rose Another important part of a map is the compass rose. Arrows show the directions *north, south, east,* and *west.*

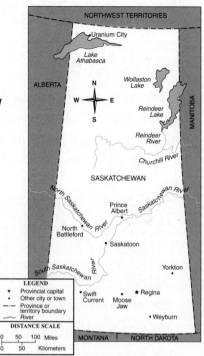

Diagrams

A diagram shows how something is put together or how it works. To understand a diagram, read the captions and all the labels.

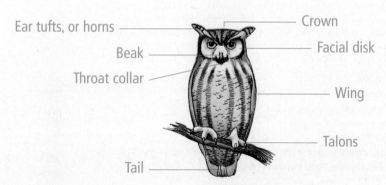

GREAT HORNED OWL

Ear tufts, or horns — Crown — Facial disk

Beak

Throat collar

Wing

Talons

Tail

If a diagram uses unfamiliar words, check the text near it for definitions. If you found this owl diagram in a book and did not understand the term *facial disk,* you would read the paragraphs near the diagram. You might discover that a facial disk is the ring of short feathers surrounding the owl's eyes.

Research and Study Skills

Taking Notes

Whether you are reading, listening to a speaker, or watching a movie, taking notes will help you remember what you read, hear, or see. Good notes will help you remember much more than what you actually write down. The following guidelines tell you important things to remember when taking notes.

Guidelines for Taking Notes

1. Don't copy what you read. Summarize main ideas in your mind, and restate them in your own words.

2. Use quotation marks to give credit for someone's exact words.

3. Write only key words and phrases, not entire sentences.

4. Below each main idea, list the details that support it.

5. Keep careful records of the sources you are using.

Here is text from an encyclopedia entry about Robert E. Lee. A card with notes is also shown. Notice that the card lists the source of the information.

> **LEE, ROBERT EDWARD** (1807–1870), American soldier and educator, was born at "Stratford," Westmoreland Co., Va., on Jan. 19, 1807. On account of business losses and ill health, his father, Gen. "Light-Horse Harry" Lee, moved with his family to Alexandria, Va. Here young Robert attended school until appointed to the United States Military Academy at West Point, from which he graduated in 1829, standing second in his class.

> **Lee's early life**
> – born January 19, 1807
> – father was "Light-Horse Harry" Lee
> – grew up in Alexandria, Virginia
> – attended West Point
> – graduated second in class in 1829
> Collier's Encyclopedia, 1999 Volume 14, page 440.

Facts
Volume number
Page number(s)
Source

Taking Notes While Listening When you take notes while reading, you can always look back and check facts to see if you missed anything. When listening to a speaker, you have just one chance to hear what is being said. Use the following guidelines to help you take good notes while listening.

Guidelines for Taking Notes While Listening

1. Keep your mind on what the speaker is saying.

2. Pay careful attention to the speaker's introduction and conclusion. A good speaker will outline the speech in an introduction and sum up the main points in the conclusion.

3. Listen for cue words, such as *first, the main point,* and *most important,* that signal important information.

4. Don't write everything. Write only key words or phrases.

5. Go over your notes after the speech to make sure you have included all of the main points.

6. Note the speaker's name, the location, and the date of the speech.

Taking Notes While Viewing It takes practice to view something, think about it, and take notes all at the same time. Unless you are watching a video, you can't stop the action and watch the film again. In addition to the general guidelines for taking notes, the following guidelines will help improve your note-taking skills.

Guidelines for Taking Notes While Viewing

1. Prepare for the film or event by reading related material ahead of time.

2. Look and listen carefully during the introduction.

3. Be selective. Don't write everything. Listen for important ideas and write only the key words.

4. Use symbols and abbreviations, such as *w/* for *with* and *#* for *number*.

5. Even though you can't watch while taking notes, listen to the dialogue and learn new information.

6. As soon as the film is over, go over your notes and fill in missing details while they are still fresh in your mind.

7. Be sure to record the title of the film.

more ▶

Outlining

An **outline** is a useful tool for sorting out main ideas and supporting details when you are reading or writing. When you use an outline to organize a piece of writing, it helps you plan the best order for your ideas.

An outline has a title and is made up of main topics, subtopics, and details. A **main topic** tells a main idea. **Subtopics** give supporting facts or details for the main topics. **Details** give more information about a subtopic. Use the following guidelines to write an outline.

Guidelines for Writing an Outline

1. Use a Roman numeral followed by a period to show each main topic.

2. Use a capital letter followed by a period to show each subtopic.

3. Use a number followed by a period to show each detail.

Here is an example of a topic outline. Note that the outline has a title. Usually the topics, marked with Roman numerals, are answers to questions about the subject.

Help for Blind People ——————— Title
I. Help with reading and learning ——————— Main topic
  A. Braille
  B. Talking books ——————— Subtopics
  C. Enlarged-print books
    1. Each letter enlarged by special machine
    2. Readers feel large letters ——————— Details
II. Help for moving about
  A. Special walking cane
  B. Trained dog
  C. Sonar device

Topics, subtopics, and details can be words, phrases, or sentences. The first word in each entry begins with a capital letter. There should always be at least two main topics, two subtopics under a main topic, or two details under a subtopic.

Summarizing

Summarizing helps you remember key points when you are reading or studying. A summary includes only the most important information.

Summarizing an Article Suppose that you read a lengthy article. Writing a summary can help you understand and remember details in the article. Read this summary of an article about sea otters, found on pages 369–370.

> Sea otters make great swimmers. Their bodies are shaped to move easily in water. Using front paws that are like hands, sea otters can pick up clams and other food. They have back feet that they use to push through the water. Sea otters can grow to be several feet long.

Notice that this summary begins with a clear statement of the main idea. The other sentences give details that support this main idea. The following guidelines should help you to write your own summary of an article.

Guidelines for Summarizing an Article

1. State the main idea of the article clearly and briefly.

2. Look for key words and important names, dates, and places from the article.

3. Use these facts to write sentences that support the main idea.

4. Be sure to explain events or steps in the correct order.

5. Use as few words as possible. Put the facts into your own words without changing the meaning of what you have read.

more ▶

Summarizing a Story When summarizing a story, briefly retell what happens. Be sure to include all the important characters and events. Read the following summary of "Crows," the story found on pages 298–299.

> Two crows with beautiful feathers and wonderful voices used to live in a forest. One crow was curious and one crow was careful. The curious crow talked the careful crow into flying near a forest fire. They were burned by the hot fire. Their feathers turned black, and they lost their beautiful call. They never went back home.

Notice that this summary includes the main events of the story. It also describes the characters' actions and their results. Use the following guidelines when you summarize a story.

Guidelines for Summarizing a Story

1. Decide what is the most important feature of the story. If it is a mystery, you might write about the plot. If the story is about friendship, you might write about the characters.

2. Write clear, brief sentences stating the most important ideas. Include important names, dates, and places from the story but don't include other details.

3. Be sure to give enough information so that the summary makes sense. The order of events in a summary should be the same as the order in the story.

4. To catch the tone or mood of the story, describe a specific character's actions or give a direct quotation.

Word Analogies

Many tests ask you to complete **word analogies** that show how two pairs of words are alike.

Wet is to *dry* as *hot* is to ___cold___ .

In this example, *wet* and *dry* are opposites. *Cold* completes the word analogy correctly because it means the opposite of *hot*. Now both pairs of words show opposites.

Often a word analogy is set up with colons. To help you answer it, think of it as a sentence.

Wet : dry :: hot : _____

Wet is to dry as hot is to _____.

This chart shows some ways words can be related.

Word Relationship	Example
antonyms (opposites)	*Fast* is to *slow* as *narrow* is to *wide.*
synonyms (same meanings)	*Surprising* is to *amazing* as *unhappy* is to *sad.*
a part to the whole thing	*Toe* is to *foot* as *finger* is to *hand.*
a whole thing to one of its parts	*Car* is to *wheel* as *airplane* is to *wing.*
a thing to a category that it belongs to	*Banana* is to *fruit* as *carrot* is to *vegetable.*
a person to something he or she does	*Farmer* is to *planting* as *doctor* is to *healing.*
a thing to one of its characteristics	*Ball* is to *round* as *knife* is to *sharp.*

more ▶

Word Analogies *continued*

Guidelines for Completing Word Analogies

1 Figure out how the first two words are alike.

2 If the analogy uses colons, say it as a sentence.

3 If you are asked to choose the second pair of words from a list, choose the pair that has the same relationship as the first pair.

4 If you are asked to fill in the last word, write a word that will make the second pair of words have the same relationship as the first pair.

Practice

A. Choose the pair of words that best completes each word analogy.

1. *Bark* is to *dog* as
   a. *scratch* is to *cat.*
   b. *tail* is to *pig.*
   c. *hoot* is to *owl.*
   d. *bark* is to *tree.*

2. *Chair* is to *furniture* as
   a. *car* is to *automobile.*
   b. *shirt* is to *clothing.*
   c. *paper* is to *book.*
   d. *dog* is to *poodle.*

3. *Day* is to *night* as
   a. *tall* is to *short.*
   b. *happy* is to *glad.*
   c. *car* is to *engine.*
   d. *horse* is to *pony.*

4. *Quiet* is to *silent* as
   a. *unhappy* is to *joyful.*
   b. *eager* is to *bored.*
   c. *sloppy* is to *messy.*
   d. *hour* is to *minute.*

B. Write the word that best completes each analogy.

5. Chef : cook ::
   pilot : _____.
   a. eat   b. write
   c. build   d. fly

6. Month : year ::
   classroom : _____.
   a. teacher   b. school
   c. chalk   d. study

7. Pie : slice :: door : _____.
   a. doorknob   b. house
   c. tall   d. window

8. Hurry : rush ::
   jump : _____.
   a. fall   b. swim
   c. leap   d. high

Open-Response Questions

Sometimes on a test you must read a passage and then write answers to questions about it. Remember these guidelines to help you write a good answer.

Guidelines for Answering an Essay Question

1. Read the question carefully. Find clue words that tell what kind of answer to write, such as *explain, compare, contrast,* and *summarize.*

2. Look for other clue words that tell what the answer should be about.

3. Write a topic sentence that uses clue words from the question. Write other sentences that give details to support the topic sentence.

4. Answer only the question that is asked.

Read the following passage and follow the instructions at the end.

Animals in the Arctic

The Arctic is the region at the top of the world. Because it lies so far north, it has very cold, long winters. The temperature can drop to sixty degrees below zero!

Even though the Arctic has bitter winters, many kinds of animals make their home there year round. If you went for a walk on the tundra, you might see caribou, a polar bear, or an arctic fox. These animals have thick fur coats that keep them warm. Some animals that live part-time in the water, such as seals and walrus, also have fur. They also have a thick layer of blubber under their skin to help warm them in the icy water.

The arctic hare, which looks like a rabbit, and the lemming, a mouselike rodent, are small furry animals that protect themselves from the cold by living in tunnels under the snow.

more ▶

Open-Response Questions *continued*

Birds have their own warm coats made of feathers. However, they have a special problem because they have no "leggings" to warm their feet and legs. Only a few birds whose feet and legs can stand very low temperatures, such as the ptarmigan, live in the Arctic.

There's one kind of animal you will rarely find, though—snakes and other reptiles. Very few of these cold-blooded animals could survive an Arctic winter!

Summarize why arctic animals are able to survive the cold winters.

Read these two answers to the instruction. Which one is a better answer?

The Arctic is at the top of the world. It's really, really cold there. Sometimes it gets as cold as 60 degrees below zero. A lot of furry animals live there but few snakes! There are the polar bear, the arctic fox, seals, walrus, and the lemming. If you don't know what a lemming is, it's a rodent that looks like a mouse. Birds and insects live there too because they don't freeze.

Animals in the Arctic have different ways that help them survive the cold winters. Some animals, such as the polar bear, have thick coats of fur. Water animals like seals have fur and blubber. Some small animals live in tunnels in the snow. The birds have feathers and special feet and legs that don't get too cold. These are the ways the animals stay alive in winter.

The first answer names the kinds of animals in the Arctic, but it doesn't tell about why they are able to survive. It also gives facts about the Arctic that the question doesn't ask for.

The second answer uses clue words from the instruction in the topic sentence, such as *survive* and *cold winters.* The other sentences summarize the main points about how the animals survive the cold. This answer gives only the information asked for.

Technology Terms

Computer Terms

Your school may be equipped with computers, or you may have your own. Try to become familiar with the following terms to understand how the computer works.

Floppy disk

Hard copy

Monitor

Keyboard

Printer

CD-ROM	A flat, round, plastic disc where computer data or music can be stored and read with a laser; many computers have built-in CD-ROM drives.
cursor	The blinking square, dot, or bar on a computer screen that shows where the next typed character will appear.
disk drive	A device that can read information from a disk or write information onto a disk; you insert a disk into a disk drive through a thin slot.
document	A written or printed piece of writing.
floppy disk	A somewhat flexible plastic disk coated with magnetic material and used to store computer data.
font	Any one of various styles of letters in which computer type can appear.
hard copy	A computer document that is printed on paper.
hard drive	A computer disk that cannot be easily removed from the computer; hard disks hold more data and run faster than floppy disks.
hardware	The parts of a computer system, including the keyboard, monitor, memory storage devices, and printer.
keyboard	A part of the computer containing a set of keys.
menu	A list of computer commands shown on a monitor.

more ▶

Using Technology

Using Technology

modem	A part of a computer that allows it to communicate with other computers over telephone lines. It can be a separate device or inside the computer.
monitor	A part of a computer system that shows information on a screen.
printer	A part of a computer system that produces printed documents.
software	Programs that are used in operating computers.

Word-Processing Commands

These commands are often used in word processing. You can give each command by typing a series of keys or by selecting it from a menu.

Close	Closes the displayed document.
Copy	Copies selected, or highlighted, text.
Cut	Removes selected, or highlighted, text.
delete	Removes selected, or highlighted, text.
Find	Locates specific words or phrases in a document.
New	Opens a new document.
Open	Displays a selected document.
Paste	Inserts copied or cut text in a new location in the same document or in another document.
Print	Prints the displayed document.
Quit	Leaves the program.
return	Moves the cursor to the beginning of the next line.
Save	Stores a document for later use.
shift	Allows you to type a capital letter.
Spelling	Activates the spelling tool.
tab	Indents the cursor to the right.

Using E-mail

Writing an e-mail is different from writing a letter or talking on the phone. Follow these guidelines to write good e-mail messages.

Guidelines for Using E-mail Effectively

1. Give your message a specific title in the subject line. The person receiving your message should know the subject before opening it.

2. Use short paragraphs. Long paragraphs are difficult to read onscreen.

3. Skip a line instead of indenting when you begin a new paragraph. Your message will be easier to read onscreen.

4. Remember that special type, such as italics or underlining, may not show up on the other person's screen.

5. Be careful how you use humor. The other person can't hear your tone of voice and may not be able to tell when you're joking.

6. Even though an e-mail may seem more casual than a letter, you should still follow the rules of good writing.

7. Proofread your messages, and fix all capitalization, punctuation, usage, and spelling mistakes.

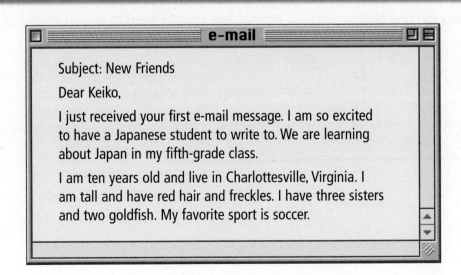

e-mail

Subject: New Friends

Dear Keiko,

I just received your first e-mail message. I am so excited to have a Japanese student to write to. We are learning about Japan in my fifth-grade class.

I am ten years old and live in Charlottesville, Virginia. I am tall and have red hair and freckles. I have three sisters and two goldfish. My favorite sport is soccer.

Using a Spelling Tool

Your word-processing program's spelling tool can help you proofread your writing. Having a spelling tool on your computer doesn't mean you don't have to know how to spell, though.

Look at this paragraph. Do you see any misspelled words? If you do, you're smarter than a spelling tool because it didn't find any of the mistakes.

A spelling tool can't tell the difference between homophones.

A spelling tool can't find a misspelled word that is the correct spelling of another word.

A spelling tool doesn't know whether two words are supposed to be one word.

Document

Summer Vacation

This summer my family and I went on a vacation to the beech. I can still remember the scent of the ocean and the feel of the sand under my bare feet. I spent ours helping my little sister build a sandcastle with a pail and a shovel. One day we saw a pair of star fish. There is no place like the beach!

Think of a spelling tool as a proofreading partner. The spelling tool can help you find mistakes in your writing, but you still need to proofread to make sure the spelling tool didn't miss anything.

Computers and the Writing Process

Computers can help you plan, draft, revise, proofread, and publish your writing more efficiently. Here are some ideas for using a computer in the writing process.

PREWRITING

Type your thoughts as you think of them. Don't worry about finishing your sentences or grouping ideas. You can use the Cut and Paste features to make changes later.

Dim the screen to help you concentrate on your thoughts rather than on correctness.

Create outlines, charts, or graphic organizers to help you plan your writing.
Tip: Some word-processing programs have ready-to-use graphic organizers that you just fill in.

Document

Benjamin Franklin's Career

I. What Ben Franklin printed
   A. City laws
   B. Notices of meetings and events
   C. Pennsylvania Gazette

II. Other jobs Ben Franklin had
   A. Statesman
   B. Scientist
   C. Inventor
   D. Writer

DRAFTING

Save your prewriting notes and ideas under a new file name, and then expand a list or outline into a draft.

Double-space your draft so that you can write revisions on your printout.

Boldface or underline words you may want to change later.

Save early and often!

more ▶

Computers and the Writing Process **H39**

Computers and the Writing Process *continued*

Using Technology

REVISING

Save a copy of your file under a new name before you begin making changes.

Have a conference with a partner right at the computer. Read your draft aloud and discuss any questions or problems you have. Then insert your partner's comments in capital letters. Later you can decide which comments you agree with.

Use the Find and Replace functions to check for overused words. Enter words such as *and, then, pretty,* or *nice* in the Find function. When the word is found, highlight it and click Replace. You can also simply boldface the word and revise it later.

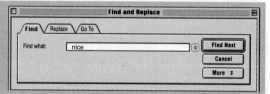

Use the Cut and Paste functions to make changes. Move or delete words, sentences, or paragraphs with just a few clicks. **Tip:** If you're unsure about cutting something, just move the text to the end of your document. You can always cut those "throwaways" later.

Rewrite problem sentences or paragraphs under your original text. Boldface your new text and compare the different versions. Delete the version you don't want.

Use the electronic thesaurus in your word-processing program to find synonyms. Be careful to choose a synonym that has the meaning you want.

PROOFREADING

Check your spelling with your word processor's spelling tool. Then check for errors a spelling tool won't catch! See "Using a Spelling Tool" on page H38.

Turn your sentences into a list. Place the cursor after each end punctuation mark and press Return. Now you can easily spot sentences that are too long or too short, run-on sentences, and fragments. You can also make sure that each sentence begins with a capital letter. When you're finished proofreading, simply delete the extra returns.

Computers make publishing your writing a snap. Here's how you can create professional-looking final products.

Choose your fonts carefully. Designers suggest using no more than three fonts per page.

Helvetica Century

Times Roman

Choose a type size that can be read easily, but remember, type that is too big can look silly. Twelve-point type is usually a good choice.

8 pt

12 pt

16 pt

Use bullets to separate the items on a list or to highlight a passage. Typing Option + 8 usually produces a bullet.

Design your title by changing the type size or font. Make a separate title page, if you like, and use your word processor's Borders and Shading functions to make the page fancy.

Add art to your paper or report.

- **Use the computer's Paint or Draw features** to create your own picture.

- **Cut and paste** clip art, which comes with some software.

- **Use a scanner** to copy images such as photographs onto your computer. You can then insert them electronically into your document.

If you don't have the equipment to create electronic art, simply leave a space in your document, print out a hard copy, and draw or paste in a picture.

Other key combinations will make special pictures and symbols called dingbats. See how many you recognize.

Using Technology

more ▶

Using Technology

PUBLISHING

Create tables, charts, or graphs to accompany your writing. For example, you can chart or graph the results of a class survey on birthdays.

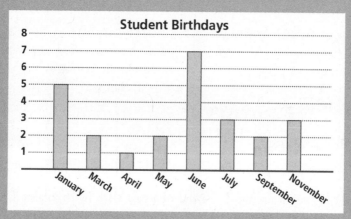

Student Birthdays

Choose your paper. White paper is always fine, but sometimes you may want to try colored paper or stationery with borders or pictures. **Tip:** Check with an adult before changing the printer paper. Paper that is too thick or heavy can jam your printer.

Create newsletters, magazines, or brochures using word-processing templates. Look at examples of real newspapers and magazines to see what kind of type to use, how big to make titles, and where to put pictures. Try combining electronic files to create a class newsletter that contains articles written by each of your classmates.

Organize your writing in electronic folders. Create separate folders to store poems, stories, research reports, and letters. You can also make a folder for unfinished pieces. Think of your computer as a giant storage cabinet!

Start an electronic portfolio for special pieces of your writing. You can create a portfolio folder on your hard drive or copy your files onto a floppy disk. Add pieces you choose throughout the year.

The Internet

What Is the Internet?

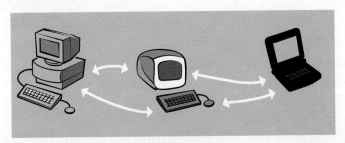

The **Internet** is a network of computers that connects people, businesses, and institutions all over the world. It lets computer users communicate with other computer users quickly and easily. Here are some of the many things you can do on the Internet.

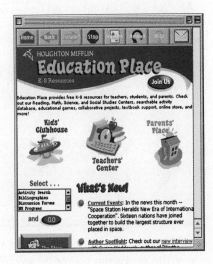

- Do research. You can watch a volcano erupt, take a tour of the Smithsonian, or hear music from the Revolutionary War. You can search for current articles or historical documents.

- Visit an electronic bulletin board or a chat room, where users "meet" to discuss specific topics. Here you can join an online book club, chat with other students who enjoy playing basketball, or debate current events.

- Send e-mail to your friends and family. Anyone who is online is reachable. See "Using E-mail" on page H37.

Tech Tip
Visit Education Place at www.eduplace.com/kids/hme/ for fun activities and interesting information.

more ▶

The Internet *continued*

- Use special software to create your own Web site. You design the page, write the text, and choose links to other sites. Your school may also have its own Web site where you can publish your work.

Tips for Using the Internet

Although the Internet can be a great way to get information, it can be confusing. Use these tips to make the most of it!

- Search smart! Use a search engine to help you find Web sites on your topic or area of interest. Type in a key word or search by topics. Most search engines give tips on searching. Some search engines are designed just for kids.

- Write down the source of any information you find on the Internet just as you would for a book. Along with the author, title, date of the material, and online address (URL), make sure you include the date you found the information. Information on the Internet can change daily.

- Check your sources carefully. The Internet is full of information, but not all of it is reliable. Web sites published by well-known organizations may be more trustworthy than those published by individuals.

- Protect your privacy. Never give your full name or address in a chat room.

Creating an Electronic Multimedia Presentation

An electronic multimedia presentation is a combination of words, pictures, and sound. It lets you express much more than you could with just words. For example, an electronic multimedia presentation on rain forests could contain descriptions of the plants found in a rain forest, recordings of animal sounds, photographs of the Amazon rain forest, and a video of flying squirrels.

Equipment

Here is what you need:

- a personal computer with a large memory
- high-quality video and audio systems
- a CD-ROM drive
- a multimedia software program

Check with your school librarian or media specialist to find out what equipment is available.

Parts of an Electronic Multimedia Presentation

An electronic multimedia presentation may include text, photos and video, sound, and animation.

Text The text of your presentation may include informative summaries, descriptions, directions, or photo captions. How the text appears onscreen is also important. You can adjust the font, size, and color of your text. **Tip:** Don't make your letters too small or put too many words on a single screen. Text should be easy to see and to read.

more ▶

Creating an Electronic Multimedia Presentation *continued*

Photos and Videos Pictures can be powerful, so choose them carefully. Here are some ways you can include pictures.

- Include video you film yourself.
- Scan in photos or artwork.
- Generate your own computer artwork.

Animation Computer animation lets you create objects and then bring them to life. Here are some things you can do with animation.

- Tell a story with animated figures.
- Show an experiment being performed.
- Track changes in a chart or graph.
- Show how something is put together.
- Show how something grows.
- Display an object from all sides.

Sound Sound can help make an image or text come alive. Imagine viewing a video of the track star Jesse Owens. Then imagine viewing the same image while listening to the cheers of the crowd and the crackle of the announcer's voice. Here are some suggestions for using sound in your multimedia presentation.

- Add appropriate background sounds— birds calling, water dripping, bells ringing.
- Use music to set a mood.
- Include songs that represent a time in history or emphasize a theme.
- Include a button to let users hear the text read aloud.
- Include audio to accompany video clips.

Designing an Electronic Multimedia Presentation

The process of designing an electronic multimedia presentation is similar to that of creating a piece of writing, but here are some additional things to consider.

Types of Media If you are planning a presentation on the moon, you might come up with the following list:

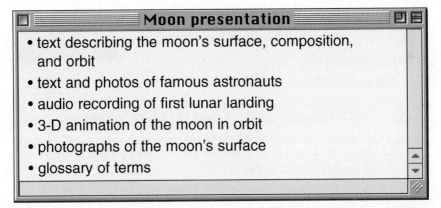

> **Moon presentation**
> - text describing the moon's surface, composition, and orbit
> - text and photos of famous astronauts
> - audio recording of first lunar landing
> - 3-D animation of the moon in orbit
> - photographs of the moon's surface
> - glossary of terms

Order of Presentation Will the presentation have a specific order, or will you allow the user to choose his or her own path? A diagram, such as the one below, will help you plan.

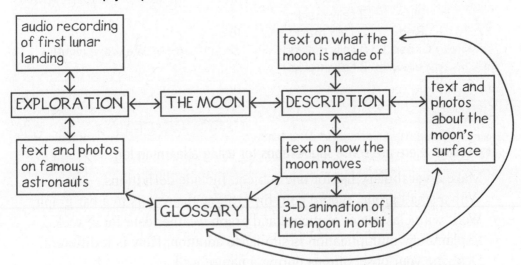

Designing and creating a multimedia presentation can be challenging and fun! **Tip:** As always, cite your sources and write text in your own words.

Keeping a Learning Log

A **learning log** is a notebook for keeping track of what you learn in different subjects. It is a place to write facts as well as your thoughts about each subject.

Getting Started Write the date at the top of the page. Then use words, charts, or pictures to help you remember what you have learned. An example from one student's learning log is shown below.

November 17
Subject: Math

1. Our class put ten colored cubes in a bag: one yellow, two blue, two green, and five red cubes
2. Question: If we pick cubes from the bag, which color will we pick most often?
3. Our Predictions: We will pick yellow least often and red most often.
4. We picked cubes to test our predictions.

Our Results

	Tally	Total
Blue	7 tally marks	7
Red	16 tally marks	16
Green	5 tally marks	5
Yellow	2 tally marks	2

← We were right!

Try It Out Here are some suggestions for using a learning log.

- Make a vocabulary list for one subject. Include definitions.
- With a small group, record coin flips. Show the results in a bar graph.
- Work with classmates to record and graph weather data for a week.
- Explain how multiplication is similar to addition. How is it different?
- Describe your observations during a nature walk.
- Record what you know about your state. What do you want to know?
- Summarize what you have learned in a lesson in school.

Keeping a Writer's Notebook

A **writer's notebook** is a kind of notebook you can keep just for writing. You can record words you like, write about authors you enjoy, and make notes about ideas for stories, essays, or poems. Relax and write freely about anything that interests you. You never know what might be useful later!

When Do I Use It? Open your writer's notebook whenever you have a writing assignment. Look there for topic ideas, exact words, details, and dialogue, even facts and examples to support a goal or an opinion. Parts of pages from one student's notebook are shown below.

Words I Like

parched	alarming	appetizing	astounded	bulky
creepy	husky	scorch	cranky	sloshing
splatter	creep	gallop		

Grandpa's Stories

Last night my grandpa told me all these stories about growing up on a farm. He had to do chores like feeding thirty cows and carrying heavy buckets of water. Then he went to a one-room schoolhouse, and there wasn't a bus. Sometimes he and his sister rode one pony together. His sister was older so she got to steer, which always made him mad. In warm weather, he didn't wear shoes. I can't imagine going to school without any shoes.

Try It Out Start your own writer's notebook. Try some of these suggestions.

- Write your thoughts or feelings about a new rule at school.
- Copy a favorite sentence or two from a book you enjoyed. Be sure to include information about the source.
- List reasons why you like a sport or other activity.
- Record a funny thing you heard someone say.
- Write details about a place you like.
- List new words.

Graphic Organizers

Are you stuck for an idea to write about? Are you confused about how to organize your ideas? Try using these graphic organizers to help you explore and plan your ideas.

Clusters or webs are good for brainstorming topics, exploring ideas, or organizing information. Write your topic in a center circle. Write details about your topic, circle them, and connect them to the center circle. Add more details to each circle.

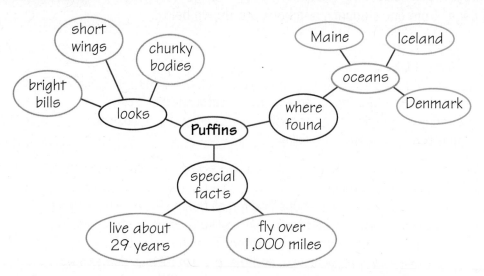

Inverted triangles can help you narrow topics that are too big. Write a broad topic in the first section of the triangle. Then write one part of that topic below it. Then write one part of the second topic. Keep going until you get a focused topic.

You can also use an inverted triangle to organize your details from most to least important.

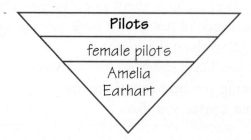

Planning charts ask you to think about your purpose, your goals, and your audience before you begin to write. These decisions will affect how you end up writing about your topic.

My Topic _____

My Purpose	My Goals	My Audience
Circle one or more.	*Name at least one.*	*Answer these questions.*
• to tell a story • to explain • to persuade • to share • to plan • to learn • other _____ _____ _____ _____		1. Who is my audience? 2. What do they already know about my topic? 3. What do I want them to know? 4. What part of my topic would interest them most?

Writer's Tools

Observation charts organize details gathered through your five senses. Use them to add details to your writing. Try to write notes in each column. Depending on your topic, you may have more details in one column than in another, or no details at all.

My Trip to the Beach				
Sight	**Sound**	**Touch**	**Taste**	**Smell**
umbrellas choppy water kites	crashing waves kids shouting boat motor	sizzling sand slimy jellyfish	gritty sandwiches	salty air

 Go to www.eduplace.com/kids/hme/ for graphic organizers.

Graphic Organizers *continued*

T-charts organize information into two groups. Use T-charts to list details about two people, places, or things. They are also helpful for exploring two sides of an argument, showing likenesses and differences, listing materials and steps for instructions, or showing two points of view.

Draw a large *T*. Write your subjects at the top. Write details about each subject in the column below it. You may want to match the information in the columns.

Summer	Winter
swimming	sledding
bathing suit	boots
watermelon	hot chocolate

E-charts show a main idea and its details. Write the main idea and underline it. Then draw an *E* next to it. Write details that support the main idea on each line of the *E*.

my grandma is special	tells funny stories
	wears crazy hats
	cooks yummy paella

KWL charts show what you already know about a topic, what you want to know about it, and what you learn after doing research.

Grizzly Bears		
What I Know	**What I Want to Know**	**What I Learned**
hibernate are very dangerous	Do they eat when they hibernate? What do they eat?	don't eat for several months eat soapberries and salmon

ISP charts show **information (I), sources (S),** and, if appropriate, the **page references (P)** where you found the information.

I	S	P
Adult grizzlies can weigh about 850 pounds! Mother grizzlies will adopt strays or orphaned grizzlies.	Know-It-All Encyclopedia Mr. Ed Ucation, tour guide at the Natural History Museum	246 139

Step-by-step charts help you to plan your instructions. List the materials that are needed to follow your instructions. Then write each step in order. Include details your audience needs to know to complete each step.

Materials	
Steps	**Details**
Step 1	
Step 2	
Step 3	
Step 4	
Step 5	

more ▶

Graphic Organizers *continued*

Story maps help you to gather details for your stories. Write notes about your character, setting, and plot.

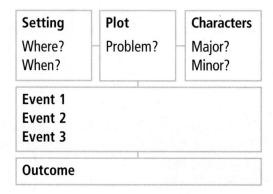

Setting	**Plot**	**Characters**
Where?	Problem?	Major?
When?		Minor?

Event 1
Event 2
Event 3

Outcome

Time lines show events in order and tell when they happened. Draw an arrow, and write events along it in order from left to right. Add dates for each event.

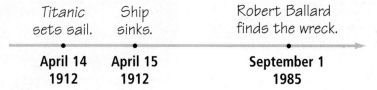

Titanic   Ship   Robert Ballard
sets sail.   sinks.   finds the wreck.

April 14   April 15   September 1
1912   1912   1985

Venn diagrams are used to compare and contrast two subjects. Write details that tell how the subjects are different in the outer circles. Write details that tell how the subjects are alike where the circles overlap.

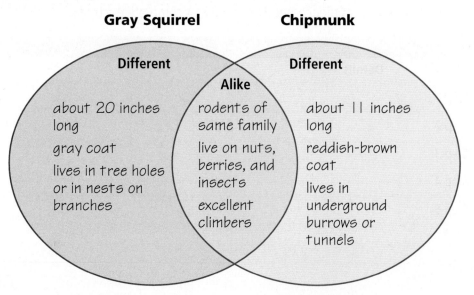

Gray Squirrel   **Chipmunk**

Different — **Alike** — **Different**

about 20 inches long

gray coat

lives in tree holes or in nests on branches

rodents of same family

live on nuts, berries, and insects

excellent climbers

about 11 inches long

reddish-brown coat

lives in underground burrows or tunnels

Writer's Tools

Guide to Capitalization, Punctuation, and Usage

Abbreviations

Abbreviations are shortened forms of words. Most abbreviations begin with a capital letter and end with a period. Use abbreviations only in special kinds of writing, such as addresses and lists.

Titles		
Mr. *(Mister)* Mr. Juan Albino		Sr. *(Senior)* John Helt Sr.
Mrs. *(Mistress)* Mrs. Frances Wong		Jr. *(Junior)* John Helt Jr.
Ms. *(Any Woman)* Leslie Clark		Dr. *(Doctor)* Dr. Janice Dodds
Note: *Miss* is not an abbreviation and does not end with a period.		

Words used in addresses		
St. *(Street)*	Blvd. *(Boulevard)*	Mt. *(Mount or Mountain)*
Rd. *(Road)*	Rte. *(Route)*	Expy. *(Expressway)*
Ave. *(Avenue)*	Apt. *(Apartment)*	
Dr. *(Drive)*	Pkwy. *(Parkway)*	

Words used in business	
Co. *(Company)*	Inc. *(Incorporated)*
Corp. *(Corporation)*	Ltd. *(Limited)*

Other abbreviations

Some abbreviations are written in all capital letters, with a letter standing for each important word.

P.D. *(Police Department)*	P.O. *(Post Office)*
J.P. *(Justice of the Peace)*	R.N. *(Registered Nurse)*

The United States Postal Service uses two capital letters and no period in each of its state abbreviations.

AL *(Alabama)*	IL *(Illinois)*	MO *(Missouri)*
AK *(Alaska)*	IN *(Indiana)*	MT *(Montana)*
AZ *(Arizona)*	IA *(Iowa)*	NE *(Nebraska)*
AR *(Arkansas)*	KS *(Kansas)*	NV *(Nevada)*
CA *(California)*	KY *(Kentucky)*	NH *(New Hampshire)*
CO *(Colorado)*	LA *(Louisiana)*	NJ *(New Jersey)*
CT *(Connecticut)*	ME *(Maine)*	NM *(New Mexico)*
DE *(Delaware)*	MD *(Maryland)*	NY *(New York)*
FL *(Florida)*	MA *(Massachusetts)*	NC *(North Carolina)*
GA *(Georgia)*	MI *(Michigan)*	ND *(North Dakota)*
HI *(Hawaii)*	MN *(Minnesota)*	OH *(Ohio)*
ID *(Idaho)*	MS *(Mississippi)*	OK *(Oklahoma)*

more ▶

Abbreviations *continued*

Other abbreviations (continued)	OR *(Oregon)* PA *(Pennsylvania)* RI *(Rhode Island)* SC *(South Carolina)* SD *(South Dakota)*	TN *(Tennessee)* TX *(Texas)* UT *(Utah)* VT *(Vermont)* VA *(Virginia)*	WA *(Washington)* WV *(West Virginia)* WI *(Wisconsin)* WY *(Wyoming)*

Initials are abbreviations that stand for a person's first or middle name. Some names have both a first and a middle initial.

E.B. White *(Elwyn Brooks White)*
T. James Carey *(Thomas James Carey)*

Titles

Italicizing/ Underlining	**The important words and the first and last words in a title are capitalized. Titles of books, magazines, TV shows, movies, and newspapers are italicized or underlined.** *Oliver Twist (book)* *Cricket (magazine)* *Nova (TV show)* *Star Wars (movie)* *The Phoenix Express (newspaper)*
Quotation marks with titles	**Titles of short stories, songs, articles, book chapters, and most poems are set off by quotation marks.** "The Necklace" *(short story)* "Home on the Range" *(song)* "Three Days in the Sahara" *(article)* "The Human Brain" *(chapter)* "Deer at Dusk" *(poem)*

Quotations

Quotation marks with commas and periods	**Quotation marks are used to set off a speaker's exact words. The first word of a quotation begins with a capital letter. Punctuation belongs *inside* the closing quotation marks. Commas separate a quotation from the rest of the sentence.** "Where," asked the stranger, "is the post office?" "Please put away your books now," said Mr. Emory. Linda whispered, "What time is it?" "It's late," replied Bill. "Let's go!"

Capitalization

Rules for capitalization	**Capitalize the first word of every sentence.** What an unusual color the roses are!
	Capitalize the pronoun *I*. What should I do next?
	Capitalize proper nouns. If a proper noun is made up of more than one word, capitalize each important word. Emily G. Messe District of Columbia Lincoln Memorial
	Capitalize titles or their abbreviations when used with a person's name. Governor Bradford Senator Smith Dr. Ling
	Capitalize proper adjectives. We ate at a French restaurant. She is French. That is a North American custom.
	Capitalize the names of days, months, and holidays. My birthday is on the last Monday in March. We watched the parade on the Fourth of July.
	Capitalize the names of nationalities, races, religions, languages, organizations, buildings, and companies. Able Supply Company Chinese Central School American Kennel Club Protestant African American
	Capitalize the first, last, and all important words in a title. Do not capitalize words such as *a, in, and, of,* and *the* unless they begin or end a title. *From the Earth to the Moon* *The New York Times* "The Rainbow Connection" "Growing Up"

	Capitalize the first word of each main topic and subtopic in an outline.
	1. Types of libraries
	  A. Large public library
	  B. Bookmobile

	Capitalize the first word in the greeting and the closing of a letter. Dear Marcia, Yours truly,

more ▶

Punctuation

End marks	**There are three end marks. A period (.) ends a declarative or imperative sentence. A question mark (?) follows an interrogative sentence. An exclamation point (!) follows an exclamatory sentence.** The scissors are on my desk. *(declarative)* Look up the spelling of that word. *(imperative)* How is the word spelled? *(interrogative)* This is your best poem so far! *(exclamatory)*
Apostrophe	**To form the possessive of a singular noun, add an apostrophe and -s.** doctor's boss's grandmother's family's
	For a plural noun that ends in s, add only an apostrophe. sisters' families' hound dogs' Smiths'
	For a plural noun that does not end in s, add an apostrophe and -s to form the plural possessive. women's mice's children's geese's
	Use an apostrophe in contractions in place of dropped letters. Do not use contractions in formal writing. isn't *(is not)* can't *(cannot)* won't *(will not)* wasn't *(was not)* we're *(we are)* it's *(it is)* I'm *(I am)* they've *(they have)* they'll *(they will)* could've *(could have)* would've *(would have)* should've *(should have)*
Colon	**Use a colon after the greeting in a business letter.** Dear Mrs. Trimby: Dear Realty Homes:
Comma	**A comma tells your reader where to pause. For words in a series, put a comma after each item except the last. Do not use a comma if only two items are listed.** Clyde asked if we had any apples, peaches, or grapes.
	Use commas to separate two or more adjectives that are listed together unless one adjective tells how many. The fresh, ripe fruit was placed in a bowl. One red apple was especially shiny.

Punctuation *continued*

Comma *(continued)*	**Use a comma before the conjunction in a compound sentence.**
	Some students were at lunch, but others were studying.
	Use commas after introductory words such as *yes, no, oh,* and *well* when they begin a sentence.
	Well, it's just too cold out. No, it isn't six yet.
	Use a comma to separate a noun in direct address.
	Jean, help me fix this tire. How was your trip, Grandpa? Can you see, Joe, where I left my glasses?
	Use a comma between the names of a city and a state and between a city and a country.
	Chicago, Illinois Sydney, Australia
	Use a comma after the greeting in a friendly letter.
	Dear Deena, Dear Uncle Rudolph,
	Use a comma after the closing in a letter.
	Your nephew, Sincerely yours,

Problem Words

Words	Rules	Examples
a, an, the	These words are articles.	
a, an	Use *a* and *an* before singular nouns. Use *a* before a word that begins with a consonant sound. Use *an* before a word that begins with a vowel sound.	a banana an apple
the	Use *the* with both singular and plural nouns. Use *the* to point out particular persons, places, or things.	the apple the apples The books that I like are long.
can	*Can* means "to be able to do something."	Nellie can read quickly.
may	*May* means "to be allowed or permitted."	May I borrow your book?
good	*Good* is an adjective.	The weather looks good.

more ▶

Problem Words *continued*

Words	Rules	Examples
well	*Well* is usually an adverb. It is an adjective only when it refers to health.	She swims well. Do you feel well?
its	*Its* is a possessive pronoun.	The dog wagged its tail.
it's	*It's* is a contraction of *it is*.	It's cold today.
let	*Let* means "to permit or allow."	Please let me go swimming.
leave	*Leave* means "to go away from" or "to let remain in a place."	I will leave soon. Leave it on my desk.
raise	*Raise* means "to move something up," "grow something," or "increase something."	Our principal raises the flag. Julio and Myra raise rabbits. The bus line raised its prices.
rise	*Rise* means "to get up or go up."	This ski lift rises quickly.
sit	*Sit* means "to rest in one place."	Please sit in this chair.
set	*Set* means "to place or put."	Set the vase on the table.
teach	*Teach* means "to give instruction."	He teaches us how to dance.
learn	*Learn* means "to receive instruction."	I learned about history.
their	*Their* is a possessive pronoun.	Their coats are on the bed.
there	*There* is an adverb. It may also begin a sentence.	Is Carlos there? There is my book.
they're	*They're* is a contraction of *they are*.	They're going to the store.
two	*Two* is a number.	I bought two shirts.
to	*To* means "in the direction of."	A squirrel ran to the tree.
too	*Too* means "more than enough" and "also."	I ate too many cherries. Can we go too?
who	Use the pronoun *who* as a subject.	Who can solve the math problem?
whom	Use the pronoun *whom* as a direct object.	Whom did she ask for an autograph?
your	*Your* is a possessive pronoun.	Are these your glasses?
you're	*You're* is a contraction for *you are*.	You're late again!

Adjective and Adverb Usage

Adjective or adverb?	**Adjectives describe nouns or pronouns. Adverbs describe verbs.** Lena is a quick runner. *(adjective)* Lena runs quickly. *(adverb)*
Comparing	**To compare two things or actions, add *-er* to adjectives and adverbs or use the word *more*.** This plant is taller than the other one. It grew more quickly.
	To compare three or more things or actions, add *-est* or use the word *most*. This plant is the tallest of the three. It grew most quickly.
	Use *more* or *most* with an adjective or adverb that has two or more syllables, such as *careful* or *politely*. Do not add *-er* or *-est* to long adjectives or adverbs. agreeable–more agreeable–most agreeable slowly–more slowly–most slowly
good, bad	**The adjectives *good* and *bad* have special forms for making comparisons.** good–better–best bad–worse–worst

Negatives

	Do not use double negatives in a sentence. INCORRECT: We didn't go nowhere. CORRECT: We didn't go anywhere.

Pronoun Usage

Agreement	**A pronoun must agree with the noun to which it refers.** Kee bought a newspaper. Mary read it. Jeff and Cindy came to dinner. They enjoyed the meal.
Double subjects	**Do not use a double subject—a noun and a pronoun—to name the same person, place, or thing.** INCORRECT: The food it was delicious. CORRECT: The food was delicious.

more ▶

Pronoun Usage *continued*

Capitalization / Punctuation / Usage

I, me	**Use *I* as the subject of a sentence and after forms of *be*. Use *me* after action verbs or prepositions such as *to, in*, and *for*. (See subject and object pronouns below.)** Jan and I are going to the show. She is taking me. Will you hold my ticket for me?
	When using *I* or *me* with nouns or other pronouns, always name yourself last. Beth and I will leave. Give the papers to Ron and me.
Possessive pronouns	**A possessive pronoun shows ownership. Use *my, your, his, her, its, our*, and *their* before nouns.** My report was about our trip to the zoo.
	Use *mine, yours, his, hers, its, ours*, and *theirs* to replace nouns in a sentence. Hers was about a visit to the museum.
Subject and object pronouns	**Use subject pronouns as subjects and after forms of the verb *be*.** He composed many works for the piano. I am she. The most talented singers are we.
	Use object pronouns after action verbs and prepositions like *to* and *for*. Clyde collected old coins and sold them. *(direct object)* Let's share these bananas with her. *(object of preposition)*
	Use the pronoun *who* as a subject. Use the pronoun *whom* as an object. Who traveled around the world? Whom did they see? To whom did they speak?
Demonstrative pronouns	**A pronoun that points out something is called a demonstrative pronoun. It must agree in number with the noun it points out or with its antecedent. Use *this* and *these* to point to things nearby. Use *that* and *those* to point to things farther away.** This is a jellyfish. These are sand dollars. That is a shark. Those are striped bass.

Pronoun Usage *continued*

Compound subjects and compound objects	To decide which pronoun to use in a compound subject or a compound object, leave out the other part of the compound. Say the sentence with the pronoun alone. Lu and _____ ride the bus. *(we, us)* We ride the bus. Lu and we ride the bus. I saw Dad and _____. *(he, him)* I saw him. I saw Dad and him.
***We* and *us* with nouns**	Use *we* with a noun that is a subject or a noun that follows a linking verb. INCORRECT: Us girls are the stagehands. CORRECT: We girls are the stagehands. INCORRECT: The ushers are us boys. CORRECT: The ushers are we boys. Use *us* with a noun that follows an action verb or that follows a preposition such as *to, for, with,* or *at*. INCORRECT: Dr. Lin helped we players. CORRECT: Dr. Lin helped us players. INCORRECT: She talked to we beginners. CORRECT: She talked to us beginners.

Verb Usage

Agreement: subject-verb	A present tense verb and its subject must agree in number. Add *-s* or *-es* to a verb if the subject is singular. Do not add *-s* or *-es* to a verb if the subject is plural or if the subject is *I*. The road bends to the right. Mr. Langelier teaches fifth graders. These books seem heavy. I like camping. Change the forms of *be* and *have* to make them agree with their subjects. He is taking the bus today. Have you seen Jimmy? They are going swimming. Mary has a large garden.
Agreement: compound subjects	A compound subject with *and* takes a plural verb. Jason, Kelly, and Wanda <u>have</u> new dictionaries.

more ▶

Verb Usage *continued*

could have, should have	Use *could have, would have, should have, might have, must have*. Avoid using *of* with *could, would, should, might,* or *must*. She could have (*not* could of) spoken louder. Juan would have (*not* would of) liked this movie. We should have (*not* should of) turned left. I might have (*not* might of) left my wallet on my desk. It must have (*not* must of) rained last night.
Irregular verbs	Irregular verbs do not add *-ed* or *-d* to form the past tense. Because irregular verbs do not follow a regular pattern, you must memorize their spellings. Use *has, have,* or *had* as a helping verb with the past tense.

Verb	Past	Past with helping verb
be	was	been
begin	began	begun
blow	blew	blown
bring	brought	brought
choose	chose	chosen
come	came	come
fly	flew	flown
freeze	froze	frozen
go	went	gone
have	had	had
know	knew	known
make	made	made
ring	rang	rung
run	ran	run
say	said	said
sing	sang	sung
speak	spoke	spoken
steal	stole	stolen
swim	swam	swum
take	took	taken
tear	tore	torn
think	thought	thought
wear	wore	worn
write	wrote	written

Words Often Misspelled

You probably use many of the words on this list when you write. If you cannot think of the spelling of a word, you can always use this list. The words are in alphabetical order.

A
again
all right
a lot
also
always
another
anyone
anything
anyway
around

B
beautiful
because
before
believe
brought
buy

C
cannot
can't
caught
clothes
coming
could
cousin

D
didn't
different
don't

E
enough
every
everybody
everyone
everything

F
family
field
finally
friend

G
getting
girl
goes
going
guess

H
happened
happily
haven't
heard
here

I
I'd
I'll
I'm
instead
into
its
it's

K
knew
know

L
letter

M
might
millimeter
morning
mother's
myself

O
o'clock
off
once
other

P
people
pretty
probably

R
really
right

S
Saturday
school
someone
sometimes
stopped
suppose
sure
swimming

T
than
that's
their
then
there
there's
they
they're
thought
through
to

tonight
too
tried
two

U
until
usually

W
weird
we're
where
whole
would
wouldn't
write
writing

Y
your
you're

Spelling Guidelines

1. A short vowel sound before a consonant is usually spelled with just one letter: **a, e, i, o,** or **u.**

staff	grasp	slept	dwell	mist
split	fond	crush	bulb	

2. The |ā| sound is often spelled **ai, ay,** or **a-consonant-e**. The |ē| sound is often spelled **ee** or **ea**.

claim	sway	stake	fleet	greet	lease
brain	stray	male	speech	seal	beast

3. The |ī| sound is often spelled **i, igh,** or **i-consonant-e**. The |ō| sound is often spelled **o, o-consonant-e, oa,** or **ow**.

mild	thigh	strike	stole	loaf	sow
slight	stride	stroll	hose	boast	flow

4. The |o͞o| or the |yo͞o| sound is often spelled **ue, ew,** or **u-consonant-e**. The |o͞o| sound may also be spelled **oo** or **ui**. The |o͝o| sound is often spelled **oo** or **u**.

hue	brew	flute	boom	wood	put
clue	fume	troop	cruise	brook	bush
dew	duke	mood	bruise	poor	pull

5. The |ou| sound is often spelled **ou** or **ow**. The |ô| sound is often spelled **aw, au,** or **a** before **l**. The |oi| sound is spelled **oi** or **oy**.

ounce	coward	claw	fawn	fault	bald	joint	loyal
sour	scowl	hawk	haunt	stalk	moist	royal

6. The |ûr| sounds are often spelled **ir, ur, er, ear,** or **or**. The |îr| sounds are often spelled **eer** or **ear**.

squirm	blur	stern	pearl	worm	smear
chirp	hurl	germ	earl	steer	rear

7. The |ôr| sounds are often spelled **or, ore,** or **oar**. The |âr| sounds are often spelled **are** or **air**. The |är| sound is usually spelled **ar**.

lord	tore	bore	hare	snare	flair	scar	barge
torch	sore	soar	fare	lair	harsh	carve	

8. Homophones sound alike but have different spellings and meanings.

loan lone	flea flee	berry bury

9. The final |ər| sounds in two-syllable words are often spelled **ar, or,** or **er.**

lun**ar**	burgl**ar**	maj**or**	clov**er**	thund**er**
pill**ar**	hum**or**	tract**or**	bann**er**	

10. The final |l| or |əl| sounds in two-syllable words are often spelled **le, el,** or **al.**

sing**le**	whist**le**	bush**el**	norm**al**	loc**al**
ang**le**	jew**el**	ang**el**	leg**al**	

11. Compound words may be spelled as one word, as a hyphenated word, or as separate words.

railroad	afternoon	ninety-nine	seat belt
watermelon	classmate	baby-sit	post office

12. A word with the VCCV syllable pattern is divided between the consonants.

at | tend	of | fer	traf | fic	tun | nel
sur | vive	es | cape	em | pire	wit | ness

13. If the consonants in a VCCV word are different and form a cluster or spell one word, divide the word before or after the two consonants.

a | fraid	de | gree	se | cret	ma | chine
rock | et	chick | en	oth | er	pack | age

14. If the first vowel sound in a VCV word is long, divide the word into syllables before the consonant.

pi | lot	fe | ver	sto | len	ba | sic
be | have	na | tion	de | tail	pre | fer

15. If the first vowel sound in a VCV word is short, divide the word into syllables after the consonant.

cab | in	hab | it	tal | ent	mod | ern
van | ish	rap | id	rec | ord	shad | ow

more ▶

16. When two different consonants in a VCCCV word spell one sound or form a cluster, divide the word into syllables before or after those two consonants.

dis | trict	al | though	com | plain	or | phan
mon | ster	or | chard	dol | phin	com | plex

17. When two vowels in a VV pattern spell two vowel sounds, divide the word into syllables between the vowels.

po | em	gi | ant	li | on	sci | ence
cru | el	di | al	cre | ate	qui | et

18. The **-ed** or **-ing** ending may simply be added to some words. A final **e** is usually dropped before adding **-ed** or **-ing**.

arrest**ed**	attend**ing**	seek**ing**	borrow**ed**	ris**ing**	freez**ing**
offer**ed**	direct**ing**	await**ing**	squeez**ing**	amus**ing**	provid**ing**

19. In one-syllable words ending with a single vowel and consonant, the consonant is usually doubled when **-ed** or **-ing** is added. In two-syllable words ending with an unstressed syllable, the final consonant is usually not doubled.

win**n**ing	bra**gg**ing	shi**pp**ed	stu**nn**ed	suffering	covered
hi**tt**ing	wra**pp**ed	whi**pp**ed	cho**pp**ed	gathering	wandered
swi**mm**ing	dro**pp**ed	be**gg**ed	spo**tt**ed	visiting	ordered

20. A suffix is a word part added to the end of a base word.

dread**ful**	breath**less**	count**less**	active**ly**	settle**ment**	soft**ness**

21. The final |ē| sound in a two-syllable word is often spelled **y** or **ey**.

read**y**	sorr**y**	beaut**y**	monk**ey**	hock**ey**
lonel**y**	hobb**y**	turk**ey**	vall**ey**	

22. Final |ĭj| sounds are often spelled **age**. Final |tĭv| sounds are often spelled **tive**. Final |tĭs| sounds are often spelled **tice**.

bagg**age**	post**age**	langu**age**	crea**tive**	prac**tice**
lugg**age**	voy**age**	cap**tive**	defec**tive**	jus**tice**
sav**age**	yard**age**	na**tive**	detec**tive**	no**tice**

23. The |k| sound in a one-syllable word is often spelled **k** or **ck**. In a two-syllable word, it is often spelled **k, ck,** or **c**. The |ng| sound before **k** is spelled **n**.

shar**k**	trac**k**	ja**ck**et	musi**c**	jun**k**	blan**k**
ris**k**	la**ck**	atta**ck**	a**c**tive	drin**k**	sin**k**
stru**ck**	mista**k**e	publi**c**	topi**c**	ran**k**	blan**k**et

24. The final |j| sound is usually spelled **dge** or **ge**. The final |s| sound is often spelled **ce**.

lo**dge**	bri**dge**	do**dge**	chan**ge**	chan**ce**	glan**ce**	fen**ce**
e**dge**	ri**dge**	stran**ge**	ca**ge**	twi**ce**	sin**ce**	

25. Final |n| or |ən| sounds may be spelled **ain**. Final |chər| sounds may be spelled **ture**. Final |zhər| sounds may be spelled **sure**.

capt**ain**	mount**ain**	fix**ture**	expo**sure**
fount**ain**	crea**ture**	lec**ture**	trea**sure**
curt**ain**	adven**ture**	mea**sure**	plea**sure**

26. Prefixes are added to beginnings of words or word roots. Suffixes are added to ends of words.

decide	**un**known	**ex**cuse	pain**ful**	care**less**
improve	**com**fort	**pre**fix	move**ment**	

27. The suffix **-ion** changes verbs to nouns. Sometimes the spelling changes.

correct	reduce	explode
correct**ion**	reduc**tion**	explo**sion**

28. If a word ends with a consonant + **y**, change the **y** to **i** when adding **-es, -ed, -er,** or **-est**.

hobb**ies**	sp**ied**	nois**ier**	tin**iest**	lonel**iest**
abilit**ies**	cop**ied**	earl**ier**	happ**iest**	

29. The suffixes **-able, -ible, -ant,** and **-ent** are added to words or word roots.

suit**able**	valu**able**	horr**ible**	vac**ant**	differ**ent**
comfort**able**	poss**ible**	serv**ant**	stud**ent**	

30. Some words have unexpected spellings.

acre	special	lamb	says	guide	knight

Diagramming Guide

A diagram of a sentence is a set of lines that show how the words of that sentence are related. You will begin by diagramming the most important words in the sentence. In beginning lessons, sentences contain words that you do not yet know how to diagram. Work only with the words that you are asked to diagram. You will learn about the others as you work through the lessons.

Simple Subjects and Simple Predicates

The simple subject and the simple predicate are written on a horizontal line called the **base line**. The simple subject is separated from the simple predicate by a vertical line that cuts through the horizontal line.

Find the simple subject and the simple predicate in the sentence below.
Wheat has lost its Number 1 place.

Study this diagram of the simple subject and the simple predicate from the sentence above.

Wheat	has lost

Find the simple subject and the simple predicate in this sentence. Note that the subject, *you*, is understood.
Guess the largest crop.

Study the diagram of this sentence.

(you)	Guess

Practice

Diagram only the simple subjects and the simple predicates in these sentences.

1. Rice has gained first place.
2. It must have a hot, wet climate.
3. Name some rice exporters.
4. The biggest growers are in the Rice Bowl.
5. This area stretches from Japan to Indonesia.

Compound Subjects

Each part of a compound subject is written on a separate horizontal line. The word *and* is written on a vertical dotted line that joins the horizontal lines.

Find the compound subject in this sentence.

India and China grow the most rice.

Study this diagram of the compound subject.

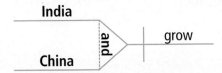

A compound subject can have more than two parts. Find the compound subject in this sentence.

Japan, Myanmar, and South Korea export more.

Study the diagram of this sentence. Note that the conjunction *and* is placed on the dotted line that connects the parts of the compound subject.

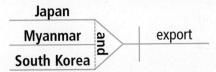

The word *or* can also join the parts of a compound subject.

Does Brazil or the United States grow more rice?

Although the sentence above is a question, it is diagrammed just like a statement. Study the diagram.

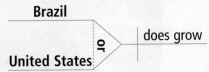

Practice

Diagram the subjects and the predicate in each of these sentences.

1. Rice and corn supplied Native Americans.
2. Quebec, the Midwest, and Louisiana had wild rice.
3. Europe and colonial America liked white rice better.
4. Is rice, potatoes, noodles, or tortillas your favorite food?

more ▶

Compound Predicates

Each part of a compound predicate is written on a separate horizontal line. The words *and, or,* and *but* are written on a vertical dotted line that joins the horizontal lines.

Find the compound predicate in this sentence.

We dressed and raced outside.

Study this diagram of the compound predicate.

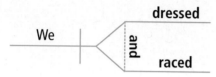

A sentence may have both a compound subject and a compound predicate.

My twin and I stumbled, slipped, and skidded along.

Study this diagram. Note where each *and* is placed.

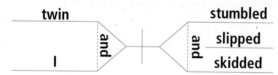

Practice

Diagram only the subjects and the predicates in each sentence. Either or both may be compound.

1. Our yard sparkled and shone after the winter storm.
2. Each branch and twig had grown and had changed.
3. Pine needles looked and felt like diamond spikes.
4. Trees groaned and complained to the wind.
5. The heavy ice bent, broke, or cracked many branches.

Direct Objects

A direct object is diagrammed on the base line after the verb. A vertical line is placed between the verb and the direct object. Notice that it does not cut through the base line.

Find the direct object in this sentence.

Paul needed some new clothes.

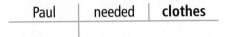

A verb can have more than one direct object. Find the compound direct object in this sentence.

Yesterday he bought boots and a jacket.
Study this diagram of the compound direct object.

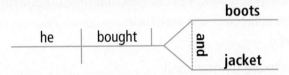

Each verb in a compound predicate can have its own direct object. Read this sentence. Find each verb and its direct object.

He liked the boots but disliked the jacket.
Study the diagram of the compound predicate and its separate direct objects.

Practice

Diagram only the subjects, the verbs, and the direct objects in these sentences.

1. First, Paul found boots.
2. Then he saw a red wool jacket.
3. It had a hood and yarn cuffs.
4. Paul paid half and charged the rest.
5. Later he changed his mind and returned the jacket.

Diagramming Guide

Linking Verbs

A linking verb is diagrammed differently from an action verb. A slanting line, not a vertical one, follows a linking verb.

Remember, a linking verb joins the subject of a sentence with a word in the predicate. The word after the slanting line may name the subject or describe what it is like.

Find the linking verb in this sentence.

A cold feels horrible.

Now study this diagram. Notice that the slanting line points back toward the subject but does not cut through the base line.

| cold | feels \ | horrible |

More than one word can follow a linking verb to describe the subject. Find the two words that describe the subject of this sentence.

Sally is miserable and cranky.

Study how these compound parts are diagrammed.

Sally | is \ and — miserable / cranky

Practice

Diagram each linking verb and the two parts of the sentence that it joins.

1. Meals are not fun for a cold sufferer.
2. Food was tasteless yesterday.
3. Today my nose is red.
4. I am feverish and dizzy.
5. This head cold is a real pain.

Adjectives

Adjectives are diagrammed on a slanting line right below the word that they describe.

Find the adjectives in this sentence.

I have brown, curly hair.

Study this diagram of the sentence.

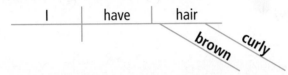

The words *a, an,* and *the* are diagrammed like adjectives.

My older sister has a long ponytail.

Study this diagram of the sentence.

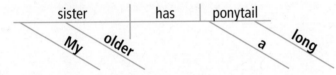

More than one adjective can describe the same word. Sometimes the word *and, or,* or *but* joins adjectives.

A long, braided, or straight hairstyle is not for me!

Note the position of the word *or* in this diagram.

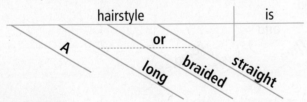

Practice

Diagram all the words in these sentences.

1. This magazine has funny costumes.
2. See the blue, pink, and green wig!
3. That outfit wins the ugly prize.
4. I like that red satin cape.
5. You have unusual taste.

more ▶

Adverbs

Adverbs are diagrammed in the same way that adjectives are. An adverb is placed on a slanting line below the word that it describes. Find the adverb and the verb that it describes in the following sentence.

We patiently watched the tadpoles.

Study this diagram of the sentence.

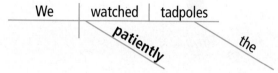

An adverb can appear anywhere in a sentence. It is not always right next to the word that it describes. Find the adverb in this sentence.

Soon the tadpoles became frogs.

Study this diagram of the sentence.

Several adverbs can describe the same word. In this sentence, find the adverbs and the words that they describe.

Then they changed swiftly and completely.

Notice the position of the word *and* in this diagram.

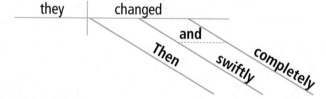

Practice

Diagram all of the words in these sentences.

1. Recently a box arrived.
2. We put a heater nearby.
3. It had twelve eggs inside.
4. Monday we heard one faint peep.
5. Now all the chicks peep constantly and happily.

Prepositional Phrases

A prepositional phrase is diagrammed below the word that it describes. Prepositional phrases that tell where, when, or how often describe verbs. On the other hand, a prepositional phrase that tells what kind, how many, or which one describes a noun.

Find the prepositional phrase in this sentence. What word does it describe?

I like stories about twins.

Study this diagram of the sentence. Notice that the preposition is written on a slanting line below the word that it describes.

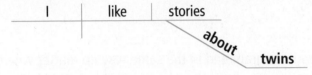

Find the prepositional phrase in this sentence. What word does it describe?

We have two sets in our family.

Study the diagram of this prepositional phrase.

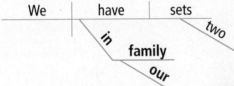

more ▶

Practice

Diagram all of the words in the following sentences.

1. Jamie lives near me.
2. He plays with some twins.
3. Once we wrote invitations for his party.
4. Jamie drew a funny picture on one invitation.
5. The two girls laughed about it.

Diagramming Guide

Diagramming Guide *continued*

Nouns in Direct Address

Diagram a noun in direct address on a short line above and just to the left of the base line.

Find the noun in direct address in this sentence.

Students, today we are having a quiz.

Study this diagram of the sentence.

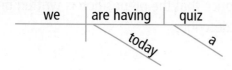

A noun in direct address is diagrammed in the same way no matter where the word appears in the sentence. Find the noun in direct address in this sentence.

Share that book with Aaron, Suzie.

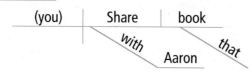

Practice

Diagram all of the words in these sentences.

1. Mr. Savchick, I have a problem.
2. My only pencil, sir, just broke.
3. You may use this pen, Liz.
4. Listen carefully, class.
5. Everyone, I will read each question twice.

How to Use This Thesaurus

Why do you use a thesaurus? One reason is to make your writing more exact. Suppose you wrote the following sentence:

The thin ballerina twirled gracefully.

Is *thin* the most exact word you can use? To find out, use your Thesaurus Plus.

Look up Your Word Turn to the Thesaurus Plus Index on page H86. You will find

thin, *adj.*

Entry words are printed in blue type. Because *thin* is blue, you can look up *thin* in the Thesaurus Plus.

Use Your Thesaurus The main entries in the Thesaurus Plus are listed in alphabetical order. Turn to *thin*. You will find

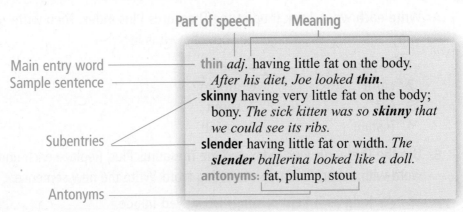

Part of speech   Meaning

Main entry word — thin *adj.* having little fat on the body.
Sample sentence — *After his diet, Joe looked* **thin**.
skinny having very little fat on the body; bony. *The sick kitten was so* **skinny** *that we could see its ribs.*
Subentries — slender having little fat or width. *The* **slender** *ballerina looked like a doll.*
Antonyms — antonyms: fat, plump, stout

Which word might better describe the ballerina in the sentence at the top of the page? Perhaps you chose *slender*.

more ▶

Thesaurus Plus

How to Use This Thesaurus *continued*

Other Index Entries There are two other types of entries in your Thesaurus Plus Index.

splendid nice, *adj.*
spotless clean, *adj.*
spring jump, *v.*
sputter say, *v.*
spy look, *v.*

1 The slanted type means you can find other words for *splendid* if you look under *nice*.

2 The regular type tells you that *start* is the opposite of *finish*.

start finish, *v.*

Practice

A. Write each word. Look it up in the Thesaurus Plus Index. Then write *main entry, subentry,* or *antonym* to show how it is listed.

1. required
2. calm
3. get
4. instant
5. ask
6. gloomy
7. shout
8. smash

B. Use the Thesaurus Plus Index and the Thesaurus Plus. Replace each underlined word with a more exact or interesting word. Write the new sentence.

9. As long as it kept raining, we stayed inside.
10. It was really too cold to go out anyway.
11. Later we looked at a great rainbow.
12. We were nervous about the weather.
13. We had to start planning our museum trip.
14. Clara was worried that there was little time.
15. Jim thought she was being comical.
16. Jim's thoughts angered Clara.
17. Mrs. Lee helped us to create a plan.
18. We decided to stick to her plan.
19. We were grateful for Mrs. Lee's help.
20. Everyone was now happy.

Thesaurus Plus

Thesaurus Plus Index

A

abandon leave, *v.*
able good, *adj.*
abnormal common, *adj.*
absurd funny, *adj.*
accept argue, *v.*
accomplish do, *v.*
achieve do, *v.*
achieve succeed, *v.*
acquire get, *v.*
act do, *v.*
active, *adj.*
actual real, *adj.*
additional further, *adj.*
admirable good, *adj.*
admirable nice, *adj.*
after before, *adv.*
agree, *v.*
agree argue, *v.*
agreeable nice, *adj.*
alarming scary, *adj.*
allow let, *v.*
also, *adv.*
alternative choice, *n.*
amaze surprise, *v.*
amiable nice, *adj.*
amusing funny, *adj.*
ancient new, *adj.*
angry, *adj.*
annoyed angry, *adj.*
answer ask, *v.*
antique new, *adj.*
anxious nervous, *adj*
appealing nice, *adj.*
appealing pretty, *adj.*
appetizing good, *adj.*
appreciative grateful, *adj.*
approve agree, *v.*
approve argue, *v.*
argue, *v.*
arid wet, *adj.*
arrive leave, *v.*
artificial real, *adj.*

as long as while, *conj.*
ask, *v.*
assemble gather, *v.*
assert think, *v.*
astonish surprise, *v.*
astound surprise, *v.*
at the end last, *adv.*
attain do, *v.*
attractive pretty, *adj.*
audacious bold, *adj.*
avoid look, *v.*
awful good, *adj.*

B

bad good, *adj.*
bark say, *v.*
be worthy of deserve, *v.*
beautiful pretty, *adj.*
before, *adv.*
begin finish, *v.*
begin start, *v.*
believe think, *v.*
bellow say, *v.*
besides also, *adv.*
big, *adj.*
blubber laugh, *v.*
boast, *v.*
bold, *adj.*
bored eager, *adj.*
boring, *adj.*
brag boast, *v.*
brave, *adj.*
break, *v.*
bright dark, *adj.*
bright shiny, *adj.*
brilliant pretty, *adj.*
build make, *v.*
bulky big, *adj.*
bumpy rough, *adj.*
bury hide, *v.*
buy get, *v.*

C

cackle laugh, *v.*
calm, *adj.*
calm angry, *adj.*
calm nervous, *adj.*
calm upset, *adj.*
capable good, *adj.*
careful, *adj.*
caring good, *adj.*
carry bring, *v.*
cause effect, *n.*
cautious bold, *adj.*
cautious careful, *adj.*
change, *v.*
changeable faithful, *adj.*
charge price, *n.*
charitable good, *adj.*
charming nice, *adj.*
charming pretty, *adj.*
cheerful happy, *adj.*
chief, *adj.*
chilly cold, *adj.*
chipper lively, *adj.*
choice, *n.*
chortle laugh, *v.*
chuckle laugh, *v.*
clash argue, *v.*
clean, *adj.*
clear, *adj.*
close finish, *v.*
close start, *v.*
cloudy clear, *adj.*
cloudy unclear, *adj.*
coarse rough, *adj.*
cold, *adj.*
cold-hearted nice, *adj.*
collect gather, *v.*
colossal big, *adj.*
come leave, *v.*
comfortable upset, *adj.*
comical funny, *adj.*
commence finish, *v.*
commence start, *v.*

more ▶

expert good, *adj.*
explore, *v.*
extraordinary common, *adj.*

fail do, *v.*
faint unclear, *adj.*
faithful, *adj.*
fake, *n.*
fake real, *adj.*
false faithful, *adj.*
familiar strange, *adj.*
fantastic great, *adj.*
fast quick, *adj.*
fat, *adj.*
fat thin, *adj.*
faulty perfect, *adj.*
fearless brave, *adj.*
feel think, *v.*
few many, *adj.*
few some, *adj.*
filthy clean, *adj.*
finally last, *adv.*
fine good, *adj.*
fine nice, *adj.*
finish, *v.*
finish do, *v.*
finish start, *v.*
first last, *adv.*
fit healthy, *adj.*
flavorful good, *adj.*
flawed nice, *adj.*
flawed perfect, *adj.*
flooded wet, *adj.*
foggy clear, *adj.*
forget think, *v.*
form make, *v.*
frank honest, *adj.*
frantic calm, *adj.*
freezing cold, *adj.*
fresh new, *adj.*
friendly good, *adj.*
friendly nice, *adj.*
frightened brave, *adj.*

frightening scary, *adj.*
fulfill do, *v.*
fuming angry, *adj.*
funny, *adj.*
furious angry, *adj.*
further, *adj.*
fuzzy unclear, *adj.*

gape look, *v.*
gather, *v.*
gawk look, *v.*
gaze look, *v.*
general common, *adj.*
generous good, *adj.*
gentle nice, *adj.*
get, *v.*
giant big, *adj.*
gifted good, *adj.*
gigantic big, *adj.*
giggle laugh, *v.*
give, *v.*
glad happy, *adj.*
glamorous pretty, *adj.*
glance, *v.*
glance look, *v.*
glare look, *v.*
gleaming shiny, *adj.*
glimpse glance, *v.*
glimpse look, *v.*
glistening shiny, *adj.*
gloomy funny, *adj.*
glorious pretty, *adj.*
glower look, *v.*
good, *adj.*
gorgeous pretty, *adj.*
gracious nice, *adj.*
grateful, *adj.*
great, *adj.*
great big, *adj.*
green, *adj.*
gripe say, *v.*
groan say, *v.*
grow, *v.*
growl say, *v.*
grumble say, *v.*

grunt say, *v.*
guard protect, *v.*
guarded careful, *adj.*
guffaw laugh, *v.*

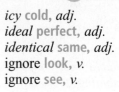

handsome pretty, *adj.*
handy useful, *adj.*
happy, *adj.*
hard easy, *adj.*
harmful good, *adj.*
hasty quick, *adj.*
haul pull, *v.*
hazard danger, *n.*
healthful good, *adj.*
healthy, *adj.*
heartless good, *adj.*
heedless careful, *adj.*
helpful useful, *adj.*
hide, *v.*
hilarious funny, *adj.*
hinder let, *v.*
hiss say, *v.*
hobby job, *n.*
holler say, *v.*
holler shout, *v.*
homely pretty, *adj.*
honest, *adj.*
honest good, *adj.*
honorable good, *adj.*
hot cold, *adj.*
howl laugh, *v.*
howl say, *v.*
huge big, *adj.*
humorous funny, *adj.*
hunter green green, *adj.*
hurdle jump, *v.*

icy cold, *adj.*
ideal perfect, *adj.*
identical same, *adj.*
ignore look, *v.*
ignore see, *v.*

more ▶

Thesaurus Plus

Thesaurus Plus

ignore think, *v.*
ill healthy, *adj.*
imagine think, *v.*
immense big, *adj.*
impostor fake, *n.*
in addition also, *adv.*
inactive lively, *adj.*
incompetent capable, *adj.*
indifferent eager, *adj.*
inefficient useful, *adj.*
inferior good, *adj.*
inferior great, *adj.*
inquire ask, *v.*
insincere honest, *adj.*
instant moment, *n.*
insulting nice, *adj.*
interested eager, *adj.*
interesting boring, *adj.*
invent create, *v.*
investigate explore, *v.*
irate angry, *adj.*
irritated angry, *adj.*

J

job, *n.*
join, *v.*
judge think, *v.*
jumbo big, *adj.*
jump, *v.*

K

keen eager, *adj.*
kelly green green, *adj.*

L

large big, *adj.*
large little, *adj.*
last, *adv.*
later before, *adv.*
laugh, *v.*
laughable funny, *adj.*
law-abiding good, *adj.*
lax careful, *adj.*

lazy active, *adj.*
lazy lively, *adj.*
leap jump, *v.*
leave, *v.*
leisure job, *n.*
let, *v.*
light dark, *adj.*
lime green, *adj.*
little, *adj.*
little big, *adj.*
lively, *adj.*
lively active, *adj.*
lively boring, *adj.*
locate put, *v.*
look, *v.*
lose get, *v.*
lovely nice, *adj.*
lovely pretty, *adj.*
loving good, *adj.*
loyal faithful, *adj.*
ludicrous funny, *adj.*
luscious good, *adj.*

M

mad angry, *adj.*
main chief, *adj.*
make, *v.*
make do, *v.*
mammoth big, *adj.*
manufacture make, *v.*
many, *adj.*
march walk, *v.*
marvelous great, *adj.*
massive big, *adj.*
masterful good, *adj.*
mature grow, *v.*
mean good, *adj.*
mean nice, *adj.*
meaning, *n.*
mend break, *v.*
merit deserve, *v.*
meticulous careful, *adj.*
microscopic big, *adj.*

mighty big, *adj.*
mindful careful, *adj.*
miniature big, *adj.*
miniature little, *adj.*
minor chief, *adj.*
minor important, *adj.*
misleading honest, *adj.*
misty clear, *adj.*
moan say, *v.*
moist wet, *adj.*
moment, *n.*
monotonous boring, *adj.*
moral good, *adj.*
more further, *adj.*
mouth-watering good, *adj.*
mumble say, *v.*
murky dark, *adj.*
murmur say, *v.*
mutter say, *v.*

N

nasty good, *adj.*
necessary, *adj.*
nervous, *adj.*
nervous upset, *adj.*
new, *adj.*
nice, *adj.*
nonsense meaning, *n.*
nonsensical unreasonable, *adj.*
normal common, *adj.*
normal strange, *adj.*
notice see, *v.*
nourishing good, *adj.*
novel new, *adj.*
numerous many, *adj.*
nutritious good, *adj.*

O

obedient good, *adj.*
observe see, *v.*
obtain get, *v.*
obvious unclear, *adj.*
offensive nice, *adj.*

offensive pretty, *adj.*
offer give, *v.*
old new, *adj.*
olive green, *adj.*
omit do, *v.*
operate, *v.*
ordinary common, *adj.*
ordinary great, *adj.*
original new, *adj.*
outstanding good, *adj.*
overlook look, *v.*
overlook see, *v.*

P

parched wet, *adj.*
part join, *v.*
particular careful, *adj.*
patch break, *v.*
peaceful angry, *adj.*
peaceful calm, *adj.*
peek glance, *v.*
peek look, *v.*
peep look, *v.*
peeved angry, *adj.*
perfect, *adj.*
perform do, *v.*
peril danger, *n.*
permit let, *v.*
persuade, *v.*
phony fake, *n.*
place put, *v.*
placid nervous, *adj.*
play job, *n.*
pleasant nice, *adj.*
pleased upset, *adj.*
plump fat, *adj.*
plump thin, *adj.*
pointlessness
  meaning, *n.*
polished rough, *adj.*
polite good, *adj.*
poor good, *adj.*
praiseworthy good, *adj.*
preference choice, *n.*
present give, *v.*
pretty, *adj.*

prevent let, *v.*
previously before, *adv.*
price, *n.*
principal chief, *adj.*
probe explore, *v.*
produce create, *v.*
produce do, *v.*
produce grow, *v.*
proper nice, *adj.*
protect, *v.*
protection danger, *n.*
protective careful, *adj.*
prudent careful, *adj.*
pull, *v.*
push pull, *v.*
put, *v.*

Q

quake shake, *v.*
qualified good, *adj.*
quarrel argue, *v.*
question ask, *v.*
quick, *adj.*
quit do, *v.*
quit leave, *v.*

R

race run, *v.*
radiant pretty, *adj.*
raging calm, *adj.*
raise grow, *v.*
rapid quick, *adj.*
rare common, *adj.*
ravishing pretty, *adj.*
real, *adj.*
receive give, *v.*
reflect think, *v.*
refreshing nice, *adj.*
refuse agree, *v.*
regular common, *adj.*
remain change, *v.*
remove put, *v.*
repair break, *v.*
repellent nice, *adj.*

reply ask, *v.*
repulsive pretty, *adj.*
required necessary, *adj.*
resolve decide, *v.*
resolve do, *v.*
result effect, *n.*
return leave, *v.*
reveal hide, *v.*
revolting pretty, *adj.*
ridiculous funny, *adj.*
risk danger, *n.*
roar laugh, *v.*
roar say, *v.*
rough, *adj.*
rude nice, *adj.*
run, *v.*
run walk, *v.*

S

sad funny, *adj.*
sad happy, *adj.*
safety danger, *n.*
same, *adj.*
satisfied upset, *adj.*
saturated wet, *adj.*
say, *v.*
scan look, *v.*
scary, *adj.*
scatter gather, *v.*
scowl look, *v.*
scream say, *v.*
screech say, *v.*
scrumptious good, *adj.*
second-rate good, *adj.*
security danger, *n.*
sedate calm, *adj.*
see, *v.*
selection choice, *n.*
sense meaning, *n*
separate gather, *v.*
separate join, *v.*
serene calm, *adj.*
serious funny, *adj.*
set put, *v.*
several many, *adj.*
several some, *adj.*

more ▶

unselfish good, *adj.*
unusual common, *adj.*
unworthy good, *adj.*
upright good, *adj.*
upset, *adj.*
upset angry, *adj.*
upstanding good, *adj.*
use operate, *v.*
useful, *adj.*
useless useful, *adj.*

valiant brave, *adj.*
varied boring, *adj.*
vicious nice, *adj.*
view look, *v.*
view see, *v.*
vigilant careful, *adj.*
vile nice, *adj.*

wail laugh, *v.*
walk, *v.*
walk run, *v.*
warm cold, *adj.*
wary careful, *adj.*
watchful careful, *adj.*
water-logged wet, *adj.*
wee big, *adj.*
weep laugh, *v.*
weird strange, *adj.*
well healthy, *adj.*
well-mannered good,
   adj.
well-mannered nice, *adj.*
wet, *adj.*
wettish wet, *adj.*
while, *conj.*
whimper laugh, *v.*
whimper say, *v.*
whimsical funny, *adj.*
whine say, *v.*
whisper say, *v.*
whisper shout, *v.*
wicked good, *adj.*

wild calm, *adj.*
win get, *v.*
wish, *v.*
witty funny, *adj.*
wonderful great, *adj.*
work do, *v.*
work job, *n.*
work operate, *v.*
work out do, *v.*
worried upset, *adj.*
worthless important,
   adj.
worthless useful, *adj.*

yell say, *v.*
yell shout, *v.*
yummy good, *adj.*

Thesaurus Plus

A

active *adj.* full of movement. *Tennis is an **active** sport.*

energetic full of strength and energy. *My **energetic** friend Janet is always busy.*

lively full of life, alert. *The **lively** puppy kept tugging at his leash.*

antonyms: lazy, sluggish

agree *v.* to express willingness. *My parents **agreed** to get a dog.*

consent to say yes. *Did Judy **consent** to your plan?*

approve to say officially that something is correct or should be done. *The principal **approved** of the field trip.*

comply with to follow a request or a rule. *Please **comply with** the rules when you visit the museum.*

antonyms: deny, refuse

also *adv.* too. *Peter likes that album, but he likes this one **also**.*

in addition plus, as well. *We went to the park and to the zoo **in addition**.*

besides together with, over and above. *Tom plays two instruments **besides** the guitar.*

How **Angry** Were You?

angry *adj.* feeling or showing displeasure.

1. slightly angry: *displeased, annoyed, irritated, peeved*
2. very angry: *upset, cross, mad*
3. extremely angry: *furious, enraged, irate, fuming, outraged*

antonyms: calm, peaceful, delighted, happy, pleased

argue *v.* to give reasons for or against something, especially to someone with a different opinion. *Jo favored a town pool, but Jean **argued** against it.*

quarrel to have a fight with words. *We **quarreled** about who was smarter.*

clash to be against one another on an issue. *Employers and employees **clashed** during a recent strike.*

disagree to have a different opinion. *The senators **disagreed** with each other.*

antonyms: accept, agree, consent

ask *v.* to put a question to. *I will **ask** Donna to come with me.*

question to try to get information from. *Please **question** him about his plans.*

inquire to try to find out information. *We **inquired** about her address.*

antonyms: reply, answer

B

before *adv.* in the past. *He was excited since he hadn't been to Texas **before**.*

earlier sooner or at a past time. *The game ended **earlier** than usual.*

previously taking place in the past. ***Previously** she wore her hair long.*

antonyms: after, later

Word Bank

big *adj.* of great size or importance.

huge	colossal
immense	mammoth
large	enormous
mighty	gigantic
jumbo	sizeable
bulky	great
massive	
giant	

antonyms: little, tiny, miniature, small, wee, petite, microscopic

boast *v.* to praise oneself, one's belongings, or one's actions. *Sara always boasts about how fast she runs.*

brag to use words about oneself to show off. *Leroy bragged about everything.*

crow to utter a cry of delight or victory. *Pat grinned and crowed, "I won!"*

bold *adj.* not timid or fearful. *Mary Read was a bold woman.*

daring brave enough to take on a big challenge; adventurous. *Two daring climbers reached the top at last.*

audacious not afraid of any risk. *One audacious bear came up to our tent.*

antonym: cautious

boring *adj.* not interesting. *The TV show was boring so I fell asleep.*

dull lacking excitement. *Not one player scored during the dull soccer match.*

dry tiresome. *It was hard to finish reading the lengthy, dry report.*

monotonous not interesting because always the same. *Monotonous songs repeat the same words over and over.*

antonyms: exciting, lively, interesting, varied

brave *adj.* able to face danger or pain without fear. *You seemed brave when the doctor set your broken leg.*

courageous able to face difficult situations. *That pilot is courageous.*

valiant acting with great courage. *The valiant soldiers risked their lives.*

fearless without fright. *The fearless cat stood still as a dog ran toward it.*

antonyms: cowardly, frightened

break *v.* to separate into pieces as the result of force or strain. *A beam broke under the weight of the snow.*

shatter to come apart suddenly into many pieces. *The delicate cup shattered against the floor.*

smash to crush into pieces. *The car smashed into the orange crates.*

crack to come apart with a sharp sound.

Dale cracked the bat when he hit the ball.

antonyms: mend, patch, repair

---

calm *adj.* without excitement or motion. *The calm water looked like a mirror.*

peaceful without worry or trouble. *Their argument spoiled our peaceful day.*

tranquil quiet and undisturbed. *We found a tranquil picnic spot.*

sedate composed; dignified. *He remained sedate during the trial.*

antonyms: excited, frantic, raging, wild

Shades of Meaning
careful *adj.* giving serious thought and attention to what one is doing.
1. alert for danger or trouble: *cautious vigilant watchful*
2. wise and thoughtful: *prudent, studious, mindful*
3. paying attention to details: *meticulous, conscientious, particular, thorough, strict*
4. showing lack of trust: *wary, guarded, protective*
antonyms: heedless, careless, thoughtless, slack, lax

change *v.* to make or become different. *I like how you changed your hair.*

convert to put something to a new use. *They converted the barn into a house.*

transform to alter completely the form of something. *We know how to transform fuel into energy.*

antonyms: continue, remain

chief *adj.* highest in rank or importance. *The chief product of the state is wheat.*

main most important. *The main library is bigger than its branches.*

more ▶

principal leading all others. *The panda's principal food is a kind of bamboo.*
antonyms: minor, unimportant

choice *n.* the act of choosing or deciding. *Please make your choice now.*

selection the act of picking one or a few out of several. *I tried on eight pairs of shoes before I made my selection.*

preference a liking for one thing over another. *My color preference is red.*

alternative decision between two or more possibilities. *The alternative is between walking or riding to school.*

clean *adj.* free from dirt, stains, and clutter. *Dad needs a clean shirt.*

spotless completely free of dirt. *The hospital operating room is spotless.*
antonyms: dirty, filthy, soiled

clear *adj.* free from clouds, dust, or anything that would make it hard to see through. *The sky was so clear that we could see the Milky Way.*

transparent able to be seen through easily. *We watched the sharks through a transparent tank.*
antonyms: cloudy, foggy, misty

cold *adj.* at a low temperature. *Cold water is the most refreshing drink of all.*

chilly not warm enough for comfort. *If you feel chilly, you can sit in the sun.*

cool at a somewhat low temperature. *The cool wind felt good in the sun.*

icy feeling like ice. *How do birds stay alive in such icy winds?*

freezing producing icy conditions. *The freezing rain made driving difficult.*
antonyms: hot, warm

common *adj.* often found or occurring; familiar. *A common response to a kind host is a thank-you note.*

familiar well known because it is often seen or heard. *The bus route home is very familiar.*

ordinary not unusual in any way. *On an ordinary day, I eat cereal.*

normal of the usual kind; natural. *It was not our normal school schedule.*

general widespread; prevalent. *The students had a general feeling of excitement before the big game.*

regular usual or standard. *They said our regular teacher was ill.*
antonyms: abnormal, extraordinary, rare, strange, unusual

create *v.* to bring into being. *Spiders create webs to trap insects.*

establish to begin or set up. *The settlers soon established a small town.*

invent to make something that did not exist before. *No one is sure who really invented the camera.*

produce to bring forth, manufacture. *How many cars do they produce?*

design to make a plan or a drawing for something. *An art student designed the school's new sign.*
antonym: destroy

danger *n.* the chance of great harm or loss. *There was no danger of getting lost if we stayed on the path.*

hazard something that could cause harm. *A blocked door can be a fire hazard.*

risk the possibility of harm in an activity. *The risk of an accident increases on icy roads.*

peril a condition that can threaten lives. *Anyone out in this storm will be in great peril.*
antonyms: safety, security, protection

dark *adj.* without light or sun. *It was so dark that we turned on the lights.*

dim not well lit. *Do not read in such dim light.*

murky very gloomy. *Evans was afraid to step into the murky cell.*
antonyms: bright, light

decide *v.* to make up one's mind. *I **decided** to buy the red bike.*

determine to make a firm decision. *Dr. Tsao **determined** to do all that he could to save the cat.*

resolve to make a firm plan. *I **resolve** to eat a good breakfast every day.*

deserve *v.* ought to have or receive. *An animal lover like Paul **deserves** a pet.*

merit earn the right to something. *June's courage **merits** high praise.*

be worthy of be good or valuable enough to receive. *The animal shelter **is worthy of** your support.*

Shades of Meaning
do *v.*
1. to carry out an action: *perform, execute, produce, make, work, act*
2. to solve something: *unscramble solve work out decode resolve*
3. to complete an action: *fulfill, finish, complete, achieve, attain, accomplish*
antonyms: omit, undo, fail, quit

E

eager *adj.* full of strong desire. ***Eager** campers set up their camp early.*

keen full of enthusiasm and interest. *Ben is a **keen** football fan.*

interested involved or concerned with. *Peg is an **interested** committee member.*

antonyms: bored, indifferent

easy *adj.* not difficult. *Tad solved the **easy** puzzle quickly.*

simple not complicated. *Use a **simple** drawing of a few lines.*

uncomplicated not hard to understand, deal with, or solve. *We followed Dad's uncomplicated directions with ease.*

effortless easily done. *The athlete made weightlifting seem **effortless**.*

antonyms: complex, difficult, hard

effect *n.* something brought about by a cause. *The moon has an important **effect** on the ocean tides.*

consequence a direct outcome of something. *The fine performance was a **consequence** of practice.*

result something that happens because of something else. *The broken branches are the **result** of the storm.*

antonyms: cause, source

explore *v.* to look into or through closely. *Katie **explored** every inch of her closet for her missing shoe.*

study to examine closely and carefully. *Doris **studied** her notes before class.*

probe to search into thoroughly. *An investigator **probed** Rick's background.*

investigate to research carefully. *Who will **investigate** the jewel's disappearance?*

F

faithful *adj.* worthy of trust. *Ben knew his **faithful** friend would keep quiet.*

loyal offering constant support to a person, country, or cause. *The spy insisted that he was **loyal** to his country.*

true trustworthy and devoted. *Ariel was a **true** friend when I needed her.*

antonyms: changeable, treacherous, false

fake *n.* someone or something that is not what he, she, or it pretends to be. *We realized that the actor's moustache was a **fake**.*

fraud a person who lies about himself or herself. *That **fraud** claimed that he got us free tickets, but he did not!*

phony an insincere person. *Pete tries to act friendly, but he is a **phony**.*

impostor a person who pretends to be another person. *Was that woman really the queen or only an **impostor**?*

more ▶

Thesaurus Plus

fat *adj.* having much or too much body weight. *We put our **fat** dog on a diet.*

plump rounded and full in shape. *Her baby brother has **plump** cheeks.*

stout large and heavy in build. *Al is slim, but his brother Ben is **stout**.*

antonyms: skinny, slender, slim, thin

finish *v.* to get done. *When you **finish** cleaning, you may go for a bike ride.*

end to bring or come to the final moments. *The first half **ended** when the whistle blew.*

complete to get to the end of something. *I **completed** the test as the bell rang.*

stop to come to a halt. *The engine **stopped** when the car ran out of gas.*

conclude to be or cause to be over. *Ms. Wang **concluded** her speech.*

close to come to or bring to an end. *The play **closed** with a joke.*

antonyms: begin, commence, start

How **Funny** Was It?

funny *adj.* causing laughter or amusement.

1. somewhat funny: *amusing, droll, whimsical, witty*
2. quite funny: *humorous, laughable, comical*
3. extremely funny: *ridiculous, hilarious, sidesplitting, ludicrous, absurd*

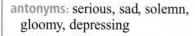

antonyms: serious, sad, solemn, gloomy, depressing

---

further *adj.* added or other. *The news station released **further** storm bulletins.*

more greater in size, quantity, extent, or degree. *We need **more** ice for the bowl.*

additional extra. *Take **additional** socks in case one pair gets wet.*

gather *v.* to bring or come together in one place. *They **gathered** around the campfire and sang songs.*

assemble to bring or come together as a group. *The band members must **assemble** in the auditorium at noon.*

collect to bring things together. *Tina has **collected** twenty different baseball hats in only one year.*

antonyms: scatter, separate

get *v.* to receive. *Did you **get** any payment for your work in the garden?*

earn to gain by working or by supplying a service. *Jay **earns** five dollars a week by baby-sitting for families in his neighborhood.*

obtain to gain by means of planning or effort. *Carol took a test to **obtain** her driver's license.*

win to receive as a prize or reward. *Did Joe **win** a prize in the school essay contest?*

acquire to gain by one's own efforts. *Ed worked many hours to **acquire** his typing skill.*

buy to gain by paying a price for. *Ana used her allowance to **buy** a gift for her mother.*

antonym: lose

give *v.* to hand over to another. *Sara **gave** her sister a small music box for her birthday.*

offer to put forward to be accepted or refused. *Jan **offered** Ina half of her sandwich and apple.*

supply to make available something that is needed. *Blood **supplies** oxygen to the brain.*

present to make a gift or award to. *Coach Hart **presented** the trophy to the captain of our basketball team.*

antonyms: receive, take

Shades of Meaning

good *adj.*

1. well-behaved: *polite, obedient, well-mannered, courteous*
2. trustworthy: *honest, decent, honorable, law-abiding, upstanding, upright, moral*
3. aiding one's health: *healthful, nutritious, nourishing*
4. pleasant-tasting: *delicious, tasty, flavorful, mouth-watering, yummy, appetizing, luscious, scrumptious*
5. having much ability: *skilled, able, capable, talented, gifted, masterful, expert, qualified, experienced*
6. kind: *considerate, caring, thoughtful, generous, unselfish, friendly, loving, charitable*
7. better than average: *outstanding, excellent, fine, superior, praiseworthy, admirable*

antonyms: awful, unkind, harmful, bad, evil, wicked, disagreeable, disgusting, unworthy, cruel, mean, nasty, heartless, inferior, poor, second-rate

glance *v.* to look briefly. *I **glanced** at him quickly.*

glimpse to get a brief view of. *She only **glimpsed** the passing car.*

peek to look briefly. *He **peeked** around the corner.*

grateful *adj.* feeling or showing thanks. *The Smiths were **grateful** when their neighbors helped rebuild their barn.*

appreciative expressing or feeling gratitude. *The **appreciative** man thanked Lori for finding his cat.*

thankful showing an understanding of how fortunate one is. *Dad was **thankful** that no one was hurt.*

great *adj.* remarkable. *Pearl took **great** pictures of the baseball game.*

terrific excellent. *A **terrific** swimmer like Natalie should make the team.*

fantastic extraordinary. *There is a **fantastic** view of the ocean from here!*

wonderful astonishing. *This is a **wonderful** museum.*

marvelous notably superior. *Your speech was **marvelous**.*

antonyms: inferior, ordinary

Shades of **Green**

green *adj.* having the color of grass; a mix of blue and yellow.

olive: light yellowish-green, like green olives
lime: bright yellowish-green, like limes
kelly: bright green, like grass or clover
emerald: bright, slightly dark green, like emeralds
hunter: dark green, like pine trees and cucumbers

grow *v.* to become or cause to become larger. *Rain helped the plants **grow** tall.*

raise to promote the development of. *Kate **raised** her puppy with love.*

produce to bring forth; yield. *Kansas **produces** wheat.*

mature to develop fully. *Has the fruit **matured** enough to be picked?*

antonym: stunt

happy *adj.* showing or feeling pleasure or joy. *Tina was **happy** because she got the lead part in the play.*

cheerful being in good spirits. *It is pleasant to be near **cheerful** people.*

glad pleased. *Sam was **glad** to be home.*

antonyms: sad, sorrowful

healthy *adj.* free from disease or injury. *The **healthy** plants grew tall.*

fit being in good physical shape. *Drew feels healthy and **fit**.*

more ▶

sound having no damage or disease.
*The old house still had a **sound** frame.*

well not sick. *Even during the flu
season, Molly stayed **well**.*
antonyms: diseased, ill, sick

hide *v.* to keep or put out of sight.
*The cat **hid** under the bed.*

conceal purposely to keep from being
seen or known. *Allan **concealed** his
sadness behind a happy face.*

bury to cover from view. *The dog **buried**
another bone under the rose bush.*
antonyms: reveal, show

honest *adj.* straightforward; truthful. *The
honest witness told the truth in court.*

direct to the point. *I will be **direct** and
not waste time.*

frank free and open in expressing
thoughts or feelings. *In a **frank** talk,
I told Lina how I felt.*
antonyms: deceitful, insincere,
misleading

--- **J** ---

job *n.* something that must be done.
*Would you prefer the **job** of scrubbing
or waxing?*

work things that must be done. *You have
enough **work** to keep you busy.*

task an assignment or a chore. *Adam's
task was to sweep the hall.*

employment an activity by which one
earns money or to which one devotes
time. *Teaching is a wonderful form of
employment.*
antonyms: play, hobby, leisure

join *v.* to put together or attach. *We all
joined hands to form a circle.*

connect to link things together. *A bridge
connects the two cities.*

unite to bring together to form a whole.
*The thirteen colonies were **united**.*
antonyms: part, separate

jump *v.* to rise up or move through the
air. *The cow in the nursery rhyme*

jumps over the moon.

hurdle to go over a barrier. *The horse
hurdled the fence and galloped away.*

leap to jump or cause to jump quickly
or suddenly. *Carl **leaped** away from
the falling tree.*

spring to move upward or forward in
one quick motion. *I **spring** out of bed
when my alarm rings.*

--- **L** ---

last *adv.* after all the others. *Add the ice
last so that it does not melt.*

finally after a long while. *After waiting
two hours, the train **finally** arrived.*

at the end at the conclusion. *Flo
stumbled **at the end** of her speech.*
antonym: first

Shades of Meaning
laugh *v.* to make sounds to express amusement.
1. to laugh quietly: *giggle, chuckle, titter*   2. to laugh in a mean or sly way: *snicker, snigger*   3. to laugh loudly: *cackle, chortle, guffaw, roar, shriek, howl*
antonyms: whimper, weep, cry, wail, sob, blubber

leave *v.* to go away from. *Please **leave**
this dangerous place at once!*

abandon to go away from because of
trouble or danger; to desert. *The crew
abandoned the sinking ship.*

quit to depart from. *Phil wants to **quit**
Seattle and move to Tulsa.*
antonyms: arrive, come, return

let *v.* to give permission to. *Ron took the
leash off his dog and **let** her run free.*

allow to say yes to. *Please **allow** me to
go to Jenny's party.*

permit to consent to. *The state law **permits** sixteen-year-olds to drive cars and motorcycles.*
antonyms: prevent, stop, hinder

little *adj.* not big in size or quantity. *Leroy is six feet tall, but he looks **little** next to that thirty-foot statue.*
tiny extremely reduced in size. *Dan could not read the **tiny** print without his glasses.*
small reduced in size. *I cannot wear this coat because it is too **small**.*
miniature reduced from its usual size. *Ella built a **miniature** city with toothpicks and glue.*
antonyms: enormous, large

lively *adj.* full of energy, active. *They were out of breath after dancing a **lively** polka.*
chipper full of cheer. *Ike felt **chipper** on this lovely morning.*
energetic full of strength and action. *The **energetic** children played on the swings all morning.*
spirited full of life. *Our team played a **spirited** game and won.*
antonyms: inactive, lazy

Shades of Meaning
look *v.* to focus one's eyes or attention on something.
1. to look quickly: *glimpse, glance, scan* 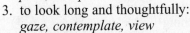
2. to look secretively: *spy, peep, peek, snoop*
3. to look long and thoughtfully: *gaze, contemplate, view*
4. to look steadily and directly: *stare, gape, gawk*
5. to look with anger or displeasure: *glower, glare, scowl*
antonyms: overlook, dismiss, ignore, avoid, shun

M

make *v.* to shape or put together out of materials or parts. *Mrs. Lewis **made** that rug from pieces of old clothes and curtains.*
build to put up something with materials or parts. *Dad **built** a tree house in our yard.*
construct to make by fitting parts together. *Will the town **construct** a bridge over the river?*
form to shape. *Ali **formed** a bird out of her piece of clay.*
manufacture to put things together with machines. *That factory **manufactures** many popular toys and games.*
antonyms: destroy, dismantle

many *adj.* adding up to a large number. *Jay learned to identify the **many** different birds on the island.*
several more than two but not a large number. *The power was out for **several** hours after the storm.*
numerous made up of a large number. ***Numerous** people lined up outside the factory to apply for a job.*
antonym: few

meaning *n.* the intended thought or message of something. *Ms. Clark explained the **meaning** of the poem to her puzzled students.*
significance the special message or intention. *What is the **significance** of the maple leaf on the Canadian flag?*
sense the many ideas implied by a word. *The **sense** of a word usually depends on its use in a sentence.*
antonyms: nonsense, pointlessness

moment *n.* a very short period of time. *Please wait just a **moment**, and a salesperson will help you.*
instant a second in time. *In an **instant**, before anyone could blink, the clown had disappeared.*

more ▶

N

necessary *adj.* having to be done. *It is **necessary** that you complete this form.*
essential very important, basic. *Regular brushing is **essential** to healthy teeth.*
required called for or needed. *The exam **required** careful thinking.*

nervous *adj.* shaken and jittery because of fear or challenge. *The **nervous** actor forgot his lines.*
anxious upset or fearful about something uncertain. *Olive feels **anxious** about her exam.*
edgy tense. *Bill was **edgy** the night before the exam and could not sleep.*
antonyms: calm, placid

new *adj.* never used, worn, or thought of before. *We finally bought a **new** car.*
fresh just made, grown, or gathered. *These are **fresh** beans, straight from Grandfather's garden.*
original not copied from or based on anything else. *The brilliant inventor came up with another **original** idea.*
novel strikingly different. *The detective's **novel** method of investigation was successful.*
antonyms: old, ancient, antique

Shades of Meaning

nice *adj.*

1. pleasing: *pleasant, agreeable, appealing, delightful, refreshing, lovely, charming, enchanting*
2. good: *fine, skillful, admirable, splendid, superb, excellent*
3. kind: *sweet, companionable, gentle, sympathetic, friendly, amiable, mild*
4. polite: *gracious, considerate, proper, well-mannered, courteous*

antonyms: insulting, offensive, displeasing, repellent, terrible, flawed, vile, mean, contemptible, vicious, rude, cold-hearted, crass

O

operate *v.* to run. *Can you **operate** a bulldozer?*
work to perform a function. *Who knows how to **work** the computer?*
use employ for some purpose. *Did you **use** my saw to build the bookcase?*

P

perfect *adj.* having no errors, flaws, or defects. *A **perfect** day for sailing is sunny and slightly breezy.*
ideal thought of as being the best possible. *Casey has an **ideal** job that allows her to travel.*
excellent of the highest quality. *The chef made our **excellent** meal from the freshest ingredients.*
delightful very pleasing. *A **delightful** breeze cooled the hot beach.*
antonyms: faulty, flawed

persuade *v.* to cause someone to do or believe something by pleading, arguing, or reasoning. *I **persuaded** Jim to clean my room for me.*
convince to cause someone to feel certain. *I **convinced** my mother that I was telling the truth.*
antonyms: dissuade, deter

Word Bank

pretty *adj.* pleasing to the eye or ear.

attractive	beautiful	radiant
cute	appealing	brilliant
charming	handsome	
dazzling	gorgeous	
ravishing	glorious	
stunning		
lovely		
glamorous		

antonyms: ugly, unattractive, homely, offensive, unappealing, disgusting, repulsive, revolting

Thesaurus Plus

price *n.* the amount of money asked or paid for something. *The price of this shirt is $10.95.*

charge a fee asked or paid, particularly for a service. *Is there a charge for washing the car windshield and windows, or is it a free service?*

cost amount of payment for a product or a service. *The cost of a concert ticket has increased ten dollars.*

expense something paid out. *Can we afford the expense of piano lessons?*

protect *v.* to keep safe from harm or injury. *Calvin wears a helmet to protect his head when he rides his bike or goes roller skating.*

guard to defend or keep safe from danger. *The police guarded the museum against theft.*

antonym: endanger

pull *v.* to apply force to in order to draw someone or something in the direction of the force. *I pulled the door toward me as hard as I could.*

drag to draw along the ground by force. *Jim dragged the heavy trash barrel across the lawn.*

haul to draw along behind, usually with great effort. *The horse hauled the heavy wagon up the mountain.*

tow to draw along behind with a chain or a rope. *With a strong rope, the big boat towed our canoe into the harbor.*

antonyms: push, shove

put *v.* to cause to be in a particular position. *Put your bike in the shed.*

place to lay something in a certain space. *Place your hands on your hips.*

locate to establish something in a certain area. *Locate your garden in a sunny place.*

set to cause to be in a particular location. *Set your books on the table.*

antonyms: remove, take away

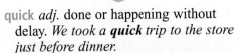

quick *adj.* done or happening without delay. *We took a quick trip to the store just before dinner.*

fast moving or acting with speed. *Traveling by plane is faster than traveling by car.*

hasty in a hurried way. *Jim scribbled a hasty note and then ran out the door.*

rapid marked by speed. *The rapid subway train zoomed through the tunnel.*

swift able to move at great speed. *You will need a swift horse if you want to get to the farm before dinner.*

speedy able to get from one place to another in a short time. *A speedy little rabbit outran my dog.*

antonym: slow

real *adj.* not imaginary, made up, or artificial. *This apple looks real, but it is wax.*

actual existing or happening. *Tory's visit to the palace was an actual event, not just a dream.*

true in agreement with fact. *Whether or not you believe it, the story is true.*

antonyms: artificial, fake

rough *adj.* full of bumps and ridges. *The carpenter sanded the rough wood.*

bumpy covered with lumps. *The bumpy road made us bounce in our seats.*

coarse not polished or fine. *The surface of sandpaper is coarse.*

uneven not level. *Because the floor was uneven, the table didn't sit straight.*

antonyms: smooth, polished

run *v.* to move quickly on foot. *Please do not run in the halls.*

dash to move with sudden speed. *We dashed out the door to get the mail.*

race to rush at top speed. *Leon raced to catch the bus.*

antonyms: walk, stroll

S

same *adj.* being the very one. *This train is the same one that I rode last week.*

equal being alike in any measured quantity. *We got equal test scores.*

identical exactly alike. *The twins were identical; no one could tell them apart.*

antonym: different

Shades of Meaning

say *v.* speak aloud.

1. to say quietly or unclearly: *whisper, murmur, mutter, sigh, mumble, grunt*
2. to say in an excited or nervous way: *exclaim, cry, stammer, sputter*
3. to say loudly: *yell, scream, screech, shout, holler, bellow, roar, howl*
4. to say in an angry way: *snarl, snap, growl, bark, hiss*
5. to say in a complaining way: *whine, moan, groan, grumble, whimper, gripe*

scary *adj.* causing fear. *Your story was so scary that I was afraid to walk home.*

alarming causing a feeling of approaching danger. *The police siren was alarming to drivers.*

frightening causing sudden, great fear. *The frightening noise was thunder.*

terrifying causing overpowering fright. *The elephant made a terrifying noise.*

see *v.* to take in with the eyes. *Julie could not see the bird in the tree.*

notice to pay attention to. *Ron entered quietly, but we noticed he was late.*

observe to watch carefully. *The cat observed the bird in the tree.*

view to look at. *We viewed the city from the top of the mountain.*

antonyms: ignore, overlook

shake *v.* to move back and forth or up and down with short, quick movements. *The leaves on the oak tree shook in the wind.*

quake to move suddenly, as from shock. *The ground quaked when the herd of cattle moved by.*

shiver to move without control, as from cold or nervousness. *The child shivered in the cold rain.*

shudder to move with sudden, sharp movements, as from fear or horror. *Al shuddered when he read the story.*

tremble move back and forth gently or slightly, as from cold or fear. *My lips trembled as I began my speech.*

shiny *adj.* reflecting light. *Craig's shiny new bike sparkled in the sun.*

bright giving off strong rays of light. *Bright sun can be harmful to your eyes.*

gleaming glowing with light. *The gleaming runway lights showed the pilot where to land.*

glistening sparkling. *The sun turned the lake into a glistening pool of light.*

antonyms: dark, dim, dull

shout *v.* to call out at the top of one's voice. *The fans at the football game shouted, "Go, team, go!"*

yell to make a loud outcry, often in anger. *Helen yelled, "Your dog is eating my glove!"*

cry to utter a special sound or call. *Jeremy cried out in sudden pain.*

holler to call out to. *"Sue, come in for dinner!" I hollered.*

antonym: whisper

some *adj.* being an unspecified number or amount of. *Joanne invited some friends to play volleyball.*

few a small number of. *Few people today get enough exercise.*

several more than two but not a large number. *Carl moved several blocks away, but we can still walk there easily.*

start *v.* to take the first step in an action. *Joan turned to page one and **started** to read her book.*

begin to get a process underway. *I will **begin** my homework right after school.*

commence to perform the first part of an action. *The graduation ceremony **commences** at noon.*

antonyms: close, end, finish, stop

strange *adj.* different; unfamiliar. *I felt **strange** on my first day at the new school.*

weird odd or peculiar. *My brother has a **weird** sense of humor.*

odd out of the ordinary. *I read a story about an **odd** animal with three bumps!*

peculiar hard to understand or explain. *There is nothing **peculiar** about a green apple, but what do you think about a purple orange?*

unusual rare or different from what might be expected. *Her **unusual** name was hard to say.*

antonyms: normal, familiar, common, ordinary

surprise *v.* to cause to feel wonder because of the unexpected. *The sudden thunder **surprised** the picnickers in the park.*

amaze to fill with wonder or awe. *The skilled juggler **amazed** the crowd.*

astonish to startle greatly. *The unexpected news **astonished** the world.*

astound to strike with great wonder. *People were **astounded** by the speed of the new plane.*

thin *adj.* having little fat on the body. *After his diet, Joe looked **thin**.*

skinny having very little fat on the body; bony. *The sick kitten was so **skinny** that we could see its ribs.*

slender having little fat or width. *The **slender** ballerina looked like a doll.*

antonyms: fat, plump, stout

Shades of Meaning

think *v.*

1. to use one's mind:
   consider
   evaluate
   reflect
   study

2. to have an opinion:
   feel
   judge
   assert
   believe

3. to suppose:
   imagine
   conceive
   dream
   speculate

antonyms: forget, ignore

unclear *adj.* not easy to see, hear, or understand. *Those complicated directions are **unclear**.*

fuzzy blurred. *The TV picture was too **fuzzy** to see any details.*

confusing mixed up. *The recipe was so **confusing** that we could not follow the steps.*

cloudy hazy; not clear. *The powder made the water **cloudy**.*

faint not distinct or bright. *The star was only a **faint** speck in the sky.*

antonyms: distinct, obvious, sharp

upset *adj.* sad or unsettled. *I was **upset** when I heard the bad news.*

worried uneasy because of fear. *Janet was **worried** about getting lost.*

nervous shaken and jittery because of fear or challenge. *Dean was **nervous** because he had to give a speech.*

troubled concerned because of pain, fear, or sadness. *Phil was **troubled** by his father's illness.*

disturbed being bothered or feeling

more ▶

unsettled. *They were **disturbed** by some noisy fire engines.*

antonyms: calm, comfortable, pleased, satisfied, composed

useful *adj.* being of service. *A rake is **useful** for cleaning up the yard.*

handy convenient, easy to use. *A wastebasket is a **handy** thing to have in each room of the house.*

helpful providing assistance. *I found this book **helpful** when I was looking for facts about the battle.*

antonyms: inefficient, useless, worthless

walk *v.* to move on foot at a steady pace. *Gabriel can **walk** to the store to get milk.*

march to move forward with regular and measured steps. *The band **marched** around the stadium as they played.*

stride to take long steps. *You **stride** so fast I cannot keep up with you.*

stroll to go forward in a slow, relaxed way. *Shall we **stroll** through the park after dinner?*

antonyms: run, stand still

How Wet Was It?
wet *adj.* covered or moistened with liquid.
1. extremely wet: *drenched, saturated, soaked, water-logged, sopping, flooded*
2. quite wet: *dripping, soppy, soggy, sodden*
3. slightly wet: *moist, damp, dank, dewy, wettish*
antonyms: parched, arid, dry, dehydrated

while *conj.* at the same period of time as. *I was waiting at the airport for Lois **while** she was waiting at the train station for me.*

as long as for an entire length of time. *We vowed to remain friends **as long as** we lived.*

wish *v.* to want, hope for. *What sights do you **wish** to see in the city?*

desire to want strongly. *More than anything else, Jan **desired** to travel around the world.*

crave to long for intensely. *The thirsty runners **craved** a cool drink.*

Glossary of Language Arts Terms

abbreviation   a short form of a word.

action verb   a word that tells what people or things do.

adjective   a word that describes a noun and can tell what kind or how many.

adverb   a word that describes a verb and tells how, when, or where.

apostrophe   a punctuation mark (') that takes the place of any missing letters in a contraction and is used to form possessive nouns.

articles   the adjectives *a, an,* and *the.*

audience   person or people who read or listen to something.

brainstorm   to think of different ideas.

cluster   See **web.**

comma   a punctuation mark (,) used to separate words in a sentence.

command   a sentence that tells someone to do something. It ends with a period.

common noun   names any person, place, or thing.

complete predicate   includes all the words in the predicate.

complete subject   includes all the words in the subject.

compound predicate   made by using *and* to combine the predicates of two sentences with the same subject.

compound sentence   two related, short sentences that have been combined, using a comma and the connecting word *and, but,* or *or.*

compound subject   formed by using *and* to join the subjects of two sentences with the same predicate.

contraction   a shortened form of two words joined together. An apostrophe replaces the missing letter or letters.

conventions   the standard rules of spelling, grammar, usage, capitalization, and punctuation.

details   exact facts or information.

direct quotation   someone's exact words.

drafting   the part of the writing process when the writer first attempts to put his or her ideas on paper in the form of a composition.

elaborate   to give more details.

exclamation   a sentence that shows strong feeling. It ends with an exclamation point (!).

future tense   shows action that will happen.

helping verb   a verb that comes before the main verb, such as *have, has, had.*

ideas   thoughts that form the main points of a composition.

indent   to begin the first line of a sentence a few spaces in from the margin.

irregular verbs   verbs that do not add *-ed* to show past action.

linking verb   a verb that joins the subject to a word in the predicate that names or describes the subject.

main idea   the most important thought or point.

main verb   the most important verb.

noun   a word that names a person, a place, or a thing

negative   a word that means "no."

order words   words that signal sequence, such as *first, next, last, then, when,* and *later.*

organization   the structure of a composition.

paragraph   a group of sentences that tell about one main idea.

past tense   a verb that shows action that has already happened.

phrase   a group of words that does not have a subject or a predicate.

plural noun   names more than one person, place, or thing.

plural possessive noun   shows ownership. It is formed by adding an apostrophe to a plural noun.

more ▶

possessive noun   a noun that shows ownership. It is formed by adding an apostrophe and *s* to a singular noun.

predicate   tells what the subject of a sentence does or is.

preposition   a word that shows the connection between other words in a sentence, such as *at, for, with, after,* and *about.*

prepositional phrase   a group of words that begins with a preposition and ends with a noun or pronoun.

present tense   a verb that shows action that is happening now.

presentation   the way in which writers show and share their compositions with their audience.

prewriting   the part of the writing process when the writer chooses a topic and plans the composition.

pronoun   a word that replaces one or more nouns.

proofreading   the part of the writing process when the writing is checked for errors in grammar, usage, mechanics, and spelling.

proper noun   a word that names a particular person, place, or thing and is capitalized.

publish   the part of the writing process when writers make a final copy of their composition.

purpose   the goal of a composition.

question   a sentence that asks. It ends with a question mark.

quotation marks   punctuation used before (") and after (") a direct quotation.

revising   the part of the writing process when the writer tries to improve the working draft by adding, deleting, reorganizing, and rewriting.

run-on sentence   has two complete thoughts that run into each other.

sensory words   words that describe how something looks, sounds, feels, tastes, or smells.

sentence   a group of words that tells a complete thought.

sentence fluency   the structure and order of sentences so that a composition reads smoothly.

series   a list of three or more words in a sentence.

simple predicate   the main word in the complete predicate. It tells exactly what the subject does or is.

simple subject   the main word in the complete subject. It tells exactly whom or what the sentence is about.

singular noun   names one person, place, or thing.

statement   a sentence that tells something. It ends with a period.

subject   tells whom or what a sentence is about.

supporting sentences   sentences that tell more details about a main idea.

tense   the form of a verb that identifies whether something happens in the present, past, or future.

topic   the subject of a discussion or a composition.

topic sentence   a sentence that states a main idea about a subject.

transitional words   words that connect sentences or ideas, such as *also, however,* and *for example.*

voice   the use of words to show the writer's personality.

web   words in connected circles that show how ideas are related.

word choice   the selection of interesting, exact words.

working draft   a composition that is still being revised or proofread and not yet final.

writing conference   a discussion between a writer and a reader about the writer's composition.

writing process   a series of steps (prewriting, drafting, revising, proofreading, publishing) that a writer follows to write a composition.

Index

386–390, 397,
428–430, 436, 441,
462–464, 470, H40
using graphics, 389
telling about one idea,
269, 273
topic sentence, what is a,
269, 273
types
address book, 175
advertisement, 37, 137,
171, 475
announcement, 99
biographical sketch, 67
book report, 435–436
book review, 147, 433
business letter, 469–470
caption, 205
cause-effect paragraph,
101, 336
classificatory, 422–434
comic strip, 245, 316
compare/contrast,
359–364
compare/contrast
paragraph, 335
conversation, 183
description, 13, 15, 17,
19, 21, 23, 25, 27,
140
dialogue, 277, 285,
300, 308, 312, 315,
321, 323, H49
e-mail, H37
explanation, 422–434
fact sheet, 65
fantasy story, 317
food column, 167
friendly letter, 295–296
geography report, 143
how-to activity book,
356
instructions, 97, 217,
338–358
interview, 43, 215
invitation, 296

letter, 109, 235,
295–296, 467,
469–470
letter to the editor, 432
list, 45, 71, H40, H41
nature report, 219
news article, 396–397
opinion, 115, 145, 173,
207, 407–433
paragraph of
information, 81, 331,
337
personal narrative, 75,
113, 177, 209, 273,
275–294
persuasive essay,
447–468
persuasive plan, 181
picture book, 316
play, 249, 319–323
poem, 41, 111, 149,
249, 437–441
poster, 356
problem-solving, 394,
395
program, 79
research report,
369–393
review, 77
riddles, 185
rules, 243
sign, 47
song, 117
speech, 73
sports report, 107
sportscast, 239
story, 75, 113, 177,
209, 305–316
summaries, 187
thank-you note, 105,
213, 296
travel brochure, 39, 241
Computer, using in writing,
361, H37–H44.
See also Technology, using
Conclusions, writing, 272,

273, 287, 363, 385,
397
Conflict. *See* Problem, in plot
Conjunctions
coordinating, 211, H71,
H72
Connecting words, 359,
360, 363
Content areas, writing in
art, 317, 357, 393, 433
career education, 393
health, 293, 393, 467
math, 357, 393, 467
physical education, 293,
357, 393
science, 357
social studies, 293, 467
Contractions, 116–117, 121,
134, 157, 216–217,
218–219, 223, 224, 231,
242–243, 256, 258, 431
Contrast. *See* Comparison
and contrast
Conventions
grammar, 32–33, 36–37,
38–39, 64–65, 66–67,
70–71, 72–73, 74–75,
76–77, 78–79, 82–83,
84–85, 86–87, 88–89,
90–91, 92–93, 94,
96–97, 98–99, 100–101,
102–103, 104–105,
106–107, 108–109,
110–111, 112–113,
114–115, 116–117, 119,
120–121, 122–124,
125–134, 136–137,
138–139, 140, 141,
142–143, 144–145,
146–147, 150–151,
152–153, 154, 155–158,
159–164, 189–190,
204–205, 206–207,
208–209, 210–211,
212–213, 214–215,

Index

Index

Index

Index

Acknowledgments *continued*

"Knuckle Down That Taw!" by Beth Kennedy from *Highlights For Children* Magazine, January 1999 issue. Copyright ©1999 by Highlights for Children, Inc., Columbus, Ohio. Reprinted by permission of the publisher.

"A Play" from *Childtimes: A Three-Generation Memoir* by Eloise Greenfield and Lessie Jones Little. Copyright ©1979 by Eloise Greenfield and Lessie Jones Little. Used by permission of HarperCollins Publishers.

From *The Sea Otter* by Alvin, Virginia and Robert Silverstein. Copyright ©1995 by Alvin, Virginia and Robert Silverstein. Used by permission of The Millbrook Press.

Poetry

"Keziah" from *Bronzeville Boys and Girls* by Gwendolyn Brooks. Copyright ©1956 by Gwendolyn Brooks Blakely. Used by permission of HarperCollins Publishers.

"A Matter of Taste" from *There Is No Rhyme for Silver* by Eve Merriam. Copyright ©1962, 1990 by Eve Merriam. Used by permission of Marian Reiner.

"My Name Is . . ." from *Silver Bells and Cockle Shells* by Pauline Clarke. Copyright ©1962 by Pauline Clarke. Reproduced by permission of Curtis Brown Ltd., London.

"Penguin" from *The Llama Who Had No Pajama: 100 Favorite Poems* by Mary Ann Hoberman. Copyright ©1973 by Mary Ann Hoberman. Reprinted by permission of Harcourt, Inc.

Book Report

Little House on the Prairie by Laura Ingalls Wilder, illustrated by Garth Williams. Illustrations copyright 1953 by Garth Williams, copyright renewed 1981 by Garth Williams. Used by permission of HarperCollins Publishers.

Student Handbook

Definitions of "floppy disk," "harbor," "mineral," "mingle," and "printer" from *The American Heritage® Children's Dictionary* by the Editors of the American Heritage® Dictionaries. Copyright ©1998 by Houghton Mifflin Company. Reproduced by permission of *The American Heritage Children's Dictionary.*

Definition of "hard disk" from *The American Heritage® Student Dictionary.* Copyright ©1998 by Houghton Mifflin Company. Reproduced by permission of *The American Heritage Student Dictionary.*

Pronunciation key on page 25 from *The American Heritage® Children's Dictionary* by the Editors of the American Heritage® Dictionaries. Copyright ©1998 by Houghton Mifflin Company. Reproduced by permission of *The American Heritage Children's Dictionary.*

From "Robert Edward Lee" from *Collier's Encyclopedia,* Volume 14, page 440. Copyright ©1997 by Atlas Editions. All rights reserved. Used by permission.

Getting Started: Listening

Bees Dance and Whales Sing: The Mysteries of Animal Communication by Margery Facklam, illustrated by Pamela Johnson. Illustrations copyright ©1992 by Pamela Johnson. Reprinted by permission of Sierra Club Books for Children.

Cricket Magazine, May 1999 issue, Volume 26, Number 9. Copyright ©1999 by Carus Publishing Company. Reprinted by permission of *Cricket* Magazine.

One Minute Warm-up

4/1 *A River Dream* by Allen Say, published by Houghton Mifflin Company, 1988. Used by permission.

4/1 *The Great Yellowstone Fire* by Carole G. Vogel and Kathryn A. Goldner, published by Sierra Club Books, 1990. Used by permission.

Acknowledgments

4/2 *From Sea To Shining Sea: Florida* by Dennis Brindell Fradin, published by Children's Press, 1992. Used by permission.

4/2 *Natural Resources* by Damian Randle, published by Wayland (Publishers) Ltd., 1992. Used by permission of Hodder Children's Books.

4/2 *Sarah, Plain and Tall* by Patricia MacLachlan, published by HarperCollins Publishers, 1985. Used by permission.

4/2 *Yang the Youngest and His Terrible Ear* by Lensey Namioka, illustrated by Kees de Kiefte, published by Little, Brown and Company, 1992. Used by permission.

4/3 *Cam Jansen and the Mystery of the Circus Clown* by David A. Adler, illustrated by Susanna Natti, published by Puffin Books, 1983. Used by permission.

4/3 *Radio Man: A Story In English and Spanish* by Arthur Dorros, published by HarperCollins Publishers, 1993. Used by permission.

4/3 *The Secret Shortcut* by Mark Teague. Copyright ©1996 by Mark Teague. Used by permission of Scholastic Inc.

4/3 *The Story of the Olympics* by Dave Anderson, published by William Morrow & Company, 1996. Used by permission.

4/3 *Why Doesn't My Floppy Disk Flop?* by Peter Cook and Scott Manning, illustrated by Ed Morrow. Text copyright ©1999 by Peter Cook and Scott Manning. Illustrations copyright ©1999 by Ed Morrow. Reprinted by permission of John Wiley & Sons, Inc.

4/4 *Akiak: A Tale from the Iditarod* text and illustrations by Robert J. Blake, published by Philomel Books, 1997. Used by permission.

4/4 *Charlotte's Web* by E.B. White, pictures by Garth Williams, published by HarperCollins Publishers, 1952. Used by permission.

4/5 *Carlos and the Skunk/Carlos Y El Zorrillo* by Jan Romero Stevens, illustrated by Jeanne Arnold, published by Rising Moon Books for Young Readers, 1997. Used by permission.

4/5 *Fables* written and illustrated by Arnold Lobel, published by HarperCollins Publishers, 1980. Used by permission.

4/5 *Justin and the Best Biscuits in the World* by Mildred Pitts Walter, illustrated by Catherine Stock, published by Lothrop, Lee & Shepard Books, 1986. Used by permission.

4/5 *Sadako* by Eleanor Coerr, illustrated by Ed Young, published by G. P. Putnam's Sons, 1993. Used by permission.

4/6 *A Llama in the Family* by Johanna Hurwitz, illustrated by Mark Graham, published by Morrow Junior Books, 1994. Used by permission.

4/6 *Clambake: A Wampanoag Tradition* by Russell M. Peters, photographs by John Madama, published by Lerner Publications Company, 1992. Used by permission.

4/6 *Creepy, Crawly Baby Bugs* by Sandra Markle, published by Walker and Company, 1996. Used by permission.

4/7 *The Sunday Outing* by Gloria Jean Pinkney, pictures by Jerry Pinkney, published by Dial Books for Young Readers, 1994. Used by permission.

Student Writing Model Contributors
Elizabeth Allen, Aimee Carney, Carolin Castillo, Wesley Crane, Asa Horvotz, Jeremy Jones, James Lee, Jessica Liu, Colin McMillan, Jane Sawyer, Jillian Tully, Jack Welch, Andrea Zawoyski

Credits

Illustrations

Special Characters illustrated by: Sal, the Writing Pal by LeeLee Brazeal; Pencil Dog by Jennifer Beck Harris; Enrichment Animals by Scott Matthews.

Yvette Banek: 101
Mary Jane Begin: H14
John Bendall-Brunello: 23, 100 (top), 140, 471
Lisa Chiba: 244
Chris Demarest: 148, 220, 246, 269, 286, 306, 311, 349, 351, 427, H13
Eldon Doty: 37, 108, 204, 242
Rita Durrell: H92
Kate Flanagan: 114 (bottom), 141, 142, 146, 183, 186, 216
Jim Gordon: 240 (top)
Jennifer Harris: 100 (bottom), 166, 234
True Kelley: 208
Rita Lascaro: H17
Jared Lee: 144, 180
Rosanne Litzinger: 1-7
John Manders: 184 (bottom)
Patrick Merrell: 36 (top), 170 (bottom)
John Meza: 174
Laurie Newton-King: 70
Chris Reed: 38, 94, 114 (top), 170 (top), 218
Scot Ritchie: 112 (bottom), 240 (bottom)
Tim Robinson: 74
Ellen Sasaki: 184 (top)
Lauren Scheuer: 103, 118, 138, 248, 249 (center), 285, 287, 336, 358, 456, 460
Susan Spellman: H20, H25
George Ulrich: 44, 80, 106, 112 (top), 182, H88, H89, H91, H93-H96, H99, H100
Matt Wawiorka: 188 (center, bottom), 200, 307, 309, 379, 380, 408, 410, 423, 437, 438
Garth Williams: 9,10
Jean Wisenbaugh: 473
Amy L. Young: 36 (bottom), 209
Debra Ziss: 119 (bottom), 249 (bottom)

Photographs

iii © Lester Lefkowitz/The Stock Market. iv © Telegraph Colour Library/FPG International. v © Lori Adamski Peek/Tony Stone Images. vi © David Young-Wolff/PhotoEdit. vii © David Stewart/Tony Stone Images. viii © David Madison/Tony Stone Images. ix © Dewitt Jones/Tony Stone Images. x © Zigy Kaluzny/Tony Stone Images. xi (t) © Daryl Benson/Masterfile. (b) Courtesy NASA. xii © Lori Adamski Peek/Tony Stone Images. xiii (t) © Julie Habel/CORBIS. (b) © Nova Stock/FPG International. 31 © Lester Lefkowitz/The Stock Market. 32 © Barbara Filet/Tony Stone Images. 33 © Bob Calhoun; Clara Calhoun/Bruce Coleman/Picture Quest. 34 (tl) © David R. Frazier Photolibrary. (tr) © Len Rue, Jr./Animals Animals. (bl) © PhotoLink/PhotoDisc, Inc. (br) © R. Cetera/Mammoth Cave National Park. 35 © Jeremy Woodhouse/PhotoDisc, Inc. 38 (t) © PhotoDisc, Inc. (b) © M. Bridwell/PhotoEdit. 39 © PhotoDisc, Inc. 40 © Kurgan-Lisnet/Liaison International. 41 © Alan Pappe/PhotoDisc, Inc. 42 © Brian Bailey/Tony Stone Images. 43 © PhotoDisc, Inc. 44 Courtesy U. S. Space Camp, Mountain View, CA. 45 © CORBIS. 46 (t) © Culver Pictures. (frame) Image provided by MetaTools. (b) © Jeff Greenberg/PhotoEdit. 47 © Albert J. Copley/PhotoDisc, Inc. 48 (l) © CORBIS. (c) © Michael Newman/PhotoEdit. (r) © Bob Daemmrich/The Image Works. 49 © Jeffry W. Myers/The Stock Market. 56 © Tom Benoit/Tony Stone Images. 57 © PhotoDisc, Inc. 58 © David Madison/Tony Stone Images. 59 (t) © Bachmann/Stock Boston. (b) © PhotoDisc, Inc. 60 © Joe Atlas/Artville. 61 © SuperStock, Inc. 63 © Telegraph Colour Library/FPG International. 64 © Jeff Greenberg/PhotoEdit. 65 © PhotoDisc, Inc. 66 © Nada Pecnik/Visuals Unlimited. 67 © Bettmann/CORBIS. 68 © Cartesia. 69 © The Granger Collection, New York. 70 © Jeff Lepore/Photo Researchers, Inc. 72 © Jane McAlonan/Visuals Unlimited. 74 © Donna Ikenberry/Animals Animals. 77 © James L. Fly/Unicorn Stock Photo. 78 (t) © PhotoDisc, Inc. (b) © SuperStock, Inc. 79 © PhotoDisc, Inc. 81 © Bettmann/CORBIS. 86 (l) © CORBIS. (r) © Coco McCoy/Rainbow/Picture Quest. 87 © Jim Cummins/FPG International. 88 © Stella Snead/Bruce Coleman, Inc. 89 © Corel Corporation. 90 © SuperStock, Inc.

92 © Lee Snider/CORBIS. 95 © Lori Adamski Peek/Tony Stone Images. 96 © Robert Brenner/PhotoEdit. 97 Image provided by MetaTools. 98 © Bob Daemmrich/Tony Stone Images. 99 © PhotoDisc, Inc. 102 © PhotoDisc, Inc. 104 © Jim Whitmer. 106 © Jim Cummins/FPG International. 107 © PhotoDisc, Inc. 108 © Esbin/Anderson/The Image Works. 109 © Joseph Sohm; ChromoSohm, Inc./CORBIS. 110 © Tony Freeman/PhotoEdit. 111 (t) © PhotoDisc, Inc. (b) Image provided by MetaTools. 115 © Nigel Shuttleworth/Life File/PhotoDisc, Inc. 116 © Sonda Dawes/The Image Works. 121 © PhotoDisc, Inc. 125 © Wood Sabold/International Stock. 126 © David Young-Wolff/PhotoEdit. 127 © J. & P. Wegner/Animals Animals. 128 © Bonnie Kamin/PhotoEdit. 129 © M. Siluk/The Image Works. 130 (t) © Michael Newman/PhotoEdit. (b) © PhotoDisc, Inc. 131 © David Madison/Tony Stone Images. 132 © Mark Junak/Tony Stone Images. 133 © Horst Oesterwinter/International Stock. 134 © Myrleen Ferguson/PhotoEdit. 135 © Stuart Westmorland/Tony Stone Images. 136 © Layne Kennedy/CORBIS. 137 © Adalberto Rios Szalay/Sexto Sol/PhotoDisc, Inc. 139 © CORBIS. 141 © Glenn M. Oliver/Visuals Unlimited. 142 © SuperStock, Inc. 143 © Cartesia. 144 © Arthur Hill/Visuals Unlimited. 145 © Santokh Kochar/PhotoDisc, Inc. 155 © SuperStock, Inc. 156 (b) © PhotoDisc, Inc. 157 © John Giustina/FPG International. 158 (l) © Alan G. Nelson/Animals Animals. (tr) © Eye Wire, Inc. (br) © Willard Luce/Animals Animals. 159 © Myrleen Ferguson/PhotoEdit. 160 (t) © Lawrence Migdale/Tony Stone Images. (b) © Reuters Newmedia Inc./CORBIS. 161 Image provided by MetaTools. 162 © CORBIS. 163 © CORBIS. 165 © Art Wolfe/Tony Stone Images. 168 © Doug Menuez/PhotoDisc, Inc. 171 © Myrleen Ferguson/PhotoEdit. 172 © Baron Wolman/Tony Stone Images. 173 © Blaine Harrington, III/The Stock Market. 174 © Bill Bachmann/PhotoEdit. 176 © Steve Starr/Stock Boston/Picture Quest. 177 © Digital Vision/Picture Quest. 179 (t) © PhotoDisc, Inc. (b) © Artville. 180 © SuperStock, Inc. 181 © Mark Newman/International Stock. 194 © Gerard Lacz/Animals Animals. 195 © National Portrait Gallery, London/SuperStock, Inc. 196 © Bob Daemmrich/The Image Works. 198 © American Museum, Bath, England/Bridgeman Art Library, London/SuperStock, Inc. 199 © Bob Trehearne/Stock Connection/Picture Quest. 201 © J. P. O'Neill/VIREO. 202 © Comstock, Inc. 203 © David Young-Wolff/PhotoEdit. 204 © PhotoDisc, Inc. 205 © Corel Corporation. 206 © PhotoDisc, Inc. 208 © Benn Mitchell/The Image Bank. 211 (tl) © David R. Frazier Photolibrary. (tr) © Don Lowe/Tony Stone Images. (bl) © Walter Chandoha. (br) © Lester Lefkowitz/The Stock Market. 212 © Walter Hodges/Tony Stone Images. 214 © Renee Lynn/Tony Stone Images. 215 © SuperStock, Inc. 217 (t) © CORBIS. (b) © David Young-Wolff/PhotoEdit/Picture Quest. 218 © Tim Davis/Tony Stone Images. 219 © Alan and Sandy Carey/PhotoDisc, Inc. 220 © PhotoDisc, Inc. 223 © PhotoDisc, Inc. 226 © Leonard Lee Rue, III/Animals Animals. 227 © Robert Lubeck/Animals Animals. 228 © Jeff Schultz/Alaska Stock Images/Picture Quest. 229 © Topham/The Image Works. 230 © Robert Maier/Animals Animals. 231 © PhotoDisc, Inc. 232 © C.C. Lockwood/Animals Animals. 233 © David Stewart/Tony Stone Images. 235 © Culver Pictures, Inc./SuperStock, Inc. 237 (tl) © Nigel Francis/ZEFA/The Stock Market. (tr) © Michael Andrews/Earth Scenes. (b) © Corel Corporation. 238 © ADAMSMITH/FPG International. 239 Courtesy of Special Olympics, Inc. 242 © Tony Freeman/PhotoEdit. 244 © Gayna Hoffman/Stock Boston. 247 © Randy M. Ury/The Stock Market. 248 © Walter Bibikow/FPG International. 251 Courtesy NASA/Finley Holiday Film. 255 © CORBIS. 256 (t) © SuperStock, Inc. (b) © Alvis Upitis/The Image Bank. 257 © PhotoDisc, Inc. 258 © Barbara von Hoffman/Animals Animals. 259 © Andy Sacks/Tony Stone Images. 260 © Bob Daemmrich/Stock

Boston. **261** © Bob Daemmrich/The Image Works. **262** © Ken Cole/Animals Animals. **263** © Richard During/Tony Stone Images. **266** © David Madison/Tony Stone Images. **266-7** © Dewitt Jones/Tony Stone Images. **267** (b) © Jerry Kobalenko/Tony Stone Images. **268** © PhotoDisc, Inc. **270** © Dennis O'Clair/Tony Stone Images. **271** © SuperStock, Inc. **272** © Inga Spence/Visuals Unlimited. **274** © David Madison/Tony Stone Images. **275** Courtesy Eloise Greenfield. **279** © Breck P. Kent/Earth Scenes. **297** © Jerry Kobalenko/Tony Stone Images. **310** © William Delzell/Tony Stone Images. **317** © *Carrie and Cocoa,* Robert Vickrey/Oklahoma City Art Museum. **328** © Zigy Kaluzny/Tony Stone Images. **328-9** © Daryl Benson/Masterfile. **329** (b) Courtesy NASA. **330** (l) © PhotoDisc, Inc. (r) © Daniel J. Cox/Tony Stone Images. **331** © Patti Murray/Animals Animals. **333** © Lester Lefkowitz/The Stock Market. **335** (l) © Rob Tringali, Jr./Sportschrome East/West. (r) © Lori Adamski Peek/Tony Stone Images. **338** © Zigy Kaluzny/Tony Stone Images. **339** © Kelly-Mooney Photography/CORBIS. **340** © Kelly-Mooney Photography/CORBIS. **364** (l) © Tony Freeman/PhotoEdit. (r) © Tony Hutchings/Tony Stone Images. **366** © Douglas Pebbles/Words & Pictures/Picture Quest. **368** Courtesy NASA. **369** © Kevin Schafer/CORBIS. **373** © Dani/Jeske/Earth Scenes. **381** © Art Wolfe/Tony Stone Images. **382** (l) © Gary Braasch/CORBIS. (r) © Wolfgang Kaehler/CORBIS. **392** (l) © Tim Flach/Tony Stone Images. (r) © Michael & Patricia Fogden/CORBIS. **393** © *Nino En Rojo,* Rufino Tamayo/ Christie's Images. **398** © Terry Vine/Tony Stone Images. **402** © Roger Ressmeyer/CORBIS. **404** © Lori Adamski Peek/Tony Stone Images. **404-5** © Julie Habel/CORBIS. **405** (b) © Nova Stock/FPG International. **409** © Lori Adamski Peek/Tony Stone Images. **412** © Lori Adamski Peek/Tony Stone Images. **413** © Paul Buchbinder. **414** (tl) © George Ancona. (bl) (r) © George Ancona/International Stock Photo. **415** © Leo Hsu. (inset) © George Ancona. **433** © *Black Camel with Blue Head and Red Tongue,* Alexander Calder (1898-1976),

1971. Sheet metal/cut, bent and painted (21 ¹/₈ inches), National Gallery of Art, Washington/Gift of Mrs. Paul Mellon, in honor of the Fiftieth Anniversary of the National Gallery of Art. Photo by Philip A. Charles. **444** © Joseph Sohm; ChromoSohm, Inc./CORBIS. **446** © Nova Stock/FPG International. **447** © Joe McDonald/CORBIS. **448** © Clive Druett; Papilio/CORBIS. **452** © Arthur Tilley/FPG International/Picture Quest. **458** (l) © PhotoDisc, Inc. (r) © Frank Siteman/Rainbow/Picture Quest. **469** © Bob Winsett/Index Stock Imagery/Picture Quest. **H8** © Spencer Grant, III/Stock Boston/Picture Quest. **H10** © Pablo Corral V/CORBIS. **H11** © Digital Vision. **H15** © EyeWire, Inc. **H17** © John Gerlach/Animals Animals. **H23** © PhotoDisc, Inc. **H31** (tl) © Comstock. (tr) (bl) © PhotoDisc, Inc. (br) © CMCD/PhotoDisc, Inc. **H46** (t) © Bettmann/CORBIS. (b) © Brown Brothers. **H51** © Telegraph Colour Library/FPG International. **H52** © Mark Newman/Stock Connection/Picture Quest. **H53** © Johnny Johnson/Animals Animals. **H72** © Wolfgang Kaehler/CORBIS. **H74** © Index Stock Photography. **H77** © CORBIS. **H78** Image provided by MetaTools.

Cover Photograph

Cover Stuart Westmorland/Tony Stone Images.